Indira Gandhi,
the 'Emergency',
and Indian Democracy

Indira Gandhi, the 'Emergency', and Indian Democracy

P.N. DHAR

OXFORD
UNIVERSITY PRESS

OXFORD
UNIVERSITY PRESS

YMCA Library Building, Jai Singh Road, New Delhi 110001

Oxford University Press is a department of the University of Oxford. It furthers the
University's objective of excellence in research, scholarship, and education
by publishing worldwide in

Oxford   New York

Athens   Auckland   Bangkok   Bogota   Buenos Aires   Calcutta
Cape Town   Chennai   Dar es Salaam   Delhi   Florence   Hong Kong   Istanbul
Karachi   Kuala Lumpur   Madrid   Melbourne   Mexico City   Mumbai
Nairobi   Paris   Sao Paolo   Shanghai   Singapore   Taipei   Tokyo   Toronto   Warsaw

with associated companies in   Berlin   Ibadan

Oxford is a registered trade mark of Oxford University Press
in the UK and in certain other countries

Published in India
By Oxford University Press, New Delhi

ISBN   0 19 564 899 4

Typeset in Adobe Garamond
by Guru Typograph Technology, New Delhi 110045
Printed by Pauls Press, New Delhi 110020
and published by Manzar Khan, Oxford University Press
YMCA Library Building, Jai Singh Road, New Delhi 110001

For my grandchildren

Preface

This book is the result of much exhortation by many friends. They all argued that since I was closely associated with Indira Gandhi and the Government of India over a momentous period in contemporary Indian political history, I should set down my recollections of the period, or at least its more memorable episodes and events. In the main, this is what I have done.

Those who persuaded me to write this book also pleasantly jibed that we Indians have little sense of history. People involved in policy-making seldom leave behind records of how they formulated policies and made decisions. Interest in institutional memory is not deep rooted in India. In Britain, in France, and in the USA, the tradition of penning analytic political memories is strong and well developed. Richard Crossman, George Kennan, Barbara Castle, John Kenneth Galbraith, George Ball and Henry Kissinger are some of the writers who come to mind when one thinks of this genre of writing. In the works of these writers it is apparent that holding positions of power did not damage their ability to remember acutely and intelligently and write persuasively. In India the practice has not quite taken hold, though there are some distinguished specimens of this kind of writing, for instance V.P. Menon's *The Story of the Integration of the Indian States*.

This dearth is partly due to our rigid laws regarding official secrets and their sweeping coverage. Besides, our documentation leaves much to be desired. In the 1970s, the information available seemed to me woefully inadequate even for top-level political purposes, and methods of storage and retrieval were quite primitive. Unlike American officials, Indians do not, as a rule, maintain diaries or personal journals. Even when they have been so inclined, the traditional working style in government offices seldom allows them the leisure for such activities. It is therefore not surprising that Indian writing of this mould has not reached the standards it has in the West.

For me, writing this memoir has been a bit of a tall order. I had no access to official records, not even to my own notes and memoranda that I had left behind in the prime minister's secretariat. My impressions of individuals and events, a few scrappy notes and personal papers, scattered jottings in appointment diaries, and a fading memory had to suffice for what I thought was expected of me. As head of the prime minister's secretariat under the prime ministership of Indira Gandhi, I had the opportunity of being both a witness and a participant in some major decisions of that eventful period. This book is largely made up of observations that derive from my involvement with affairs of state during my tenure. If the witness in me overshadows the participant, it should be attributed more to my temperament and academic background than to any wish to evade responsibility. Even while actively participating, I often had the feeling that I was standing a little outside the ring and watching events. I can only hope that this infirmity has helped my account to be dispassionate, coherent and readable.

The 1970s were a tumultuous decade in India, indeed in the subcontinent. It was a period of high hope and deep disappointment. Several dramatic things with lasting consequences for the region happened at this time. The political map of the subcontinent was redrawn: Bangladesh came into existence and Sikkim merged with India. India and Pakistan fought a decisive war that was followed by a peace agreement at Simla which had all the appearance of permanence. It was during this period that the two-nation theory, on the basis of which India was partitioned in 1947, appeared to have collapsed, only to be followed by the rise of religious fundamentalism—itself the result of the sudden enrichment of Saudi Arabia and the oil-producing Gulf sheikhdoms. The most outstanding leaders of the region—Zulfikar Ali Bhutto, Mujibur Rehman, Indira Gandhi, Jayaprakash Narayan—reached towering heights of success and depths of defeat at about this time. The Congress party's revival after a landslide electoral victory under the leadership of Indira Gandhi in 1971 was followed by humiliating defeat in 1977. Bhutto's success in reviving a residual Pakistan after its bifurcation in 1971 was followed by the army coup in 1977 and Bhutto's judicial murder in 1979. The triumphant return of Mujibur Rehman from a Pakistani prison to his newly independent country was followed by his assassination in Bangladesh. From this complex of exhilarating and depressing episodes I have selected a few where I was either an observer or a participant. My recollections are thus not a history of the regime with which I was associated, but rather a blend of impression, essay, argument and empirical data teased out of the events that crowd that decade.

The decade highlights dramatically the dilemmas that India, a large, diverse and poor country in dire need of economic and social change, faces in its attempt at self-governance. On the one hand the experiment of authoritarian rule during the twenty-one months of the Emergency established beyond doubt that India has to be self-governing to be governable. On the other hand the return of Westminster-style democracy has yielded unstable governments that make governance increasingly difficult. No doubt there will always be a hiatus between self-government and good government—imperfections of human nature and man-made institutions will see to that—but political progress lies in reducing the gap. For India, it is a race against time.

The experiences described within this book are naturally those that filtered through my personal background, the peculiarities of the place and the environment in which I grew up, and that inescapable subjectivity which clothes even the most strenuous attempt at dispassionate understanding. My generation in Kashmir was affected by politics in a big way, even when we were teenagers. Politics burst upon us like a thunderstorm when we were most impressionable, but unlike a thunderstorm it did not pass, and has stayed with us. Even those of us who were not actively involved, compulsively embraced politics as a sort of permanent hobby. This, I believe, justifies the more personally oriented early chapters of this memoir, where I describe my Kashmiri origins and certain youthful impressions that gave shape to me as—in my wife's phrase—'a political animal'. My doubts about the rightness of the decision to include my early years in this volume were set aside in a bulldozingly conclusive manner by Rukun Advani, my friend and editor at Oxford University Press, who argued persuasively that my assessment of Indian politics, political episodes, and politicians have been shaped in intangible ways by my early life, which is therefore inseparable from the totality of my experience.

Even in these early chapters, I fear, politics intrudes and gives credence to my family's opinion of my species. I cannot write about my school without digressing into the nature of social relations and political tensions between the British and the Indians. I cannot write about a teaching stint in Peshawar without dwelling at some length on the complex political history of that region of the subcontinent. I cannot think of the institutions with which I was involved—S.P. College, the Delhi School of Economics, the Institute of Economic Growth—separately from the political flaws that bedevil institutions and institution-building in India. In an oblique sense, therefore, my life provides the personification for a modern maxim: 'the personal is the political'. I understand my whole life, even its seemingly apolitical and academic early years, as a jigsaw of bits and pieces that have all been touched—my wife would say 'contaminated'—by politics.

Readers who, upon their reading of the first few pages feel that they do not share this opinion and are interested only in my more overt experience of political power in proximity with Indira Gandhi, would do well to skip the first five chapters, after which my story connects directly with the high politics of India in the 1970s.

Acknowledgements

This book would not have been written but for the constant prodding of Professor André Béteille. To his persistence he added a most generous offer of help. He read every page I wrote and gave me his comments with the skill of a tutor and the affection of a friend.

Professor M.N. Srinivas encouraged me, by giving his own example, to overcome the disadvantage of my not having maintained a diary. He is famous among sociologists for having reconstructed from memory *The Remembered Village*, that classic of Indian sociology, even though all the material he had painstakingly prepared for it over many years was destroyed in a fire. His tips on how to recall were most useful. Professor T.N. Madan read a substantial part of the manuscript and made useful suggestions. G.K. Arora made several improvements in the last chapter. B.N. Tandon helped me with some facts about the prime minister's secretariat. Dr S.N. Mishra, Director of the Institute of Economic Growth, placed its facilities at my disposal.

Rukun Advani went far beyond his obligation as my editor and invested a good deal of his time in removing unnecessary fat and suggesting additions in the interests of readability and clarity.

My younger brother B.L. Dhar's silent concern and traditional deference did not inhibit him from pointing out flaws in my work. His criticism stimulated me more than he can imagine. I am also grateful for his tireless bibliographical assistance and anxiety to provide me with every facility he thought I needed.

My wife, Sheila, suffered most from this undertaking. Her absolute lack of interest in politics, politicians and their ways could not save her from my constant intrusions into her private world of literature, music and grandchildren. On my part, I could not help exploiting her multiple talents in the interests of this book. Its completion should give her much needed relief.

Finally, I would like to acknowledge the ungrudging help of Sushil Kumar Sen of the Institute of Economic Growth, and V.O. John of the Industrial Development Services, in typing and retyping the manuscript.

Contents

CHAPTER ONE

Home and School in Kashmir

My father belonged to a family of Unani hakims. As far back as he could remember, all his ancestors had been hakims and bore the family name 'Hakim'. The family lived in a comfortable, three-storeyed ancestral house in the Rainawari district of Srinagar and enjoyed middle-class respectability. The house had a large garden where medicinal herbs as well as flowers and vegetables were grown. My father's nostalgic memories of this childhood home were tinged with pain because circumstances did not allow him to grow to manhood there. He left his father's house, along with all the advantages he could have inherited, when he was only seven years old. Throughout his life he remained acutely aware of what might have happened if his father had treated him differently. Though his pride prevented him ever questioning his childhood decision to leave his father's house, he did harbour some bitterness which in later years his own immediate family sensed and shared.

He had lost his mother at the age of five. Soon afterwards his father had married a young and beautiful girl called Poshkuj, which means 'flowering shrub' in Kashmiri. Names like Poshkuj were not pet names. They were proper names common among both Hindus and Muslims. These have now been discarded in favour of Sanskrit names by Hindus and Persian and Arabic ones by Muslims.

A widower's options in the matter of choosing a partner were narrow: Poshkuj therefore did not come from the same background as her much older husband but belonged to a village near Anantnag. My grandfather was besotted with his new wife and was always looking out for ways to demonstrate how passionately fond of her he was. He imagined it would please her if he were rough with her stepson, my father. So, one day, he lost his temper with his son for a trivial reason, which no one remembers exactly, and proceeded to give him a tongue-lashing. In the course of this he used certain swear words against his dead mother which the young boy took literally. Unable to bear the abusive insults he simply walked out of the house, never to return. He found refuge with his maternal uncle, Vasudev, who was at the time running a small business which he himself was too innocently incompetent to handle. This Vasudev was intensely religious minded, a devotee of the goddess Khir Bhawani. Every month he would walk barefoot to the shrine of the goddess at Tulamula, a distance of fifteen miles from Srinagar. He remained a bachelor all his life, quite content with his reduced circumstances.

Having shifted to Vasudev's house, my father soon realized that his uncle could not afford to educate him. He himself was determined to get an education and strike out on his own. His only asset, however, was a flair for sports. This was sufficient to gain him admittance to a missionary school at Srinagar that had been set up by the Church Missionary Society (CMS) of London under the leadership of the Reverend J.H. Knowles. The school was born in 1881, the same year as my father, and had ever since then been trying unsuccessfully to introduce sports to students. The situation proved opportune for my father. With his natural aptitude and keenness on the field, he easily won a scholarship of five rupees per month. He was thereby relieved of the anxiety of being a burden upon his uncle. Soon he became a star sportsman. Luckily for him Knowles was succeeded by the Reverend C. Tyndale-Biscoe, an even bolder and more dynamic cleric whose ideas on education laid great emphasis on sports. My father became a great favourite of Biscoe, so much so that, soon after he passed his matriculation examination, he was made headmaster of one of the five schools that the CMS had established in the city.

At the time that I was born, in 1919, my father continued to live with Vasudev in his small four-room house, of which two were always locked because they were in the keeping of a relative who worked outside the city. Of the two rooms that we had, one had sunk a foot below ground. Water collected in ditches around it and one of my vivid recollections of my mother is of a woman hooded in thick woollen cloth, shovelling water into a small drain to keep it from flooding the room. The room was part kitchen and part sitting room for all of us; at night Vasudev would spread his bed and spend the night there. My parents, my sister and I had the other room.

My father spent practically the whole day out of the house. His work over, he would either be on the playing field or perched within a shop in the vicinity of the house, puffing at a hooka and watching the world go by. I spent most of my time with a friend next door. My friend had an entire room to himself. Within this exclusive arena of luxury we would study and play.

My sister, who was older by three years, was of a very sensitive nature. She had seen her older sister die of some wasting disease and attributed her death to the poverty of our housing. The loss of her older sister made her more assertive; she pressed our father to buy the two vacant locked-up rooms, which he did. I was about seven years old at the time, but I still remember how thrilled my sister and I were when we went to the room upstairs and saw the sky from our new window. My father was aware of the harmful effects of constrained space upon his growing family. He could by now have afforded better accommodation, but he would not bear the thought of tearing himself away from the house where his mother had been born.

Luckily for me and my sister, the house stood in the way of a road-widening scheme of the municipal committee. So the house was demolished and my father received a compensation of 500 rupees. A similar amount was given to Vasudev, who moved with us to a new house my father bought. Our new home was a modest one, but it dramatically changed the quality of our life. My sister and I had rooms of our own now, an experience rather overwhelmingly welcome for us both. The house was situated on a canal off the river Jhelum and commanded a magnificent view of distant mountains. On a clear sunny day we could see Gulmarg from our balcony. My father now spent more time with the family, especially with me. The proximity of the canal gave him an opportunity to teach me to swim; this helped reduce his disappointment at my not being a sportsman in his mould.

Vasudev was equally pleased with the new situation. He spent the entire amount he'd received for his ancestral property by arranging an elaborate and special shradh ceremony for his parents, his grandparents, their parents, and so on to the seventh ancestor. The ceremony was at Martand, the famous pilgrimage centre in south Kashmir. The ceremonies (the plural is more appropriate to describe what happened) were spread over twelve days. This particular kind of shradh is called *bah*, which, while sounding like a Wodehousian dismissive, means 'twelve' in Kashmiri and is supposed to end the need for all further shradhs. Since Vasudev was a bachelor, there would be no one to perform a shradh for his ancestors once he was gone. My father, whose orthodox religious beliefs had eroded in the company of European colleagues, was very annoyed with his uncle for wasting money over these rituals, which he dismissed as mumbo-jumbo. But Vasudev was very pleased with himself at having done the best he could for his ancestors. I remember him taking me and my sister out on the bank of the canal on a starry night. Flushed with the pride of piety he pointed out the *sapt rishis* (Great Bear), the particular constellation where he believed his ancestors had been catapulted by his lonely efforts.

The event I most looked forward to in the summer vacations was the visit to my mother's ancestral home at Sopore, a small town about thirty miles to the north of Srinagar. Sopore is situated on the banks of the Jhelum, where the river emerges from the Wular lake. The town has an interesting history. Its name is associated with Suyya, the famous innovative engineer of King Avanti Varma (ninth century AD) and grandson of Lalitaditya, the greatest ruler of Kashmir in pre-Islamic times. The Kashmir valley was (and still is) often faced with floods. These occur because the waters of the swollen Jhelum cannot pass quickly enough through the narrow gorge at Baramulla, their passage being blocked with boulders. Suyya had no modern dredgers to solve his problem. Legend has it that he used a method that present-day economists would call 'monetary incentives' in the most literal sense: he is reputed to have thrown money into the river where the boulders stood. Naturally, the mobs rushed in and removed all obstruction. The water flowed out, swamps got drained, fertile lands emerged, and all was well. A trading centre sprang up and, to honour one who was now regarded as a benefactor, the spot was appropriately named Suyyapura. Sopore is the Kashmiri version of that name. In recent times Sopore has grown into a very prosperous town because of the apple orchards in the surrounding areas. It was at Sopore that the Jammu and Kashmir Muslim Conference was transformed into the National Conference in 1939. This was a watershed in the evolution of Kashmir politics. It was at Sopore that the National Conference adopted 'Naya Kashmir' as its ideology and programme in 1945, in the presence of national secular leaders like Jawaharlal Nehru, Khan Abdul Ghaffar Khan and Maulana Azad. More recently, Sopore has changed radically to become the headquarters of Jamat-i Islami, a storm centre of the Muslim secessionist movement in the state.

So far as my personal attachment to Sopore is concerned, it was almost physical and began with my birth. My mother had repaired to her parental home for the delivery, as was customary among Kashmiri women, the requirement compounded in her case by the fact that my father's house had no space for an event as momentous as a birth.

My maternal grandfather's establishment in Sopore was a large joint family. Several brothers and their children lived together in an atmosphere of joyful togetherness: there were no tensions normally associated with such families. Nor were there rivalries among the cousins. Three of them were patwaris and the family was known by that name. They were all, in varying degrees, very religious. My maternal grandfather was possessed of a saintly disposition. He was a devotee of Kashmiri Shaivism and was supposed to be well versed in its mysteries and rituals. According to family lore he was a practising saint. But I have no recollection of him: he passed away before I could be aware of his existence.

My mother's cousins had gone through the traditional schooling in Persian. The atmosphere at home was relaxed. Conversations centred around literary matters and often took the form of contests and comparisons between different Persian poets and the recitation of appropriate verses to suit the arguments. They also knew their *Ramayana* and *Mahabharata*. I remember a fascinating comparison made by one of them between Karan's battle with the Pandava brothers and that of Sohrab and Rustum in Firdousi's *Shahnama*. But the third generation of the Patwari family—the generation to which I belonged—was rapidly getting out of this Persian literate ambience into that of Urdu and English. Whereas my grandfather's generation had a Persian influence even in their names—his name was Gulab Ram and his brother's Aftab Ram—my generation found such names most incongruous, if not meaningless. They also found the turbans worn by earlier generations, which looked like those one sees in Mughal miniatures, quaint, and they preferred being bareheaded in summer while using balaclavas in winter. My grandfather's generation also sported beards which resembled those of the Muslims, except that they did not clip their moustaches in the middle. In old photographs it is difficult to distinguish between a Kashmiri Pandit and a Muslim gentleman or moulvi.

Kashmiri Pandits in North Kashmir were poorer than those in the South. They considered it no indignity to be engaged in cultivating land. In a village near Sopore, a Pandit landlord's jagir lands were cultivated by Pandit tenants. Many rural Pandits were subsistence farmers. Generally speaking, these Pandits were much tougher than their counterparts in South Kashmir. To add to their meagre incomes they would ply tongas on hire or set up small retail shops in the village. They also had much closer relations with Muslims of their own class and were much less selfconscious about their Pandit identity. In my wanderings in the vicinity of Sopore I would stay occasionally with one such tenant farmer family which was related to my grandfather's. Their village, Dara Lalad, was at a distance of three miles from Sopore, near the Srinagar–Baramulla road. At the time of the tribal raid in 1947, some of the marauding tribesmen halted during their drive to Srinagar near the village and somehow came to know of the existence of a Pandit family. The Pandit house was surrounded and four brothers shot dead. The women and children had left earlier, along with other Pandit households, and taken shelter with Muslim neighbours.

Apart from my grandfather's house, Sopore held no particular interest for me. But it served as an excellent base camp when I was grown up enough to venture forth with other youngsters to explore more interesting places. The Patwaris had numerous friends and relations scattered all over North Kashmir, and we were welcome in their homes. My most favourite places were the Lolab valley and the Wular lake.

The Lolab valley is not one of those spots in Kashmir over which the Emperor Jehangir would have swooned. Nor would it have inspired Thomas Moore to conjure up the romance of Lala Rookh. It does not possess the scenic grandeur which has overwhelmed many visitors to Kashmir. But it is remarkable for the homely and pastoral beauty of its woodland and villages. The hillsides of the Lolab valley are on a human scale, close, touchable, friendly. They were clothed in those days with thick forests of deodar and pine in which one could roam and establish a kinship with its fauna and flora. Its villages were buried in park-like clumps of walnut, apple and pear trees, which provided an environment for healthy life unsurpassed. Its woodland glades remained inviolate: there were no tourists and no garbage. I have often dreamt of spending the last days of my life in one of the woodland glades of the Lolab valley, which continues to haunt me.

Wular is the largest fresh-water lake in the Indian subcontinent. My father's feat in having swum across its fourteen-mile length (his greatest triumph in life) made it of special interest to me. Besides my sentimental reasons, the lake had its own charm, most notably the absence of tourists. Sitting near the Ziarat of Baba Shukar Din, I could see a vast body of water in front, its moods changing with the weather and the hour of the day. The boatmen of Wular are experienced weathermen. They can anticipate the mood of the lake fairly accurately and know when not to annoy it. According to popular legend there is a city submerged in the middle of the lake. It is believed to be inauspicious to row over the city. Boatmen avoid it and ply their vessels nearer the shore, not merely out of respect for the legend but for a more practical reason—to avoid being caught in a storm if their judgement of the weather proves wrong. They also take out an insurance of safe voyage by invoking the aid of the Sufi saint Baba Shukar Din, whose Ziarat oversees the lake.

The Mission school, popularly known as Biscoe school, became an important part of my life even before I was enrolled as a student there. My father was, after all, its headmaster. He would often talk about the school and about its principal, whom all Kashmiris called 'Biscu sahab'. Whenever my father's colleagues dropped in at our home, Biscoe was the favourite topic. His activities and idiosyncrasies were also frequently the subject of discussion between my parents.

Some of my father's colleagues complained that Biscoe was laying more emphasis on sports and outdoor activities like swimming, boating, trekking and mountaineering than on books and classwork. They feared that students from other schools might outshine theirs in the examinations. My father, being himself a keen sportsman, was on Biscoe's side in these discussions. The way Biscoe was talked about and the things that were said about him intrigued me greatly. I was fascinated by stories about the school, which seemed a place of great fun. I could hardly wait to enrol. I was also very curious to see Biscoe Sahab, who was held in such awe by everybody. I was, at the same time, extremely nervous at the prospect.

I must have been about four years old when my father said I was to accompany him to a Christmas party at Mr Biscoe's house. I was all excitement and alarm. There were lots of English men, women and children at the party and only a few Kashmiris. This was my first time in such close proximity with the British. I had seen European tourists, collectively referred to as 'Angrez' in our lingo, from a distance as they floated down the river Jhelum in shikaras. The older boys had warned us that while it was all right to look in their direction, we shouldn't point fingers towards them as our fingers would be chopped off for such misdemeanour.

The Christmas party was also the first time I saw a bungalow from the inside. I was dazzled by the furniture, the sofa settees, the many chairs in the sitting room, and a huge dining table in the adjoining dining room laden with all sorts of eatables which I could scarcely recognize. The Kashmiri middle class homes that I knew had no furniture. The sitting room in such homes had only a single chair near the door of the sitting room for a visitor to sit down. On this he could unlace his shoes before walking on to seat himself in the carpeted area. The walls in such homes were generally bare, except for a calendar or a family photograph. In contrast the Biscoe house looked like a palace in a fairy tale.

I did not know what to do when we entered the house except clutch my father's hand. While I was taking in these surroundings awestruck, an Englishwoman said something which sounded nice, clasped both my hands, and pinched my cheeks. She was followed by several others who did the same. All this made for a friendly atmosphere which had a dramatic effect on me. My nervousness disappeared and I regained my wits. I left my father and joined the several older English boys that were around. To my surprise one of them spoke Kashmiri and called the boy with whom he was having an argument *haramuk*, the Kashmiri word for bastard. This was most exciting. I was now anxious to get home as soon as possible so that I might tell my friends all that I had seen. In particular, I was dying to tell them I had met and actually shaken hands with people whom they had only gapingly beheld from a distance.

Meanwhile I was trying to identify Biscoe Sahab in the crowd. Believing he was bound to be the most impressive looking man in the gathering, I fixed my gaze upon the tallest man I could see, quite certain he was my man. To my disappointment it turned out that Biscoe Sahab was a short man with a ruddy face and a nose tilted towards the west. It was difficult to accept these as the lineaments of the man my father had spoken so much of. The crooked nose, I discovered, was the result of a boxing match in which Biscoe had insisted on challenging a boy twice his size. This was one of many stories with which admiring colleagues and students described Biscoe's physical and moral courage.

At the party, however, I was not impressed by Biscoe. When my father finally presented me to him he was all smiles, gave me a present, and asked me in Urdu what I wanted to be in life. Without any hesitation, I responded in English, 'IN ALL THINGS BE MEN', without having the least idea what I was saying. My reply was the school's motto which, inscribed upon the medal my father had won for swimming across the Wular lake, I had lovingly memorized. I don't know what Biscoe thought of my reply but he looked flabbergasted for a second and then, with a broad smile, shook my hand and called me *badmash*. From that day, every time we met he called me *chota badmash* (little rascal) with a friendly twinkle in his eye.

Several years later I was standing in front of him, waiting to receive my 'character form'. This was an annual event when, in his capacity as principal, he handed out assessments of performance under three broad headings: Body, Mind and Soul. These all-encompassing categories covered sports, academic performance, social service, and personality. These were then broken down into some extraordinary items. For example, under Soul was a category called Colour of Heart. And in the preliminary paragraphs about boys' particulars, the item titled Father's Income contained the sub-heading 'Probable Loot' if that particular boy's father happened to be employed in the revenue, police or public works departments. Biscoe would add a figure under the subheading, no doubt after a quick calculation of the likely size of the loot. I do not remember anyone protesting against this practice.

On these occasions Biscoe's routine question to students was whether they agreed with his assessment of them. Now, instead of asking me that routine question, for which I had prepared myself, he reminded me of my reply to his question at the Christmas party and asked me to explain what I understood by the school motto. As I stood there fumbling for words he picked up a piece of paper and asked me to read it carefully at home. He said: 'This is the meaning of IN ALL THINGS BE MEN.' It read:

We mean by a man, one who is at once strong and gentle, self-reliant and self-sacrificing. The Crest embodies and the Motto proclaims this, our School's ideal of manhood. The paddle stands for self-reliance and sturdy hard work,

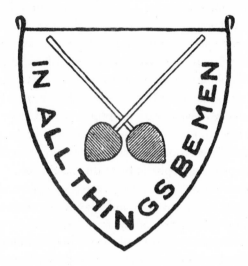

while its broad heart-shaped blade for large-hearted sympathy and fellow-feeling. The paddles are laid across to remind all men of Him who made self-sacrifice the bedrock of His life and purpose, and service to mankind the one dominating motive of His earthly existence.—A.S. Wadia.

The day I joined the school was one of the greatest excitement for me. It started with the arrival of the family priest early in the morning to initiate me in the alphabet of the Sharda script, the ancient script of Kashmir (which is now dead, for all practical purposes: its use is confined to the casting of horoscopes). The initiation ceremony was very simple. After invoking Saraswati, the goddess of learning, the priest held my index finger in his hand and ran it through some sand, which had been spread over a corner of the floor for this purpose, and made

me repeat each sound of the alphabet after him. The exercise concluded with his blessings and those of my mother. Thus solemnized for
learning, I was sent off to school.

My father took no interest in the ceremony nor did he fuss at my
joining a school where he himself was headmaster. There were no arrangements for a playful entry to the school, such as happens in pre-
school kindergartens nowadays. His chaprasi handed me over to a
magnificent looking man wearing a snow-white *dastar* and a red beard
framing a handsome, stern face. This was the famous Moulvi Sahib.
He was in charge of what was called the 'Persian Class'. The Persian
Class was a relic from the days when Persian was the official language
of Kashmiri administration. The name somehow persisted even though
Persian had long been replaced by Urdu and English.

The serious business of learning started soon after Moulvi Sahib
had introduced me to the class and allowed me to distribute some
sweets my mother had given for my classmates. While announcing my
name he did not mention my family name. In the enrolment form my
father had written 'Dhar' instead of 'Hakim'. He had explained the
reason for this change to me earlier. According to him, Hakim indicated a profession which was no longer relevant to us, whereas Dhar
(Bhardwaj), being our gotra, was a permanent point of reference in our
genealogy.

Many years later Moulvi Sahib told me the real reason for the
change. 'Your father hated the name Hakim, that's why you're a Dhar',
he said. Moulvi Sahib said his own preference had been Hakim. He
was saddened by the fact that my father had denied it, particularly
because he thought it suited me. How? He did not explain. I guess he
liked Hakim because it was a Persian word.

I was, however, pleased with the change in family name because I
didn't want to be known in the school as the headmaster's son. Alas,
the alteration in nomenclature was of no avail, for everyone knew the
truth within a day or so and I had to bear that cross throughout my days
in the school.

To come back to my first day in school: after a small ceremony of
introduction, the Moulvi Sahib immediately launched into the Urdu

alphabet, which sounded very different from the version I had heard from the family priest only an hour earlier. I was confused and wanted to go back home. I was let off but asked to come back the next day with writing materials, which consisted of a wooden slab, a small wooden container filled with chalk and water, a couple of reed pens, a rag with which to erase the writing on the slab, and a piece of glass—usually the bottom part of a bottle—to polish the slab so that the pen could run easily on it. This was an awkward load to carry and I did not like it at all. But the preparation of the slab for writing, though a laborious process, was most welcome. It saved us from repeating aloud the alphabet again and again and gave us an opportunity to talk and play amongst ourselves. The Moulvi sahib had an eagle's eye for detecting malingerers, whom he regularly threatened in Urdu, with a menacing accent on the gutturals: *Haddian tor dunga!* (I will break your bones.) But of course nothing like this ever happened.

The madrassa-like ambience was a matter of deliberate policy to induce orthodox parents to send their children to school—parents generally looked upon a playful atmosphere as a waste of time for their wards. As a consequence one had to stay in the Persian Class for a year before being promoted to the First Primary. So I spent a year learning the Urdu primer, which started with the alphabet and progressed to the formation of short sentences. We learnt the entire primer by heart over the year without knowing what the sentences meant. When my mother asked what I had learnt at school, I rattled off all my short Urdu sentences from the primer. She understood not a word either but was pleased with my performance nonetheless. She enjoyed these sessions, making me reproduce lessons which she herself would commit to memory and then recite aloud for my benefit.

My mother had a fantastic memory. She could reproduce scores of verses from *Karima*, and from Sheikh Saadi's *Gulistan* and *Bostan*. She had only to hear her cousins recite them when she was a young girl to have them by heart. Later, she found out the meaning of some of these verses and could quote them with telling effect in conversations, or when tendering advice to children and friends. She could neither read nor write, but her interest in my studies was always intense: she wanted me to be a scholar. My father, on the other hand, was passionate about developing in me an interest in sports and was deeply disappointed at my lack of enthusiasm.

Moving up to the First Primary was like moving into a different world altogether. And as we moved up from one class to the next, the change in atmosphere and activities became sharper and more exciting. We now sat on benches instead of squatting on the ground. The teachers dressed differently, not in a *pheran* like the Moulvi Sahib, but in semi-European garb, and the students were required to be in shorts and shirts in the summer months and jackets and trousers in winter. Unlike other schools, ours did not close for the long winter. After a good snowfall, students were taken out into the playing fields for snow fights. We had one and a half months of summer vacations, during which the school organized outdoor activities such as hiking, mountaineering, swimming, and sailing in the Wular lake. All these activities sharply marked out our school from the others.

The CMS schools were the first to teach English and introduce modern education in Kashmir. The indigenous educational system consisted of *maktabs*—schools attached to mosques—where Muslim boys were taught Arabic, Persian and some elementary arithmetic. The Hindu boys generally went to *pathshala* schools to learn Sanskrit, and to private tutors to learn Persian and acquire traditional knowledge. The establishment of a modern school by English missionaries prompted the maharaja's government to introduce modern education into Kashmir's moribund society.

The maharaja was suspicious of British intentions. He believed that the British regretted their decision to hand over Kashmir to his grandfather under the Treaty of Amritsar in 1846, and that they now wanted to regain the Valley and make it a British settlement. There were genuine reasons for such fears. The maharaja felt the activity of missionaries could well be a part of the larger British design. The establishment of state schools was therefore considered to be more than an educational endeavour; it could also have been a political countermove.

In the state schools education was provided free, making it possible for the children of poor families to attend. Since Muslims were slow to take advantage of these new educational facilities, a section of their more enlightened leadership established the Islamia High School. This combined modern education with an Islamic ethos. By the end of the nineteenth century Srinagar had four high schools, and Anantnag and Baramulla had one each.

Biscoe arrived on the emerging educational scene in 1891 and took charge of the CMS schools. He was a straightforwardly Kiplingesque character, full of faith in himself and his mission, and, influenced by the disparaging observations of several of his compatriots on the character of Kashmiris, was determined to lift the natives from 'the low state into which their tragic history had laid them'. A British friend of his described Biscoe as an 'apostle of cheerful and happy Christianity'. 'In all things be men' summed up the essence of his religion, for true 'manliness entails virtue and rejects vice'.

The years of missionary effort that preceded Biscoe's arrival had produced a small crop of somewhat modernized Kashmiris. These were mostly Pandits. Biscoe recruited some of them to enlarge the teaching staff of his expanding school system. Thus began what his grandson has accurately called 'an unusual but fruitful partnership between a group of Kashmiri Pandits and an English missionary'. It was unusual because the missionary made hardly any converts to his faith, and so could be judged to have failed in his task. But it was fruitful inasmuch as it became an institution which produced self-reliant men whose attitude to work, society and life in general was robust and humane. Biscoe boys were trained to unhesitatingly jump into rivers to save the drowning: indeed this was not unusual in a city situated on both banks of a river often in flood. Biscoe boys were also seen with buckets of water, trying to put out a fire, or helping children to safety, or saving goods from a burning house—this last a common occurrence because the houses were made of combustible materials. Biscoe boys picked up nails and miscellaneous sharp-edged objects off roads

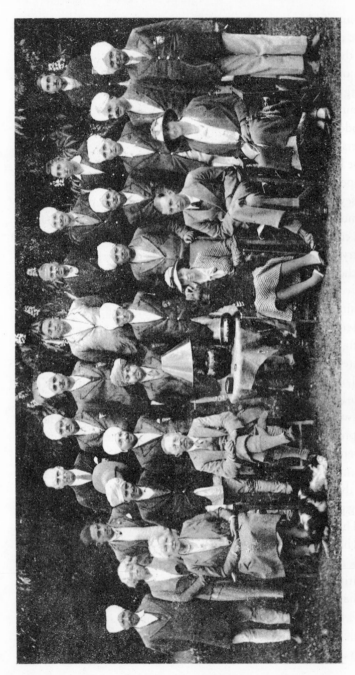

Principal Biscoe and his family with the senior staff of the school, 1934. Biscoe is seated in the front row, second from left

and out of harm's way. They did all these things unselfconsciously. These everyday altruisms became so familiar to the public that they took them for granted. 'Biscoe boys are like that', people would say.

In other ways, Biscoe boys earned no approbation. They started talking about the evils of child marriage and the desirability of allowing young widows to remarry. The Kashmiri Pandit elders, always very orthodox, were thoroughly alarmed. They blamed Biscoe for planting subversion in the minds of young and impressionable pupils. And Biscoe left them in no doubt about his own role in these matters: he was open and blunt about the need for social reform. He poured scorn over several of the cherished customs and social habits of the Pandit community. His annual reports were replete with hilarious, sometimes contemptuous, descriptions of their ways. He was determined to carry through his reformist zeal even within the narrow scope that the school administration provided. For instance, married students were required to pay twice the normal tuition fee and non-swimmers were similarly penalized.

Biscoe had his own way of handling awkward problems. Good-looking young boys in Srinagar were often harassed by goondas. The usual technique was to snatch the boy's cap and molest him if he followed his tormentors in an effort to recover the cap. If the boy did not pursue his cap he would be pursued and waylaid in a lonely spot. Rival gangs would fight for possession of the boy. Ugly stories grew around these practices. Nobody did anything about the abomination till Biscoe intervened when one of his students was victimized. He sent a group of his muscular boys to catch the goonda and his accomplices and bring them to the school, where each one of them was given a pair of boxing gloves and asked to fight it out with Biscoe boys of their own size. The goondas were no boxers; they were felled with a few well-aimed blows by the school's champion boxers. Having bitten the dust, the goondas left the school thoroughly humiliated in the presence of the entire student body. This was Biscoe's lesson to his students in what he called 'the noble art of self-defence'.

This was all to the good. But Biscoe began to teach other lessons which were deeply resented. Matters came to a head in 1902 when, during a terrible cholera epidemic in Kashmir, about 500 people died daily for a fortnight. As one of the main causes of the epidemic was the incredible filth of the city, Biscoe decided to clean it up with the help of his staff and students. This move shocked the community, for it involved scavenging, an activity undreamt of among Brahmins. There was an upsurge of anti-Biscoe feeling and he came to be looked upon as a dangerous scourge.

One does not know how these matters were presented to Mrs Annie Besant. She undertook a long journey from Madras to Srinagar, opened a school in Srinagar, and took away 300 of Biscoe's students. This was considered a retaliatory measure, a protest against Biscoe's educational methods. For Biscoe it was a year of crisis but he weathered it with his customary stoicism.

The spirit of the times was, however, in favour of Biscoe's ideas. Modern education was gaining ground and making inroads into the citadels of orthodoxy. Biscoe was ironically vindicated by a most tragic event. On a summer day in 1934, seven masters were sailing on the Wular lake when the weather suddenly deteriorated. Overwhelmed by a massive squall, they perished despite being strong swimmers. Dina Nath Warikoo, my most favourite teacher, was one of them. It was a terrible loss, for he had also become a friend of mine. He took great interest in my studies and had introduced me to the world of books outside the prescribed texts. The first book he made me read was John Bunyan's *The Pilgrim's Progress*. To make sure I had read the book he asked me to prepare a summary for him. His sudden death was an irreparable loss to me.

Of the seven dead, three were my father's colleagues at the Sheikh Bagh School. On hearing of the tragedy he rushed out of the house on a bicycle to join Biscoe, who was on his way to the lake. I pleaded with him to take me along but he refused. I wanted to see Warikoo, who I hoped was alive. Ultimately I had my way and reached the lake with Biscoe and my father.

At the lake, which looked calm and serene after the storm, the scene was one of utter confusion. Dozens of fishermen with their boats and nets and poles were looking for dead bodies. A large number of former Biscoe boys had already arrived and were frantically diving in and out of the water. In the meanwhile the relatives of the deceased began arriving, distraught and anxious. Biscoe sat on a rock alone, his eyes closed.

I tried imagining what the masters would have done when the storm hit them. Since they were all very good swimmers, I thought they might have swum across the lake and that they might still be lying in the rushes, exhausted but alive. My state of reverie was broken by a sudden clamour: a body had been found. It was the body of Nanak Chand, the captain, the best swimmer in the group. He was called Batuk, which means 'duck', because he was so fond of the water. If Nana Batuk was dead, no one could have survived. After a while dead bodies started being unloaded from the boats, one by one. Even from a distance they looked grotesque and bloated. I was too frightened to go near them. But when Warikoo's body was taken out I rushed towards it, only to recoil in horror at the sight. I went back to one of the boats moored on the shore and sat there staring at the callous calm of the lake. My father picked me up, gave me something to eat, and sent me back home.

The Wular disaster threw the small Kashmiri Pandit community into gloom. But this time there were no protests. A political leader of the community went to the lake to sympathize with a visibly shaken Biscoe and offered him support. 'For the last forty years you have taken your boys to the lake to face storms, and have turned Kashmiris into men', he told Biscoe. This was Biscoe's moment of triumph, overshadowed so completely by tragedy.

As I said, Biscoe loved to lampoon Kashmiris. There was a purpose to this: he was in search of a cause with a capital C. He found it in the upliftment of 'the poor, the forsaken and the fallen humanity of Kashmir'. There is so obviously an element of exaggeration in his stories on the weakness of the Kashmiri character. They served to cast his role in educating them in the heroic mould. Good Biscoe boys were, in his judgement, completely reconstructed human beings. My father and some of his colleagues noted the exaggerations but did not protest for they were convinced of the basic soundness of his educational methods and his passionate desire to regenerate Kashmiris. My father in fact had an unshakeable faith not only in Biscoe but in the entire English race. He was an avid reader of the war news. Just before his death in December 1940 he asked me to bring him up-to-date on the fortunes of the ongoing war. I had rushed home from Delhi on learning of his serious illness and was more interested in the state of his health and the doctors' prognosis. But he insisted, and I gave him a long list of British reverses. With a wan but confident smile he pointed towards the hills visible from his hospital window and said the British were as solid and invulnerable as those.

For people of my generation, this reverence for Biscoe and Britain did not wash long. By the time I reached college, most of us were ardent nationalists and aggressively flaunted coarse khadi clothes. I remember the shock to Biscoe when, dressed in my new garb, I ran into him on the Bund, the famous Srinagar promenade, where he was strolling. He was speechless and red in the face and shouted: 'I can't imagine Vishen Hakim's son in these silly clothes'. It was the first time he hadn't called me 'chota badmash'. At college some of my friends and I moved out of our nationalism into what we thought was a wider worldview: Marxism. Biscoe was heartbroken when one of my former teachers in the school reported what had happened to some of his 'good boys'. This was the time when his tenure in Kashmir was about to end. It was only after he left for good that we realized how much we owed to this eccentric Englishman.

Between the Annie Besant episode and the Wular tragedy drastic changes took place in the Valley. In 1910 an institution called Hindu College was established in Srinagar by Mrs Besant. It was later taken over by the state government and renamed Sri Pratap College, after the maharaja. This institution turned out a steady stream of graduates, mostly Kashmiri Pandits. As their numbers increased they found their areas of employment restricted within the state. The higher echelons of state administration were at that time dominated by Punjabi Hindus, while Kashmiri Pandits manned the lower rungs of administration in the revenue and public works departments and served as clerks in the civil administration. This position within the Dogra regime was a great comedown for them even as compared to their position during the harsh days of Afghan rule earlier.

Dogra rule lasted a hundred years. In the latter half of this period, a few Kashmiri Pandits were inducted into the administration in very senior positions. These were not more than a dozen in number, and all were immigrants to the state. They were descended from families that had migrated out of Kashmir several generations earlier. Socially, culturally and linguistically they were no part of the local Kashmiri Pandit community. In fact, Kashmiris called them *batta*-Punjabi.

In the social structure that prevailed in the early part of the twentieth century, Kashmiri Pandits by and large occupied the lower-middle-class stratum. There were no more than half a dozen families with substantial land holdings at one end of the scale, and a small percentage of rural Pandits who were tenant farmers at the other end. The rest of the community consisted of government servants who manned the lower rungs of administration; shopkeepers; and schoolteachers. The ambition of a young Pandit at the time was to be a clerk, an ambition ridiculed by Master Zinda Kaul in a popular poem entitled 'A ha ha clerki oh ho clerki'.

Despite this relative social downgrading, a whole mythology about Kashmiri Pandit domination over the Dogra administration and their oppression of Muslims has been created. The genesis of this mythology is based on the compulsions of the British policy regarding what came to be known as the Great Game, the century-long rivalry between Czarist Russia and imperialist Britain for the control of Central Asia—a nineteenth century variation of the Cold War. Since these facts have been ignored by ideologues it is necessary to go into them at some length.

By the 1870s the British government had become obsessed with fear of the Russian penetration of the defences of their Indian empire. To put a check on them, frontier defences had been strengthened. But the Gilgit region, which was thought to be particularly vulnerable to Russian designs, was outside the Indian defence schemes because it was part of Kashmir State, which, under the Treaty of Amritsar, was in 'independent possession' of the maharaja. The strategic reasons, however, required take-over of the administration of the state directly by the British government, an act which would be in violation of treaty obligations. Equally worrisome was the fact that the take-over would be looked upon as a step against a maharaja who, like his father and grandfather, had maintained most friendly relations with the government. But, as with the Cold War, strategic considerations overrode all others and a lofty reason had therefore to be found to justify the deed. This was sought by declaring that the maharaja's regime was oppressive, and he himself unfit to rule.

According to the plan prepared by the foreign office, a British officer was inducted in Kashmir as Resident for the first time. Soon after his arrival in the state he dutifully sent reports of the maharaja's 'misrule' to his government. Not only that, he even found the maharaja in 'treasonable correspondence' with Russia! A 'voluntary resignation' was secured from the maharaja and the administration of Kashmir put under the control of a council consisting of his brother and certain selected officials in British service. The council had full powers, subject to the condition that they would take no important step without consulting the Resident, and that they would act upon the Resident's advice whenever it was offered!

The role of the foreign office would have remained a sealed secret but for the efforts of the *Amrita Baazar Patrika*, a Calcutta newspaper which, in a pioneering effort of investigative journalism, unearthed and published the secret documents behind the drama of the take-over. The *Patrika* scoop created a sensation in the country and greatly embarrassed the viceroy. It also inspired William Digby to write his book, *Condemned Unheard*, in which he exposed the plot and established beyond doubt that the maharaja was deposed not because of misrule but because 'Gilgit was wanted for strategic purposes by the

British government'. Digby's findings completely falsified the statement of the secretary of state for India wherein he had said, 'It is quite true that we did interfere in the matter of Kashmir, and why? Because the people of Kashmir were so ground down by the tyranny and ill government of maharaja that we were bound as the paramount power to interfere for the protection of the 'interest of the inhabitants of that country.'[1]

This is not to say that the feudal administration of Kashmir was less oppressive than that of other feudatory states, or for that matter that of the provinces under the direct rule of the British. The village patwaris and revenue officials, for instance, were getting their 'rasoom', an institutionalized bribe sanctified by custom for their work—a phenomenon prevalent all over the subcontinent since the Mughal days of Todar Mal. But as Digby says, 'certain Anglo-Indian newspapers picked on Kashmir and wrote continually about its misgovernment' in order to provide the rationale for British intervention. Kashmiri peasants, no doubt, were poor like their counterparts in India, but their poverty was highly exaggerated to suit policy. Sir Walter Lawrence, who conducted the first land settlement survey in the Valley and who has been widely quoted on the prevalence of bribery in the state, also recorded the following observation: 'If one looks at the purely material condition of the villagers, I should say the Kashmiri peasant is, in every respect, better off than his fellows in India. He has ample food, sufficient clothing, a comfortable house, and abundance of fuel, and he obtains these without much effort. There is general comfort, but no luxury and the process of distribution of wealth, by which a country is divided into the very poor and the very rich, has not yet commenced in Kashmir.'[2]

The purpose of this digression was to explain the British need to present the maharaja's administration as an oppressive regime. Kashmiri Pandits were fitted into this set-up but were minor cogs in the administration. Be that as it may, the alleged oppressiveness of Kashmiri Pandits has not only survived into our times but has received regular

---

[1] William Digby, *Indian Political Agency* (London: 1890), p. 34.
[2] Walter R. Lawrence, *The Valley of Kashmir* (rpt, Srinagar: Chinar, 1992), p. 255.

support from Nationalist and Marxist writers, and has thus become a part of political correctness. Even Sheikh Mohammad Abdullah, who knew Kashmir so well, fell victim to this propaganda. In a reference to these times he says, in his autobiography, that the word 'Pandit' was synonymous with 'ruler'. To lend substance to this view, he says that Kashmiri Pandits are addressed by villagers as 'mahara', an abbreviated form of 'maharaja'. This is a misunderstanding. The fact is that juniors address seniors as 'mahara' if they are Pandits and as 'haz' (an abbreviated form of 'hazrat') if they are Muslims. 'Mahara' and 'haz' are nothing more than polite forms of address used in ordinary parlance; they do not signify a servile attitude, as insinuated by Sheikh Abdullah.

It was not local Pandits but Punjabi Hindus who dominated the administration. Their domination started with the appointment of Diwan Jawala Sahai, a rich Punjabi from Aminabad, as the first prime minister whose office remained hereditary for many years. He had earned this bonanza for the help he had rendered to Maharaja Gulab Singh in putting together the sum of 75 lakh rupees, which he had to pay the British government in lieu of the war indemnity imposed on the Lahore durbar.

In the unsettled circumstances of the time, it was natural that the diwan and his family should prefer to bring into the administration their own people, whose loyalty they could trust implicitly. This trend created a Punjabi Hindu ruling class in the state. They not only occupied places of trust and power in the administration but also became a dominant element in the commercial field, particularly in wholesale trade, thus making inroads into the economic space previously occupied by Kashmiri Muslims. There was not much social intercourse between Punjabis and Kashmiris. Punjabis settled in clearly demarcated areas of the city of Srinagar, where they formed an enclave of their own with hardly any social contact between them and the local people, whom they called *hattos*, a contemptuous term used for coolies. The resentment of Kashmiris against the growing Punjabi domination gave birth to the demand of 'Kashmir for Kashmiris' which has undergone several mutations: from the exclusion of outsiders ('non-state subjects') in the matter of acquiring property in the state during the maharaja's days, to special status for the state under article 370 in the Constitution of India, and now to the demand for azadi, which has become an international issue.

After lagging behind by a generation, Muslims were taking to higher education. Their arrival on the scene coincided with the deteriorating economic situation and increased competition for jobs. The world-wide economic Depression which started in 1929 hit Kashmir very hard. The steep fall in agricultural prices reduced farmers to a state of destitution. It was distressing to see farmers come down from their villages to sell rice in the city for just two rupees a *khirwar* (a corruption of the Persian word *kharbar*, i.e. a donkey-load equivalent to 77 kgs). The fall in state revenues and the general decline in economic activity aggravated unemployment, especially among the educated.

One of the new arrivals from these emerging educated Muslims was Sheikh Mohammed Abdullah, who had a Masters degree from Aligarh Muslim University. Frustrated in his quest for a job which would do justice to his education, he set up reading rooms and study circles where small groups of young men discussed political questions. It was from these reading rooms that a powerful movement arose which attracted the educated unemployed, the frankly communal, the religious crusaders, and the poverty-stricken peasantry.

This movement began with communal overtones. The 13th of July 1931 is now generally recognized as the day when the freedom movement began in Kashmir. On that day twenty-two Kashmiri Muslims who were demonstrating outside the Central Jail in Srinagar were gunned down by the Kashmir police. The demonstrators were expressing their sense of solidarity with one Abdul Qadeer, a non-Kashmiri who was being tried in the jail premises for having made seditious speeches and inciting people to violence against the state. Qadeer was rumoured to be in the employ of the British Resident in Srinagar. Sheikh Abdullah has described him as a *khansaman* (cook) of a British major from the Yorkshire Regiment who was sojourning in Kashmir. In any case

Qadeer seems, by all accounts, to have been a shadowy character. The tragic and unprecedented firing led to large-scale rioting in downtown Srinagar. Several Hindus were killed, and their houses and shops looted. These events led to communal tensions which made us, Kashmiri Pandit students, aware of our status as members of a minority community for the first time in our lives. My mother's younger sister lived in the riot-stricken area. My father had to rescue her and her two young children and bring them to our place for safety.

The communal tension abated only after some years. Sheikh Abdullah strove valiantly to restore the old amity between the communities and finally succeeded, in 1939, in converting the Muslim Conference into his National Conference. In the process he lost some of his influence among Jammu's Muslims. However, he gained the confidence of the minorities. Several Hindu and Sikh leaders now joined him in his nationalist endeavour. As a result of these political changes, the Kashmiri Pandits' sense of their separate identity became less sharp.

Muslim demands for proportionate employment in the state's services received a positive response from the government but had an ominous meaning for us: we felt threatened. Some of our seniors started an agitation against the recommendations of a commission which had been set up under the chairmanship of Sir Bertrand Glancy to look into popular grievances. The commission had recommended a better deal for educated Muslims. Kashmiri Pandits, who had known very few avenues of employment outside government service, now felt threatened and disheartened by what they thought was a bleak future. The more enterprising among my fellow students began talking rather more positively about trade and business as alternative sources of employment. This trend received encouragement from Kashap Bandhu, a Kashmiri Pandit leader who had spent the formative years of his life in Punjab. He arrived in the Valley soon after the 13th July episode to provide leadership to the rudderless Kashmiri Pandit community.

Kashap Bandhu started a movement of social reform which went beyond earlier attempts to allow the remarriage of widows and end the dowry system and curtail extravagant expenditure on marriages and so on. He wanted to change the very look of the men and women of his community. He argued against wearing the pheran, the loose

Kashmiri gown, which he said made men lazy and effeminate. He ridiculed the habit of wearing earrings by young Kashmiri Pandit boys. He exhorted people to take to professions other than government clerkships. As a result of his efforts Kashmiri Pandit women substituted saris for the pheran and men opened shops in an effort to sell textiles, hardware, pharmaceuticals, and leather shoes. They even set up tailoring shops, which were considered pretty low in the social scale. Kashap Bandhu and his colleagues were, however, rather more successful in widening economic choice than in the reform of traditional social customs.

It was in this politically surcharged atmosphere that I joined the S.P. College, as it was known, in 1934. After centuries, it seemed, Kashmiris were shaking off their passiveness and, like the rest of India, demanding freedom from feudal oppression and political servitude. Strong political winds blew all over the state.

The composition of the teaching staff had changed by the mid-thirties, when I joined the college. The non-local element, consisting of Bengalis and Punjabis, had sharply declined and was replaced by Kashmiris, mainly Pandits. Ours was what is called a *mufassil* college, where students could only get a simple B.A. or B.Sc. There were no arrangements for honours and postgraduate studies. The college was isolated from the university to which it was affiliated in distant Lahore. Such institutions are usually intellectual backwaters. Ours was saved from that fate to some extent by the fact that Srinagar attracted teachers from the plains during their summer recess. Some of these were invited to the college for special lectures. I remember L.C. Jain, economics professor at Punjab University, and B.N. Ganguli of Delhi University addressing economics students at my college while vacationing in Kashmir. The college sometimes managed distinguished visitors for a public lecture: Tej Bahadur Sapru lectured to an overflowing audience on the essence of liberalism; C.P. Ramaswami Aiyer spoke on the Hindu conception of truth; K.M. Munshi discussed Indian culture; Hafeez Jalandari, the poet, recited to an ecstatic crowd his famous poem Rakkasa. These were exciting events, long remembered and talked about. But all said and done they were sporadic and could not sustain intellectual life at a satisfactory level.

Barring Professor Jaya Lal Kaul, who taught English, none of our teachers was outstanding, though most were devoted to their students and always available for advice. But with none amongst them could we converse on the kind of political and economic problems which were engaging us. We had to go outside the campus in search of such people. At this time, along with some of my classfellows, I came in contact with Ghulam Mohammad Sadiq, a young and upcoming Kashmiri politician with radical views. He was very unusual among Kashmiri politicians. Not a great public speaker like Sheikh Abdullah—who could sway the masses whichever way he liked—Sadiq was too sophisticated to be a mob orator and too honest to resort to catchy phrases. Nor was he an organization man like Bakshi Ghulam Mohammad, for he was too aloof to be on backslapping terms with party workers. Sadiq was an intellectual who believed in the power of ideas. His ideas were not mere abstract notions culled from books, but rather ideas wrested from a deeper understanding of the problems of Kashmir. Under Sadiq's influence we became more and more interested in Kashmir's politics. My own interest in these ideas remained deep within me and found realization much later, when I moved out of Kashmir. As for the rest of our group, within which D.P. Dhar was the most prominent, several joined the National Conference and became colleagues of Sadiq. Another prominent member was N.N Raina who joined the Communist Party and established a party cell in Kashmir.

I continued my association with Sadiq. He introduced me to B.P.L. and Freda Bedi, and to K.M. Ashraf. The Bedis were regular summer visitors to Srinagar, their activities being centred around the top political leadership, especially Sheikh Abdullah. They were a glamorous couple and too elite for the politically uninitiated. My contact with them was brief but intense and fateful. I was asked by Sadiq to help Bedi in the preparation of a document on political and economic reforms for the National Conference. The document, called 'New Kashmir', was later adopted by the Conference as the sheet anchor of its ideology and became part of its programme of action after it came to power in 1947. I did nothing more than assemble some data and prepare a few notes for Bedi. That was the end of my contact with him. Though mine was a minor contribution, the police found this out and put me under 'Category B' of political undesirables.

My association with K.M. Ashraf lasted longer. He came to Srinagar to address a conference organized by the Students Federation. Though very young, he had already achieved a countrywide reputation. He addressed the open session of the conference twice, first in English and later in Urdu. Both these occasions became the main events of the conference and had a tremendous impact on the audience. On the podium he was a star performer; his marshalling of facts was impressive, his arguments persuasive, his eloquence torrential. Young students like me were swept off their feet. I felt greatly privileged when I, along with a hundred others, had tea with him. We felt sure we were meeting a great leader who was bound to play an important role in moulding the fortunes of India. When I met him in Delhi a few years later he seemed to have lost his elan, and by the time he became an academic in Delhi University he was burnt out as a political activist.

The Great Depression of the early thirties had, as I said, hit the Kashmir economy hard. My classfellows, like students in the rest of India, were in ferment and receptive to 'dangerous thoughts'. Those of us who were influenced by Marxism were convinced that the Depression was a crisis in capitalism. We began to pay more and more attention to what was happening at the broader, national level in India. We were thrilled when a large number of Congressmen—though not the majority—turned to socialism. Nehru was their leader and we were keenly interested in all that he said. As Congress President he declared in April 1936 that the only key to the solution of the world's problems, and of India's, lay in socialism. 'When I use this word', he said 'I do so not in a vague humanitarian way but in the scientific, economic sense.'[3]

To our utter surprise our Muslim friends were less attracted by this increasing focus on socialism within public debate. Since they always emphasized the backwardness and the poverty of their community, we presumed they would be even more enthusiastic about socialism than

[3] Presidential Address to the National Congress (Lucknow, 1936), in *India and the World*, p. 82.

we were. On the contrary, they seemed sceptical of our certitudes, especially of our assertion that socialism was a panacea for all social evils. Some of them were inclined to agree with what Jinnah said in his presidential address to the annual session of the Muslim League a year after Nehru had addressed the Congress session in the same city. Jinnah protested that 'all this talk of hunger and poverty was intended to lead people to socialistic and communistic ideals.' At this time Jinnah was still an unknown and remote figure to us in Kashmir.

It was not Jinnah the politician but Iqbal the poet who was compelling attention for my politically-minded Muslim friends. Iqbal's poetry became very popular with them, even while we were all proud of Iqbal's Kashmiri descent. The fact that his ancestor was a Sapru, a Pandit, added to his attraction for us. There were poignant verses among his compositions lamenting the poverty and backwardness of Kashmir. Sheikh Abdullah, aided by his musical voice, made effective use of Iqbal during his campaigns for political mobilization in the state. The Sheikh was careful in his selection of Iqbal's verses, using only those which served his political cause. Radicals and reactionaries could quote him equally effectively; both drew support from him for what they professed or sought to do.

Iqbal had graduated out of his nationalistic phase and, by the time of his death in 1938, had become the prophet of the Indian Islamic renaissance. The crisis in western society, according to his devotees, was the result of its irreligious, or rather un-Islamic, character, and the remedy was a return to the pre-capitalist society of early Islam. To my Kashmiri classfellows Iqbal's Islamic fervour was less evident than his poetic and political support to Sheikh Abdullah and his struggle against the feudal regime. Iqbal was without doubt the most influential member of the All India Kashmir Committee which had been set up in Lahore to lend support to the political movement in Kashmir.

It was only when I went to Delhi for my postgraduate studies that I saw Iqbal's influence in full bloom. His magnificent poetry was leading Muslims into a romantic view of medievalism, soothing the minds of young men distressed and baffled by the contemporary malaise. His poetry generated an atmosphere which was congenial for the emergence of a Fuhrer. Like Nietzsche, Iqbal had unbounded admiration for 'those rare great minds' who alone can shape the destinies of nations; Qaid-e Azam was the natural outcome of his lyricism. Muslim intellectuals who were sympathetic to the Muslim League were quick to realize this potential. They appropriated the immense prestige of his authority for their own purpose, and it was distressing to see Muslim friends, whom Iqbal called to a New Sinai, avidly consuming medieval political ideas. Yet simultaneously Sheikh Abdullah made devastatingly effective use of Iqbal's poetry to raise the political consciousness of his people. Iqbal had denounced the Treaty of Amritsar, under which Kashmir was acquired by the Dogra ruler, as 'a sale deed'. In powerfully emotive verses he exhorted the morning breeze to blow over Geneva and convey to the League of Nations his torment at the sale not only of peasants, pastures and meadows, but of an entire nation at a throwaway price. I still remember the response of the audience when the Sheikh recited such verses in his emotionally charged, trembling voice, concluding in a reverberating roar of denunciation against the treaty and the ruler.

CHAPTER TWO

College in Delhi

I was a good student and did well in the examinations, often standing first in my class, especially in Economics. So I was keen to do my Masters in that subject after graduating in 1938. Most of my friends decided to go to Lucknow University, but my father was against my going there. He had strong views on the subject for he had heard that Kashmiri students in Lucknow formed a group of their own, stayed in the same hostel, had a mess of their own, and did not interact with other people. Moreover, most Kashmiri students combined a law degree with their Masters, this being allowed in UP's universities. The acquisition of a law degree was a kind of insurance against failure to get a proper job, but my father believed this was a ruinous programme and he was sure it would result in the Kashmir bar being overcrowded with briefless lawyers. Forman Christian College at Lahore could have been an alternative, but my father had disqualified the institution after he found perfumed face creams in the hostel room of a friend's son on an earlier visit.

Nobody in Kashmir had heard of Delhi University. Only two students from the Valley had ever gone there, though both had done well and had returned to Kashmir in 1938. One of these was J.N. Bhan, who had been a favourite student of Dr B.N. Ganguli. It was Bhan who had invited Dr Ganguli to our college for a lecture and he was keen to send his younger brother, a classfellow of mine, to Delhi for his Masters in mathematics. He persuaded my father to allow me to venture there as well. And so it was that Bhan's brother Ram Narain and I became the second pair from Kashmir to join Delhi University.

Ram Narain and I left Srinagar on the 3rd of October 1938, a few days before the colleges were to open in Delhi. It was our first trip out of the Valley; neither of us had ever seen the other side of the Banihal tunnel. The way my parents, especially my mother, bade me farewell gave the impression that I was going to Mars, never to return. She was full of advice and prayers for my safety.

We left by bus for Jammu where, after a night's rest, we were to take the train to Delhi. En route we keenly observed the changing landscape. Jammu looked like a different world. Everything seemed different: people, language, dress, manners, even the structure of houses. The terrain was rocky, there was no greenery, and the atmosphere was hazy with dust. Ram Narain did not like what he saw and felt homesick.

We had never seen a train and were looking forward to our first railway journey with the excitement of young boys. We had tickets for a third-class compartment. The coolie, who insisted on carrying our four heavy suitcases all by himself, suddenly vanished in the jostling crowd. Having lost contact with him we did not know what to do. Panic-stricken, we rushed around and finally discovered him at the door of our compartment and were shoved in by him. The compartment was jampacked and we were able to get places to sit only at Sialkot. After that we were so afraid of losing our seats that we never got down till we reached Delhi. We ate what we could buy from hawkers through the window.

In Delhi we stayed with a friend of the elder Bhan. Ram Narain was keen to join St Stephen's College. I too was carrying a letter for a St Stephen's professor, C.B. Young. This was at the instance of my father. I myself had no desire to join that college. I had heard from Mohan Kishan Tiku, the other Kashmiri student who had preceded us, that St Stephen's was an exclusivist and elitist institution full of boys from toady families, while Hindu College, despite its name, attracted students from every section of the community. It was also reputed to have the blessings of freedom fighters. Talking to our host, I also discovered that co-operative teaching arrangements between St Stephen's and Hindu College had broken down. The only economics professor I had heard of was Dr Ganguli, and he was at Hindu College. But we had first to go to St Stephen's College. Ram Narain was promptly admitted. Before I could meet C.B. Young I ran into K.C. Nag, the head of the economics department. I told him that J.N. Bhan had suggested I approach him. He looked incredulous and said in a brusque manner: 'You are mistaken, he must have asked you to join the college across the street.' This suited my purpose very well. I could tell my father that after this summary treatment I did not see C.B. Young. I went across the street.

The sight of the Hindu College building depressed me. A chaprasi guided me to the staff room. The look of the staff room was even more depressing, it was so dark and dingy. Ganguli was sitting in a corner reading a book. He was most pleased to know that his favourite Kashmiri student had sent me to meet him. He arranged my admission and the allotment of a room in the hostel forthwith. He was most encouraging and told me he hoped that I would do as well as Bhan, who had secured first position in the M.A. examination, which had upset Professor Nag of the rival college.

The department of economics at Hindu College consisted of just three teachers. Dr Ganguli was, of course, a very good economist and an expert on international trade. He was also an excellent teacher. He was my only anchor in that otherwise disappointing set-up. The other two teachers were no better than those in Srinagar. I realized quite early that we were going to be a self-taught group. We exchanged notes with students in St Stephen's. This exchange was strictly on barter terms: they were interested in our notes from Ganguli's lectures, we were interested in their theory notes. Underlying this friendly exchange was intense rivalry between the two colleges. The competition goaded us to hard work and did us a lot of good.

Our hostel had no common dining arrangements. There were five kitchens run by five cooks and one could join a group attached to each cook. The arrangement was supervised by the students themselves. The college authorities took no interest in these matters except ordain that only vegetarian food was cooked in these kitchens. This enforced vegetarianism was no hardship for the residents, almost all of them being vegetarians. However, they were divided into two main groups, the Jats and the Banias. I joined one of the Jat kitchens. Each of the Jat boys had a small tin of pure ghee which he would carry to the kitchen at mealtimes to smother his chapatis with, and it would then be properly locked if left with the cook. They used to make a great show of the large quantities of ghee they could consume. This Jat obsession with ghee made it more than an item of food for them: it was a symbol of their macho outlook on life. The segregation of Jats and Banias in different kitchens had nothing to do with their food habits. It was caste feelings and politics that separated them. The Jat boys were all votaries of Sir Chhotu Ram, the leader of Haryana's Jats and a member of Sir Sikander Hayat Khan's Unionist ministry in Punjab. The Bania boys were all pro-Congress. The Jat boys were proud of their physical prowess, the Banias of their brains. Whenever they met and talked politics, one could feel the tension in their relations, but it never flared into outright quarrel. I became fond of both groups. I used to go on long walks with a Jat boy and have after-dinner discussions with the Banias. Since I was the only one from outside their region, I was a bit of a curiosity and prized for that reason.

Ram Narain, my fellow Kashmiri at St Stéphen's, missed Kashmir so much that he decided to go back after only a month's stay. Each time we met during that month he would intone in a sad voice: 'what do they know of Kashmir who only Kashmir know?' I tried to curb his nostalgia for Kashmir but it proved of no avail. I learnt later that it was not Kashmir beckoning him as much as a girl there that he wanted to marry. I would have missed him bitterly but for the abundant warmth of my Jat and Bania friends.

Almost all my classfellows had done their honours in economics and the syllabus for the M.A. course was easy for them. I had to make up for the deficiency. This hardly left any time for anything else. I worked hard but, even so, was surprised to get the highest marks in the first-year examination. The only extramural thing I did during that year was attend and occasionally participate in debates in the college parliament. The Hindu College parliament was not the usual college debating society. It was the replica of a parliament, with the full paraphernalia of a prime minister, his cabinet, a leader of the opposition, and so on. It had its own building, built after the fashion of a Greek amphitheatre. The debates were of a high standard and members would quote May's *Parliamentary Practice* after the style of accomplished parliamentarians. Many members of the Central Legislative Assembly used to participate in these debates. I heard Bhulabhai Desai, leader of the Congress legislative party and his deputy, Khan Abdul Qayum Khan, participating in these debates.

The academic year 1939–40 began with the outbreak of war and the atmosphere in the college changed as abruptly as in the rest of the country. Everyone discussed the war and how the international situation would affect India. The Indian leaders' attitude to the war was the hottest subject of public debate. Most students were disappointed by the reactions of the top Congress leadership. They were furious with Gandhiji, who had said two days after the war was declared: 'I am not thinking just now of India's deliverance. It will come, but what will it be worth if England and France fall, or if they come out victorious over Germany, ruined and humbled.' Nehru's attitude to the Nazis and Fascists was well known: he was passionately opposed to them. But students were more in tune with Subash Bose's opinion that Britain's difficulty was India's opportunity. One of my hostel friends had a radio set on which we would listen to Berlin Radio's special broadcasts beamed to India. German victories would thrill most students. As for myself, in the discussions that would follow the broadcasts I was more on Nehru's side, for I was anti-Nazi without being pro-British.

Despite the opposition of the Indian political class, mobilization in aid of the Allies started in right earnest. Centres for recruitment to the armed services sprouted all over the country. One such centre was opened in the vicinity of our college, near the Red Fort. We could see long lines of sturdy men offering to enlist. Attractive advertisements appeared in the newspapers proclaiming career opportunities in the armed services. Two of our fellow hostellers who were very vocal in their denunciation of the British informed us calmly, one day, that they had received 'offers' of commissions in the army and were leaving within a week. Without waiting for questions, they said that an independent India would need experienced army officers, and that was why they had volunteered.

The indifference of the British government to India's political aspirations put the Congress party, which was in power in eight states, in an awkward situation. The Congress leadership was prepared to help in the war effort provided the British government made a clear statement about the post-war political status of India. Since there was no satisfactory response, the Congress ministries resigned in protest in November 1939. Though it was not realized at that time, in retrospect this seems to have been a great tactical blunder. Jinnah, the great tactician, took full advantage of the ensuing situation. To begin with, he called on Muslims to celebrate the departure of Congress provincial governments as 'a day of deliverance and thanksgiving'. He opened up his campaign against Congress by organizing 'atrocity' propaganda against their ministries. Several reports in which these 'atrocities' were catalogued were prepared and circulated to denounce Congress as the great menace to Indian Muslims—much greater than British imperialism.

The reports were well written, from the propaganda point of view. Conclusions were not arrived at after careful reasoning. What was sought was to play upon feelings and to produce an emotional effect on people. Various Congress governments issued press notes denying the allegations, but this had no effect on my Muslim friends, most of whom were fellow Kashmiris at Aligarh Muslim University. Having known their earlier views, I was amazed at the impact of the League propaganda. They had become deeply suspicious of Hindus. Even the impartial pronouncements of provincial governors did not allay their suspicions. For instance Sir Henry Haig, the governor of UP, wrote in the *Asiatic Review* of August 1940 that 'they [his Congress Ministry] acted with impartiality and a desire to do what was fair. Indeed, towards the end of their time they were being seriously criticised by the Hindu Mahasabha on the ground that they were not fair to the Hindus . . .' My friends, like other Muslims, continued to believe people who informed them that the history of the 'atrocities committed on Muslims in the Congress provinces was simply heart-rending and could only be compared to that of the post-mutiny days, and even worse.'[1]

A Muslim friend who was studying at the Law College showed me a short note on propaganda techniques meant for League workers which was given to him by an Aligarh professor. It quoted Goebbels: 'whether propaganda has been good is shown when it has had the chance of working for a certain time on the type of people whom it aims at inspiring and winning for its ideas. . . . So no one can say your propaganda is too crude, too vulgar or too brutal or it is not respectable enough; for these are not characteristic indications of its specific nature. It is not its business to be respectable or mild or tender or humble.' Whether inspired by it or not, the League propaganda showed all the characteristics of the Hitler technique—exaggeration, menace, instilling fear into the masses, producing a sort of ecstasy and wild excitement in the crowd. It succeeded in creating a persecution complex among Muslims. They suspected even the Wardha scheme of education—which attempted to combine 'mental with manual training' and gave a vocational bias to education—as part of an anti-Muslim agenda. That the author of the scheme was the famous Muslim educationist Dr Zakir Hussain, the head of Jamia Millia Islamia, made no difference to them.

I have digressed to give a detailed description of the League propaganda because I find that, in order to be politically correct, history is being subverted. Even a thoughtful writer like Sunil Khilnani feels it necessary to say in his otherwise excellent book *The Idea of India*: 'there is a real force to the point that practical experience of Congress rule in the Indian provinces after the election of 1937 was instrumental in encouraging Muslim political alienation. Congress governments, subject in many cases to the influence of nationalist Hindus, lost the trust of Muslims . . .'[2]

In conversations with Muslim friends I ran into concepts which I had not heard before. One such was 'Bania imperialism'. The term 'Bania' was used the way the Nazis used the term 'Jew'. It was not an

[1] K.S.Abdur Rehman Khan, MLA (Berar), in *Eastern Times*, 26 April 1940.
[2] (London: Hamish Hamilton, 1997), p.163.

analytical concept like 'bourgeois' in Marxism, but a term of abuse and hatred. 'Bania' personified all those forces of evil which frustrated the destiny of 'the Muslim nation' in India. Gandhi, the arch-Bania, naturally came in for vigorous attack for standing between Muslims and the Millennium. In this heated atmosphere, Banias, Congress and Hindus became interchangeable terms. The Congress, as an organization of 'Banias' in particular and Hindus in general, was said to be plotting to crush Muslims. These so-called crusaders against Islam were described in lurid colours. Here is a specimen of such writing: 'Scraggy, chocolate-coloured longevity seekers, sitting in loin cloths and weaving metaphysical hocus pocus with subtle schemes of economic pressure, five feet four inch processionists with flat noses and bulging cheeks, shouting outlandish slogans in shrill voices—all this smelling strongly of usury, untouchability and an inordinate fear and hatred of the Muslims.'[3] In contrast, the League provided hope in the form of a resolution which was passed at its Lahore session in March 1940, and which has become famous as the Pakistan Resolution. The passage of this resolution had an immediate impact everywhere in the country, including our little student community at Hindu college. There was a great deal of anxiety and anger among the Hindu students. Although it was the examination time—my final M.A. examination—everyone was talking about Pakistan and which areas would constitute it. Would it materialize? Could it survive? Everyone had a view, mostly in the negative.

Soon after my examinations, I decided to leave for home. While saying goodbye to my friends I realized how much, without my knowing it, Delhi had entered into my life. I postponed my departure for a week, went around Delhi with one of my friends, and saw the history of India scattered all over the city and its surroundings. I did all this with a feeling of desperation, believing it was my last opportunity to see what I had missed during my two years' stay.

[3] El Hamza, *Pakistan: A Nation*, p.114.

When I reached home, I found that the war-promoted boom in the Indian economy had had beneficial effects on Kashmir as well. The gloom of the Depression years had lifted. Economic activity was getting more diversified and employment opportunities had multiplied. The number of tourists visiting Kashmir had visibly increased. More important was a change in the political atmosphere. It was a change in sharp contrast with what was happening in the rest of the country. The National Conference, which had come into existence in the previous year, was going to have its first annual session in September at Baramulla in North Kashmir. The transformation of the Muslim Conference into the National Conference was a remarkable event, considering the fact that in March the All India Muslim League had, in its Lahore Resolution, demanded that 'geographically contiguous units are demarcated into regions which should be so constituted, with such territorial re-adjustment as may be necessary, that the areas in which Muslims are numerically in a majority, as in the North-West and Eastern zones of India, should be grouped to constitute "Independent States" in which the constituent units shall be autonomous and sovereign.' Having seen the impact of League propaganda about the 'two nation theory' on my Muslim friends in Delhi and Aligarh, it was refreshing to see the National Conference asserting its own heritage of a deeply rooted and composite culture, and its own national vision of the future. Sheikh Abdullah, the undisputed leader of the Conference, was stating emphatically that the goal of the movement he was leading was to break the old shell of an archaic economic and political set-up.

It is not generally known that after attending the Ramgarh session of the Congress as a special invitee, Sheikh Abdullah attended the Lahore session of the League. He himself recorded this episode in his autobiography. He says he just wanted to get a feel of League politics directly, by sitting in the audience and observing its proceedings. But his conspicuously tall figure betrayed him. Sardar Aurangzeb Khan, the League leader from the North West Frontier Province, spotted him and invited him to take a seat on the podium. The Sheikh declined and said he had come to listen and not speak.

Sheikh Abdullah is very critical in his description of what he saw and heard, but what appalled him most was a speech by Nawab Bahadur

Yar Jung, the fiery orator from Hyderabad. In his speech the Nawab, after sympathizing with Kashmiris and endorsing their demand for responsible government, rejected a similar demand on behalf of the people of his own state on the plea that Hyderabad was acquired by Muslims with the help of the sword and Muslims would keep it that way. The Sheikh left the meeting in disgust and, next day, called on Maulana Ghulam Rasool Mehr and Abdul Majid Salik, editors of the influential Urdu newspaper *Inqilab*. He told them of the speech by Bahadur Yar Jung and asked them if they could explain the Nawab's contradictory attitude to Kashmir and Hyderabad. This irritated Mehr. Responding sharply he said, 'We can sacrifice lakhs of Kashmiris for Hyderabad.' Terminating the conversation, the Sheikh says he kept his cool and told Mehr politely: 'You may want to sacrifice Kashmiris but are Kashmiris prepared for it?'

Jinnah's 'two nation theory' went against the grain of feelings among Kashmiris at this time. With the exception of a few families who had come in with the Muslim invaders, all Kashmiri Muslims were converts from Hinduism, and their descendants. Jinnah had visited Srinagar in 1936. He was received by people as a distinguished Indian leader. The Muslim Conference had organized a reception in his honour and presented him a public address. Jinnah had then advised them not only to befriend non-Muslims but consider them components of the economy and polity of one country. But, as the Sheikh wryly points out in his autobiography, this was before Jinnah had become Qaid-i Azam.

Some time in June, our examination results appeared. I was delighted to receive a telegram from Dr Ganguli saying I had passed in the first division and that the college was going to offer me one of the two tutorial fellowships that had been instituted a year earlier. The other Fellow was being nominated from the mathematics department. We were expected to take some tutorials and work for a research degree.

This arrangement suited me very well. Back in Delhi I found another piece of good news awaiting me. Sir Maurice Gwyer, the new vice-chancellor, was anxious to build a proper campus for the university. To begin with he offered large plots of land to the premier colleges affiliated to the university. St Stephen's started constructing its buildings right away. Our college delayed its construction programmes on account of financial problems but used several bungalow-type buildings on the land allotted to it as staff quarters. The principal, Dr Ganguli, and some other members of staff, including myself as a Tutorial Fellow, were accommodated in these buildings. For me it was a great luxury to have two rooms with an attached bathroom all to myself. To have the Delhi Ridge, with its numerous and well shaded trails, in the close neighbourhood was unbelievable good luck. This part of Delhi was in those days very open and quiet. The land now occupied by the bustling neighbourhoods of Kamla Nagar and Shakti Nagar was part of an abandoned golf course. The only habitation was Chandrawal village near Malkaganj Chowk. During the Mutiny of 1857 its inhabitants had harassed British soldiers camping on the Ridge. A young man from the village was now a chaprasi of the principal. He would regale us with stories of the brave deeds of his ancestors against British and Mughal rulers. The police kept a stern eye on the village. Now, of course, the village has been swallowed up by the urban sprawl.

I had hardly spent two months in these new and bracing surroundings when I received an ominous telegram from Kashmir informing me of my father's serious illness. Only two months earlier, he and I had cycled to Sopore. Throughout the journey he cycled ahead of me and our only stop to rest had been because I was tired out.

I left for home the same evening. When I reached I found him in a hospital, where he had been operated upon for a carbuncle on his neck. His doctor told me that he had earlier been diagnosed as a diabetic but apparently he had taken no notice.

On the third day he passed away at the age of fifty-nine. It happened at dead of night. My mother and I were alone with the dead body. She herself was sick and looked desolate as she sat clasping my hand. To my horror I found that when I tried to say something to her, no words came. I rushed out of the room and tried to talk to the nurse on duty and found I had suddenly lost all speech. I loathed myself for this. I thought of my father and was ashamed at how disappointed he would have been at my state. Speechless, I listened to my mother's instructions on the funeral arrangements. She told me what I had to do as the oldest son. The thought of lighting the pyre was something I felt quite beyond me.

In the morning, when I went home to make the necessary arrangements I found my seven-year-old brother trying to find out what had happened. His whole innocent manner brought tears to everyone's eyes and speech to me. I was able to speak to my brother and asked him to find our father's pet dog, who had suddenly disappeared during the night. I went through the rites and ceremonies mechanically but the thought of lighting the pyre did not leave me. As we neared the cremation grounds I felt my fright was becoming visible. At the cremation ground one pyre was already ablaze and a young boy, not much older than my little brother, was going around it. The sight of this orphan suddenly gave me courage and I went through the rites without disgracing myself.

My father's death changed my research plans. I had become the head of a family consisting of a sick mother and four small children. I could no longer handle my new responsibilities with the fifty rupees that I earned in Delhi from my fellowship, most of which I had to spend for my own survival. I looked for a job in Srinagar and was told an economics lecturer's post was to be filled in a couple of months' time. I applied for the job and left for Delhi after a month's stay at home. In Delhi I gave some private tuitions to supplement my meagre income. To my surprise I was not called for the interview and the job was offered to a Muslim candidate with a third class M.A. degree. I was furious, even though I knew it was not anything personal against me: this was a case of positive discrimination, as recommended by the Glancy Commission, to raise the percentage of Muslims in the services.

Nevertheless, when I went back to Srinagar during the summer holidays, I was persuaded by my friends to seek redress from the prime minister, Gopalaswamy Ayyangar. I was granted an interview, which was considered to be a hopeful sign by my friends. Mr Ayyangar had acquired a great reputation in Kashmir for being an outstandingly able and firm administrator. His photographs gave the impression of a stern, unsmiling man. When I was ushered into his office room I found I had to walk quite some distance to reach his desk. He looked exactly like his photograph, only a little more grim. He beckoned me to sit with a slight nod of his head and listened to my complaint patiently, without any expression on his face. When I stopped, he simply said, 'Young man, these are haphazard times here; try your luck next time.' I was too intimidated to ask what he meant.

Meanwhile I applied for jobs to several colleges outside Kashmir. In late August 1941 I was called for an interview at Edwardes College, Peshawar.

CHAPTER THREE

Among the Pathans of Peshawar

I went to Peshawar because I needed a job, the place had no attraction for me in other respects. The thought of living among Pathans intimidated me, for I had read and heard many horror stories associated with Afghan rule over Kashmir.

The proximity of Afghanistan with Kashmir and the economic, political and cultural exchanges between the two territories have a long and varied history. In the folk tradition of Kashmir, however, the ancient links seem to have been long forgotten. Knowledge of Buddhist contact during the Kushan age, when Peshawar was the imperial capital and Kashmir part of the Kushan empire, is confined to the more obscure parts of history books. What stands out in the collective memory of Kashmiris, particularly among the Pandits, is the barbarities they suffered at the hands of Afghans.

Most of the people in the train that took me from Rawalpindi to Peshawar were Pathans, or 'Pakhtuns' as they preferred to call themselves. One of the many harsh things I had heard Kashmiris say about Pathans came to my mind during the journey: '*Peshi een sangdillan sar bureedan chu gul chidan ast*', which means 'For these stony-hearted people, beheading a person is no more cruel than plucking a flower.'

Even while such thoughts assailed my mind, the fierce-looking Pathan sitting next to me offered me tea, which he had ordered for us both as a matter of course. When he spoke to me in Urdu his tone changed dramatically from the raucous, guttural accents of Pashto to a soft and gentle, almost feminine, sound. I later found that this was true not only of my fellow passenger but of all Pathans when they spoke

Urdu. I have never understood the reason for the change. My Pathan companion, whose hospitality I accepted with some hesitation, turned out to be a fruit merchant. I found him very amicable during the rest of our journey, during which he tried politely to educate me about the many varieties of grapes and their fine differences.

My first impressions of Peshawar were positive, both physically and psychologically. The college was situated in the cantonment area, which was neat and tidy, as such areas always were under British military administration. But Peshawar cantonment was reputed to be among the best such places. Sir Colin Campbell, a distinguished military commander in Crimea, laid it out with great care. He situated it in relation to the Khyber pass—the traditional gateway for invaders of India—in a manner that would 'make the defence of the city and the valley of Peshawar easy while keeping the living conditions of the troops comfortable.' The result of his efforts was a pretty little town. With well planned avenues radiating from a central hub called Company Bagh, movement in the town was easy for pedestrians and vehicular traffic. The small population of 40,000 enabled one to escape the claustrophobic feeling of being in an Indian town. The near and distant mountains provided glorious vistas, mornings and evenings. It was an island of modernity surrounded by people who seemed to linger in medieval times with unbelievable passion and vigour.

Peshawar city, as against the cantonment, was I discovered an ancient urban centre steeped in the romance of history. Its history was punctuated by a variety of names: to the geographer Hectaeus of Miletus writing in 500 BC, i.e. even earlier than Herodotus, it was Kaspapuros; to Huen Tsang, the Chinese pilgrim, it was Po-lu-sha-po-lu; in Sanskrit texts it is called Purushapura; al-Beruni describes it as Pushabur; and present-day Pakhtuns call it Pekhwar. To me the city was straight out of the pages of the *Arabian Nights*, with its narrow streets, crowded with men in a variety of dresses, speaking different languages. Bazaari-kissa Khani, the 'street of storytellers', where traders and caravans once broke journey and regaled themselves with travellers tales, was the heart of the city and gave it an undiminished medieval ambience. It was in this bazaar that I spent my first day in Peshawar. It was a Sunday and I remember vividly the bustle and sights and sounds of the place.

Next day I visited the college campus, where I was interviewed for the post of lecturer in economics. The interview took just half an hour, at the end of which I was offered the job and asked to join right away, which I did. I was also allotted a two-room suite in the hostel, which was very comfortable.

The college itself was small, with a student body of not more than 250 and a staff of about 15 teachers. Small numbers led to close contact between teachers and students; everybody seemed to know everyone. This was a unique experience for me. My colleagues, mostly either Hindus or Christians, were very friendly. There was only one Muslim member of staff—he taught Persian. There was no local person on the teaching staff. The principal, the Reverend Mr Dalaya, was a Maharashtrian Christian, while the rest of the teaching staff came from Punjab and UP. Dalaya was an Oxford man and very proud of the campus layout with its quadrangles, which he had arranged and now maintained with loving care. His Oxford training also made him strictly enforce the rule that teachers move about the college premises wearing black gowns.

I was pleased to learn that the college was started by the same Church Missionary Society which had established my school in Srinagar. The mission had launched its educational programme in the North West Frontier Province in 1855, a whole generation before extending it to Kashmir. The college had grown stage by stage after starting off as a high school and bore the name 'Herbert Edwardes', this Edwardes being among the first men of the empire to appear in Peshawar at the end of the Sikh wars. According to Olaf Caroe, historian of the Pathans, Edwardes and his junior but more famous colleague General Nicholson (who died in Delhi in the assault on Kashmiri Gate in 1857), passed for heroes even in their own day. Edwardes was said to have been a deeply pious Christian in the evangelical tradition and it was he who, as commissioner of Peshawar, introduced Christian missions to the Frontier and founded the college which upholds his memory.

The atmosphere in the college was calm and serene but intellectually unexciting. As an established liberal arts college it formed the nucleus of the intellectual and cultural community of the province. Many of its bright students had made their mark in public life. The students were most respectful with their teachers and indiscipline was unheard of. I had an instructive experience in this respect. While invigilating an internal examination, I caught a student copying from notes which he had smuggled in. I was furious and turned the boy out of the examination hall. My colleagues told me that this was unprecedented, besides being indiscreet. Having heard stories of the Pathan passion for revenge when their self respect was trifled with, I began to worry about the consequences of my action, but this did not last long. Two days later I was told I had a visitor. When I saw the formidable figure of a burly Pathan rising from a chair in the common room where he was waiting for me, I missed a heartbeat. But to my utter surprise he salaamed me most respectfully and introduced himself as the luckless father of an unworthy son. He apologized profusely for what his son had done and begged me to pardon him. That was the end of the matter.

This, I was told, could not have happened at Islamia College in the same city. Islamia College had a much larger student body and the contact between teachers and students was more distant and diffused. The macho culture of the Pathans was more prominent there than at Edwardes. Islamia boys would often be seen sporting pistols, the ultimate badge of Pathan manhood. Such a sight was rare at Edwardes. There was not much contact between the two colleges, except for the occasional sports match. The main reason for this lack of contact was a physical barrier: Islamia College, being situated outside the walled city, was cut off after dusk when the city gates were closed.

Edwardes College had built up a very good reputation among the forward-looking sections of Pathan society. The more religiously oriented preferred Islamia College, founded by Ross-Keppel, another well-known frontier officer who is said to have been responsible for what is called the Pathan renaissance. Ross-Keppel was assisted in this task by Sahibzada Abdul Qayyum, also a civil servant who later became a minister in 1932, when limited self-government was introduced in the province. Comparing the two colleges, Olaf Caroe says:

Both Edwardes and Islamia Colleges at Peshawar stood for a tradition, each in its own way. The greater self-consciousness of Pathan nationhood, induced by memories of the Sahibzada and the challenge of the Islamia's location in the tongue of the Khaibar, was balanced by the more tolerant and eclectic syncretism taught in the classrooms which remembered Herbert Edwardes. It was no accident that most of the men who subsequently filled key posts in the all-important Provincial Services were Islamia alumni, while Dr Khan Saheb, with his all-India view and admiration for Sher Shah, owed allegiance to the older college. Both streams were needed, the one to supply the educational background for a local Pathan renaissance, the other to suggest the place which the Pathan might fill in the development of a sub-continent.[1]

I taught two courses, one on economic theory and the other on Indian economic problems. The Pathan students showed more interest in the latter. They were interested in the causes of the economic backwardness of India, and quite a few of them would come to my rooms to discuss these problems. They wanted to go beyond my classroom lectures, which were narrowly focused on matters like savings and investments, into broader questions such as belief systems, cultural attitudes, and the political institutions responsible for economic development. I found I was not adequately equipped to answer their questions. Nor was there any material available in the library that could have helped me. In retrospect, I found they had raised questions of economic and political sociology that economists addressed more than a decade later, when development economics became a sub-discipline of economics.

What prompted my Pathan students to raise these questions was Afghanistan's failure to modernize itself under Amir Amanullah Khan. They shared the Amir's conviction that modernization was absolutely necessary for Afghanistan's economic development, cultural renaissance, and national rebirth. But they attributed his failure to his mechanical imitation of the policies of Kemal Pasha in Turkey, blaming him for not taking into consideration the greater backwardness of Afghanistan. They were particularly critical of his crude attempt to

---

[1] *The Pathans, 550 B.C. to A.D. 1957* (London: Macmillan and Co. Ltd., 1958), pp. 429–30.

bludgeon the religious establishment. They believed that Islam, if properly interpreted and rescued from the clutches of mullahs, is in harmony with progress and modernization. And in this respect they had great faith in education, which they believed would blend modern civilization with tradition. The most powerful weapon in the hands of reformers and modernists, in their opinion, was the Koranic injunction 'to seek knowledge even if you have to go to China for it.'

I soon found that most of the students who visited me after lectures were sympathetic to the Khudai Khidmatgar movement, started by Khan Abdul Ghaffar Khan in 1921 to bring about social reform in Pathan society. It was said that he was inspired to serve his community by the selfless example of the Reverend Mr Wigram, principal of the Mission High School, the earlier incarnation of Edwardes College, where he had been a student. He became interested in establishing a network of schools in the province to combat the widespread ignorance of his fellow Pathans and bring about religious and social reformation within tribal society. He had watched Amanullah Khan's programme for the modernization of Afghanistan with great admiration. In fact he had migrated to Afghanistan during the Hijarat Movement, after a brief flirtation with the Khilafat Movement. It is said that it was Amanullah Khan who had asked him to go back to India. He had later returned, in 1921, vowing to inspire a sense of national consciousness among Pathans in order to achieve their liberation.

The Khudai Khidmatgar movement rapidly grew into the dominant political force of the province, both in the settled districts and in the tribal areas. Ghaffar Khan cast the struggle for emancipation within the larger framework of the Indian freedom struggle. He linked his movement to the Indian National Congress and himself came under the influence of Mahatma Gandhi. In the provincial elections of 1937, the Congress Party came out victorious and formed the government under the leadership of Dr Khan Sahib, the older brother of Ghaffar Khan. While implementing the programmes of the movement, Khan Sahib's ministry worked against the traditional supporters of the British Government, namely the big landowners. The privilege of being honorary magistrates and *zaildars*, bestowed on them by the British to enhance their power and influence, was taken away. Many of the big Khans were also *inamdar*s and, as such, did not have to pay land revenue. *Inam*s were withdrawn by the new Congress government. All these measures gave a wider social base to the party among the lower classes.

The two Khan brothers who dominated the political scene in the province were very different from each other. Ghaffar Khan, the younger brother, was the senior leader. He was puritanical in his way of life and a stern disciplinarian in the Gandhian mould. He wore his charisma effortlessly. Khan Sahib, the British educated medical doctor with an English wife, was a simple, straightforward Pathan. As chief minister he did not prove a great administrator, but all were impressed by his honesty of purpose. He had set up a modest clinic where he treated patients free of charge, except those with venereal disease. He made them pay for their treatment because, according to him, they had spent money to become infected. The bare walls of his clinic had just one plaque on which was inscribed a Persian line: 'Do not sell the dust of your country for foreigners' gold.' Because of his connection with Edwardes College, I met him on several occasions. It was greatly refreshing to meet such a transparently sincere man.

The British government detested both brothers. It was alarmed by the growth of the massive all-Pakhtun movement which they led. The fact that Khudai Khidmatgars wore shirts dyed with brick dust earned them the sobriquet 'Red Shirts' or *surkhposh*, and made them suspect in the eyes of the British and the mullahs. Luckily for the British government, the Khan Sahib ministry resigned office along with the other Congress ministries in November 1939. Only when the Congress was replaced by the pro-British Muslim League ministry did the British become somewhat confident of preventing Khudai Khidmatgars from posing a threat to their war effort.

Sir George Cunningham, the governor, an old frontier hand who spoke fluent Pushto and was quite familiar with the Pathans and their ways, used his administration to build up the Muslim League as a counter to Ghaffar Khan and his movement. Aurangzeb Khan, who headed the Muslim League ministry which replaced the Congress, was known to be a creation of the British. According to the governor's diary note of 19 July 1943, 'Aurangzeb is extremely amenable and anxious to do what I want. He seems to have forgotten that the function of a Minister is to advise the Governor. Nearly every file comes from him with a note, "I solicit the advise of H.E. the Governor".' With Aurangzeb at his disposal, it was not difficult for the governor to tell the tribesmen to 'prevent Congress volunteers wearing red jackets from entering your villages. They call themselves Khudai Khidmatgars (Servants of God), but in reality, they are servants of Gandhi. They wear the dress of Bolsheviks. They will create the same atmosphere as you have heard exists in the Bolshevik dominion.'[2]

How successful Cunningham was is now a matter of history. Even in our college we could see the shadow of Iskander Mirza, the deputy commissioner of Peshawar. His daughter was a frequent visitor to the College—she came to play tennis. Mirza, who later became president of Pakistan, was a trusted Cunningham man. There are many stories about his efficiency in the service of his master. I am tempted to narrate one. During the turbulent days of the Red Shirt Movement there was an occasion when the administration expected large-scale violence in the wake of a protest procession. The governor was against using the army, fearing that it might lead to greater violence. Iskandar Mirza offered to take full responsibility for handling the situation to the satisfaction of the governor. On the fateful day, all that he did was to ask his agents to mix *jammal gota* (a strong purgative) with the cold drinks provided at stalls which had been set up by the organizers for the convenience of the demonstrators. As the procession moved on, it became thinner and practically melted away by the time it reached its destination. Everyone including Dr Khan Sahib, who led the procession, was impressed by Mirza's neat trick.

Students as well as staff knew who Mirza's agents were and what they were up to. Their job was to find out the enemies of the British government and harass them in all sorts of ways, including getting mullahs to issue fatwas against them. Suspicions of Cunningham's activities are fully borne out by his diaries and papers, now available

[2] Vartan Gregorian, *The Emergence of Modern Afghanistan* (Stanford: Stanford University Press, 1969), p. 327.

at the India Office Library. In September 1942 his policy note says: 'Continuously preach the danger to Muslims of connivance with the revolutionary Hindu body. Most tribesmen seem to respond to this.'

The Pathan boys who were in touch with me were apparently aware of the network of mullahs the governor had recruited for his anti-Congress and anti-Hindu campaign. They were scornful at the very thought of Hindu domination. In this respect they were very different from my Muslim friends in Delhi, for whom the fear of Hindu domination once the British left had become an obsession. The Pathan boys were anti-British, proud of their history, and conscious of the fact that several Pathan rulers had held dominion over India. They were particularly proud of Sher Shah Suri, whom they described as the greatest Afghan.

The brightest of my Pathan students was called Ayub. He came from the unadministered territory called Ghair Ilaqa or Yagistan (land of rebels). The border between the settled districts and those of Ghair Ilaqa was artificial. Ayub was very proud of his tribe, the Waziris, because they had not enlisted in the service of the British, as had the Afridis and Yusafzais. He described how an entire British brigade was destroyed by the Waziris, whom even their enemies recognized as the finest fighters in the world. But he deplored his fellow tribesman's attitude to education and educated people. For Waziris, he told me, reading books, particularly English books, meant studying Satan's works. They looked down upon educated men as unmanly and unfit for action. Evidently his father had taken a great risk when sending Ayub to college.

Ayub was keen that I visit his home in Waziristan. So I went off with him, despite the warnings of my colleagues, who thought it a risky business. Waziristan had been declared a disturbed area at the time.

The visit to Ayub's house had the thrill of an adventure for me. I was dressed in Ayub's *shalwar* and long shirt, which fitted me very well as he was more or less my size; he was probably my age too. He was sure I looked an Afghan in my borrowed garb and would pass unnoticed.

Ayub's house was in a barren, rocky wilderness. It was scarcely visible until one reached it. Its flat roof was only a few feet above the ground—a device to protect it against aerial bombardment, which the

British resorted to in their pacification campaign against the Waziris. It was a small, two-storey mud house with one of its storeys under ground. In contrast to its unremarkable exterior, the room we entered was luxuriously covered with carpets. His father welcomed me with the respect due to a teacher, and the three of us sat on the floor. An elaborate meal, consisting mainly of fatty lamb, rice and chicken stuffed with nuts, was produced in my honour. I learnt a good deal here about the ethnic consciousness and pride of simple tribal Pathans.

When Ayub's father talked about Afghan rule in Kashmir, his tone changed from that of a solicitous host to that of a member of a superior race destined to be conquerors. According to him, Kashmiris were incapable of establishing order in their country. The collapse of Mughal rule gave them a chance to be independent, but instead they sent a prayer to Ahmed Shah Abdali to take over their country. This was a reference to the historical fact that two Kashmiri notables, in the course of factional rivalry, had indeed invited Abdali to invade Kashmir. That Kashmir fascinates Pathans was clear by the ecstatic manner in which he raved about the beauty of the Valley. I heard from Ayub's father, as I did from several other Pathans, the proverb: 'Unto every man his own country is Kashmir' (*Har cha ta khpal mulk Kashmir day*). To me it sounded more like an assertion of their patriotism than an expression of desire for Kashmir. However, I was not too sure of my understanding of the Pathan mind: Pathans express themselves in diverse ways. For instance Zaman Khan, a direct descendant of Khushal Khan Khattak, the legendary Pathan patriot and a poet like his great ancestor, composed the following verse (as translated by Olaf Caroe):

> They say Kashmir is a paradise now,
> Today the prisoner of an infidel foe.
> Soldier, set free this paradise on earth,
> If thou to very Paradise would go.

And once, in a lighthearted mood at a dinner, Dr Khan Saheb told us that every time he heard the word 'loot' his blood rushed to his veins and he felt like rushing out to grab something. And when the lure of loot combines with religious zeal, he said, nothing holds back the tribesman. I did not know, at the time, that we would witness the grim truth of this observation a few years later, when Pathan tribesmen raided Kashmir in 1947.

Ayub and a number of his fellow students had, at my suggestion, formed an informal study circle where economic and political questions that interested them were discussed. They would sometimes invite teachers and others to participate. But they were careful about whom they invited. Anyone they suspected of being a toady was carefully kept out. I thought they were paranoid in their suspicions, but apparently they knew better. I became almost a regular member of the group, which I found far more lively than the staid intellectual club in the city, called the Khyber Athenaeum, where a few teachers, lawyers and publicists met for intellectual discussion.

Khan Abdul Qayum Khan, the deputy leader of the Congress Party in the central assembly, was a frequent guest of the student group. He was a barrister with a degree from the London School of Economics. He was writing his book, later published under the title *Gold and Guns on the Pathan Frontier*. His analysis of British policy was most impressive. We became very friendly and exchanged ideas freely. I could never have imagined that a man with his views would join the Muslim League just three years later.

He was not the only one to change his political creed in such a drastic manner. In neighbouring Punjab, Mian Iftikhar-ud-din, a stalwart Congressman, had joined the Muslim League even earlier and set a precedent for Muslim politicians of so-called progressive views to follow. This new trend was predicated on the assumption that the League had become a people's party and was now representing the urge of Muslim nationalists for freedom. The intellectual underpinnings for this view were provided by the Communist Party of India in terms of what became popularly known as the Adhikari thesis. Syed Mir Qasim, who later became the Congress chief minister of Jammu and Kashmir, was at that time a student at Aligarh Muslim University. In his auto-biography he candidly confesses that under the influence of leftist parties he worked hard for the election of Nawabzada Liaquat Ali Khan, the Muslim League leader. One cannot tell whether it was the growing popularity of the League amongst the Muslims, or the cogency of Adhikari's argument, that proved irresistible for people like Khan Abdul Qayum Khan.

With his height, which was six feet, and his heavy build, Qayum looked to me a big burly Pathan with Khan at both ends of his name. It was therefore a bit of a surprise to learn that this double-barrelled Khan was not a Pathan but a Kashmiri whose family had migrated from Pattan, a village midway between Srinagar and Baramulla, where he still had some relatives. His family name was Wani. Peshawar had quite a sizeable number of Kashmiri Muslim Settlers. The 1941 census report listed them separately as a community. Kashmiris were not considered Pakhtuns, even though they were settled in Peshawar for several generations, and even when they dressed and behaved like the natives. All the same, they were doing well in various trades. Some of them had sent their sons to Edwardes College. Unlike Qayum Khan, they carried their Kashmiri surnames and did not hide their identity.

Though keen to project himself as a Pathan leader, Qayum was quick to use his Kashmiri connection to his advantage. After August 1942, when the Congress Party started the Quit India movement and Congressmen in the N.W.F.P. were being arrested, he left for Srinagar and started a law practice there. His stay in Kashmir not only saved him from being jailed by the British but also gave him an opportunity to establish contacts in the state, which he used in 1947 to organize the tribal raids.

The students taught me much about the competing roles of Pakhtun ethnicity and Islam within the politics of the area. The Pathans were highly conscious of their cultural and linguistic identity. They were proud of their Bactrian and Kushan heritage which had recently been uncovered for them by French archaeologists in Afghanistan. In matters of ethnicity, culture and language they considered themselves part of the larger Afghan family. The Durand Line, which divides the N.W.F.P. from contemporary Afghanistan, was to them a British device to keep them divided. They resented the notion that Afghanistan was merely a corridor between Central Asia, Persia and India; that it was a recent creation of Ahmad Shah Abdali; and that it had no history and no distinct culture. To them Afghanistan was the country of the ancient Aryans. They believed that the Avesta and the earliest Vedas were the fruits of Afghan creativity. Panini, the Sanskrit grammarian, I was told, was a resident of Charsada in Peshawar district. And in Muslim times they claimed Sanai, Maulana Rum, Unsari, Farrukhi, and Anwari—all great names in Persian literature—as Afghans. Ibni Sena (Avicenna), Abu Hanifa, and al-Beruni were also brought into their fold.

I was amazed to hear Pathan boys say: 'For a thousand years we have been Muslims, but for five thousand years we have been Pakhtuns.' To them, love of the motherland was sanctioned by Islam and patriotism was the duty of every devout Muslim. They would quote their famous poet-warrior Khushal Khan Khattack (1613–89), whose martial songs still stir the Pathans. Khushal's poetry is inspired by hatred for the Mughals, especially Aurangzeb, the most religious minded of them all, against whom Khushal fought.

Their proud history did not make the boys oblivious of weaknesses in their society. They were acutely aware of these, chief of which was inter-tribal rivalry and strife. How to detribalize society was for them the greatest challenge they faced. To consolidate Pathan society they were prepared to amend Pakhtunwali, their celebrated code of honour, of which they were very proud. Along with chivalrous virtues, such as the provision of asylum to fugitives and the extension of hospitality to visitors, this code enjoined Pathans to seek revenge against their enemies. My students were trying to redefine these 'enemies'. In this context they applauded the efforts of Khan Abdul Ghaffar Khan, who was mobilizing Pathans against British rule by appealing to their ethnic pride. The broad assumption was that the British were the main hurdle in their path to prosperity and progress. Once the British left, they believed it would be easy for them to tame the mullahs and modernize their tradition-bound society. They were convinced it was the British Indian government that had mobilized the Afghan mullahs against Amir Amanullah. Even though I myself had faith in social engineering at that time, I was a bit sceptical of their over-optimistic assumptions.

By the time the summer vacation started, I had spent nine months in Peshawar. During this short period my involvement with these Pathan students and their society had become so intense that I would gladly have skipped going home for the holidays had my mother not needed me to look after family matters. On her urging I had to abandon my visit to Kabul, which I had planned with Ayub and his friends.

On my arrival in Srinagar, I learnt that the college that was my alma mater was being reconstituted into two separate colleges to cope with the increasing number of students seeking admission. The desire for higher education among Muslim latecomers received great encouragement from the political leadership. As recommended by the Glancy Commission, the state government had appointed a special inspector of schools to promote education among Muslims. The first inspector for Muslim education was Ghulam Ahmad Ashai, who was not only an able educationist but also a highly politically motivated person. In fact he was one of the small group of Kashmiris who launched Sheikh Abdullah on his political career. His political zeal gave a keen edge to his efforts to spread education among Muslims.

By 1941 the number of students at S.P. College, as it was called, had crossed the figure of two thousand, and the management of such large numbers had reached breaking point. The government therefore decided to establish another college under its own aegis, since no non-official body was forthcoming to undertake the task. The college was restructured under the able guidance of Khwaja Ghulam-u-Saiydain, an eminent educationist who was persuaded by Gopalaswamy Ayyangar to accept the post of director of education. Saiydain was keen to revamp the educational system in the state. In order to raise the academic calibre of the teaching staff he was even prepared to tilt on the side of merit, as against strict adherence to the ratios of reservation prescribed under the rules of recruitment for state service. These developments suddenly brightened the chances of my getting a job. When the time to apply for the newly created post of lecturer came, however, my summer holidays were nearly over and I was back in Peshawar.

I had informed Principal Dalaya in advance about my intention to apply for the Srinagar job. Dalaya also knew about my family circumstances. He was sympathetic and forwarded my application with a very handsome testimonial. When my students came to know about the possibility of my leaving Edwardes College, they were upset. A delegation of students called on the principal with a request to enhance my salary, which he readily accepted. I had a tough time convincing the boys about my compulsions in wanting to get back to Srinagar. They became so emotional that the only way I could pacify them was to promise to come back during the winter months, when the Srinagar colleges closed for the vacation, a promise which I kept for two successive winters.

There were several farewell parties before I left and many exaggerated things were said in my praise. A remark I still remember with some amusement was made by Ayub's father. He said I was such a fine man that he never thought of me as a Hindu. When the time for my departure came, fifty boys accompanied me in my train journey from Peshawar to Rawalpindi, and bade me goodbye only after I was seated on the bus bound for Srinagar.

I have changed jobs several times in the course of my life, but never have I had such an overwhelming send-off or such an emotional bus journey. Parting from my Pathan students was a wrench, but at the same time the prospect of being back in Kashmir was exciting and alluring, particularly at that time of the year.

CHAPTER FOUR

Back Home—in Kashmir and Delhi

I returned to Kashmir in mid October 1942, at a time of the year when the Valley is enveloped in shades of purple, red and yellow, and the air is alive with harvest songs. It is a season when Kashmiris shed their melancholic disposition and look upon their land and their life with a more optimistic eye. For my mother it was more than the joyful mood of the harvest season; her son had returned home for good.

She had learnt that government college lecturers were gazetted officers and therefore had the privilege of attending the maharaja's durbar. This thought pleased her no end. I did not have the heart to tell her that I loathed the idea and dreaded seeing myself dressed in a bright-coloured brocade achkan, sporting a pink turban and carrying a full-length sword, the regulation outfit of a durbari. In fact when I received the first invitation to attend a durbar where I was to present a half sovereign as nazar to His Highness, I excused myself on the grounds that I was in mourning for my grandmother. (Both my grandmothers had died decades earlier.) When I finally ran out of excuses, I did attend two such functions. They were quite amusing, except for the wording of the *hazoor minister's* (minister-in-waiting's) invitation, which threatened that 'failure to attend would amount to disloyalty to the throne and the person of His Highness'.

It was pleasant to be back at my alma matter in my new capacity as a teacher. But teaching undergraduates was no great intellectual challenge. The college atmosphere had changed since my student days: it was less intellectual and more political now. It was no more Marx versus Marshall; it was Jinnah versus Gandhi. The discussions in the staff common room were dominated by politics which revolved around issues relating to the Pakistan and Quit India movements. The participants fell into three main categories: the nationalists, the leftists—who called themselves progressive—and the pro-Muslim League members. The leftists and nationalists belonged to the Valley, while the entire pro-League group came from Jammu, Mirpur and Poonch. For the latter group the main source of inspiration was *Dawn*, the newspaper founded by Jinnah. They referred to it as 'Dawn Sharif' and read it reverentially. It was their new gospel. The discussions were often heated but left no ill will. The only unpleasant thing I recall was a Muslim colleague demanding a separate jug of water and glasses for Muslims. He started it as a joke to tease his Hindu colleagues but it gradually became a serious proposal and was actually implemented. It was something like the evolution of Pakistan, which started as a Cambridge undergraduate's fantasy and grew into a fact of history.

As the staff-room discussions tended to become repetitive, I found shelter in the library. I read extensively—economics, history, politics and sociology—and became convinced that economics by itself was a narrow discipline. To do justice to it, economists must possess a wider perspective, particularly if they were involved in policy-making. Since their services were being used to run the war economy, they were sure to be used even more for post-war reconstruction. I could not get my economist colleagues interested in these problems. They too were absorbed in the immediate world, which was dominated by the politics that hung heavy over the state.

The summer of 1944 was full of political excitement in Kashmir. It turned out to be one of those times when the fate of a country is decided. Jinnah arrived in June and was given a welcome reception by Sheikh Abdullah and the National Conference. He was received as a distinguished visitor and was not expected to interfere in the political affairs of the state. But unlike the neutral posture of his previous visit, this time Jinnah spent his entire six weeks mobilizing the support of Kashmir Muslims in favour of the dormant Muslim Conference. His success elsewhere in the country had made Jinnah grossly underestimate the Sheikh's standing among Kashmiri Muslims. Sheikh Abdullah accepted Jinnah's challenge and launched a counter-offensive against him; he roused Kashmiris to a pitch that compelled Jinnah to abandon his visit. Jinnah left Kashmir a disappointed man, bitter against Sheikh Abdullah and his party. These events further politicized the atmosphere in the college and made me increasingly uneasy about the quality of academic life in Kashmir.

In December 1944, when the winter vacation started, I left for Peshawar, where I had to go to redeem the promise I had made to my Pathan students. This time I reduced my stay there by two weeks and decided to go on to Delhi. I reached Delhi in mid January 1945 and was happy to find that under the dynamic Sir Maurice Gwyer, its first full-time vice-chancellor, Delhi University was fast developing into a major university. Sir Maurice had appointed V.K.R.V. Rao, a brilliant economist, as the first university professor of economics. After his stint as statistical adviser to the ministry of food, Rao was expected to join the university in 1946. In the meanwhile postgraduate teaching at the university had been revived with the help of a few college teachers. Hindu College was also in the process of expanding its department of economics. Both Principal Thadani and Dr Ganguli of Hindu College wanted me to join the college and asked me to apply for the post of lecturer. When I told them that I could apply only through the proper channel, i.e. the ministry of education of the Kashmir government, they said my candidature would be considered by the selection committee even without my applying. I had never seen Dr Ganguli, known for his sedate nature, as excited as he was on this occasion about the new prospects opening up for the university. His excitement infected me, and the thought of returning to Delhi gripped me.

A couple of months after my return home to Srinagar I received a letter from Principal Thadani offering me the job. I was pleased, but in a dilemma. None of my friends and colleagues whom I consulted was in favour of my leaving Srinagar. They thought it foolish to give up a pensionable government job for a private college job far away in Delhi, with no appreciable increase in salary. Nor did I discuss this matter with my mother, who I was sure would be upset. But she picked it up in the course of my discussions with friends. To my surprise she not only approved of the possible shift to Delhi but helped me make up my mind. Without saying it in so many words, she did not want me to turn down the Delhi offer on her account. She put her advice in a Persian aphorism—*safar vasilai zafar ast* (travel is a means of success).

I knew that my mother had suppressed her own feelings at the prospect of my leaving Kashmir once again. I also knew that she was not going to leave Kashmir to be with me. Kashmiris are a stay-at-home people. They leave Kashmir only when pushed out by adverse circumstances, seldom because of the attraction of opportunities outside; they have left Kashmir in large numbers from time to time, but mainly to escape oppressive regimes: in the twentieth century there was no migration till the tribals raided Kashmir in 1947. In 1945, when I received the job offer, I had no apparent compulsion to leave. My friends remained unconvinced about the rightness of my decision. My mother alone supported the idea. I took six months to make the final decision.

I reached Delhi in October, after the summer session. Hindu College was not able to provide me with residential accommodation. While I was looking for private lodgings I stayed as the guest of an old friend in University Hall, the postgraduate hostel. Sir Maurice had lavished all his care on that building, and at the time a Fellows Court, meant for research fellows, was being added to it. Sir Maurice would visit the site every evening before going to the Cecil Hotel, where he stayed. He could not walk around, being on crutches, and would sit on a boulder to watch the building take shape. On one such occasion I ran into him and, thinking I was one of the residents, he started talking to me about what he wanted the Fellows Court to be like. He asked me about my background and was much interested in Biscoe, about whom he said he had heard a great deal. After a couple of such chance encounters, he invited me to tea in his hotel room and asked me if I would like to be resident warden of the hall. I was excited at the prospect but reminded him that, not being a university teacher, I could not be considered for the appointment. He brushed this aside, saying that since I was participating in the postgraduate teaching at the university there would be no objection. I was certain that this specious argument of the former chief justice of the federal court would not be accepted. But he had his way; nobody objected when I was appointed resident warden of what came to be known as Gwyer Hall after Sir Maurice left the university.

At about this time Professor Ishtiaq Hussain Qureshi was appointed provost. He was an eminent historian, an authority on medieval Indian history, as well as a leading intellectual associated with the Muslim League and an ardent advocate of the two-nation theory. His ideological passions did not seem to go well with his scholarly disposition and sophistication. As a teacher he had earned the admiration of his students, but as provost he was ill at ease with the residents of the hall, who belonged to a variety of disciplines. But for his personal charm,

Sir Maurice Gwyer

the hostel residents would have been completely alienated from him. Most of them were not Muslims, yet were very respectful to him. He stayed aloof and participated only in formal functions, as the head of the institution. His relations with me were courteous and correct but never informal, except towards the end of his stay, when he had to leave Delhi as a refugee under tragic circumstances. That happened later in August 1947, and I will digress to recount a characteristic Partition story.

The arrival of Hindu and Sikh refugees had created an explosive situation in Delhi. Hardly a mile away, at Kingsway, was a large refugee camp. Refugees roamed all over the university campus, narrating horror stories. Though there was no violence, the atmosphere was tense and we were fearful of what might happen. On the advice of the provost, my Muslim wards had already left the Hall and joined their families. Qureshi himself stayed on.

Over this period I was in constant touch with him. He was badly shaken by what was happening in the country: he had lost faith in the administration's ability to keep peace and ensure the safety of Muslims and their property. He felt that Gandhiji, who was expected in the city on a peace mission, was the only hope. I was surprised at this sudden change in his attitude, for only a couple of months earlier, during one of his rare conversations on politics with me, he had called Gandhiji a hypocrite. The night before he left India he called me several times and requested me to find out from my friend, Dwarka Nath Kachru, Nehru's private secretary, when Gandhiji was expected to arrive in Delhi, as though he was expecting a rescue mission from Pakistan. Since I had no definite information to give, he became desperate and decided to leave. In those days S.L. Poplai, lecturer in history at Hindu College, was my only colleague with a car. He readily agreed to drive me and Professor Qureshi to the residence of Rafi Ahmed Kidwai, from where Qureshi went to Karachi, later becoming a member of Liaquat Ali Khan's cabinet.

On my return to the university I was shocked to see the provost's lodge completely ransacked. Qureshi's household goods had all gone and his books were lying scattered everywhere: all this had happened over the three hours that I had been away. I felt ashamed and took the students to task for not trying to prevent the pillage. They helped me to collect Qureshi's books and papers but looked sullen and unrepentant.

But to come back to 1946. The academic year 1946–7 proved to be a turning point in the growth of the university's department of economics. V.K.R.V. Rao rejoined the university after the summer recess in 1946. He brought with him a vision of a world-class institution and abundant energy to translate it into reality. He had his office in one of the barracks near the university cricket ground. It was one of many flimsy structures that had been hastily put up in the campus to house British military personnel during the war. From this ramshackle office, supported by a typist-cum-clerk personal assistant and a typewriter, Rao started thundering about his plans to all who visited him. His main activity at this stage was the organization of public lectures. Almost every afternoon he would either chair a public lecture by a guest speaker or be the speaker himself. This lecture programme was very successful. It gave what later became the Delhi School of Economics a great deal of publicity about its 'existence' and its plans. The lectures were mostly on current policy questions and the speakers were always distinguished. The lecture programme became the chief intellectual activity of the university outside classrooms and laboratories. The only other place for such activities was the Indian Council of World Affairs, which was expected to be the Indian counterpart of the Royal Institute of International Affairs in London, with Sapru House aspiring to rival Chatham House.

Being conveniently located it was easy for me to attend the public lectures. On the second or third such lecture, Rao persuaded me to take notes and release them to the press on his behalf. Thus began my affair with what was beginning to be the Delhi School of Economics.

The summer of 1946 was a year of great hopes as well as of dire foreboding in India. Independence was on its way, we were all sure. The probability of Partition worried Ganguli and me but Rao was excited about India's arrival on the international scene as an independent country. His association with the National Planning Committee,

set up by Subhas Chandra Bose under the chairmanship of Jawaharlal
Nehru in 1938, had made him most interested in the role economists
would play in the development of the country. Newspapers were full
of stories about post-war reconstruction in Europe and the Soviet
Union. The viceroy had set up a department of planning and development under Sir Ardeshir Dalal, a member of his executive council.
Indian industrialists had already expressed their hopes over India's
economic future and outlined how success could be achieved by for-
mulating the Bombay Plan.

In the midst of all this excitement Rao felt that the economics profession in India was not adequately prepared for the tasks that would
inevitably have to be undertaken. Most Indian economists were home-
spun, and even those who had been abroad, mainly to British universities, had been there for postgraduate research on Indian subjects.
Their treatment of economic problems was generally historical, and
descriptive in nature. Professor Vera Anstey of the London School of
Economics, whose main interest was in the history of Indian economy,
was a great draw for Indian students.

Though Indian economists had concerned themselves with policy
questions, they had hardly produced any coherent set of policies or
plans for India's economic future, not even something like, say, the
Bombay Plan. Individual economists had written articles on specific
policies here and there, and some were associated with sub-committees
set up by the National Planning Committee. This committee published twenty-five reports on different sectors of the economy and brought
together a great deal of useful data, though it did not produce a national plan. Jawaharlal Nehru, the chairman of the committee, summed
up the position: 'we have not at this stage considered it necessary or desirable to collate all this vast material or to pronounce judgement on
the many recommendations made. That is a matter now for the National Government to take up.' Professor K.T. Shah of Bombay, who
was General Secretary of the committee, brought out in 1948 a volume
entitled *National Planning, Principles and Administration* which emphasized all the desirable things the national plan should aim at, but
he did not say much about how to realize them.

Indian economists had developed a strong nationalist tradition in their approach to the government policies of the day. Ever since Dadabhai Naoroji wrote his classic *Poverty and Un-British Rule in India,* Indian economists had taken a more or less well-articulated anti-government patriotic stand. Controversies over the 'drain theory', disputes about the rupee–sterling exchange rate and 'discriminating protection', the accumulation of 'sterling balances' as a result of India's war effort, and similar issues about the wrongs done to the economy had excited academic interest in a manner that made their contributions a part of the national movement. But they were less preoccupied with and frequently technically unequipped for the the problems that regeneration of the Indian economy through planning would pose.

Younger economists like Rao were also very nationalistic, but they were less concerned with the wrongs of the past than with building the future. Young lecturers like me were with him in this. We paid more attention to what Alfred Marshall, the great guru, had said to one of his Indian students, B. Mukerjee of Lucknow University: 'For twenty years I have been urging Indians in Cambridge to say to others. "How few of us when we go the West think of any other aim save that of our *individual culture?* Does not the Japanese nearly always ask himself in what way he can strengthen himself to *do good service to his country* on his return? Does he not seek real studies? Does he not watch the sources of Western power? Is not that the chief reason for Japan's quick progress? Cannot we imitate her?" '[1]

Rao was convinced that the country needed high-calibre economists and researchers to meet the requirements of independent India. He also wanted them to be committed to the cause of India's progress. His constant refrain was that India needed economists who had both technical competence and social awareness. These needs could not be fully met only by sending bright students abroad, as was attempted by the government soon after the war. He felt India should have its own first-rate teaching and research institutions for this purpose.

The first memorandum on the objectives of the Delhi School of Economics envisaged an institution which would combine the activities of the department of economics and an all-India research centre.

[1] *Memorials of Alfred Marshall,* ed. A.C. Pigou (New York: Kelley & Millman, 1925), p. 472.

Besides the basic research which is appropriate for a university depart-ment, the memorandum stressed that the School should undertake research on development policies relevant for a developing economy like India. The task Rao envisaged for this purpose was to set up no less than a world class School of Economics, and he went about it in a de-termined manner. But despite his furious efforts to hurry things through, the results came in very slowly. It took him a year to get the post of a reader created in the department. Ganguli, who was an honorary reader under the cooperative teaching arrangement, joined the university in late 1947. I joined the department as a lecturer after a further lapse of one year, in October 1948. Rao had to work hard to get the post of lec-turer—for one year in the first instance—sanctioned by the university. He was very surprised when I did not ask my college for leave or for a lien on my job and accepted a temporary post instead. Much to my embarrassment, he took every opportunity to quote this fact to illus-trate the commitment of his colleagues to the idea of a school—which was no more than an idea at the time.

The fact is that I was a much disappointed man at that time and wanted a change. I had been selected to go to Cambridge under the post-war scholarship scheme of the Government of India. I could not avail of this because of my adverse Kashmir police record—on account of my help in the preparation of the 'New Kashmir' document. At this time, the opening Rao offered me was most welcome. I was also sure that Rao would succeed in his plans; he had just then turned down the invitation of Lord Boyd Orr, the director-general of FAO, to join the organization.

The first major step to establish the School was the enrolment of students to the M.A. course in economics in the academic year 1948–9. As a result, the university acquired, for the first time in its history, a student community that did not belong to an affiliated college. The first batch of such students came only from Delhi and its environs. This was not good enough for an institution that aspired to all-India status. To try and attract the brightest minds from all parts of the coun-try became a primary concern for the School, and many ways were thought of to achieve this. One was to invite internationally known economists on the staff. Rao succeeded in persuading the Reserve Bank of India to provide financial support for a visiting professorship to Sir John Hicks of Oxford University. After this, visiting professors became a regular feature of the School. Another attractive scheme that was aimed at the student community was the organization of a summer school in Srinagar, in 1949. The response was tremendous. We were deluged by applications from all over the country. After careful selection, fifty students were admitted. A young American couple, Clare and Harris Wofford, who were interested, were allowed in. Wofford wrote a book on his Indian experience entitled *India Afire.* (He is at the time of writing a senator in the U.S. Congress.) The summer school was very successful in projecting the School to the student community, but the organizational effort involved was too great for it to be institutionalized into a regular feature.

What Rao had in mind for the School needed big money and much planning: money on the required scale was not available then, either from the government or private sources. The choice was either to wait for better times and greater resources or to launch the institution without even the basic physical and human infrastructure. Rao chose the latter course. This decision imposed on him and his small band of colleagues a burden which in retrospect seems unbelievably heavy. All the work had to be shared between just three persons: Rao, Ganguli and myself. Enrolling founder members, lobbying government officials, persuading potential donors and preparing notes for public addresses took a major part of Rao's working day. In the midst of this hectic activity he had also to teach a course on monetary economics, conduct tutorials, and supervise the work of some research students.

Ganguli had a temperament which determined his sphere of activity automatically. No two persons could have been more different from each other than Rao and Ganguli, but together they made a splendid team. Ganguli was the teacher par excellence. Students had easy access to him. He was always there, ready with counsel and help. He also looked after the library. Equally important was his role in the management of the crises which Rao would generate in the normal course of his activities, inside and outside the School. Rao ruffled everyone's feathers spontaneously and effortlessly; Ganguli had to smoothen them with patience and deliberation.

The estimate about the gestation period that the School project would take proved wrong. To begin with, the Delhi School of Economics was only a name given to the activities of three teachers, and that was how it remained for three more years. During that period all of us were stretched to the limit and not much worthwhile research could be done. Evidently, the School lacked the critical mass to be even a viable department of economics. But Rao drove us on and we did not seem to mind.

Perhaps I would have succumbed to a feeling of drudgery had I not got a break. In 1951 I went to Harvard on a Fulbright Smith–Mundt Fellowship. While at Harvard, apart from my own research work I was asked to study the case method at the Business School and prepare a comprehensive note for the ministry of education because Rao was getting the ministry interested in introducing courses on business management at the School and elsewhere in the country.

The expansion of the School began in 1953. By this time the School had already shifted to the new Arts Faculty building and the ample space available there was getting rapidly filled up. Significant additions were made to the academic and administrative staff. A statistical unit under Sivasubramonian was established and a number of research assistants and research fellows appointed. A notable appointment was that of K.N. Raj as Professor of Monetary Economics. Economic planning had become intellectually challenging and a sub-discipline of development economics was emerging. The Planning Commission was the cynosure of economists' eyes. Much glamour was attached to persons working in such an institution. Raj brought some of this glamour with him when he joined the School.

It was also in 1953–4 that preparations for the Second Plan were in full swing in the Planning Commission. There was a feeling in the commission that its in-house research needed to be supplemented from outside to provide adequate back-up for the Plan. Accordingly, the commission set up a research programme committee which formulated elements of research which were to be farmed out. The School received substantial grants to conduct research on river-valley multipurpose projects, small-scale industries, and the economics of urbanization. With this big jump in research activity and the starting of a journal, *Indian Economic Review,* the School began to take shape as a centre for research as well as teaching.

But before these basic activities could be consolidated, Rao launched a programme of further expansion and diversification. Two diploma courses in economic statistics and economic administration were introduced, followed a little later by an evening diploma course in Business Management. An Orientation Centre for foreign technicians was set up with the assistance of the Ford Foundation. The centre organized a crash programme of lectures, seminars and group discussions for the U.S. personnel who came to India under various technical assistance programmes. All such persons were required to attend the course before they took up their jobs in India. K.R. Narayanan (now president of India) was seconded from the ministry of external affairs to organize the centre. The earlier slow growth was now compensated by feverish growth.

With the rapid increase in its size and activities the School was outgrowing its premises in the Arts Faculty building. More important than the need for extra accommodation, Rao wanted the School to have its own building and campus to suit its own specific current and future requirements. For this project the university provided a nine-acre plot of land and Sir V.T. Krishnamachari, chairman of the board of governors secured a donation of Rs 600,000 from the Birla Educational Trust for the building. Lady Ratan Tata gave Rs 100,000 for the library. The name given to the library was part of the terms of the grant. The Birla Educational Trust had also stipulated that the building be called 'Birla Bhawan'. It is interesting that while everybody calls the library by its donor's name, nobody associates the building with its donor despite a big bronze plaque proclaiming the name on the front door of the building. In fact the impression one gets is that no one, not even the faculty, seems to have noticed the plaque. I have often wondered about the difference in general attitude to the two main donors of the School.

A separate campus was not the only distinction Rao wanted the School to have. He wanted members of the School to be recognized by their distinctive appearance and a certain social outlook. Accordingly, a formal silver grey *band gala* jacket was chosen as the School uniform and an enamelled pin designed to be worn on the left breast pocket with the Rig Vedic prayer *Tamaso ma jyotir gamaya* embossed on it. The faculty and students were exhorted by Rao, lecture after lecture, to combine the acquisition of technical skills with social awareness and concern for the poor and downtrodden. He hesitated to formally prescribe an ideology but avidly promoted a vague variant of democratic socialism and a Hindu view of humanism derived, in large measure, from the teachings of Sri Ramakrishna and Swami Vivekananda. He was so affected by this philosophy that after his retirement he wrote a book called *Swami Vivekananda: Prophet of Vedantic Socialism.*

Rao also introduced the concept of a 'school fraternity' to be constituted by members of the staff and the student body. Social get-togethers and other activities were organized to develop the fraternal spirit, and the celebration of Founder's Day was the high point of these activities. The fraternity also produced a wall paper called *DSE Courier*. The first editor of the paper was Krishna Raj, now editor of the *Economic and Political Weekly*, Bombay. One of the earliest and most memorable events of the fraternity was a visit by Jawaharlal Nehru, who spent two informal hours with the members, discussing a variety of subjects, sitting on a writing table, his legs swinging free. The fraternity also attracted the attention of eminent visiting professors from abroad. Shigeto Tsuru was a great favourite of the students. Unlike many of his compatriots, he was a good mixer and enjoyed playing chess with them in the Junior Common Room, the centre of the fraternity's activities. Phelps-Brown of the London School of Economics wanted to fraternize with students of a working-class background. We did not have such students, but that did not prevent him from having a cluster of 'them' around him: evidently, some students had sufficiently declassed themselves to qualify for the professor's company. Maurice Dobb, despite his ideological inclination to be friendly, kept his donnish distance; he found it difficult to relax even with like-minded people. The most thrilling moment of his stay with us was when he had a hole-and-corner meeting with Arun Bose who, at that time, was an underground communist student leader.

The senior common room was meant for the academic staff. Here they gathered for a cup of tea around 4 o'clock in the afternoon. It was easily the most lively place in the School. It became an arena for all kinds of discussions on economics, politics, and current affairs. Distinguished visitors who were not inclined to give formal lectures were invited for informal discussions at tea sessions. Jayaprakash Narayan came along one afternoon and thought aloud about the Bhoodan Movement he was planning to launch. It was in the Senior Common Room that Professor Joan Robinson threw a cup of tea at a sceptic when she was holding forth on the efficiency of the backyard steel furnaces in Mao's China. She had actually seen, she announced, Chinese peasants making ball bearings!

With the rapid expansion of the School between 1953 and 1957, its dual character of a university department as well as an autonomous institution of research and training became less and less tenable. The university authorities complained that the School had the best of both worlds. Some university departments resented the autonomy that the School enjoyed and used the levers of power in academic and executive councils to curb it. They particularly resented the rapid increase in the number of senior appointments. Since the University Grants Commission's (UGC's) funds to the School had to be routed through the university, it was easy for these authorities to interfere in the affairs of the School and whittle down the autonomy it enjoyed.

By the beginning of 1957 the pressure to redefine the position of the School *vis-à-vis* the university reached a critical stage. It had to choose between being an autonomous institution, with the attendant uncertainty of funding, and returning to the safe grooves of the university. Rao stood for autonomy; he did not want the School to be shackled by the cumbersome rules and regulations of the university. He also felt that the progress of the School would be hampered if it stayed back as a university department because no vice-chancellor would like to be seen as less than even-handed in the promotion of different departments. In these circumstances, he thought it would be difficult for a centre of excellence to emerge within the university matrix.

Within the School, the staff members, especially the younger ones, were sceptical about Rao's ideas on the question of autonomy. Autonomy was associated in their minds with what was described as Rao's authoritarianism. The real issue about autonomy, however, was to find financial resources to replace the UGC grants. Rao was prepared to shoulder the responsibility of raising funds from other sources but he found, to his great disappointment, that his own colleagues were not with him in this endeavour. Rao was a sad man the day the School returned to its original status of a university department, or, more accurately, a cluster of departments under the nominal umbrella title of the Delhi School of Economics.

Rao did not surrender to the university completely. The building on which he had spent so much time, energy and passion was, of course, gifted to the university, but the research units of the School which were funded from non-UGC sources were held back to form the launching pad of a new institution to be called the Institute of Economic Growth. By a favourable twist of circumstances Rao himself became the vice-chancellor while the negotiations were still on. This made the transfer of the School to the university and the creation of the Institute less contentious than it might otherwise have been. The Institute was set up in November 1958. I shifted there soon after, ending my decade-long association with the Delhi School of Economics.

The Institute aimed at undertaking basic analytical studies in the field of economic development. The research programme covered important aspects of the economy such as agriculture, industry, national income, population. As senior research fellow I took charge of the section on industry, which was to study changes taking place in that sector and explore their policy implications. I did some work on the petroleum industry, which had relevance to the Third Five-Year Plan, and wrote a monograph on the role of small industry in Indian economic development, in collaboration with the British economist H.F. Lydall. This work received wide notice because it was a comprehensive critique of the government policy and was based on empirical studies. It called for a reorientation of government's policy on small industries at a time when the fashionable thesis was that 'small is beautiful'. The main point this study made was that assistance to small industry should help remove disabilities rather than confer special benefits.

The study caught the attention of Philippe de Seynes, under-secretary general, department of economic affairs in the United Nations, and it was partly on account of this that I was offered an assignment in what was then called British Guiana.

CHAPTER FIVE

In British Guiana

E arly in 1962 the United Nations Secretariat asked me whether I would be interested in taking on an assignment as economic adviser to the Government of British Guiana (BG), as it was known then. (The name 'Guyana' was adopted after independence.) The timing of the job offer was significant. BG had been in the news lately as Cheddi Jagan, the newly installed premier, was having a hard time in the wake of the very first budget his government had introduced. The budget had led to a stormy protest by opposition groups; even trade unions were up in arms against it. Their leaders had dubbed it anti-working class and the protest demonstrations had led to large-scale rioting and arson in Georgetown, the capital city. The working class opposition to Jagan seemed paradoxical because Jagan was a Marxist whose pro-labour credentials were well established. Not only that; Nicholas Kaldor, the distinguished Cambridge economist and tax expert on whose recommendation the budget was based, was also well known for his leftist political leanings.

I had met Jagan in Delhi in the company of a few leftist teachers from the university a decade earlier. Along with Forbes Burnham, he had visited India in 1953 after the dismissal of their government by the British governor on the grounds that they were trying 'to turn British Guyana into a communist state'. The two handsome young leaders gave us the background of the Guyanese people's struggle for freedom and British attempts to thwart it. Their description of events and of the policies of the British government sounded all too familiar to our Indian ears.

Jagan and Burnham made an impressive duo. Jagan looked like a born leader. He was transparently sincere and presented his ideas with verve, vigour and clarity. There was something hypnotic about his personality. His easy and informal manner made him accessible and everyone called him by his first name. Burnham was more eloquent, less emotional, and somewhat more intellectual and sophisticated. But he was self-consciously clever and there was something canny about him. Both Jagan and Burnham made a strong impression during their Indian tour and succeeded in presenting their point of view most effectively. Their audience marvelled at the fact that the two leaders, one a descendant of indentured labourers from rural Bihar and the other of slave ancestors from somewhere in West Africa, were now together leading their people. The Indian press was very supportive of their struggle against colonial power. The accusation that they were hatching a 'communist plot' was dismissed as the usual imperialist tactic in order to ensure that a compliant government was installed in decolonized countries. I had seen the anti-communist hysteria generated by McCarthy in the USA and found myself in full sympathy with the Guyanese leaders.

This was the only background I had on BG when I received the UN offer. The assignment entailed preparing a development plan for the country and helping to build up a department of planning. It was tempting, but the fact that an economist of the eminence of Kaldor had cut a sorry figure there filled me with trepidation. I finally accepted and had three months in which to prepare myself.

I used this time to read extensively on the history, economy and politics of BG and discovered that, in the nine years since I had met Jagan, much had happened which explained BG's budget fiasco. The People's Progress Party (PPP), which had led the freedom movement, had split and Jagan and Burnham had parted company. The sad thing about the split was that it had taken place more or less on racial lines. The racial divide was further accentuated by the fact that it coincided with the rural–urban divide. The party split broke up the alliance between workers on the sugar plantations and the rural poor (who were predominantly East Indians) on the one side, and urban trade unions and the lower middle class (who were mostly Blacks) on the other.

The British government had used a mix of policies that had successfully fractured society in Guiana. In the period following the suspension of the constitution and the dismissal of the government, they had tried to weaken Jagan and create a political leadership more acceptable to them. The method used was to play upon the ambitions of a few power-hungry politicians and artfully emphasize the racial and cultural differences between East Indians and Blacks in a manner that would sow distrust between the two communities, which together constituted more than 80 per cent of the country's population.

This is not to suggest that there had never been a racial problem in Guiana. Indian indentured labourers were brought to replace the slaves who had abandoned sugar plantations after the abolition of slavery in 1833. The Blacks had moved away to work in factories and towns. Occupational and geographical divisions between the two races had kept them apart. In the plantations there were only European supervisors. Finding themselves in an unfamiliar environment, the Indians withdrew into their traditional culture for sustenance. Unlike the Africans, they successfully resisted the attempts of missionaries to convert them to Christianity. Through hard work and thrift they managed to give their children and grandchildren education and a better future. When their descendants moved out of rural poverty into urban professions and business, they came into contact and conflict with their Black counterparts. Since there was resistance to their entry into government services, Indians made strenuous efforts to succeed in business and the liberal professions. Middle-class Blacks, in imitation of the whites, looked down upon such Indians as 'coolie' upstarts and the Indians, ever conscious of their ethnic identity, were dismissive of African snobbery as imitation culture.

The Africans were also worried about the fact that Indians constituted 51 per cent of the total population of the country. To highlight the sinister political implications of this demographic fact, it was alleged that Indians used 'apaan jaat', meaning one's own kind, as a code phrase to garner votes for Indian candidates. These were ideal circumstances in which racial tensions could be whipped up.

Despite its success in splitting the pro-independence alliance, the government could not keep the constitution suspended indefinitely. Times had changed. Colonialism was in retreat. The Guianese struggle for freedom had gained sympathy in the Third World, where the two

Cold War power blocs were contending for influence. Britain as a champion of freedom and democracy in the East–West contest did not want to be seen as a repressive power in any of its colonies. But it was faced with a dilemma. The independence movement of BG was led by a party which Britain and its American allies suspected to be communist in its ideology and international affiliations. Yet something had to be done. The constitution had been announced in 1956, providing a legislature in which half the members were to be elected, the other half being nominees of the governor. Under this new constitution, elections were held in 1957. Jagan's party, despite the defection of Burnham and his followers, won the majority of elected seats in the legislature. Though he was in government now, Jagan was not comfortable. He described the new government as a coalition between his People's Progressive Party and the colonial office, with the governor in the driver's seat. Jagan had gained office, not power. He felt particularly handicapped in tackling the economic issues on which he had set his heart. He was not even allowed an economic adviser of his own choice. He wanted Charles Bettelheim, the French socialist economist, who was recommended to him by Professor Mahalanobis, but his proposal was rejected by the governor.

In these circumstances Jagan felt that the only way out was to generate pressure for independence, which he did strenuously. As a result of his efforts and other compulsions a conference of Guianese political leaders was held by the Colonial Office in London in 1960 to consider the issue of independence. At the conference, Burnham, who by now had formed a separate party of his own called the People's National Congress, opposed independence except within a West Indies federation, of which BG would be a member. In the federation, Blacks would be in a majority, whereas in BG they were a minority. He added one more condition to the grant of independence, namely acceptance of proportional representation for the election to the governing assembly, as this would solidify the racial division of society and tilt the elections against the PPP. With such basic differences in the respective stands of the political parties, the conference was inevitably deadlocked. The conference suggested that the date for independence be

tied to the coming into existence of the proposed West Indies federation. For the interim period constitutional changes conferring self-
government were approved.

To implement the new constitution elections were held in 1961.
Despite US opposition to Jagan's 'communist' movement, he won 20
out of 35 legislative seats and formed the government once again.
Though the anti-communist tirade against the PPP had not succeeded
in defeating them at the polls, the forces behind it did not give up efforts to dislodge the new government, which was alleged to have plans
to expropriate property. As a result of this propaganda, businessmen
started withdrawing money from banks and sending it abroad. The
flight of capital created a scare which affected ordinary people, who
began to withdraw their savings. To prevent the situation from deteriorating, the government imposed controls over the convertibility of
the Eastern Caribbean dollar. These measures were denounced by the
press and opposition parties as dictatorial.

As the financial position of the country deteriorated, the government found it impossible to grant the demand of government employees for salary increases to offset rises in the cost of living. Government
employees had organized themselves into two trade unions, one for
senior civil servants and the other for the lower-paid employees. Both
unions were members of the Trade Union Congress (TUC), which
was under the influence of Burnham, who had, by now, become an
implacable foe of Jagan and the PPP. Faced with a precarious financial
situation and a resentful civil service, Jagan once again started his
search for funds abroad. He went to Washington to see President
Kennedy for US aid. He failed. His efforts met with the same fate in
Canada.

Jagan returned home disappointed but determined to get the economy going by mobilizing domestic resources. He secured the services
of Professor Kaldor through the UN. The budget, the only instrument
available to the government for raising resources, was at hand. It was
prepared on the basis of Kaldor's recommendations and contained tax
proposals on capital gains, gifts, wealth, semi-luxury consumer goods
and alcoholic beverages. It also included a plan for compulsory savings
under which anyone with a wage or salary income above $100 a month

was required to buy government bonds at the rate of 5 per cent of the excess income.

This was the budget that created a political storm which made media headlines around the world. *The New York Times* described it as 'courageous and economically sound'. For *The Times*, London, the budget proposals were not only courageous but also 'not far from what Guiana must have'. Similar views were expressed by the chairman of Booker Brothers, the British company that owned most of the sugar industry and other businesses and whose dominance of the economy had earned for the country the name 'Booker's Guiana' in local parlance. But in Guiana itself the local press carried a vituperative campaign against the budget, and against Jagan and his party. One newspaper denounced the budget with the headline: 'Tax avalanche will crush working classes.' Another described it as a 'Slave Whip Budget.' Jagan's efforts to soften the opposition by offering to take back the increase in duties on most of the imported commodities and to modify the compulsory savings met with indignant rejection.

From all accounts it became clear that the budget was only an instrument in the struggle for political power between Jagan and his party on one side and his opponents on the other. In view of the violence organized to support political protest, the British government set up a Commonwealth Commission to enquire into the disturbances that followed the introduction of the budget. The commission had Sir E.C. Asafa-Adjaya of Ghana and Justice G.D. Khosla of India as members, with Sir Henry Wynn Parry of England as chairman. After careful study the commission came to the conclusion that the reason for the disturbances should be 'sought in political rivalries and a feeling that Dr Jagan had strong communist tendencies and that if he were left in power his government would proceed to enact measures injurious to the proprietory rights of the upper classes and businessmen.'

It was against this background of turmoil in the country of my destination that I left for BG in early July 1962. En route I stopped in London and New York. While in England I went to Cambridge to see Professor Joan Robinson. She was critical of Kaldor. She thought Kaldor had handed over to Jagan a standard package of taxes, which he had earlier presented to India and Ghana, without taking local circumstances into consideration. Kaldor had apparently been dismissive of the opposition to his budget in a casual and facile manner.

Joan Robinson organized a meeting at her house for me to meet Kaldor. Throughout the meeting she continued to berate him for having put Jagan into trouble. When Kaldor finally said 'I have learnt my lesson in Guiana,' she tartly retorted, 'Nicky, your education has been very expensive.' She praised Jagan for his gallant defence of Kaldor. Warding off criticism of Kaldor, Jagan had taken the responsibility on himself, saying it was he who had accepted what were only the recommendations of an expert.

At the UN secretariat in New York I found that the attitude towards Jagan's government was one of indifference. My briefing was largely confined to administrative arrangements. On substantive matters I was given some statistical and other data by way of background material. For the rest, I was asked to play it by ear. A young Latin American economist whom I met accidentally gave me a copy of a report on Guiana by John Adler, an economist of the World Bank. Adler's report was sympathetic to the Jagan government's understanding of the requirements of their economy. 'It is clear to me', Adler said in his report, 'that the top priorities have been correctly selected.' The fact that Adler was more sympathetic to the Jagan government than the United Nations secretariat surprised me. I learnt later that the Adler report was pigeonholed and had no effect on the bank's policy. I also met my old friend Paul Sweezy, the editor of *Monthly Review*. Sweezy had had to leave the Harvard faculty at the height of the McCarthy hysteria. He gave me his views on the ground situation in Guiana. He was worried about Jagan's future because of the continued US hostility towards him and urged me to do whatever I could to help.

I arrived in Georgetown in mid July and was met at the Atkinson airbase by the UN resident representative and Lloyd Best, a young man from Trinidad who was to work with me. He was a fresh graduate from Cambridge University and this was his first job. Though young in years, he was fully conversant with the economic problems and political aspirations of various groups in Guiana. He knew several officials and politicians personally, which was a great advantage, particularly in the prevailing circumstances of mistrust between civil servants and politicians in the country. The two of us together, one a Black from neighbouring Trinidad and the other an Indian from distant India, were expected to give balanced advice in a country where the Blacks and the East Indians were believed to be involved in economic competition and political rivalry. Best and I were able to evolve a common approach to economic problems. Sometimes he would get emotional in argument, but eventually would take a more detached view of things. We soon became very good friends and he started calling me his older brother. In a touching gesture of warmth he gave his newly born daughter the Indian name Kamala.

We were less lucky with Dr Gyan Chand, the well-known Indian economist whom Jagan had pulled out of retirement to head the Planning Unit as an official of the government, with Clive Thomas, an able local economist, assisting him. Best and I were supposed to be consultants to the unit. Gyan Chand was an extremely pleasant person with very charming old-world manners, but he was very rigid in his economic judgements, which were dominated by his ideology. The Guianese civil servants had no time for him. Best would also get impatient with him and found it difficult to be polite in discussions. I tried hard to throw bridges between the two but failed. Gyan Chand looked upon Jagan as another Castro in the vanguard of the anti-imperialist struggle. He was blissfully unaware of the vulnerabilities of Guiana—a large but empty country with a small population of about half a million which was further divided by class, colour, race and religion, and situated in an area which the United States considered its backyard.

I had met Gyan Chand in Delhi a few times, mostly in the company of K.N. Raj, to whom he was close. I found him a great admirer of Mao's Great Leap Forward and a passionate believer in the Hindi-Chini Bhai-Bhai syndrome. In Guiana he laid stress on Afro-Asian unity, which was fine, particularly in the racial context of the country. In economic matters he was convinced that the salvation of Guiana lay in reducing, if not eliminating, foreign investment in sugar and bauxite, two of the three main segments of its economy, the third being rice cultivation, which was done by the East Indians. Gyan Chand's ideas were more in tune with the ideologically committed elements of the PPP, for whom the nationalization of large industry was essential strategy towards socialism.

Best and I had a different approach. The challenge which the leadership of Guiana faced was how to reduce the constraints imposed by the colonial economic arrangement on its lopsided economy and launch an investment programme which would prompt broad-based growth in a sustained manner. Everyone was aware that the domestic resources available for such a programme were severely limited, that foreign aid from the Western bloc had been denied, and that BG was not allowed to approach the socialist bloc. Jagan was thus faced with a cruel dilemma. Given the circumstances in which he and his party were placed, he had either to change his ideological stance in a credible manner or face a political onslaught from the colonial power.

The only way out of the dilemma was for him to create a joint front with Burnham and forge an economic programme on the basis of a consensus. Best and I thought it our duty to explore the possibility of a rapprochement between the two estranged leaders, who had once been comrades in arms in the freedom struggle of their people. Perhaps the ideological barriers were not as impenetrable as they seemed. Jagan after all had never described himself as a communist. He was, of course, a Marxist, but not doctrinaire. To be sure, some of his party colleagues had announced their communist leanings in unmistakable terms. This was no doubt awkward baggage that Jagan had on his back, but his leadership was so well established that he could throw it off without much damage. In any case, Indian workers and farmers were his steadfast supporters. Some hard-line ideologues might have abandoned him, but he would have been more than compensated by attracting some elements from the Indian middle class who had withheld their support from him because they believed him to be a communist. Above all, it was necessary for him to allay the genuine fears of businessmen and to enlist the support of the black working class in order to broaden the base of support for Independence. He had no choice but to break the political impasse by seeking the co-operation of Burnham.

With that purpose in view we arranged meetings with the two leaders. I met Jagan alone and Burnham along with Best and Thomas. My meeting with Jagan started with his reminiscing about his Indian tour in 1953. He said he was appalled at the widespread poverty in India. He compared India's efforts in alleviating poverty with those of China. He was impressed with the success China had achieved in this field in such a short time. He was very pleased, he said, with the warm reception which he and Burnham got from people everywhere in the country but was apparently disappointed with the Government of India. He felt that Nehru's government did not want to annoy the British government by supporting them officially. The way our conversation developed did not seem propitious for the sort of discussion I had in mind.

Since nothing came of this conversation, I met Jagan again, a week later. This time I took the initiative and told him that I wanted to share with him and have his reaction to the conclusions I had reached in my understanding of Guianese development requirements. Jagan listened attentively and without any interruption till I finished. I said that, given the nature of the political economy of Guiana and his own political commitments, he must have an economic plan which would ultimately benefit the rural poor, who were mostly Indians, and the urban unemployed, who were mostly Blacks. To achieve these objectives required investment in irrigation and drainage to make more land available for expanded, and more diversified, agriculture on the one hand, and a programme of industrialization based on the local production of imported industrial goods wherever feasible. It also required further investment in the sugar and bauxite industries, so that their operations could add more value to their products within Guiana. (Sugar was exported to England in semi-processed form and refined there and two-thirds of the bauxite was shipped out as raw ore.) Furthermore, a development programme of these dimensions required sizeable investment in infrastructure, particularly power, transport (especially road transport), and communications.

Even without the detailed figure work, it was obvious that a development programme of the size and composition envisaged would require investment funds way beyond what the economy could generate internally. Foreign aid could reduce the gap substantially because, being a small country, the aggregate amounts required would be small, even though they were large compared to the domestic budget. And such aid could come only from western countries and multilateral agencies which would insist on the involvement of foreign and domestic capital in the investment plan. I left it at that.

Jagan pondered over what I had said. For a minute I thought he was putting the scenario in concrete terms in his mind. In practice it meant aid from the USA, the UK, Canada, the World Bank and offering of investment opportunities to Bookers, ALCAN, ALCOA and local capitalists. An ideologically committed person like Jagan, I thought, would dismiss this scenario as a programme of surrender to foreign and domestic capitalist exploiters. But I was wrong. Jagan said it was a useful exercise but that it pointed only to one end of the spectrum of possibilities. He accepted that ideological extremism was unrealistic and that he was prepared for compromises. He said that sizeable aid from socialist countries was also possible. 'Look at Nehru,' he said. 'He got aid from both sides.' 'Despite his socialist pronouncements', I added. But Jagan doubted if Burnham would co-operate. According to him Burnham's political ambition was to be numero uno in Guianese politics, at whatever cost.

I was pleased at Jagan's sober and thoughtful reaction and felt encouraged to talk to Antony Tasker, the local head of Bookers, whom I had met several times earlier. He agreed with me that Jagan was not a hide-bound ideologue. But Jagan, according to Tasker, changed his opinion after consulting his wife Janet, who was reputed to be more doctrinaire and uncompromising in her views. Tasker, however, assured me that if the PPP moved out of its public postures on ideology, Bookers would respond positively. He left me with the feeling that the initiative would have to come from the other side. All in all, Tasker was encouraging but not enthusiastic.

While I had met both Jagan and Tasker several times after my arrival in Georgetown, I had not met Burnham, who was the third key player in the political game. He was perhaps the most important of them all because, like Jinnah in India, he held in his hands a veto on the political

future of his country. It was critical for us to know his views. Clive
Thomas set up a meeting with him for Best and me. It turned out to
be a marathon affair lasting three and a half hours. Burnham was relaxed and cordial, and talked freely on various matters, including some
of a sensitive nature. In his thinking on political and economic matters, he sounded very flexible and pragmatic. His formulations were
phrased in a manner that would leave enough room for him to move
to the right or the left, as the political chessboard might demand. He
made no secret of his contacts with US senators and trade-union
leaders. He did not show any strong antipathy to Bookers but told us
proudly that he had rejected an offer of 80,000 dollars from that firm
to fight the elections in 1956. He believed American liberals to be
progressive and approved of their insistence on monetary, fiscal and
other reforms before recommending aid. His vision for Guiana seemed
to be that of a Black-dominated polity and a mixed economy supported by US aid. In this connection, he added that to sustain growth the
country would need Black immigrants from the West Indies since they
would fit in without creating social problems. 'Immigrants from India
and Mauritius will not fit in', he added with a smile, looking intently
at me.

He spoke at length about Jagan. He told me that Jagan was not at
ease with him despite their long association. A conversation with Jagan,
according to Burnham, meandered slowly through trivialities before
Jagan could get to brass tacks. He always fidgeted with his fingers, a
sign of nervousness born out of a consciousness of intellectual inferior-
ity. Burnham was very proud of his own scholastic and academic at-
tainments; he had been the Guiana Scholar of his time in England. At
the same time, he seemed to be jealous of Jagan's fame as a leader. He
resented what he called Jagan's publicity abroad, which he said was
zealously created by communists as well as by anti-communists. Burnham complained that communists killed him with 'non-mention' and
anti-communists took him for granted. His resentment against Jagan
was so great that he would adopt any political line, however desperate, if it ensured toppling Jagan. Given the geopolitical realities of
the Caribbean, Burnham seemed to suit US foreign-policy requirements very well. He seemed to have qualified himself to fit into the US

anti-communist campaign without diminishing his self-respecting, neutralist and social posture.

For me, the meeting with Burnham was disappointing. It confirmed Jagan's assessment of Burnham. I saw no possibility of him and Jagan combining their efforts. Best had reached that conclusion even before the meeting. We decided to abandon our efforts to seek a consensus for an economic development programme. It was becoming increasingly clear to us that the solution to economic problems had to wait till the ongoing struggle for political power had run its course.

We therefore decided to confine ourselves strictly to our narrowly defined tasks. We helped in the establishment of the Planning Unit, participated in technical seminars for members of the staff, and started preparing our report on planning. The report was in two parts. In the first we presented an outline of the plan and in the second the results of a series of feasibility studies of a few small and medium-sized industries. We organized our work in a manner that would enable us to complete the report by the end of our year of assignment.

A week after our meeting with Burnham, a train of dramatic events took place which demarcated the region within the defence perimeter of the United States in the most explicit manner. On 22 October, President Kennedy, in a broadcast, disclosed information on the presence of Soviet ballistic missiles at a launching site in Cuba and announced the quarantine of all ships going to Cuba. This was the beginning of the most dangerous episode in the annals of the Cold War, when the world stood on the edge of a nuclear holocaust. Because of a previous appointment with him, I was with Jagan in his house when Kennedy made his famous speech announcing the quarantine. We both heard it on the radio in his study. When I asked Jagan about the likely Soviet response, he was sure the Soviets would not back down. Since Jagan himself had bravely broken the American blockade and traded with Cuba earlier, he was sure the mighty Soviet leaders would not succumb to American threats. Even after the crisis had blown over and the missiles removed from Cuba, Jagan refused to draw any meaningful lesson for himself or for his country from the episode.

The Cuban missile crisis roughly coincided with the Himalayan crisis. On the Sino-Indian conflict Jagan was ambivalent. His East

Indian community was in sympathy with their country of origin, but he himself was ambiguous. K.C. Nair, Indian high commissioner to the British West Indies and BG, told me how disappointed he was when he tried to elicit Jagan's views on China's aggression against India. The small group of expatriate Indians, mostly doctors and businessmen, felt forlorn and friendless. The high commissioner could not bring much cheer to them, being himself at the receiving end of a stream of bad news from Delhi. His own morale was low: he told me that the Chinese, having captured large areas in NEFA, were about to descend and spread themselves in the plains of Assam. He was irritated with me when I told him that the Chinese were not so foolish and that it was reasonable to expect them to withdraw before winter set in. I said the Chinese onslaught was like the British punitive expeditions against the turbulent tribesmen in the North West Frontier province. Though annoyed with me for what he called my 'non-serious approach' in the matter, he kept me informed of developments at home and was fulsome in his praise for my common sense when he telephoned me from Port-of-Spain in the middle of the night to give me news of the Chinese withdrawal.

To go back to Jagan. In the summer of 1963 he had to face yet another crisis. It started when the government introduced a bill to provide for a secret poll of workers by which the trade union which secured the majority of votes would be recognized as the bargaining agent. This had become necessary because of jurisdictional disputes between the trade unions. The anti-Jagan element in the trade-union movement, represented by the Trade Union Congress (TUC), looked upon the bill as a challenge to their leadership. They denounced it as a threat to the existence of free and democratic trade unions! The minister of labour, in a bid to mollify them, held consultations with the TUC and employers' associations, as a result of which several amendments were made in the bill. But the TUC remained dissatisfied and there was no let-up in the demonstrations. The impression of the people who were in the know was that there was no chance that the TUC or the opposition at large would consider the bill on its merits. As in the case of the budget the previous year, the bill became an instrument of political warfare. Demonstrations and protests were organized under the directions of Burnham. He used all his famed oratorical skills to rouse his followers to action, reminding them of their power which 'no hell or high water' could stop. The tempo of the agitation rose day by day and climaxed on 6 April, when the presence of two Soviet ships loading rice in Georgetown harbour became a pretext for violence. A rumour was spread that the ships were carrying arms for Jagan's followers. Crowds came out, attacked the police, and indulged in widespread rioting in a prelude to a countrywide general strike.

Jagan's response to the crisis was very impressive. He was determined to keep the economy going. He managed to keep essential services like electricity, water, and ferries running despite the strike. His greatest worry, however, was about the stoppage of oil supplies because Guiana was critically dependent on oil imports. Supplies of oil from Trinidad, the neighbouring oil-exporting country, dried up. Jagan sought the governor's help to get oil from Venezuela through the British government or through the British Navy. The governor turned down the suggestion as impractical. In these circumstances, Jagan was driven to appeal to the Cuban government for help. The Cuban response was positive and prompt but it carried obvious political costs. Though the blockade resulted in shortages, Jagan made sure that there was no scarcity of food. As the strike dragged on, week after week, people began to find life difficult. It was Jagan's leadership and organizing ability that made the majority of people accept their hardships with fortitude during this eighty-day period of the longest general strike in the world.

The strike finally ended on 7 July, through the intervention of the British Trade Union Congress, whose representative persuaded the leaders of the strike to settle the dispute. The strike ended because the financial burden on the sympathizers of the strike was proving too heavy and the striking workers themselves were psychologically exhausted.

Jagan weathered the storm but it was certainly not the end of political strife in Guiana. The US government now seemed determined to get Jagan out of power and was putting pressure on the British to help. Only three days after the end of the strike *The New York Times* reported that Dean Rusk, the US secretary of state had told the British government that the continuation of the PPP government would intolerably heighten American difficulties with Cuba. It also reported that Prime Minister Macmillan had assured President Kennedy that early independence was not contemplated for Guiana. It was now only a question of time and suitable tactics to achieve Jagan's ouster in a plausible manner.

The political parties having failed to reach an agreement, it was not difficult for the British government to impose a settlement on lines that would ensure that Guiana had a government that suited them and the United States. The device used was the system of proportional representation for the election of a new government. The London *Economist* described the device as 'considerably more extreme than even the main opposition party has recently been demanding'. It brought out the consequences of the imposition of proportional representation in the following terms: 'it is likely to lead to more directly racial voting . . . it appears remarkably like a device for ensuring the defeat of Dr Jagan's government . . . the imposition suggests that the policy of obstruction and sometimes of violence followed by certain opposition groups in the last two years has secured for them a vastly more favourable solution than could have been obtained had the forms of democracy been observed.' As expected, the new constitutional arrangement ensured Burnham's rule for twenty-one years, till his death on 6 August 1985.

My year's stay in Guiana and the general strike ended at about the same time. My contract came to an end on 11 July. Despite the difficulties we had to face during the strike, Best and I were able to complete our report on time. The United Nations wanted both Best and me to continue for another year, but both of us thought that no useful purpose would be served by our continuation or by the appointment of substitutes by the United Nations. In my capacity as Resident Representative, an additional charge I had to undertake since November on account of the sudden death of the incumbent, I advised the UN secretariat accordingly during my debriefing session in New York. So with our departure the UN assistance to Guiana for this particular project ended.

In any case I could not have stayed longer in Guiana. The reason was that Dr Rao was being appointed a member of the Planning Commission and of the board of governors of the Institute of Economic Growth and had decided to offer me the post of director of the institute in his place.

I returned from Guiana a sad man, fearful about Jagan's political future and that of his people. They both deserved better than what seemed likely. Jagan had many qualities necessary for leadership. He was a man of sincerity, integrity and courage. His love for his people, both African and Indian, was genuine. Their suffering over the dark days of slavery and indenture were a part of his living memory. He was very articulate and persuasive. He was the most charismatic leader of all Caribbean politicians. And yet, in 1963, it did not seem likely that he would succeed. This gloomy prospect was not because the odds against him were formidable, which, indeed they were. It was because of his habit of viewing problems through the distorting lenses of ideological stereotypes that were created by the Cold War. He viewed all social conflicts and tensions in terms of an overarching class conflict. This way of looking at problems in a multi-racial, multi-religious society made it impossible for him to avoid confrontational politics. Jagan made it easy for his ambitious and unscrupulous political rivals, racial bigots and foreign vested interests to combine against him. Since, according to his theory, all these elements constituted an alliance— 'reactionaries in collaboration with imperialists'—he made no attempt to break the alliance. He was in danger of becoming a willing victim of his own theory.

For me, Guiana proved to be a place where one could see many contemporary problems in their stark reality and the year I spent in BG was a period of intense education. Everything here was on a laboratory scale, and it did not take much mental effort to see individual strands of social and political realities separately and in their juxtaposition. In

this laboratory one could see imperialism in action without any confusing and contradictory explanations; the recklessness with which
plural societies can be set upon self-destructive courses by ambitious
leaders; the power of multinationals for good and evil; the ways by
which the working classes can be divided and made to play what
ideologues call 'reactionary' roles; and the ease with which gifted leaders can be beguiled into self-defeating policies by their ideological
certitudes. I also saw the absurd lengths to which the mad logic of the
Cold War could drive a super power; how a liberal American president
could be manipulated by opportunist politicians from a tiny land in
the name of fighting communists.[1]

---

[1] A decade and a half later, George Ball, undersecretary of state with President Kennedy, admitted that 'A great deal of time, money and effort—including a substantial
amount of President Kennedy's own time—was expended in 1962 in trying to keep
Mr Cheddi Jagan from coming to power in Guyana, although most Americans could
not find the country on the map . . .' George W. Ball, *Diplomacy for a Crowded World*
(Little Brown Company, 1997), pp. 222–3.

CHAPTER SIX

Between Academics and Policy-makers

S oon after my return from BG I took over the directorship of the Institute of Economic Growth from V.K.R.V. Rao. The institute had started with a small research programme which it had inherited from the Delhi School of Economics. With that small beginning it was able to expand and diversify the programme at a pace and in a manner that made it, by 1965, the country's leading institution for economic research and training. The programme was organized in and around a number of separate units relating to studies on population, agriculture, industry, labour, planning and development, and energy. Barring the section on energy, the entire programme was financed by the corresponding ministries and the Planning Commission. The energy section was funded by the Burmah Shell Company. Besides research work the institute also ran two training programmes; one for probationers of the Indian Economic Service for the home ministry and the other on project evaluation for the Planning Commission.

The institute also inherited an orientation centre which was expanded to include non-US technical personnel. The centre now focussed on presenting to them as objectively as possible a picture of India in transition—a traditional rural economy transforming itself into a modern economy. The institute was also intimately connected with the UNESCO Research Centre for Social and Economic Development, which was housed in the premises of the institute. The work of the centre extended to the South East Asian region. I was ex-officio chairman of the steering committee of the centre. The centre gave us an opportunity to study the changes that were taking place in countries whose experience might be relevant to India and other developing countries.

In managing this highly diversified complex of activities, I was lucky to have a brilliant band of colleagues to work with: A.M. Khusro, Raj Krishna, Dharm Narain, Arjun K. Sengupta, T.N. Madan, Ashish Bose, P.C. Joshi and C.H. Hanumantha Rao. All of them distinguished themselves as research analysts and high-ranking advisers. Their co-operation made it easy for me to run the institution smoothly for seven and a half long years.

Since the research programme was almost entirely funded by the government and its agencies, it was feared that the institute might lose its academic independence and the government might try to influence the research findings. Not only did that not happen, I often found that it needed some effort to get the ministry seriously interested in the outcome of programmes they had funded. The only time we would have a discussion with the ministry was at the initial stage, when the research proposal was being sanctioned. Once it was accepted, the implementation of the proposal would become the responsibility of the accounting branch of the ministry. It was their job to make sure that the money had been spent according to rules and a report of work done submitted at the end of the financial year. They would be annoyed with a serious research worker if his work did not keep pace with the flow of funds released for it, and, exemplifying the soul of bureaucracy, they were satisfied with a shoddy report merely because it was submitted in time. Whether the money was well spent or not was no part of their thought process.

In these circumstances there was not much scope for the utilization of research findings for policy purposes. There were, of course, some officers who took interest in policy-oriented research but their interest was personal and not institutionalized in the ministry as a consumer of research. The ministers, as a rule, were even less interested. My colleague Raj Krishna used to say they are 'knowledge-proof'. C. Subramaniam was the only minister who took keen interest in research relevant to him in his capacity, first as minister for steel and later as minister for agriculture. He was receptive to new ideas and used to invite researchers to his house for in-depth discussions. It was he who changed the agenda of development for agriculture in India. For the rest, the ideological atmosphere generated by the planning strategy crafted by Mahalanobis and popularized by Nehru was so overwhelming that the revision of existing policies was unthinkable. But this was not true only of the political leadership, it was equally true of the intellectual elite.

And yet this was precisely the time when India needed to look again at the policies it had been following. Since the early sixties the economy had performed poorly. Food shortages were becoming chronic, industrial output was running much below the targets, while idle capacity was expanding. The economy was becoming increasingly dependent on foreign aid. Aid-giving countries and institutions were becoming stridently critical of India's investment priorities and its policies to implement them. The external criticism of India's economic plans was matched by domestic frustration on account of increasing unemployment and unrelieved poverty.

The optimism generated at the start of planning, a decade earlier, had disappeared. In sum, Indian planning was in crisis and formulation of the fourth five-year plan was becoming a game of snakes and ladders for econometricians of the Planning Commission. In the troubled days of the 1930s, R.H. Tawney noted that reflecting upon alternative futures is 'uncongenial to the bustling people who describe themselves as practical people, because they take things as they are.' He proceeded to tell his fellow Englishmen: 'The practical thing for a traveller who is uncertain of his path is not to proceed with utmost rapidity in the wrong direction; it is to consider how to find the right one. And the practical thing for a nation which has stumbled upon one of the turning points of history is to consider whether what it has done hitherto is wise and if not wise to alter it.' India had stumbled into a situation which required from its leaders clear decisions on the future course to follow.

Lal Bahadur Shastri, the unassuming prime minister who had succeeded the charismatic Nehru, seemed an unlikely person to face up to this situation. But in his own quiet way he did initiate a series of steps which would have not only brought the economy out of the existing crisis but possibly put it on a high-growth path in the long run. He wore no ideological blinkers; he saw facts as they were in all their starkness. Chronic food shortages made him shift investment from basic industries to agriculture. Roaring black markets persuaded him to make a relative shift from controls to incentives, and the glaring inefficiency of the public sector made him accept a larger role for the private sector and foreign investment. He also took measures to shift the locus of economic decision-making from the Planning Commission to the ministries and from the centre to the states. These measures reduced the influence of the Planning Commission—which had developed a rigid, almost doctrinaire outlook on economic policies—and at the same time decentralized decision-making.

Shastri's pointed references to the yawning gap between promise and performance of the five-year plans and his plea for reordering development priorities drew criticism from leftists in general and the two communist parties in particular. Within three months of his assumption of the office of prime minister he had to face a no-confidence motion in parliament. But Shastri stood his ground. In his reply to the debate, he referred to the charge of deviation from Nehru's economic policies and boldly asserted: 'In a democracy there is every opportunity for re-thinking and freedom of the formation of new schemes and policies.' In fact the Second Plan, which laid the foundation of planning, had clearly stated that its objectives 'were not rooted in any doctrine or dogma . . . It is neither necessary nor desirable that the economy should become a monolithic type of organization offering little play for experiment in either form or as to modes of function.'

I was a direct witness to this process of reorientation by virtue of my being nominated to the National Planning Council, which was set up by the government in February 1965. While announcing the decision Lal Bahadur Shastri indicated that he had felt it would be an advantage if more non-official experts could be associated with the preparation of the Fourth Plan. The members of the Planning Commission, however, did not take Shastri's low-key announcement at its face value. They looked upon the council as a rival body set up to erode the authority of the commission.

The seventeen-member council was composed of industrialists, scientists, rural workers, economists and trade unionists. Besides me, P.S. Lokanathan, director-general of the National Council of Applied Economic Research (NCAER), was the only other economist in the council. Apart from considering and advising on policy issues, members were expected to undertake studies on problems suggested by the council or by the government. The council set up a number of groups to consider selected problems in different sectors of development. Thus the scope and direction of the council's work ran parallel to that of the Planning Commission. Council members were expected to work in close and continuous association with the commission. Although the council and its committees met several times and had very useful discussions and prepared several papers, it could not function the way Shastri wanted because of the hostile attitude of the commission.

There were other difficulties. Only those members could undertake independent studies who had their own organizations to work for them. In that respect both Lokanathan and I had the advantage of having the back-up of independent research organizations. But before we could mobilize our resources, the ongoing work for the Fourth Plan was overtaken by the crisis which had developed as a result of the outbreak of hostilities with Pakistan and the consequent suspension of aid by the United States. The council met in November 1965 and considered reorienting the plan. Two months later Lal Bahadur Shastri died and with him died the inspiration behind the search for a revised policy framework for India's economic development.

As war-time leader Shastri had attained a stature which he lacked when he took over as prime minister. During the brief period of his stewardship he had acquired his own popular political support that would, I believe, have given him added confidence to pursue an agenda of economic reform of the kind that was taken up only twenty-five years later, in 1991. In the event, his initiatives turned out to be no more than a minor episode in the history of India's economic reforms.

After Shastri's death I got some more opportunities to look at the way our economic policies were operating on the ground. In particular, I got a closer view of the working of our public sector when the new government nominated me on the board of directors of Hindustan Steel and the State Bank of India. I learnt enough from the working of these two companies—one the largest industrial enterprise and the other the biggest commercial bank in the country—to be sceptical about the exaggerated role that had been assigned to the public sector in our plans. In the Industrial Policy Resolution of 1956, perhaps the most important statement of economic policy and which has had far-reaching consequences on India's economic growth and well being, it was stated clearly that the government expected the public sector to generate surpluses on an increasing scale. In fact Mahalanobis, the architect of Indian planning, believed that there would be no need for additional taxation in about fifteen years time, i.e. by the beginning of the 1970s!

The actual results have been very disappointing. Public-sector enterprises had no compulsion to be cost effective because the government carried the losses they incurred. In the board of directors of Hindustan Steel, I remember a manager who used to explain away losses glibly by invoking social cost/benefit analysis and reminding us that we should not confuse public-sector culture with the crass commercial notions of the private sector. The imposition of social obligations on public-sector enterprises gave them an alibi for inefficiency. P.L. Tandon, who also served on the Hindustan Steel board, put this point succinctly: 'when the management of a steel-making enterprise has to run large housing colonies, clubs, schools, polytechnics, hospitals, temples, colleges, waterworks, lighting roads, sanitation, bus services, shops and cooperatives, it will inevitably have less time to concentrate on its main function, to make steel.'

In the Indian experience the disabilities of a public-sector enterprise begin right from its conception: from the first stage when it is identified, appraised and selected for inclusion in the public investment programme. The sponsoring agency, such as a central ministry, and associated interests such as the government of the state where the project is to be located, are keen to see that the project is included in the investment programme. To improve the prospects of acceptance, costs are often underestimated. Inadequate technical capability in the analysis of projects at different points in the decision-making process makes for poor preparation. The fact that projects are often modified in the course of implementation shows the generally poor quality of project preparation. Since the approval of the project has to filter through general administrative structures, more time and energy is spent on observing procedures than on ensuring technical and economic viability. The results are indifferently prepared projects, with costly delays and an adverse impact on the economics of such projects. The financing of projects takes place through annual budgets, which makes the implementation of these vulnerable to the vagaries of the budget, regardless of time schedules and construction schedules. The planning and implementation of public enterprises is thus biased in the direction of higher capital costs and longer gestation periods.

In theory, public-sector enterprises are owned by the people and run in their interest. In practice, they have spawned a number of economic interests and political constituencies which wield formidable power. Public-sector undertakings project the power of the government, the minister, his ministry and his political party over large groups of men and large amounts of money. This is particularly true in the case of the public sector in the states, where it provides an arena for the distribution of sinecures and patronage in return for political support. This is the major reason for the spread of the public sector to activities which are outside the key or strategic area originally demarcated for it. The political process as it has evolved has made the public sector an omnibus apparatus for undertaking tasks and responsibilities that belong to the state and society at large. A case in point is the bailing out of 'sick' units in the private sector, which are dumped on the public sector. All parties in power, regardless of their ideological inclination, have found that the public sector lends itself to political use.

The political success of the nationalization of banks had made nationalization a kind of magic formula, a sort of 'open sesame' to gain political power. Early in 1972, while the Congress Party was preparing for the state elections which were to be held in March that year, the prime minister summoned me to her house. Mohan Kumaramangalam and C. Subramaniam were there already. Mrs Gandhi told me that they were discussing Mohan's suggestion that the Tata Iron and Steel Company (TISCO) should be nationalized. She asked for my reaction to this idea. Mohan had talked to me about this on an earlier occasion and had advanced some technical and ideological reasons in support of the notion. I had countered his suggestion on the grounds that Tisco was a well run company which could by example spur other steel companies in the public sector to perform more efficiently. After this casual conversation I had heard nothing further on the subject from Mohan, who was the minister for steel. My response to Mrs Gandhi's question was that the nationalization of TISCO would send an ominous message to the private sector and demoralize it. It would also work against the development of a healthy mixed economy which she had recently spoken about in a public speech. She said that Mohan was of the view that such a move would be very popular and therefore of political advantage. I told her that if the only purpose of Mohan's proposal was to influence voters and gain political advantage, it was unnecessary at that point because the two-month old victory over Pakistan had already ensured that the Congress Party would win the forthcoming elections.

All this has now the status of common knowledge, and some effort is being made to change the governing philosophy of India's public sector, but it was not so at all in the 1970s.

I first met Indira Gandhi around the middle of August 1965, when she was minister for information and broadcasting. I had met her, or more accurately seen her, once before, in 1963, at a breakfast to which I was invited by her father, who wanted me to give him a first-hand account of the happenings in British Guiana. K.C. Nair, Indian high commissioner to British West Indies and British Guiana, had mentioned my name to the prime minister. Mrs Gandhi had not joined us for breakfast. After that I had no occasion or reason to meet her, and so I was puzzled when I received an urgent phonecall from her house asking me to see her. No reason was given.

I went to her Safdarjung house in the afternoon the same day and was ushered into the sitting room where she was waiting for me. She seemed restless and was plucking at her sari involuntarily, then rearranging it on her knees. 'What are your thoughts on the internal situation in Kashmir?' she asked, without preliminaries. A couple of weeks earlier Pakistan had begun infiltrating into the Valley and the situation there was heating up.

I was unprepared for the abruptness of her question. I had written an article in the monthly magazine *Seminar* a while earlier, but she made no reference to that. But since I had kept in touch with several friends in the Valley, I was able to respond to her question in some detail. Among other things, I warned her of the existence and potential for mischief of pro-Pak lobbies because I believed that newspaper reports from Srinagar on the co-operative attitude of the local population were excessively optimistic. I asked her what the ministry was doing to counter the psychological warfare that Pakistan had unleashed alongside the induction of its guerillas. She was acutely aware of anti-Indian sentiment among sections of the Kashmir population as a result of Sheikh Abdullah's continued imprisonment and Bakshi Ghulam Muhammad's high-handed and corrupt ways. She said her ministry was doing what it could, but it needed assistance. She was full of praise for Sushital Bannerji, a senior officer of the state, and N.L. Chawla, the station director of Radio Kashmir. She told me she had been wondering how to win the battle for the hearts and minds of Kashmiris and wanted to know if I had any views on the subject. She said she was meeting me at the suggestion of Romesh Thapar. I felt this was a matter for professionals but promised to put my thoughts, for what they were worth, on a piece of paper. I prepared a short paper and sent it to her a few days later.

Upon getting the note she sent for me again. She had read the note very carefully and discussed some of the suggestions I had made. I was impressed by her knowledge of everybody who was anybody in Kashmir politics. She liked my suggestions but said neither the prime minister nor the home minister would care for her opinion. She made several such comments which indicated that there was no rapport between her and Prime Minister Lal Bahadur Shastri. I gathered that she thought he lacked leadership, and she certainly seemed to hold a poor opinion of his handling of foreign affairs. What seemed to have hurt her personally was a belief that he had positioned her in his cabinet more as a political necessity than as a valued colleague. Yet that had not put her off. Her patriotism was transparent and she was keen to help in facing the Pakistani threat to India's security and secularism. As minister of information and broadcasting she took keen and detailed interest in Radio Kashmir and was in personal touch with the head of that organization.

On 1 September 1965, when the situation created by Pakistani infiltrators deteriorated sharply, she decided to visit Jammu city and Srinagar and sought the prime minister's permission. After a delay of three days he reluctantly gave his consent. She asked me to accompany her and I readily agreed. On 4 September, when we were scheduled to fly out, it started pouring. At the airport we were told that the Indian Airlines plane could not land at Jammu, so we flew straight to Srinagar. At Srinagar airport there was no one to receive Mrs Gandhi except Chawla and a police officer. She was taken to the state guest house, and I went off to Nedou's Hotel. Half an hour later, when I went to see her at the guest house, she was already closeted with Ghulam Mohammad Sadiq, the chief minister.

After ascertaining his views on the local situation, she addressed the various Congress workers who had been brought in at short notice. More than her words, it was her presence in the Valley that impressed them most. She was the only central minister or political leader who had arrived in their midst at a time when they were confronted with a serious external threat and the danger of internal sabotage. After the meeting was over she discussed with Sadiq suggestions about building up local resistance to infiltrators along the lines we had discussed in Delhi. By the time we finished it was late evening. Sadiq and I were tired and about to leave and have a drink at his house when she suddenly sprang a surprise: she felt she should visit soldiers at the front. Sadiq said he would talk to the corps commander and find out about arrangements.

En route to his house Sadiq told me he felt humbled before her bravery. Apparently her desire to visit the front was not as sudden as it had seemed to me: Sadiq had earlier given her the lowdown on the situation, which was very grim, and told her that the failure of the infiltrators to incite Kashmiris to revolt had incensed the Pakistanis, and that they were making a determined bid to breach the Srinagar–Jammu–Leh roads so as to isolate Kashmir militarily and politically. She had listened coolly to his briefing and told him finally that 'in these circumstances our jawans must know that the country is behind them. I must visit them before I leave.'

The visit to the front, however, never came off. Next morning when I went to the guest house to see her, she was busily packing her things and talking to Chawla and other officers of Radio Kashmir. In the midst of this bustle she took me aside and briefly told me the prime minister wanted her to fly back to Delhi immediately. I stayed behind and heard on the radio that evening that Pakistan had bombed Amritsar. Nedou's was swarming with journalists. One of them woke me early next morning to say that war had broken out across the Punjab border. As a consequence civilian flights were cancelled and I was grounded in Srinagar.

While in Srinagar I had enough time to go around the city—which, of course, I knew very well—and meet friends and relatives. I was amazed at how well informed people were about the Pakistani plans. They knew the job of the infiltrators was to create confusion and thereby provide an opportunity to the locals to rise in revolt on 9 August, the day Sheikh Abdullah's government was dismissed and he himself arrested in 1953. Since nothing spectacular had happened on that day, people felt instinctively that the infiltrators had failed in their primary mission. There were, of course, groups of people in the city and reportedly in some villages who received the infiltrators as freedom fighters. Some government officials were also reported to be sympathetic to them. But the bulk of the people were indifferent to their appeals. They paid no attention to the proclamation broadcast from Sada-e-Kashmir, the clandestine radio station Pakistan had set up in Pakistan Occupied Kashmir. A sizeable section, particularly those who had seen and remembered the depredations of the tribal raiders in 1947, were actively hostile to the infiltrators.

I had to be in daily touch with Sadiq, who promised to find some way of sending me back to Delhi. On 13 or 14 September Sadiq sent me a message to rush immediately to the airport. With great difficulty I was able to hire a taxi with the tempting offer of Rs 75 to the driver. Within a couple of miles to the airport I saw army vehicles abandoned on the road and soldiers lying flat on its edges. They were astonished to see a taxi merrily speeding away. Apparently there was an air raid warning, or perhaps an exercise was on. The taxi driver took no notice of his surroundings. He was very pleased with the killing he had made and delivered me safely to my destination.

Within a few minutes of my arrival at the deserted terminal building a convoy of cars drove up and, after the dust settled, D.P. Dhar (state home minister), Sushital Bannerji (development commissioner), Mangat Rai (chief secretary) and Nayantara Sehgal (Jawaharlal Nehru's niece) became visible. We were all led to the spot on the runway where two helicopters were ready to take off. We were about to get in when the siren went off and we were ordered to lie in ditches some distance away. We had to do this thrice. After an hour or so we shook off the dust and got into the helicopter, all except Mangat Rai, who had come to see off his friend Nayantara.

During the flight our helicopter seemed to hug the Pirpanjal mountains. We flew so low that we could see the mountain sides, rock by rock. At Udhampur we were transferred to an airforce Dakota which took a most circuitous route to Delhi. Once again we flew very low so as to stay below the reach of Pakistani radar. It was nerve racking to find oneself flying just over tree tops, but D.P. Dhar kept us all in good cheer with his banter, assisted by much whisky, which he had thoughtfully brought along. He was at his best when a Pak airforce plane flew over us, which it did twice.

After the Srinagar visit my meetings with Indira Gandhi became more frequent. During these she discussed only Kashmir and foreign policy questions, particularly those relating to the Kashmir problem. I do not remember a single occasion when she asked me anything relating to economic questions, which was my professional area of interest. The silence on economic matters intrigued me: it could not be for lack of interest. In her critical remarks on Shastri she had complained that he was under the influence of people who did not like Nehru's economic policies. Could it be that she had bracketed me with the same group because I had been nominated a member on the National Planning Council which Shastri had set up to help the Planning Commission?

After she became prime minister in January 1966 there was a sharp change; she mostly talked about the economic problems she faced. This was particularly so after the devaluation of the rupee in June that year.

The decision to devalue the rupee had proved widely unpopular. She felt she had been let down by her advisers and started looking for non-official opinions on economic issues facing the country. L.K. Jha, her secretary at that time, convened a conference of economists and young business executives to ascertain their views on these matters. I presented a paper on the need for foreign investment, in which I argued that we must welcome such investment, particularly in priority areas, and not be afraid of political subversion, as was feared by some of her political colleagues. We were not a banana republic, I maintained.

This was not a fashionable point of view. After the conference I got a letter from her saying L.K. Jha would call meetings of a small group which would discuss economic policy matters from time to time. However, nothing came of it as her confidence in Jha's advice on economic matters had been eroded by what was perceived to be his role in the devaluation episode. Jha was a senior ICS officer with considerable experience of economic administration. He was known to be in favour of policies recommended by the World Bank. This made him very unpopular with all who were critical of the World Bank. Mrs Gandhi thought he had become a political liability.

In my meetings with her I got the impression that Indira Gandhi had a broad economic philosophy but was less sure about how that philosophy was to be translated into policies. The main components of her economic philosophy were national self-reliance, elimination of

No. 1463-PMO/66

September 10, 1966.

Dear Prof. Dar,

     I am anxious that in the shaping of economic policy not only the experience and the expertise which exists within Government but also the advice of economists as well as people directly engaged in economic activities should play a significant role. A number of Committees and Panels have been set up by the Planning Commission or by individual Ministries.

     My object in writing to you is to enquire whether you would find it possible to help by your advice and guidance on a somewhat personal basis. What I have in mind is not the setting up of yet another Committee or Panel but something much more informal. On important issues, a small official group will prepare a paper which will be sent to you as well as to a few other economists on a strictly confidential basis. Thereafter, depending upon the subject-matter and the convenience of those addressed, we could either have a meeting to discuss the matter further or you could send your comments in writing. In addition, should you feel that a particular topic should be considered, you might send a note which would be circulated and dealt with.

     This proposal can only be given shape after detailed thinking. But I felt that even at this stage it would be worthwhile to have your reactions to this idea and to invite your suggestions regarding the procedure which I have tentatively outlined. Shri L.K. Jha will be responsible for the general coordination of this work and will arrange to have the papers prepared and circulated, and to fix meetings as and when necessary.

     I hope you will be able to spare some time for this work. Your assistance will be welcome and valuable.

Yours sincerely,

(Indira Gandhi)

Letter from Indira Gandhi to P.N. Dhar, 10 September 1966

poverty, and the modernization of India's economy. She imbibed these concepts only partly from her father, but mostly from her own experience, some of which was quite bitter.

The back-to-back droughts of 1965 and 1966, which had made the country desperately dependent on food aid, and had reduced it to what was called a 'ship-to-mouth' state, taught us a very hard lesson in self-reliance. The devaluation episode, a policy sold to her as the price for getting more foreign aid, further emphasized the need for self-reliance. Without this experience she might have withheld her powerful political support to the new strategy for agricultural development that initiated what is popularly called the Green Revolution. The strategy aimed at raising the output of foodgrains from areas with assured water supply by combining high-yielding varieties of seeds and chemical fertilizers. Additionally, farmers were offered attractive prices if they sold their produce to government agencies. Radical elements in the ruling party as well as outside it were critical of the strategy. So were most social scientists: they feared that the strategy might accentuate interpersonal and interregional disparities in the distribution of income and wealth. They also feared that increased profitability from the adoption of this strategy might encourage mechanization and induce a large-scale eviction of tenants. Despite her own political inclinations being similar to those of these critics, she supported the new strategy because it promised avoidance of dependence on aid.

Indira Gandhi had travelled extensively in different parts of the country and seen poverty: it was not to her a matter of statistics about per capita income and the poverty line. She had seen poverty in the emaciated bodies of the men and women who comprised her audiences. She believed that eliminating poverty was the central economic and political problem of India. The anti-poverty programmes, which have multiplied in recent years, were first inspired by her. Regarding the third component, namely modernization of the economy, she believed that without a modern technological and industrial base it would not be possible to provide either welfare to the people or security to the country.

As regards the precise policies to achieve these broad economic goals, Indira Gandhi was ambiguous. Unlike her father, she had no strongly held ideological preferences about specific approaches to economic problems. This pragmatism could have served India very well, particularly in the mid-sixties, when she took charge of the country. This was the time when India's economic circumstances and security environment had deteriorated. Wars with China and Pakistan and the levelling off of foreign aid had left the economy in poor shape. The failure of monsoons in the year of her ascension to power, in 1966, followed by another drought, had resulted in a decline in national income, in absolute terms. The droughts had created widespread food scarcity; inflation and black-marketing were rampant. Serious doubts had arisen not merely in the way the plans were implemented, but in planning itself. These were circumstances which demanded a self-assured and determined leadership with a pragmatic outlook, qualities which Indira Gandhi demonstrated she possessed—but only after she consolidated her power. However, the path to that position ran through struggles in which ideologues rather than pragmatists became her allies and advisers.

Perhaps the ideological shift in favour of the Congress Left was inevitable in the situation in which Mrs Gandhi was placed. Under the Kamaraj Plan her father had removed from his cabinet critics of his economic policies such as Morarji Desai and S.K. Patil, and some conservative and allegedly corrupt chief ministers like C.B. Gupta of U.P. and Bakshi Ghulam Mohammad of Jammu and Kashmir. Under this Plan, evolved by K. Kamaraj (chief minister of Tamil Nadu) and Nehru in early August 1963, cabinet ministers and chief ministers were expected to offer their resignations and work for the party. 'Party before Post' was the slogan used to weed out political undesirables from positions of power. But Shastri had brought some of these back in the cabinet or placed them elsewhere in influential positions. Most of them lacked popular appeal. The media derisively nicknamed them 'the Syndicate'. In the public perception they were not very different from members of the Swatantra Party, a rightist group which was identified with princes, large landholders and big industrialists. They had failed to present even their sensible economic policies as relevant to India's circumstances. Indira Gandhi had also personal reasons to dissociate herself from the Syndicate. She was full of resentment against them because they had tried to manipulate and dominate her when she succeeded Shastri in 1966.

Above everything else, the intellectual climate of the country was predominantly against right-wing politics. Nehru had succeeded in converting a whole generation of the urban intelligentsia to his views on economic planning and associated policies. Academic economists, barring a notable few like Jagdish Bhagwati and T.N. Srinivasan, had become devout votaries of the Nehru–Mahalanobis model of economic growth. Any deviation from the fundamentals of that model was considered politically incorrect. Mrs Gandhi, surely, was not going to deny herself the advantages of this legacy in her struggle for power.

The Congress Party fared badly in the general elections of 1967 and was voted out of power in several northern states. It was the first general election held after Nehru and was generally considered a watershed in the political development of India. More was read into the Congress defeat than was warranted. A factual analysis of the electoral results revealed no marked ideological shifts. The decline in the dominance of the Congress Party was due to the electoral alliances of opposition parties and not because of any abrupt change in voter preferences.

The leftists, however, interpreted the reduced Congress vote as a verdict against the Syndicate and the policies of retreat from socialism that were associated with them in public perception. The humiliating defeats of certain Syndicate leaders such as Kamaraj in Madras, Atulya Ghosh in West Bengal, and S.K. Patil in Bombay, lent credence to leftist views. In this situation, Indira Gandhi could retrieve her image as a 'progressive' and strive for independent leadership for herself by supporting radical elements in her party. These elements, variously known as the Congress Forum for Socialist Action, and the Young Turks, believed in the radicalization of economic policies as a method of rejuvenating the Congress Party and making it an effective instrument for the social transformation of India—as envisaged by Nehru. The forum had succeeded in projecting itself as the custodian of Nehru's thinking and ideas. They were supported by some elements in the Communist Party which believed it was possible for their party to gain leverage in determining the national agenda by such a tactic. Mohan Kumaramangalam had argued for such a tactic since 1964 within the councils of the Communist Party of India (CPI). He ultimately left the party in 1966 to pursue his thesis on his own, which he did with considerable success.

Under the persistent pressure of radicals in the Congress Party, differences on policy matters were becoming more and more polarized. Indira Gandhi's attempts to find a consensus were not yielding any tangible results, except to delay the open rupture. While she felt beholden to the radical elements in the incipient power struggle, she had instinctive doubts about the soundness of some of their policies. But she kept her reservations to herself. I would not have known about her dilemma if she had not asked me, in April 1967, to prepare for her a note on socialist programmes under democratic constraints. This request came at the end of a discussion at her house in which participants laid great emphasis on distributive justice as a means to promote both growth and equity. In the course of a discussion I quoted what a Jat peasant told me: 'you want to distribute cooking oil free, do it by all means; but tell me, is anyone collecting oil seeds? Remember, you get oil from oil seeds.' This was a folksy observation which raised only a laugh from the smart fellows, but it was a bit of robust commonsense that apparently made an impression on her.

In the paper I prepared for her I said that the redistributive aspect of socialism presupposes a high level of development and productivity. A country like India, which is at a lower stage of development and is struggling to accelerate its economic growth, must first achieve a genuine economic breakthrough before it can afford to practice full-scale socialism. Otherwise there is the danger of the country missing both socialism (in the sense of redistribution of income in favour of lower-income groups) as well as economic growth. I defined the problem facing the country as being how to resolve, or at least minimize, the conflict between the needs of economic growth and the claims of socialism. (I redefined the concept of equality as an equitable distribution of income-earning opportunities rather than of existing incomes.)

In a country where unemployment was widespread, one of the principal means of reducing the disparity of incomes would be the rapid creation of employment opportunities.

To this end, the paper supported the idea of a rural works programme prepared by P.S. Lokanathan, director-general of the National Council of Applied Economic Research, and argued for flexible labour markets; prevention of the substitution of capital for labour because of militant trade unionism; profit sharing for the working class in organized industry via bonus shares; rapid expansion of primary education; implementation of what was at that time called the 'socialist charter for children', and so on. To increase industrial output, the paper argued against extending the public sector and for more efficient use of existing government-owned undertakings, as well as for a drastic reduction of controls and bureaucratic power. The paper obviously contained several suggestions which were anathema to doctrinaire socialists, but my purpose was to highlight the basic issues in a straightforward manner, bereft of ideological verbiage, so that she could think about them herself.

I had prepared myself to answer her questions, arising out of what I had said in the paper. Apparently she did not need further explanation and she sent the paper, as it was, to her cabinet colleagues and to some members of the Planning Commission, and to B.G. Verghese, her information adviser at the time, for their reactions. The recipients did not know who the author was. Mrs Gandhi sent me copies of the comments made by these colleagues.

Morarji Desai, Sardar Swaran Singh, Chenna Reddy, Ashok Mehta and several others commended several of the suggestions made in the paper. Jagjivan Ram was critical. The opening sentence of his comments was: 'This hackneyed slogan of "redistributing poverty" has been carried too far. It may convince a theoretician and a secluded economist but it has no appeal to the people.' Dr V.K.R.V. Rao, after affirming his faith in socialism, ended his comments favourably, though in a complicated manner. His conclusion was: 'Under the circumstances, it is worth considering whether one should not frankly admit failure on the socialist front, reaffirm faith in socialist ideology, emphasize the need for more preparation and planning for moving in that direction, and meanwhile follow a pragmatic economic policy, essentially based on expediency but intended only for the short period, and frankly admit its rational and compulsive character in the context of the current economic and international position of the country.'

I was very pleased with myself, hoping my paper would become the starting point of a debate which might produce a consensus on economic issues. I was hopelessly wrong. The struggle for power in the party took a very sharp ideological turn. By the middle of 1967 P.N. Haksar replaced L.K. Jha as the prime minister's secretary. The change was made by the prime minister after great deliberation. Haksar was a socialist of conviction whom she knew as a student in London. He had several friends in the Communist Party of India and among Congressmen of the left persuasion. Soon after he took over he began to cement these elements into an influential political group loyal to Indira Gandhi. His prime concern was to strengthen the prime minister politically. He honestly believed that leftist politics were also good economics and that the two together were in the best interests of the country.

I had met Haksar for the first time in London in May 1966, where I was invited to give a lecture in honour of Rabindranath Tagore at the School of Oriental and African Studies. Haksar was in the audience and seemed pleased with what I had said, even though I had argued for more foreign aid to accelerate India's economic growth. That was the beginning of our friendship. After he joined the prime minister's secretariat he had seen my paper on socialism and had thought it ambivalent. What he did not like were my reservations about the nationalization of commercial banks, which I had expressed in an interview conducted by *The Statesman* for its issue of 15 November 1967. Nevertheless, he continued to discuss economic matters with me from time to time, sometimes on Mrs Gandhi's suggestion, as he told me. I had several meetings with him on the nationalization of banks. I particularly remember two such meetings. In one, Krishna Menon made the startling point that if we nationalize banks we do not have to bother about mobilizing resources! The other meeting, along with K.N. Raj, was at Haskar's house. I learnt later that the second meeting was at the suggestion of the prime minister, who was keen to know Raj's views on the subject. Raj was wholeheartedly for nationalization and said it would take at least six months to prepare for it and that it should be done as an elaborate but secret exercise. Three days later banks were nationalized.

In a separate meeting with him I told Haksar that I could see bank nationalization as a powerful weapon in the factional fight against the Syndicate, but if it was just a flash in the pan, unaccompanied by constructive steps to accelerate growth, it would yield no long-term economic and political benefits. Indeed, I feared it might just trigger off a movement of vulgar populism. I sensed the danger of populism from the manner leftist Congressmen and Communist Party intellectuals presented the case for bank nationalization. But quite frankly I did not realize that my apprehensions would come true almost immediately after the deed was done.

However, despite the tremendous political boost she received from this single act, one thing was clear to me—that Indira Gandhi had no ideological fixations in economic matters. This impression was confirmed by a formal interview I had with her after the nationalization of banks, when the euphoria generated by it was at its height. The interview was arranged by Pran Chopra and published by him in *The Citizen and Weekend Review* in early 1970. Answering a question on the new direction to economic policies, she said: 'In the circumstances here in India it would be difficult to change entirely and suddenly what we have been committed to. We have been committed to the concept of a mixed economy. Within that there is considerable room for movement. As far as I am concerned, and I think my party is concerned, we believe we should remain centrists but left of centre, if I may put it that way. Personally I do not feel that the words left or right have much meaning. But they seem to make things clearer to people sometimes. That is why I am using them...And I think mixed economy is a viable concept and it can be the means of attaining a socialistic society.'

It was therefore no surprise to me that, despite knowing my views on several issues which did not tally with those of some of her favourite advisers, she wanted me to join her office. In fact I got the clear impression that it was because of my being something of a Doubting Thomas that she wanted me around. What was really surprising was that Haksar too wanted me to be on her staff, despite his view that economists have no political sense, and despite some of his progressive friends complaining against my being a reactionary.

But it was I who was full of misgivings about the prospect that was now held up in front of me. After much procrastination, spread over months, I finally landed up as an adviser in the prime minister's secretariat in November 1970.

CHAPTER SEVEN

The Prime Minister's Office*

T he nature of my work in the secretariat, as described by Haksar to me, was very vague. In view of my background as an economist the general impression was that I was going to be an economic adviser, although my designation carried no such qualifying term. In fact Haksar felt it necessary to assure I.G. Patel, who was secretary for economic affairs in the ministry of finance, that he need not worry about any dilution in his work or authority because of my appointment. Haksar was deliberately vague about my field of work. He joked about being an odd-job man himself and suggested that I too should not confine myself to economic matters. In fact the first note I prepared was on the pros and cons of a mid-term election. Haksar did not want to tell me at that stage that I was expected to succeed him nine months later, when he retired. My stint as adviser, I discovered later, was essentially a familiarization course.

I called on the prime minister a day before I joined her office. Since the nature of my job seemed amorphous I asked her if there were specific problems she would like me to examine. Knowing her reticence I started the conversation by mentioning some of the broad issues thrown up by the euphoria generated by bank nationalization. Populist reactions to this event had begun worrying me. She was quiet; perhaps she was disappointed with what I said. After a pause she said what seemed to me something out of the immediate context: 'we must do something about education also', and added: 'I hope you will not be a bureaucrat.'

'I cannot be one even if I try, it's too late in the day,' I said, to lighten the atmosphere.

*The prime minister's secretariat was renamed 'prime minister's office' in 1977.

She greeted that remark with a feeble smile. It was all over in five minutes. N.K. Seshan, her personal assistant, had booked me in for fifteen minutes. I wondered whether her demenaour meant that my time was up and that I should leave or whether I should continue the conversation. I proceeded on the latter assumption and by some strange quirk of conversational sequence I told her that the 'people's car' idea was irrelevant in the prevailing circumstances in India, and that we must think in terms of cheap and quick public transport. I described the people's car idea as fraudulent. She did not respond; she just looked blank. Haksar, whom I met soon after and to whom I repeated the conversation, was amazed at what he called my naivete. He told me I had dropped a big brick; the PM might think, he said, that I was referring to Sanjay's Maruti car project, about which I knew nothing at the time.

In my new circumstances I could not help feeling that I had moved into a different cultural zone. In the morning a battery of chaprasis would line up in the parking lot in front of South Block and wait to open car doors and carry brief cases for their sahibs. Not accustomed to this, I carried my brief case myself. But this was only for a few days. My chaprasi, a chubby and strong-muscled rustic, did not like it. I could see that I had hurt him. My private secretary, an experienced Tamil Brahmin steeped in the culture and lore of the secretariat, said my chaprasi was crestfallen because he had been denied the opportunity to carry my brief case. I decided to talk to the chaprasi about this. After some persuasion he told me shyly that my prestige would suffer if I continued to carry my own brief case. So I gave up and got acclimatized to the new environment with my chaprasi walking proudly ahead of me, brandishing my brief case.

Being a senior officer, I had two chaprasis. The older and senior one had seen better days. He had been in service in South Block during the days of its imperial glory. He showed this legacy in his manner and vocabulary. Opening the door for Sam Manekshaw, he would announce the general as 'Jungi Lat Sahib'. He deployed his hands with authority and contempt, indicating to lesser people that they should move aside when I happened to walk through the corridors. I found him too much of a relic and decided to change his duties to prevent him embarrassing me. He took it philosophically but felt, I was told, sorry for my lack of 'robe-daab'.

Another thing I learnt was that my colleagues never called each other by their names even in conversation. They called each other by their designations, like J.S.(I), J.S.(II), D(I), and so on. Also, as a matter of general practice, a senior officer seldom went to the room of a junior officer. This lesson I learnt in a dramatic manner. Among my new colleagues I had earlier known only H.Y. Sharada Prasad. A couple of days after I joined the secretariat I went to see him in his room. As soon as his chaprasi sighted me and divined my intention, he flung open the doors almost in panic and with full force, without the slightest warning to the occupant. I was most embarrassed to see Sharada Prasad looking startled by the manner of my entry. Getting over his surprise he very thoughtfully told me that his chaprasi was not to be blamed: I had broken convention by visiting him. I should have called him to my room, he said. However, I continued to disregard this hoary practice and dropped in on colleagues when I thought it necessary and convenient for work. It saved a lot of time.

The role of chaprasis in the bureaucracy and governance of India is a fit subject for a doctoral dissertation. The institution is said to be as old as the Mughals, and the term chaprasi is supposed to be the corruption of a compound word consisting of *chap-o-raast* which in Persian mean left and right, i.e. a man who must appear in the direction in which the sahib happened to cast his gaze. I am firmly convinced that without chaprasis the sahibs would look naked and bereft of awe-inspiring authority, for the chaprasi, even more than the personal assistant, generates the required atmosphere of power around an officer. Some chaprasis I have seen are far more impressive-looking than their bosses. They are also first-rate quick-change artistes. The ease with which they change their facial expressions and tone of voice and use their hands to suit the status and the circumstances of a visitor would do credit to a talented actor.

I must hasten to add that, unlike the ministries, the PM's secretariat (PMS for short) did not function on a strict hierarchical principle. Excepting the most important matters, which went up to the PM through the principal secretary or secretary, other officers often dealt directly with the PM, keeping their seniors fully informed. This method reduced delays and encouraged officers to take responsibility for their assessments. The success of the arrangement was essentially due to the fact that the senior officers worked as a team. Much of the credit for this belonged to Haksar. With his warm personality and wide-ranging intellectual interests, he was able to relate with ease to colleagues of different backgrounds, interests and specializations. He did have pro- nounced ideological preferences and held them strongly, but he also displayed the ability and willingness to understand the other person's point of view. This made him approachable; his colleagues imbibed an *esprit de corps* rare in government offices.

The secretary was the first person the PM met every day, as a matter of routine. During the time Haksar and I were on the PM's staff we used to meet her separately. We met her together only when our points of view were either complementary or when there was some difference of approach or judgement between us. I must say to Haksar's credit that this was his way of conveying to her that our differences were hon- est differences.

These meetings were usually brief, focused and purposive, but not always. She was quite capable of diffusing the concentration of a seri- ous discussion she might herself have initiated by suddenly introduc- ing something trivial and unconnected, mostly to do with hearsay about personalities. At first I was puzzled by these sudden changes in the level and scope of our discussions, but over time I realized that it was an expression of her loneliness, her need for lighter conversation, even a little gossip. The fact that she was a woman at the top in a male- dominated society had only made this need greater. For her it was not always a simple matter to relax with colleagues. In our conservative environment it could hurt her image, as she had discovered to her cost in the early days of her prime ministership. For instance, a minister she knew well had taken advantage of her informality with him to boost his own position. She had learnt to be wary and maintain her distance from her colleagues, who were mostly men. This accentuated her naturally reserved demeanour and earned her the reputation of being aloof, secretive and haughty. It took me a while to understand her position and get used to her style. But it did present a practical problem: because one could not always depend on her undivided attention in face-to-face encounters, it was not easy to cut through preliminaries, and long hours had to be spent writing unnecessarily detailed notes.

She also had a disconcerting habit of reading papers lying on her desk while one was talking to her. The first time this happened to me, I stopped talking. She raised her head and asked me to go on, adding that she could do several things at the same time. In the beginning I found her multiple activity in the course of a presentation or an argument very discouraging. But I soon got used to it. She did not mean to be impolite; it was merely an awkward habit of which she was unaware and for which, naturally, no one had ever had the temerity to upbraid her.

She practised this style sometimes even in her meetings with foreign dignitaries. I remember vividly an occasion when the Shah of Iran was talking rather earnestly to her in his Niyavaran palace in Tehran about the future prospects of the oil industry. She suddenly turned her gaze away from him towards a window, from where she could hear the twittering of bulbuls. Sardar Swaran Singh swiftly stepped in to save the situation by appearing to hang on every word the Shah uttered and nodded his head vigorously, while I increased the speed of my note-taking. But I cannot say what the Shah thought of it. Her mental resistance against following complicated arguments was partly responsible for this kind of reaction in her. After my first experience of this sort, I realized that to get her considered reaction a problem had to be presented to her in writing before one discussed it.

The longest and most tedious meetings with Indira Gandhi had to do with the preparation of her speeches. She took great pains over these exercises, regardless of the importance of the occasion or the subject matter she had to deal with. Sharada Prasad, her information adviser and speech writer, bore the brunt on these occasions. He wrote very well and his command over sources of information on a variety of subjects was remarkable. But what impressed me most was his ability to produce a coherent and lucid piece out of the vaguest briefing he would get from her, and from the inchoate assistance he received from his colleagues. His drafts often emerged as finished pieces in themselves. Their finalization with the PM took much more time than he would have spent in preparing them. And the process of finalization not only caused unnecessary delays but also tensions and turmoil: everything else had to wait till these speech-writing exercises were over.

Indira Gandhi's contributions to these were of an editorial nature. She would break a long sentence into shorter ones, substitute a difficult word with a simpler expression. This way she put her own stamp on her speeches. Sharada once said that she was the best sub-editor he had ever known. All this would have been fine, but for her desire for 'quotations'. The search for appropriate quotations was a time-consuming process for Sharada and for some of her personal friends who constituted the search party. She herself maintained a notebook of quotations. Haksar once said to her in exasperation: 'a prime minister should not quote but be quoted', but it had no effect.

Her passion for quotations once caused me a great deal of personal embarrassment. In a major speech on economic matters she quoted, without attribution, Mahbub-ul Haq—the Pakistani economist who was at the time working for the World Bank. Haq had written an article in a Hong Kong journal which someone had passed on to her. In fairness to her, she had circulated Haq's paper to me and several others for an opinion. I had made a written comment which was critical; I had then participated in the preparation of her speech and seen its final version. Usually, she did not depart from the written text, but on this occasion she added, in an impromptu manner, some sentences from Haq's paper. When a journalist discovered this, all hell broke loose. The matter was reported all over India and abroad. Haq became famous overnight and her speechwriters were accused of plagiarism. *Motherland*, the RSS newspaper, named me as the culprit. When N.K. Seshan, her personal assistant, sent her the newspaper cutting, she wrote on the margin: 'I am sorry I have got Shri Dhar in trouble. I did use Haq's article deliberately, I meant to put the words in inverted commas. I did not take his name because I thought there might be narrow-minded prejudice against a Pakistani. There was no intention to pretend—I had already sent copies of the article to Shri C. Subramaniam, Mohan Kumaramangalam, and others.' She also cleared my name in a press conference. But the story became a hardy annual for several years. Every time Haq visited India and met journalists, he made tongue-in-cheek observations about Indira Gandhi's open-mindedness and about ideas having no frontiers and national boundaries.

The other occasion when we ran into difficulties with speech writing was even more serious, but in a different manner. On 3 December 1971, when Pakistan attacked our air bases on the western front and war began, Indira Gandhi was in Calcutta. Sam Manekshaw gave me the news at about six in the evening. Lots of things had to be done as a result of the outbreak of hostilities. One of them was preparation for a radio address to the nation by Indira Gandhi. In the midst of a welter of activities that burst upon us in the office, a text of the speech was prepared for her. I went to the airport to brief her about the war situation. On our way back to the city she asked me, among other things, about the speech. She showed some annoyance when she found I was not carrying the text with me: she could not wait to see it. The delay in reading the speech was going to be compounded by her having to go first to her house, where the chiefs of staff were awaiting her.

After she had finished with the chiefs she rushed to the office. She arrived in a bad mood as her car stalled on the way. When she saw the text of the speech she flew into an almighty rage. It was not up to the mark, she said. One of the ministers who fancied himself as a writer offered to help—with pitiful results. He made life even more difficult for us than it was already by saying that her speech ought to be of Churchillian standards. The result was a delay which took her beyond the scheduled time announced for her speech. The All India Radio personnel were getting desperate because we were not in a position to tell them the exact time of her speech; and their listeners were wondering what was happening. She finally spoke an hour or so after the announced time.

These idiosyncrasies—some might say failings—apart, Indira Gandhi was no ordinary person; she was a great leader by any standard. She possessed abundant common sense, a natural ability to assess individuals and circumstances, and remarkable practical sense. She packed enormous energy into her frail body and could work without rest or pause for hours. She was courageous and determined and undeterred by obstacles. And unlike most Indians, she was not a risk-averse person. She was truly the 'only man in her cabinet'.

She was also fiercely patriotic and had absolute faith in the destiny of India. She passionately desired India to be a prosperous, modern and strong country. In these matters she was her father's daughter. In other ways she was very different from him. Although immensely proud of her patrimony, she believed Jawaharlal Nehru was a weak man. She suspected his weakness was rooted in his goodness. She often said: 'People call Gandhiji a saint, actually it was my father who was a saint.' To achieve her political objectives she herself did not hesitate to manipulate men and events in a manner that would have been anathema to her father. She did not have much use for what she called public-school morality, and she did not mind her critics calling her amoral and ruthless. Yet she was shrewd enough to realize the incalculable value of the Nehru legend. She enriched the legend by combining a projection of Nehru as a national hero with what one might call a Nehru of Camelot, and she made herself the sole inheritor of this legend. She tried to pass this on to her sons, even though Sanjay Gandhi did everything possible to prove he did not deserve the legacy and Rajiv Gandhi made it obvious that he was being dragooned into this inheritance. It was not given to Indira Gandhi to weave the Nehru legend with the traditions of the Congress Party.

When I joined the PMS its prestige stood very high. The secretariat had played a crucial role in the preceding year, during which the ruling Congress Party had split. Morarji Desai (the deputy prime minister and finance minister) had resigned, and commercial banks had been nationalized. These events had shifted the balance of political power in favour of Indira Gandhi, even though she was heading a minority government and was dependent on the support of small opposition parties in parliament.

The secretariat headed by Haksar had played a key role in these developments. The successful management of crisis situations had brought Haksar into the limelight and dramatized the role of the prime minister as the ultimate custodian of power and bearer of responsibility. This leadership role was further enhanced by Indira Gandhi's sweeping electoral success in March 1971. She became the head of a strong and stable government with an overwhelming majority in parliament. She was now the unquestioned leader of the Congress Party. It was from this position of strength that she was called upon to face the crisis in East Pakistan, which had brought ten million refugees into India from that province. The outstandingly successful handling of the crisis further confirmed the pre-eminent position of the prime minister in India and the emergence of her secretariat as the key element in its governance.

No doubt all these crises were handled by the prime minister with the assistance of the organs and agencies of government, but the secretariat had to play a leading role in co-ordinating the effort. This was inevitable because in a parliamentary democracy the prime minister is so overwhelmingly the focus of power and responsibility. The fact that decisions in situations of crisis are left to the prime minister does not mean that decisions taken by others in normal circumstances are less important, and indeed these other decisions may be more important in terms of their consequences for the country and the people. In the Indian case princely and feudal rule has endowed the prime minister with an extra halo.

The prime minister's secretariat, however, became a victim of its successes. And it had quite a run of these successes—the split in the ruling party in 1969 which eliminated the prime minister's rivals from the party, the crisis of 1971 resulting in the emergence of Bangladesh, the successful management of the economic crisis of 1974 triggered by the first oil shock of the previous year, and the dangerous situation created by the actions of the Chogyal in Sikkim and its eventual accession to the union in 1975.

The dramatic aspects of crisis management have created an exaggerated impression of the nature and reach of the prime minister's power, not only in India but also in other established parliamentary democracies. Since there has been a great deal of criticism of the power wielded by the prime minister's secretariat in India, a digression on the prime-ministerial system is in order.

A prime minister is certainly the most powerful person in a parliamentary democracy. He is at the apex, but the apex, it must be remembered, is only a small part of the pyramid. Regardless of constitutional and other restraints, the personal power of the prime minister is limited by the constraint of time and the sheer size of government. A day cannot be stretched beyond a few hours. No one, howsoever capable, can master the complexities of international affairs, economic policies, defence and security problems, and the complex host of thorny questions which daily land on his desk. The quality of a prime minister's leadership depends on how and when he realizes the limits of power and, having done so, is clear about the uses to which he puts the power at his command. How he relates the apex to the rest of the structure determines the reach of his influence and sets the tone and temper of his government and administration.

As party leader, as dispenser of patronage, as chairman of the cabinet, as the most important representative of government and people in parliament and in the mass media at home and abroad, the prime minister wields vast powers. The security of the state and the welfare of the people depend on how and to what purpose that power is wielded. The manner in which the prime minister influences his colleagues and administration is a vital question which has largely been left to speculation, conjecture, and motivated accounts. In the process a vast body of mythology has developed around the prime minister's office (the PMO, as it is called now), with the result that there is a general tendency to regard the office as some kind of a super-cabinet, exercising power in a manner that undermines the democratic process. In view of the mythology that has grown around the PMO it would be a good idea to demystify it, but any adequate attempt would really need to be on a scale similar to that undertaken by John Mackintosh and his colleagues in the United Kingdom.[1] Here I shall confine myself to a presentation of some basic propositions based on my experience as head of the PMO for five years.

Media discussion of this subject has generally been based on the assumption that under the cabinet system the prime minister only sketches certain lines of policy and lays down general guidelines which his colleagues and subordinates are expected to follow, and that for these functions the prime minister does not need a substantial office. The notion has received further support from the belief that Prime Minister Nehru functioned according to this classical pattern. There has not been much scholarly work on the subject. A couple of doctoral theses I have seen do not do justice to the topic. A pioneering attempt was made by Harish Khare in a short monograph, but it does not seem to have been followed up.[2]

The concept of the collegiate system of the cabinet, in which the prime minister is but the chairman of a council of ministers, or first among equals, has been obsolete in the country of its origin for more than a century and is now only a hoary and pedantic anachronism. As Richard Crossman points out, 'even in Bagehot's time it was probably a misnomer to describe the premier as chairman, and *primus inter pares*.' Bagehot's classic study of the English constitution remains, according to Crossman, 'an accurate and vivid account of how Cabinet Government worked *before* the extension of the suffrage, *before* the creation of the party machine, and *before* the emergence of an independent Civil Service administering a vast, welfare state.'[3] Even before

[1] *British Prime Ministers in the Twentieth Century*, 2 volumes, edited by John P. Mackintosh (Weidenfeld and Nicholson, 1980).

[2] Harish Khare, 'The Indian Prime Minister', in *The Journal of Constitutional and Parliamentary Studies*, Jan.–March 1971.

[3] R.H.S. Crossman in his introduction to Walter Bagehot, *The English Constitution* (London: The Fontana Library, 1965), p. 35.

some of these developments, which have enhanced the power and authority of the prime minister in a modern democracy, Gladstone debunked Bagehot's notions. He wrote about the deviation of political realities from political myths connected with the British prime minister: 'nowhere in the wide world does so great a substance cast so small a shadow; nowhere is there a man who has so little to show for it in the way of formal title or prerogatives.' Lord Salisbury is reported to have described collective responsibility in 1880 as a 'constitutional myth'.[4] Thus, over the years Bagehot's cabinet system has become what has been called the prime-ministerial system in Great Britain.

The Indian parliamentary system, unlike its British counterpart, was born *after*, not *before* the political parties and their caucuses, and after a civil service active in the social and economic fields had come into existence. Universal adult suffrage and the parliamentary system were introduced as a single political package. There was no gradual enlargement of the franchise, as happened in Great Britain, and Indian leaders who came to dominate parliamentary parties were established leaders who had led the freedom struggle and acquired popularity and charisma in the process. In the Congress Party that led the freedom movement, there was a high command already in existence years before it became the ruling party. This was probably a necessary institution for the Congress Party when it was fighting the British in the streets as well as in the pre-independence legislative councils of the provinces. In India, therefore, the prime-ministerial system was rooted in the circumstances of its political history.

There are several other, and more mundane, reasons for the lack of a collective deliberate body in the sense in which Bagehot conceived the cabinet. The most important of these is the heavy workload that governmental activity throws up for cabinet decisions. In India the load has been excessive. To be sure, some items of the cabinet agenda can be eliminated without damage, but even after that the volume of business is too large for any meaningful deliberations except in very general terms. Cabinet deliberations are therefore centred more around the elimination of overlaps and jurisdictional conflicts and the

---

[4] Anthony Sampson, *New Anatomy of Britain* (London: Hodder and Stoughton, 1971), p. 74.

harmonization of viewpoints of various ministries. In other words, cabinet work is largely devoted to problems of co-ordination rather than in-depth analysis of policies or debates on policy choices.

This is not to belittle the problem of co-ordination. To make policies more coherent they have to be co-ordinated. But even in this area basic work is done in the parallel committees at the secretariat level, where the cabinet secretary and the prime minister's office play a central role and wield corresponding power. To cope with the growing volume of work handled by the cabinet, the device of cabinet committees is being used increasingly. This reduces the workload of the cabinet and improves the quality of decisions because more in-depth discussion becomes possible in a smaller group. At the same time it makes the cabinet as a whole less important in the decision-making process as the cabinet usually endorses the views of the committees. Moreover, the committee system enhances the power of the prime minister because it is his prerogative to appoint members of the committees according to his judgement.

The cabinet room is a very different place from the houses of parliament. There is no gallery here and therefore no scope for rhetoric, speeches, posturing and play-acting. What is needed in cabinet meetings is the ability for careful and lucid presentation of a case; knowledge of various aspects of the problem under discussion; and mastery of detail. Given these requirements, each cabinet minister normally concerns himself mainly with his own items of the agenda and avoids critical observations on those relating to other ministries, unless his ministry is involved in an inter-ministerial issue. Ministers adopt this stance not only for reasons of prudence—they do not like their colleagues to pry too much into their ministries—but also for the more substantial reason that they would have to work and think a lot more to be able to present an alternative view on a subject with which they are not directly concerned. They usually think it is enough to keep themselves informed of the goings-on in other ministries.

There is also the problem of the varying calibre of ministers. As the politicization of the electorate has deepened in India, the quality of the people's representatives has undergone a vast change. The earlier representatives were better educated and more competent in handling technical matters. Their successors, though nearer the people and their concerns, are much less competent to handle matters that have to be decided at cabinet meetings. This is even more true of state cabinets than of the central cabinet. The states that have registered greater progress have been those with dominating chief ministers. One has only to think of Punjab under Partap Singh Kairon, Haryana under Bansi Lal, and Kashmir under Bakshi Gulam Muhammad, to illustrate the point. To combine within a single minister the popular character of peoples' representative with an ability to govern is an unresolved question of democracy, especially that of a nascent democracy like ours.

This is not a satisfactory situation, nor is it consistent with the concept of cabinet responsibility. As an outsider, I felt that whereas the cabinet secretariat was an efficient set-up, it had no mechanism to brief ministers collectively on issues and problems about which they were supposed to take collective decisions. To be sure, ministers did come to cabinet meetings fully briefed by the officials of their particular ministries on items relating to them, but on other items they mostly behaved like uninstructed onlookers.

After seeing the cabinet at work for two years, I raised the question of its greater involvement in the decision-making process with my friend and colleague B.D. Pande, who was then the cabinet secretary. Pande was a very intelligent and hard-working official with an open mind. Both of us tried to produce a self-contained note on the subject of reform of the government in this area. For this purpose Pande consulted some of the secretaries to the government. But his colleagues raised all sorts of problems which he thought insurmountable. I suspected that the secretaries were afraid the reform might result in a reduction of their own authority. Since the results of our effort did not satisfy us, the idea was abandoned.

In the meanwhile I learnt from an official of the British high commission that their prime minister was also wrestling with the problem

of creating a genuine cabinet system which would enable his ministerial colleagues to be fully informed on the questions they were to deliberate. Prime Minister Edward Heath had set up a group called the
Central Policy Review Staff. It consisted of about a dozen intellectuals
under the leadership of the Labour peer Lord Rothschild, a scientist
and former Shell executive. The group was popularly known as the
Whitehall think-tank, although it was outside the Whitehall system.
Rothschild began his work with the conviction that 'any move towards
presidential practices would be incompatible with the British system
of cabinet government.' He was keen therefore to maintain a safe
distance from the prime minister's office, and to make clear that he
was not a part of it, but of the cabinet secretariat. Of the many tasks
Rothschild outlined for his team I was interested in his promise that
'Mr Heath and his colleagues will receive something like a progress report every six months. The idea is to chart the interaction of policies
on each other, and show up the lacunae in the planning, or where
circumstances have forced a U-turn.' I was particularly interested in
his U-turn proposals and Heath's political management of the change
that the revised policies would entail, because it was abundantly clear
to me and to some others in our officialdom that several of our policies,
particularly economic policies, needed a U-turn.

A great deal was expected from Lord Rothschild's team in his country. His appointment was described by his admirers as the most dash-
ing government appointment since Winston Churchill made Lord
Beaverbrook his minister of aircraft production. But Rothschild did
not succeed in his endeavours; he was defeated by the conventional
civil service. Indeed his failure was foretold by James Robertson, a
former member of the cabinet secretariat who was also interested in
reforms to the working of government.[5] Robertson predicted that the
Rothschild think-tank would prove 'an ineffective substitute for the
necessary research, planning and management services which a modern prime minister needs.' The prediction proved correct: Heath's attempt at being different from Harold Wilson—his predecessor, who
was accused of turning his office into a presidential office—did not

[5] See James Robertson, *The Reforms of the British Central Government* (London:
Chatto & Windus, 1971).

succeed. After Heath's failure to prop up the British cabinet system, its decline continued in that country. A later observer went to the extent of saying: 'The Cabinet seems to have disintegrated in the literal sense of that word. Every member of the Cabinet is important, but his importance depends on functions that are performed almost entirely outside the Cabinet.'[6]

In India the importance of a cabinet minister depends on his political weight and his reputation for efficiency as a minister, not on his contribution to cabinet discussions. In every cabinet, therefore, there are a few whom the prime minister consults before the meetings, as they can sort out differences among members before they crop up in the meetings. These ministers become the prime minister's confidants and constitute what is called the inner cabinet. Inner cabinet consultations sometimes result in adjustments and changes in policies to accommodate points of view held by these important, political heavyweights. Thus, in the prime-ministerial system the country is governed by a prime minister 'who leads, co-ordinates and maintains a series of ministers, all of whom are advised and backed by the civil service. Some decisions are taken by the premier alone, some in consultation between him and the senior ministers, while others are left to heads of departments, the cabinet, and cabinet committees of permanent officials.'[7] This is equally an accurate description of the Indian system, with which I was familiar when I served in the prime minister's office.

I have gone into some detail on the British attempt to revitalize the cabinet system to indicate the nature of our own analogous problems. Given our more complex situation, Pande and I had even less chance of success. For effective government, I accepted the proposition that the PMO had to be a power house. The real question was how to increase its efficiency and contain abuses of power.

Parallel to the emergence of the prime-ministerial system has been the need for a supportive administrative apparatus enabling the prime minister to initiate, co-ordinate, and monitor policies. This does not preclude the cabinet, or for that matter parliament, from influencing

---

[6] Collin Seymore-Ure, 'The "disintegration" of the Cabinets', quoted by Richard Rose, *Politics in England* (London: Faber and Faber, 1980).

[7] R.H.S. Crossman, p. 53.

policy. Their influence operates through cabinet committees and parliamentary committees with which the cabinet secretary's office and the prime minister's office are intimately associated. These offices have played a crucial role not only in India, but also in other parliamentary democracies. For instance Harold Macmillan, commenting on his prime ministership, observed that if it was possible to operate the system and yet retain the confidence of the cabinet as a whole, it was partly due to the generosity of his colleagues and partly to the skill of Sir Norman Brook (his cabinet secretary), and to his private secretaries in gaining their confidence.[8]

Our parliamentary democracy and the cabinet system trace their origins to Great Britain. The traditions of the civil service are also avowedly similar. It is not therefore surprising that the prime ministers in the two countries should function in a similar manner. Yet similarity in political institutions often disguises important differences, for below the institutional surface operate social and cultural attitudes and behaviour patterns which are dissimilar. Having noted basic reasons for the decline of the cabinet system—reasons common to all parliamentary democracies—it needs to be said that in India the trend is further accentuated by factors specific to it. Indian culture continues to be feudal, even if it is gradually changing. Our attitude to authority is based on hierarchical values. It is not therefore surprising for cabinet ministers to behave like members of a feudal court and for their colleagues in government, the party, and the services to follow suit. These behaviour patterns are part and parcel of our social system.

In Indian writings on this subject, the phenomenon is attributed exclusively to Indira Gandhi's prime ministership. This is unfair. Jawaharlal Nehru's regime too was surrounded by a feudal atmosphere. After the departure of his senior comrades—those who were part of the freedom movement—he became supreme leader of the Congress. He

[8] As quoted by John Mackintosh, op. cit.

was the chief vote-catcher and therefore dispenser of favours for people with political ambition. He became indispensable for his party colleagues in their effort to stay in power. In return they accepted his ideas and policies, whether or not they believed in them: his ministerial and party colleagues too behaved like courtiers. Several who had reservations about his policies never articulated them. This made the support for some of Nehru's policies appear overwhelming, which simply was not true. Take the case of co-operative farming, for example. There was very little support for it in Congress Party ranks, but nobody opposed it in party counsels. M.O. Mathai has described in detail, in his memoirs, how cabinet ministers used to fawn on him even though he was no more than Nehru's lowly private secretary.

It is perhaps true that Nehru was more genuinely liberal and openminded, and less temperamentally authoritarian and autocratic than his daughter. On this account, Nehru's court appears in retrospect to have been less feudal than Indira Gandhi's. In her time the feudal ethos became much more pronounced. This happened gradually and without deliberate effort, and the manner of its happening shows how democratic institutions function in an essentially pre-democratic culture.

It began in circumstances which seemed quite normal. Since Indira Gandhi had to function as an official hostess to her father, she brought together some friends to help her. She was unprepared for the tasks that had fallen to her lot. She was shy, diffident, and lacked conversation. But Nehru had no choice in the matter; she was the only available member of his family, and one whom he could trust. She had certain other advantages: she was well bred, she had good taste, she carried herself well. She was shrewd and a keen observer of what was going on around her father. All she needed was stronger intellectual equipment—this had in part been denied her by a frequently interrupted education. To supplement her own mind she brought together a small group of friends and helpers. Her proximity to her father made her and her group the magnets that attracted all kinds of favour-seekers, as happens in a feudal court. When she became prime minister, this group was transformed into what the media called her 'kitchen cabinet'.

The kitchen cabinet was described by her detractors as a shadowy group operating under the shelter of the prime minister. Its existence was looked upon as a symbol of Indira Gandhi's inadequacy rather than as an essential requirement for fulfilling the leadership role which, as prime minister, she was called upon to play. Little did these critics know that under the British parliamentary system which they held out as a model, and which we were supposed to replicate in India, prime ministers bring in special advisors to help them. According to Anthony Sampson, Lloyd George had his 'garden suburb' of experts; Churchill had his eccentric private empire; Wilson had Sir Solly Zuckerman (later Lord Zuckerman) and Lord Balogh as advisers on scientific and economic policy respectively.[9] It is true that Indira Gandhi's kitchen cabinet was too informal a set-up, and that was the reason why it attracted unfair reference. However, it did not last long.

The electoral setback in the general election of 1967 set off a power struggle in the Congress Party. Indira Gandhi was trying to release herself from the shackles of the Syndicate, the party bosses who had been discredited by the electorate but who were nevertheless trying to hold the party in their grip in the name of collective leadership. The Syndicate was also in confrontation with the younger socialist group in the party who favoured radical economic policies and supported Indira Gandhi. The struggle for power ended in 1969 when the party split, which brought Indira Gandhi into her own. By then she had disbanded the kitchen cabinet and organized a well-oiled secretariat staffed with an adequate number of aides. Her landslide victory in the general elections of 1971 brought her to the top of the political pyramid and gave her the confidence to assume the mien and manner of a confident leader. She was now not only prime minister in her own right but also the most dominant political leader and vote gatherer.

[9] Anthony Sampson, op. cit.

These developments had dramatic effects on the attitudes and behaviour of her colleagues in government and in the party. A personality cult evolved and a court came into existence.

Her court evolved as Indira Gandhi consolidated power. Courtiers changed as the opportunities and situations changed. But certain functional types remained all through and continue, in fact, to exist in the courts of all Indian prime ministers.

Each courtier evolved his own style and function according to his perception of what would promote his own, or his faction's, interests. They came in many shapes and sizes. Some were specially made to suit the requirements of the leader and the regime. But there were in my time two types which, in India, seem to have become relevant to all prime ministers. I call them 'idea' men and 'situation' men. During my years in the prime minister's office I became very familiar with both types. The 'idea' man would seek audience to present a solution of some vexed national problem. In this category could be found not only outside aspirants but also party leaders and ministers and their rivals. What drove these gentlemen to suggest 'ideas' was not their anxiety over problems facing the country but simply a desire to be noticed by the prime minister for a job or an assignment, a promotion or preferment. I remember a man who later became a minister, and who is currently a well-established public figure, spending hours in the Institute of Economic Growth to collect some ideas on economic matters and present them as his own to the prime minister. To cover his embarrassment he would shyly suggest to me that for Indiraji the man who presents the idea is as important, if not more, than the idea itself.

The 'situation' man specialized in studying and reporting on a situation in a geographical area, or relating to a group in the party. The 'situation' could relate to law and order, dissensions in the party, leadership rivalries, or someone trying to become too big for his boots. This was very important and sometimes a vital source of information for the prime minister. Mostly, such men were not keen observers of men and events; their analytical powers were severely limited. But they were avid collectors of fact, gossip, and motivated opinion, and they would sometimes become, unwittingly, a mine of misinformation or disinformation. They were also less ambitious than the 'idea' men. Indira Gandhi was more fond of these tale-bearers than of 'idea' men and would make use of them, sometimes, in ways that would ruin individuals or mar well-conceived policies. Her proclivity for such men indicates, if not an inferior level of interest in larger ideas, at least a rather different sort of intellectual orientation than her father's, which lowered the political milieu and calibre of discussion when she came to power.

Sometimes even senior politicians would behave like these storytellers to impress the prime minister with their wide-awake and deep concern for the national interest. Even chief ministers would succumb to this temptation often. Once, when Indira Gandhi was on tour in Darjeeling, I got an urgent message that she wanted to speak to me. When she came on the telephone she sounded excited and apprehensive and told me that a *coup* was imminent in Dacca and that it was going to be led by Brigadier so and so. When I expressed my disbelief she started getting impatient and wanted me to call a meeting of the cabinet committee on political affairs (CCPA) to consider the matter most urgently. Apparently she had forgotten that the putative *coup* leader was a refugee under our care—a nervous wreck who had managed to leave Dacca with just a vest and *lungi* on him. I knew the weakness of the person who had fed her this story. He had a childlike fascination for intelligence reports and loved to play cops and robbers. He used to persuade BSF intelligence people on the borders to retail to him whatever stories they would pick up before these were checked and crosschecked for veracity. He wanted, it seemed to me, to report them to the PM before the intelligence agencies did. The *coup* story was one such tale.

Be that as it may, the meeting of the CCPA was dutifully held. R.N. Kao, the head of our external intelligence, was specially invited to attend. His views were crucial. He could not say that the Brigadier was in Delhi, but he told the members in a very confident and persuasive manner that he did not believe the story. Kao's statement was received in silence by the members. Sardar Swaran Singh broke the solemnity of the atmosphere and said, 'let us wait and see and in the meantime we need not lose our sleep over it.' When the PM returned to Delhi she coolly forgot all about the *coup*. Nor did I remind her about it.

The prime minister's office cannot be insulated from the prevailing cultural milieu in which it functions. I remember constantly receiving pleas such as, 'it can only be done through your office'; 'it can only be decided at the highest level'; 'how will the prime minister feel about this suggestion?'; 'What is her mood like?' These pleas were often made by ministers, civil servants, businessmen and publicists—by people who, at the same time, complained about centralization of power by the prime minister. My colleagues had a similar experience. Senior officers often had the maturity to handle this, but their juniors, particularly those in physical proximity to the prime minister—such as private secretaries and personal assistants who worked at her residence—were usually taken over by delusions of grandeur. Private secretaries and personal assistants are important in any administrative system because they control access to bosses. In India they have been converted into minor power centres by people seeking such access for favours and contacts. This was particularly true in the case of the prime minister's office. The larger-than-life image of some of its former personal assistants underscores the point. Thus, the temptation to succumb to the feudal ethos always exists, especially for those in advantageous positions.

The tasks facing the prime minister of a country like India, which lacks social cohesion and is handicapped by a fractious history, are infinitely more complex and daunting than those of a modern, developed and homogeneous country like Britain. The federal polity and interventionist role of government implicit in the planned development of large areas of social and economic life make for far greater demands on the Indian prime minister.

During Nehru's long tenure the magnitude and complexities of our problems did not surface for several reasons. Most of his colleagues were comrades in the freedom struggle with long periods of involvement in a common endeavour. The Congress Party was in power at the centre and in the states. The leadership shared a common outlook and where there were differences they strove to keep them within manageable limits. This is particularly true of the period when Sardar Patel was deputy prime minister. The greater part of Nehru's tenure as prime minister covered a period largely devoted to the formation of the state, the laying down of the institutional framework for economic and social development, and the creation of a co-operative federal structure. On these basics there was agreement in the ruling Congress Party and in the country. There were, of course, differences on certain policies and ideological matters, but these differences were submerged under the overall consensus. Even Nehru had sometimes to assert himself formally, as he did at the time of C.D. Deshmukh's resignation in 1956 on the proposal of making Bombay a centrally administered city. In his statement to the Lok Sabha on his resignation Deshmukh attacked the official policy on Bombay and criticized Nehru's functioning as prime minister. In his reply Nehru retorted: 'I am the prime minister of India, and the prime minister is the prime minister. He can lay down the policy of the government.'

Nehru's stature as a national leader and hero, his liberal outlook, his intellectual eminence, and his habit of publicly discussing policy options, coupled with the early demise of Sardar Patel and parting of the ways with Rajagopalachari, aided his political ascendancy and invested the Nehruvian consensus with vast moral authority. Indeed some elements of this consensus, such as planning as an instrument of economic and social change, had been accepted even before independence. These circumstances enabled Nehru to operate the prime-ministerial system smoothly, with the help of a relatively small office whose activities were more restricted and less visible. His office was usually headed by an officer of the rank of joint secretary. It might be added that being his own foreign minister Nehru had the assistance of senior civil servants on foreign policy and national security matters, which fall within the prime minister's purview.

With Nehru's departure the situation changed. Lal Bahadur Shastri lacked Nehru's charisma. As prime minister he was only first among equals. To establish himself, and to make up for his comparative lack of familiarity with foreign policy and science and technology, he felt the need for a stronger office and appointed a full-fledged secretary-level civil servant, L.K. Jha, to head his office, with a consequent increase in its size.[10] Interestingly, the upgradation of the PMO in India had been preceded in the same year in Britain by a similar process.[11] Whether the British example inspired the Indian prime minister is not known, but it must have helped him allay the fears of his more suspicious colleagues and civil servants. Shastri's tenure was too brief for him to evolve a prime-ministerial system. The task was left to Indira Gandhi.

The assumption of prime-ministerial office by Indira Gandhi was accompanied by significant changes in the economic and political environment. The country was hit by a severe drought. The fragile balance-of-payments position and acute food shortages had made the economy more and more dependent on foreign aid. The United States had suspended aid in 1965 on account of India's war with Pakistan. President Johnson refused to renew the PL480 agreement on a long-term basis and kept India on a short leash in order to exercise leverage over our policies. India's food economy had become dependent on his goodwill and moods. To Indira Gandhi this was a matter of national humiliation. After sweet-talking President Johnson on the telephone

[10] The number of staff of all categories in the PMO increased from 117 in 1949 to 198 in 1965.

[11] 'Since 1965, successive PMs have had one or more personal policy advisers in Downing Street to supplement a handful of civil service advisers . . .' See Richard Rose, op. cit.

into releasing more food supplies, Sharada Prasad recalls her disgust with the situation, and her resolve to end it.

The United States and the Bretton Woods institutions had come to the conclusion that India's economic growth was held back by the government's wrong policies. The Indian economy was said to be in a 'quiet crisis'.[12] This was their view even before the back-to-back droughts of 1965 and 1966 had put the economy into a tailspin and the crisis had become loud and clear. They were critical of the heavy industry emphasis and the neglect of agriculture and foreign trade by Indian planners. In September 1964 the World Bank sent a mission to India under the leadership of Bernard Bell.

The Bell Mission presented its report to the Bank president and recommended major policy changes, which included giving high priority to agriculture, devaluation of the rupee, and the reduction of import controls. These recommendations amounted to sharp departures from the set of policies which flowed from the Nehru–Mahalanobis model. T.T. Krishnamachari, the finance minister, was opposed to devaluation and resigned on that issue. But Shastri's government had accepted the Bell recommendations in principle. They became the basis for negotiations with the government.

Before the negotiations could be completed, Shastri died. Indira Gandhi accepted devaluation and related policies on the understanding that there would be an increase in the amount and quality of aid from the donors, especially the United States. She had been assured by Ashoka Mehta, deputy chairman of the planning commission, and by L.K. Jha, her secretary, that the proposed policy package would lift the economy to a higher growth path, and what is more, the additional aid would reduce the need for it in the foreseeable future. Mehta sloganized the proposition in memorable words: more aid now to end aid later. In other words, what Indira Gandhi was promised was accelerated growth of the economy with a prospect of real self-reliance. To her this seemed like the fulfilment of her father's dream. It was too enticing a picture to reject, especially because she was politically embarrassed to

[12] See John P. Lewis, *Quiet Crisis in India* (New Delhi: Asia Publishing House, 1963).

find that her regime had become associated with what was called a 'plan holiday'.

In the event, Government of India devalued the rupee. But the enhanced aid that was promised (900 million dollars a year for a number of years) did not materialize. The donors reneged on their promise. Nature too turned hostile: the severe drought of 1965 was followed by another, which denied or postponed the economic benefits—such as increase in exports and improvement in the foreign exchange reserves—that might otherwise have accrued to the economy. In the absence of any tangible benefits from the adoption of policy changes, political attacks on Indira Gandhi gathered strength not only from the Congress Left and other radical parties, but also from Kamaraj, president of her own party. Kamaraj, who was responsible for her election as prime minister, was annoyed with her for not consulting him on devaluation. The national press too was, by and large, critical of the policy changes.

It was against this background that general elections were held in March 1967. The Congress Party lost heavily in the northern states. The party was badly shaken but Indira Gandhi's leadership was not endangered. This paradoxical result was due to the fact that the party elders, i.e. the Syndicate, fared badly in the elections; the stalwarts among them were defeated. In these circumstances, the authority of the central government was considerably eroded. The central leadership of the Congress Party was demoralized and lacked a cohesive outlook on the problems facing party and country. The cabinet did not consist of like-minded people. Few cabinets do, but Indira Gandhi's at that time was a coalition of widely ranging political views, if not ideologies. The ideas expressed ranged from the search for a nuclear umbrella and massive economic aid all the way to complete socialization of the means of production as a cure for all problems. These political weaknesses raised serious doubts in India and abroad about India's ability to cope simultaneously with the demands of national security, political independence, and economic development.

The new prime minister thus faced a two-fold challenge. The first was to establish her pre-eminence in the cabinet. The second was to forge a coherent set of policies and develop a credible political stance. These challenges were formulated in very clear terms by Kamaraj.

Soon after Nehru's death he had said: 'No person would be able to fill the void left by Jawaharlal's disappearance from the scene. The party would, therefore, have to function on the basis of collective leadership, collective responsibility and collective approach.' This statement posed the danger of a power struggle between the party president and the prime minister. A similar struggle, though in a more subdued form, had taken place twice in Nehru's time. But given his stature and standing in the country, he had emerged victorious against the contentious party president Acharya Kriplani, as well as against Purshotam Dass Tandon who had aspired to make the party presidentship a rival power centre. This time Kamaraj wanted prime-ministerial power to be shared not only with the party's central leadership but also with the state chief ministers who, he said, 'must give assent to all basic policy decisions'. The kind of fragmentation of power implied in Kamaraj's formulation would in Indira Gandhi's view have made the prime minister look like a broken reed and rendered the country ungovernable. For effective government she thought it necessary to strengthen the authority of the prime minister, a view widely shared at that time.

To meet these challenges the prime minister could not depend solely on cabinet colleagues, some of whom were political rivals who believed she was on probation and, as such, should abide by the judgement of party elders. The prime minister therefore needed aides who were not her rivals and who could give her professional assistance and advice. Presidential aides play such a role in the United States. In Britain senior civil servants play a similar role, though in a lower key, which makes them look somewhat ambiguous. The permanent under-secretary is in theory supposed to administer policies, but in actual fact he also participates in policy formulation. In any case the line that separates administration of policy from advice on policies is a thin one.

Presidential aides in the USA are more activist than British civil servants. Richard Neustadt, a presidential adviser, was once asked by a British treasury official: 'Why are your officials so passionate?' Neustadt turned the question around, asking why British civil servants were so dispassionate in relation to their activities. He concluded that American civil servants care about policies because their careers are wrapped up with the success of their departments and, even more, with their reputation for getting things done.[13]

In Indian circumstances, with conflicting advice proffered to her by politicians and civil servants and her own kitchen cabinet, Indira Gandhi thought she needed a strong secretariat staffed with people who would evaluate her bitter experience of her first months in office, her electoral reverses, and the plethora of conflicting and confusing advice she was receiving, and so come up with policy suggestions that would be technically sound and politically feasible. She felt the Congress Party needed a new image, for which she needed new ideas. L.K. Jha, who had provided her definitive advice, had lost her confidence thanks to the devaluation episode. She wanted someone in his place who would not be a dispassionate, on-the-one-hand-and-on-the-other type of aide. She found such an aide in P.N. Haksar, her acquaintance from university days in London. His appointment as secretary to the prime minister was strongly supported by some members of the kitchen cabinet. L.K. Jha was sent to the Reserve Bank of India as governor in September 1967, and Haksar appointed in his place.

Haksar was an activist, a 'one-handed' secretary, keen to make his boss a successful prime minister. He reorganized the office and raised its calibre and potential for dedicated advice and assistance. Before a person was appointed in the prime minister's secretariat, he would make sure that he or she was 'loyal' to Indira Gandhi. Given his strong left-leaning ideological preferences, he interpreted the electoral reverses of the Congress Party as a rejection of the liberalization trend in the economic policies initiated by Shastri which had climaxed in the devaluation episode. The Syndicate, according to him, lost public support because of the people's suspicion that they were deviating or retracting from Nehru's economic and foreign policies.

The new image which Indira Gandhi was seeking to establish was therefore to be based on economic radicalism with an anti-American slant in foreign policy. To fit various policies in a coherent framework,

---

[13] Richard E. Neustadt, 'White House and Whitehall', in Richard Rose (ed.), *Policy-making in Britain* (New York: Free Press, 1969), p. 292.

it was necessary to provide policymakers in different ministries with some central guidance. And this guidance could come naturally only from the PM's secretariat (PMS). On Haksar's advice, Indira Gandhi widened the span of her control, and that of her office, over the administration.

This was the formative period of the PMS and its basic structure seems to have remained essentially unchanged since Indira Gandhi reorganized it in 1967. Of all the prime ministers since then, Morarji Desai was the only one who declared it his intention to divest the PMS of its 'excessive power' and make it a small unit. All he succeeded in doing was changing its name from 'secretariat' to 'office', and reducing the staff marginally from 229 to 211. His failure was not the result of bureaucratic resistance but the recognition that it was rather necessary to keep a group of aides to assist the prime minister's multifarious tasks.

The prime minister's office assists the prime minister in his capacity as the head of government. The party expresses its policy preference in broad terms at election time, in the form of manifestos, but it is the prime minister's task to convert them into concrete policies, adjust them to the prevailing circumstances, and implement them through the administration. It is in this field that the PM's office plays a crucial though intangible role.

The prime minister's office is sometimes described as a 'think-tank', which it is not. But while P.N. Haksar and I were associated with it, it certainly did assemble ideas and policy inputs from other parts of the system, and from sources available outside the system. This role is likely to increase as more of these resources from the think-tank become available. This is not to say that the PMS does not generate ideas on its own. It does, but more often it is a transmission belt for ideas which constitute a part of the inputs that go into policy formulation. There is no defined, stereotyped manner in which this takes place. Nor is there a particular individual who can be treated as an 'idea' man. It is also an exaggeration to assert that the PMS's advice always prevails. For example, the government's decision to take over the wholesale wheat trade in 1973 was against the advice of the PMS.

The prime minister's office works in different ways under different prime ministers and secretaries, depending on their individual styles and the degree of collaboration with the cabinet secretary and the ministries. But it is most productive when it is able to mobilize its resources in conjunction with those available elsewhere in the system. Thus the efficiency of the PMO is to be judged not merely in terms of its own performance but even more in terms of its contribution in the galvanization of the entire secretariat for better performance. If it functions in a manner that curbs initiative or lowers morale elsewhere in the system, then it weakens instead of strengthening the hands of the prime minister.

What is true of policy formulation and co-ordination (where it liaises with other ministries directly and through the cabinet secretary) is even more true for the implementation and monitoring of policies at the centre and in the states. While the greater part of inter-ministerial co-ordination is done, and will continue to be done, by the cabinet secretariat, there are always issues and areas that a prime minister chooses to monitor personally. Bank nationalization in 1969, the Bangladesh crisis in 1971, the anti-inflation packages of 1974, and the twenty-point programme in 1975 are examples. Nor should it be forgotten that departments like atomic energy and electronics were from the very beginning under the direct supervision of the prime minister, requiring staff support from the PMS. In these days of summit diplomacy it is sometimes necessary for the prime minister to send officials from his own secretariat for discussion to foreign capitals.

So much for the concept and the system on which the PMS is based. How any system actually works depends on the temperament, capacities and motivations of the individuals involved, and their relationships. The human factor is of much greater significance in the PMS as it is here that the buck stops. Of crucial importance is the extent of rapport between the prime minister and his secretary, and the secretary's relations with his colleagues. The PMS is a team, with the secretary or principal secretary as chief of staff, and the office works best when it works as a team. This has been demonstrated in critical situations which needed careful, constant and concentrated attention. In the final analysis, however, one has to agree with Asquith, the British prime minister, who said: 'the office of the prime minister is what its holder chooses and is able to make it.'

CHAPTER EIGHT

The Bangladesh Crisis

O n 25 March 1971, when the Pakistan army started a holocaust in East Bengal, the fifth Lok Sabha was two days old
and the Indian prime minister's secretariat was preoccupied
with a draft of the president's address to the joint session of parliament.
The address had acquired unusual importance because, in the wake of
Indira Gandhi's landslide victory in the mid-term elections, it was
likely to be viewed as a curtain-raiser for economic and social policies
the government meant to pursue in order to fulfil promises made in
the election campaign.

While Indira Gandhi and her political colleagues were busy electioneering, her official aides were deeply involved in constructing,
from a plethora of suggestions, a set of policies which would be politically attractive and economically sensible. The sheer magnitude of her
electoral victory had convinced radicals in the Congress Party that
their ideas and opinions were right, while it had caused some worry to
others who were not so radical about the capacity of the system to cope
with populist demands. Much of the secretariat's time and energy during those days was spent on ideological disputations around the proposed economic policies.

Little did we know then that our plans to revitalize the economy
would be overtaken by events in neighbouring East Bengal. We were
certainly aware of the problems that had arisen in Pakistan in the wake
of its first general elections, on the basis of universal adult franchise,
held in December 1970. We knew this election was meant to coincide
with the dissolution of the single unit within which the four provinces
of West Pakistan had been integrated since 1955. Each province had

been promised its own legislative assembly and government. The National Assembly was expected to frame a new constitution and put an end to the martial-law regime. In our view the end of military rule and the return to democracy and a federal system of government in Pakistan were positive developments not only for Pakistanis but for the entire subcontinent. Unfortunately events did not turn out as expected; on the contrary the election results brought out the structural deficiencies in Pakistan as a nation state.

The Awami League under the leadership of Sheikh Mujibur Rehman had made a clean sweep of the polls in East Bengal. The League leadership had succeeded in converting the election into a referendum for its demand for autonomy. It won 160 directly elected seats out of 162 from East Bengal in its National Assembly of 300 members, and thus got a majority to form the government at the centre. In West Pakistan the Peoples Progressive Party led by Zulfikar Ali Bhutto emerged as the largest single party, winning 83 seats. The election results confirmed the east–west regional divide of Pakistan's party system, which turned into an irreconcilable political divide in the course of just two months.

The unexpected election results in East Bengal unnerved the military rulers and political leaders of West Pakistan, especially Bhutto, who felt threatened by the emergence of a solid political phalanx from East Bengal aspiring for a place in the establishment. In the absence of any trans-regional political support, it was obligatory for the leaders of the two principal parties to accommodate each other in order to evolve a co-operative federal polity. But what made such a development difficult was the yawning gulf that separated them in their views on the future constitution of Pakistan. Both were suspicious of each others' motives. Mujib was suspected of harbouring secessionist tendencies since March 1966, when he had first put forward his 'Six-Point Demand'. In 1970 this document became the election manifesto of the Awami League. The central and most contentious point in the manifesto, from which other demands flowed, was that the jurisdiction of the federal government be restricted to defence, foreign affairs and currency, subject to certain conditions. As a counterblast to the League's six points, Bhutto started to cast doubts over Mujib's loyalty to Pakistan and began mobilizing political elements in West Pakistan against him, with himself as leader. He cast himself in the role of defender of Pakistan's integrity as a sovereign state which, according to Mujib, was a cloak for the dominance of the West Pakistan ruling clique.

President Yahya Khan tried to bridge the gulf between them. He went to Dacca on 12 January and met Mujib, who had offered to be flexible about his demands. This encouraged Yahya Khan to declare that Mujib would be the next prime minister. He then turned to Bhutto, whom he found very hostile to Mujib, and rigid in his demand that the National Assembly should meet only after a consensus had been reached on constitutional issues and sharing of power at the centre. Having failed to get the two leaders to narrow down their differences, Yahya Khan suggested the two should meet. Towards the end of January 1971 Bhutto and Mujib met in Dacca on three occasions but nothing positive emerged. Bhutto continued to press for postponement in convening the National Assembly and reverted to the tough posture he had adopted before his meetings with Mujib, when he had asserted that 'no constitution could be framed nor could any government at the Centre be run' without his co-operation, and that the 'PPP was not prepared to occupy the opposition benches in the National Assembly.'[1] To reinforce this position Bhutto announced on 21 February that his party would boycott the assembly if it met. The resulting polarization of politics between East and West Pakistan now constituted a dangerous impasse.

It was in these tense circumstances that Yahya Khan announced an indefinite postponement of the inaugural session of the National Assembly, ostensibly to give more time to the political leaders to settle their differences. Mujib did not take the presidential announcement of 1 March at face value. He thought Yahya Khan had given Bhutto a veto on the political process. Feeling cheated, he launched a powerful civil disobedience movement to be able to negotiate from a position of demonstrated strength. His five-day protest proved beyond any doubt that it was Mujib who was in *de facto* control of the administration of East Bengal. On 6 March Yahya Khan announced that the National Assembly would be convened on 25 March. It looked as if

[1] *The Pakistan Times*, Lahore, 21 December 1970.

Yahya Khan had taken note of the ground realities. On 15 March he arrived in Dacca with a team of advisers to restart negotiations with Mujib.

Since negotiations were resumed and were apparently proceeding normally, we thought that some sort of settlement between Mujib and Bhutto was in the offing and that power would finally be transferred from the martial-law administration to a civilian government at the centre. So far as East Bengal was concerned, we were sure that regardless of the composition of the government at the centre the Awami League would form the government, as it had won 288 seats out of 300 in the provincial assembly. The emergence of the Awami League and the prospect of the return of democracy had given us hope of improved relations with Pakistan. We looked forward to greater economic cooperation, at least in the eastern region. We had good reasons for that expectation. The Awami League did not share the anti-Indian obsession of the ruling clique based in Karachi and Islamabad. The 'security threat from India', the theme song of the clique, had militarized politics in Pakistan and had resulted in the denial of democracy. This had hit East Bengal particularly hard, because it had to share the burden of a heavy defence budget, from which it got no tangible benefit. Indiaphobia had, in fact, marginalized East Bengal's influence in the governance of Pakistan. The Bengali middle class, politically the most highly conscious and articulate group in Pakistan, felt anti-Indianism had hurt their economic interests, thwarted their political aspirations, and denigrated their culture.

The suspension of trade and transit facilities after the war of 1965 had adversely affected Assam and other eastern states of India, but it had affected East Bengal even more adversely. Indo-Pak hostility had made the Pakistan government insensitive to the economic interests of East Bengal and this was bitterly resented by the Awami League leadership, who had built up a powerful protest movement against economic domination by West Pakistan. Economists in East Bengal had analysed the economic exploitation of their province by West Pakistanis. Their conclusion—that their province had been reduced to a colony—provided the Awami League the basic rationale for their demand for provincial autonomy. The League's six-point platform for autonomy sought to transfer control over foreign trade, foreign-aid allocation, and taxation powers to the provinces, so that no province could be dominated through disproportionate control of the central government's power over allocation of resources.

This was expected to be gradually redressed by the Awami League after it assumed control over economic affairs. What we expected was the emergence of two economies within a single loose federal polity. This, to us, seemed an inevitable development, given the geographical incongruity of Pakistan, the two halves of which were separated by 1200 miles of Indian territory. Such a confederational set-up would have provided a closer political link between the two physically separate and distant parts of the state. In fact that kind of relationship seems to have been envisaged in the 1940 Lahore Resolution of the Muslim League. The resolution had not used the expression 'Pakistan' but had demanded that 'the areas in which Muslims are numerically in a majority, as in the north-western and eastern zones of India, should be grouped together to constitute units which shall be autonomous and sovereign.' Thus the notion of a separate state in the eastern region was embodied in the so-called Pakistan Resolution itself. Fazlul Haq, who had moved the Pakistan Resolution at Lahore on behalf of the Muslim League, had left that organization and set up a separate secular political party which demanded full regional autonomy, as promised in the Lahore Resolution. H.S. Suhrawardy, a stalwart Pakistani turned Bengali nationalist, founded the Awami League, which carried the autonomy movement further. Under the leadership of Mujib the Awami League became a mass political party on the basis of a radically expanded concept of autonomy, which was elaborated in its six-point programme.

We were naturally interested in the normalization of economic relations with East Pakistan as this would have significantly improved economic prospects in our own eastern region. Apart from its obvious economic benefits, Awami League rule in East Bengal would also in our judgement have had a stabilizing effect on the politics of the region. The secular outlook of the leadership was expected to ease Hindu–Muslim tensions in East Bengal and, as a consequence, reduce the migration of Hindus to India. We had also hoped that the new political dispensation in East Bengal would put an end to the insurgency that the Pakistan government was supporting in some of our eastern states. These were our national interests as we saw them at the time.

According to reports reaching us it seemed that negotiations between Yahya Khan and his team from West Pakistan on one side, and Sheikh Mujib and his Awami League advisers on the other, though difficult, were continuing. Reports emanating from Dacca suggested that the talks were about to conclude and that an agreement had been reached on some substantive points. We did not know then that the last phase of the so-called negotiations was merely a diversion to enable Pakistan's army commanders to work out plans to crush the autonomy movement. We learnt later that while the negotiating teams were in session in the president's house in Dacca, Yahya Khan himself was in conference with his generals in the cantonment.

Despite knowing that military personnel in plain clothes were being transported from West Pakistan and that an army build-up in East Bengal was afoot, we were taken by surprise when news of the sudden termination of negotiations, followed by a savage military crackdown in Dacca, started coming in. First reports about the crackdown were alarming, yet we continued to believe that negotiations would be resumed after a brief show of military might. We had even interpreted the appointment of Lieutenant-General Tikka Khan—who had earned the sobriquet of 'butcher of Baluchistan' for his bloody repression of a similar movement for autonomy in that province—as part of the show. It was difficult to understand why the Pakistani rulers would go over the brink and start a full-scale civil war. For at stake were the territorial and ideological foundations of the state, matters too serious to be trifled with. Who could imagine that the Pakistan leaders would unleash terror to such an extent that Bengali Muslims would be driven to repudiate the two-nation theory, which was the *raison d'être* of their state, and reverse their decision of 1947 which had spearheaded the movement for the creation of Pakistan?

We were soon proved wrong. Yahya Khan is believed to have told his officers: 'There can be no political settlement with the "Bingos" till they are sorted out good and proper.' But it was not only the military leadership that had gone berserk. Bhutto, the great defender of Pakistan's integrity and ideology, approved of the merciless military offensive and in a public statement thanked the army and God for saving Pakistan. It did not take us long to see that the so-called crackdown was a well-thought-out operation planned not only to cow down the Bengali population through genocide but also to decapitate the Awami League leadership and terrorize intellectuals into silence. To make sure there was no armed resistance from any Bengali area, the Pakistan army attacked the police headquarters, the East Bengal Regiment, and the East Pakistan Rifles to disarm them. The attempt was only partially successful.

Among the earliest refugees in Delhi—also a friend—who gave me a first-hand account of the happenings in East Bengal was Rehman Sobhan, the eminent economist. He was Sheikh Mujib's adviser on economic issues and was known to be very close to him. He had participated in negotiations which the Sheikh had conducted with his West Pakistani counterparts and had taken great risks while fleeing from Dacca. Soon after his arrival in Delhi he contacted me and immediately threw himself wholeheartedly in the liberation movement, proving to be amongst its most persuasive spokesmen. He had little faith in the Pak military regime's intention to work out a viable political solution. He thought Bhutto even more hostile to Mujib than Yahya. Rehman was also well informed about other Awami League leaders. It was he who first told us that Tajuddin, the general secretary of the Awami League and future prime minister of Bangladesh, had crossed over to India along with some of his colleagues.

After what he had seen in Dacca and en route his escape to India,

Rehman had become apprehensive of Pakistan's intelligence agencies. He was sure that Delhi swarmed with their agents. And, being on their hit list, he was so frightened that he was afraid of being seen in Delhi. He was keen to meet the Soviet ambassador, Mr Pegov, but scared to use my staff car lest he be seen by a Pakistani agent. I had to drive him there in a friend's car so he could keep his appointment. The ambassador was amused to see me chauffeuring his visitor and gave me an undiplomatic wink. I told him Sobhan would enlighten him on the reason why I had changed my job!

Another friend who turned up in Delhi soon after was Nurul Islam, director of the Pakistan Development Institute. I had not met him since 1952, when we were both at Harvard. The impression I carried of him was of a confident young man bubbling with intellectual energy. It was distressing to see him looking forlorn and deeply depressed when I met him at the house of Ashok Mitra, chief economic adviser and later finance minister of West Bengal. Unlike Sobhan, Islam was not politically active, but even he had had to flee to save his life. It took much reassurance for Islam to regain his composure and become his normal self. Both Sobhan and Islam were sick with worry about friends and colleagues they had left behind. I used to tell them that, like refugees everywhere, they were exaggerating their fears, but they knew better and their forebodings about the Pak army unfortunately came true. 'Operation Blitz', as the army's plan was code-named, bore out their worst apprehensions.

For us the military operations really began to cause concern when refugees started pouring into India. The first to arrive were the Awami League cadres and remnants of the police and military personnel who managed to escape. They were followed by Hindus who had escaped a merciless hunt. It was only by the middle of April that we were able to see what the Pakistani rulers wanted to achieve by their military action. By driving out Hindus in their millions, they hoped to substantially reduce the political support that the Awami League enjoyed as it was the 'wily Hindu' who was supposed to have misled simple Bengali Muslims into demanding autonomy. Additionally, with the Hindus gone, Bengal would lose its majority status *vis-à-vis* West

Pakistan and not be in a position to challenge its political dominance. Pakistani rulers, according to our intelligence reports, also expected that the presence of Hindu refugees in such large numbers would provoke Hindu–Muslim riots in India, which would enable them to depict the East Bengal movement as a welter of Indo–Pakistan and Hindu–Muslim confrontations.

The international community, which was more familiar with India–Pakistan tensions since the partition of India in 1947, was likely to accept such a presentation. To ensure this Pakistan had planted *agent provocateurs* among the refugees, perhaps encouraged by the fact that some Indian Muslim leaders had condemned the Awami League and its autonomy movement. To add to our woes, Urdu-speaking Muslims, known as Biharis in East Bengal, also came in with the Bengali refugees. These 'Biharis' had migrated to East Bengal at the time of Partition, twenty-five years earlier. There they had identified themselves completely with the Pakistan army, enlisted as Razakars, and organized fanatic groups such as Al Badr to help the army suppress the Bengali autonomy movement. To escape reprisals from the enraged local population, they wanted not merely temporary shelter but a permanent home in India. The actions of the Pakistani rulers had thus converted their domestic crisis into a sub-continental one.

Immediately after the crackdown on 25 March, refugees started streaming into West Bengal, Assam, Meghalaya and Tripura. These states had borne heavy social, economic and political costs on account of earlier waves of refugees—these refugees had settled there in the wake of Partition. As a result, the entire eastern zone of India was demographically askew, economically retarded, politically unstable, and socially volatile. Extremist political groups like the Naxalites were active in West Bengal, while Naga and Mizo insurgents, helped by China and Pakistan, had converted our eastern states into disturbed areas.

The governments of these states, already saddled with the problems of rehabilitating refugees, were hardly in a position to take on the burden of new arrivals.

When the flow of refugees turned into a flood, it became a crisis for India. In the course of just five weeks, from 14 April to 21 May, their number jumped from a little more than 100,000 to about 3.5 million. And more were on their way. At first they came in at 60,000 a day, and then at a staggering 150,000 a day for several days before the onset of the monsoons. They were crossing over into India at numerous points over a porous border stretching 1300 miles. Most of them came on foot; others used bullock-carts, rickshaws, and country boats. The flow of refugees was simply unstoppable.

The Pakistan government seemed determined to pursue its military option in East Bengal to the finish. They made no secret of it. Their policy for East Bengal was openly spelled out to Anthony Mascarenhas, a senior Karachi journalist, on his visit to the eastern command head-quarters at Dacca. According to his report, published in *The Sunday Times*, London, on 13 June 1971, the policy had the following three elements:

1. The Bengalis have proved themselves 'unreliable' and must be ruled by West Pakistanis; (2) The Bengalis will have to be re-educated along proper Islamic lines. The 'Islamization of the masses'—this is the official jargon—is intended to eliminate secessionist tendencies and provide a strong religious bond with West Pakistan; (3) When the Hindus have been eliminated by death and flight, their property will be used as a golden carrot to win over the under-privileged Muslim middle class. This will provide the base for erecting administrative and political structures in the future.

According to Mascarenhas, this policy was being pursued 'with the utmost blatancy'. This was corroborated by a report from Faridpur published in *The New York Times* issue of 4 July which said: 'Although thousands of "anti-state" Bengali Muslims have been killed by the army, the Hindus became particular scapegoats as the martial-law regime tried to blame Hindu India and her agents in East Pakistan for the autonomy movement . . . The army also forced Muslims friendly to Hindus to loot and burn Hindu houses; the Muslims were told that if they did not attack Hindus, they themselves would be killed.' For us the magnitude and pace of the refugee influx established every day that Pakistan's policies were being followed relentlessly.

The very size of the refugee problem determined the Indian response to the East Bengal crisis. Refugees became a majority in the tribal area of Tripura. Even in West Bengal, there were places where refugees outnumbered the local population: the small town of Bongaigaon, with a population of 5000, had in the course of just two months been submerged under a flood of 300,000 refugees. The coalition government of West Bengal, already harassed by the CPM and the Naxalites, was too weak to handle this critical situation. In fact it had to be dismissed a month later and the state brought under president's rule.

It was only after Indira Gandhi visited the refugee camps in West Bengal, Assam and Tripura in the last week of May that she made up her mind on the Indian response to the crisis. I was with her in the West Bengal sector and saw the impact the appalling condition of the refugees had upon her. We had, of course, read the hair-raising reports that had appeared in the world press about the miserable conditions of the refugees and their suffering, but what we saw in the camps defied description. More than the stories of what had happened to them, it was their physical and mental state that assaulted our moral sensibility. In our offices in Delhi we had been preoccupied with their number, with the political fall-out of their presence, with calculations of the financial cost of maintaining them. It was an altogether different experience to come face-to-face with these terror-stricken villagers and listen to their individual tragedies. Indira Gandhi, whom everybody expected would say a few words of solace and sympathy, was so overwhelmed by the scale of human misery that she could hardly speak. When we returned to Calcutta's Raj Bhawan after the visit she said in a grim and firm voice: 'The world must know what is happening here and do something about it. In any case, we cannot let Pakistan continue this holocaust.'

Now the development of a coherent refugee policy became top

priority for the prime minister and her advisers. This was a difficult task but it would have been impossible had the mid-term poll—which she had ordered only two months earlier—not released her from the constraints of a minority government hamstrung by conflicting pressures and concerns: she would have been driven to striking postures which would only have complicated matters. After the elections she was much less vulnerable to opposition attacks and strong enough to take responsibility and provide leadership.

This is not to say that there were no critics of the policies adopted by the government in response to fast-changing situations. There were people who advocated a discriminatory attitude to the refugees—they wanted only Hindus to be allowed entry. There were hawks who wanted to stop the refugee movement at once by launching a military operation against the Pakistan army in East Bengal. They dismissed the government's restraint as 'spinelessness masquerading as caution' and as 'moderation'. Several members of the council of ministers affected by public criticism of the government's 'inaction' started demanding that the Indian army march into East Pakistan. To silence them Mrs Gandhi asked for Sam Manekshaw's opinion on the issue, knowing very well what his answer was going to be.[2] While his negative professional judgement, which went against the demand for military action, had a sobering effect on the hotheads, it gave rise to the myth that India had a plan to dismember Pakistan, a subject to which I will return later.

The media, however, continued to pillory the government for inaction. 'As a public display of national impotence, our performance has few comparisons' was a typical comment from such critics.[3] Even Jayaprakash Narayan, the avowed Gandhian, was putting pressure on the prime minister to attack Pakistan. I was astonished at his unbalanced judgement and emotionalism. (I was to witness more of these traits in this otherwise lovable human being when he started the movement associated with his venerable name in 1974.) It needed a great deal of persuasion from Haksar to make him divert his energies to mobilizing world public opinion against Pakistan instead.

[2] Manekshaw has made this little event a very colourful episode. See, F.R. Jacob, *Surrender at Dacca: Birth of a Nation*, Appendix 6 (Delhi: Manohar, 1997).
[3] *Economic and Political Weekly*, 3 July 1971.

Some people who described themselves as realists were of the view that it was a delusion to believe that the refugees would ever return to their homes. Their counsel was that India should concentrate on securing aid for their settlement. Yet others suggested exchanges of population as a way out. And extremist political groups were trying to recruit supporters from the refugees for their own revolutionary causes. Several of these suggestions found echoes in the discussions of the crisis management group. Some feared that the emergence of a sovereign Bangladesh might lead to the cessation of West Bengal and a radicalization of politics in eastern India, with unpredictable consequences for the country. In these circumstances it was her vastly strengthened leadership that enabled Indira Gandhi to formulate a national consensus to meet the crisis.

On her return to Delhi on 16 May from her visit to the refugee camps, she took a firm decision that India was not going to absorb the refugees, as it had been doing, and that Pakistan must make it possible for them to return home in safety. The need to find a political solution which would ensure the return of the refugees made India inevitably an interested party in the Pakistan civil war. It was therefore necessary to prevent the dispersal of refugees and set up camps—a herculean task, for the influx continued unabated. By December the number of refugees had climbed to about 10 million, only 7 million of whom could be housed in camps. Since no accommodation could be provided for the remaining 3 million, they melted away into informal labour markets and sweat shops, or became squatters on pavements.

This was the largest number of refugees ever to cross an international boundary in so short a period. The figure was equal to the entire population of several member countries of the United Nations. Arrangements for their housing, feeding and medical needs imposed a very heavy strain on India's financial and organizational resources, besides of course forcing the government to put on hold its plans for poverty alleviation and economic growth. This was a matter of great regret to me personally. Instead of assisting my colleagues in the ministry of finance and the planning commission to find resources for development, I found myself harassing them to raise resources to finance refugee camps. Direct expenditure on refugee relief alone cost

Rs 260 crores by the time war broke out in December 1971, and an additional sum of Rs 80 crores until they returned to their homes. This entailed a massive resource-mobilization effort over and above what had been provided for in the budget presented in May. The sum of Rs 60 crores which had been earmarked for refugee relief proved to be a gross underestimate. The government had to seek an additional 200 crores in August and another 143 crores in December through supplementary budgets.

With its long experience of handling famine relief and other disasters, the Indian administration was able to cope with the demands made on it by the refugee flood. Even so, it was not easy to organize at such short notice 1500 relief camps for up to 50,000 people per camp. I remember an exhausted camp commander, after answering the prime minister's impatient questions, telling me testily: 'Sir, please tell the prime minister that even hurry takes time.' While hurry was taking time, shelters in the form of small thatched huts made from local material, and tents made of wood-frames covered with tarpaulin, were being speedily put up. Schools, dharamshalas and public buildings were being emptied to accommodate refugees. Even so they overflowed and took up every inch of ground that could be found in the proximity of potable water.

To follow up on her decision that the refugees would have to return to their country, Indira Gandhi made an important statement to the Lok Sabha on 24 May 1971:

These twenty-three years and more, we have never tried to interfere with the internal affairs of Pakistan, even though they have not exercised similar restraint. And even now we do not seek to interfere in any way. But what has actually happened? What was claimed to be an internal problem of Pakistan has also become an internal problem of India. We are, therefore, entitled to ask Pakistan to desist immediately from all actions which it is taking in the name of domestic jurisdiction, and which vitally affect the peace and well-being of millions of our people. Pakistan cannot be allowed to seek a solution of its political or other problems at the expense of India and Indian soil . . . *conditions must be created to stop any further influx of refugees and to ensure guarantees for their safety and well-being* [emphasis added].

This statement was a reversal of the position taken by her when, immediately after the beginning of the military operation in East Pakistan, she had reminded agitated members of the Rajya Sabha that India had to act within international norms.

The crisis that India faced called for extraordinary qualities of leadership. It demanded a cool, determined and inspiring leader who could define the national purpose and effectively mobilize national effort for that purpose. In Indira Gandhi the occasion and the leader were well matched. She decided to take direct responsibility for meeting the crisis. This was adversely commented upon at that time by sections of the bureaucracy and politicians. The criticism was that she was trying to manage the crisis too tightly, with only a small group of officers to help. This group was dubbed the Kashmiri Mafia. In actual fact this group was nothing more than the kind of ad hoc committee which is often formed in the Indian administrative set-up to tackle specific problems. P.N. Haksar, secretary to the prime minister (later replaced by me), R.N. Kao, special secretary in charge of external intelligence, and T.N. Kaul, foreign secretary, were responsible for the epithet this group had earned, but it also included T. Swaminathan, the cabinet secretary, and K.B. Lall, the defence secretary. The physical proximity of their establishments made it easy for members of this group to meet informally and at short notice. The prime minister, though in direct touch with the group through her secretary, used sometimes to meet its members individually to keep herself fully informed. The core group, or the 'panchayat' as they called themselves, were also in touch with Govind Narain, the home secretary, I.G. Patel, secretary for economic affairs, and General (later Field Marshall) S.H.F.J. Manekshaw, chief of the army staff. Other officers were called in by the core group when their expertise was required. In normal circumstances it would have been a time-consuming exercise for a group like this, consisting as it did of strong personalities with different backgrounds, to agree and produce well-thought-out policy prescriptions. But there was no time to let group dynamics take its course. The immensity of the crisis and awareness that any miscalculation could be disastrous helped each mind to focus on the same points.

Nevertheless, it would be an exaggeration to say that the group functioned without friction, for there were differences of approach and assessment. There were problems of ego and temperament as well. Kaul had ready-made answers, he was impatient of intellectualism; he wanted quick action and immediate results. Haksar was for careful reflection on suggestions and mindful of the consequences of the action suggested. He looked at policies from a longer-range point of view but tended to pontificate. Kao's concern was that the intelligence supplied by him not be interpreted too imaginatively. He was jealous of the freshly gained reputation of his organization, which had been badly damaged over the Chinese attack in 1962. K.B. Lall spent much time and effort demonstrating that he was the most intelligent member of the group, an endeavour which was rebuffed, sometimes rudely, by Manekshaw, who had his own claims to a high IQ. Govind Narain, a seasoned civil servant, was a keen defender of the home ministry's turf and would resist spiritedly any inroads into his territory. Swaminathan was a good chairman, letting everybody have his say but insisting on clarity of conclusions. Differences of temperament and style notwithstanding, this group had been honed into a very cohesive team by the time I joined it in late August.

At the political level, matters connected with the crisis were considered by the political affairs committee of the cabinet, which met from time to time to review the situation and deliberate on broader aspects of the policy.

There was a great deal of sympathy for the plight of the refugees all over the world, and much concern about the grave social, economic and political implications for India. Newspapers carried eyewitness accounts of the atrocities committed by the Pakistan army and these outraged public opinion everywhere. Yahya Khan, like all dictators, remained unmoved by criticism. There was no evidence that his government felt any need to relent or find a credible political solution to the problems it had created.

The International Rescue Committee for Refugees, which had sent an emergency mission to India, submitted a report to the US government towards the end of July. While acknowledging that 'there has been an extraordinary effort on the part of the West Bengal and Indian government to organize these refugee camps and supply them with at least minimum quantities of food and water', it emphasized that 'political solutions for the return of the refugees must be found', and went on to say that 'it is imperative that India's shattering burden of caring for the refugees be shared by other nations and other peoples to create time for such a settlement.' The report warned that 'if the present trend of refugee influx continues the figure is likely to go up to seven million before July is out.' It pointed out that seven million people was the total population of Cuba and said the situation was so desperate that it could explode at any time. Such warnings and apprehensions, as well as the efforts of the government of India to mobilize international support for a peaceful resolution of the conflict, went unheeded. Most governments, while expressing deep concern, refused to put pressure on the Pakistan government for a political solution on the grounds that it was an internal matter. China and several Muslim governments accused India of interference in Pakistan's domestic affairs and extended support to Yahya Khan's military regime.

Encouraged by the lack of pressure from his countrymen and the world at large, Yahya Khan made a statement on 28 June announcing what he called 'a plan to transfer political power to civilians'. This was indeed a diabolical plan. It consisted of the appointment of Dr A.M. Malik, a Bengali gentleman, as civilian governor in place of the notorious General Tikka Khan. The secret part of the plan was to arrange sham polls for seats rendered vacant by the flight of Awami League members of the national and provincial assemblies. These reports were confirmed later in September by a press note issued by the Pakistan election commission. In the meanwhile Yahya Khan continued to denounce the Awami League leaders as traitors, with whom he said he would have no truck, and as such the ban on the League was to continue. Nor was Sheikh Mujib going to be released. It was obvious to us, as it was to the people of East Bengal, that the martial-law administration was planning to set up the façade of a puppet government in the province as its future political dispensation. Yahya Khan had no desire to open a dialogue with genuine representatives of the people. Not unexpectedly, his announcement was followed by an acceleration in the refugee influx.

All this was sufficiently worrying for us. Our worries increased further when Henry Kissinger, President Nixon's special assistant for national security, arrived in India a week or so after Yahya Khan had spoken. We were dismayed when Kissinger called Yahya Khan's 28 June announcement a conciliatory gesture. He said it was the beginning of 'an evolutionary process' which we should encourage. The 'process' would, according to him, lead to a satisfactory solution of the national aspirations of Bengalis! He made some proforma statements of sympathy for the refugees but showed no genuine understanding of India's predicament. But of course it is wide off the mark to say this about Kissinger, he being far too astute an analyst for anyone to suggest that he seemed somewhat short of understanding. The truth is that, being a cold-blooded strategist, India did not count for much in his scheme of things. We did not know then that his mind was elsewhere—in Beijing, to be exact. After his famous visit to China he told L.K. Jha, our ambassador in Washington, that if China intervened in a warlike situation between India and Pakistan we should not look to the United States for assistance.

On 2 August Yahya Khan announced in a television interview that Mujib, whom he called the 'leader of the defunct Awami League', would be put on trial for having committed acts of treason and incited armed rebellion against the state. 'How would *you* treat your criminals?' he rhetorically asked foreign media representatives at the interview.

These pronouncements by Kissinger and Yahya Khan had a decisive impact on Indian policy-making. In view of the deteriorating situation, the prime minister called for an in-depth review of the entire gamut of policies relating to the crisis. This resulted in a series of steps, the first two of these being specially important. First, it was decided that international opinion should be mobilized to pressurize Yahya Khan into abandoning Sheikh Mujib's trial. The prime minister wrote to all heads of government expressing her apprehension that this so-called trial would be used only as a cover to execute Mujib, which would aggravate the situation in East Bengal and in turn create serious problems for India. She requested them to exercise their influence with Yahya Khan and persuade him to take a realistic view in the larger interests of peace and stability. The second step was to help Bangladeshi freedom fighters who had been clamouring for arms and training facilities. The government had till then resisted these demands, except to a minor extent, and even that had been to prevent them approaching others for such help. The threat of Sheikh Mujib's trial had given a new impetus to the resistance movement. Even without help from us they had begun to intensify their attacks on the Pakistani forces. The reckless bravery of Bengali freedom fighters received wide media coverage in India. As admiration and sympathy for them grew, so did resentment and anger against the government of India for its reluctance to support them militarily. This put the government upon the horns of a dilemma. It wanted to help but at the same time it wanted to avoid open conflict with Pakistan. After much cogitation, help had been stepped up but even then it had not gone beyond the provision of sanctuaries and logistics.

Despite the detailed planning of military operations, the top leaders of the Awami League—including most of the elected members of the national and provincial assemblies and the bulk of the cadres—had been able to go underground or cross over to India. A couple of days before the actual crackdown their houses had been marked for identification to help West Pakistani soldiers deal with them. This had had the unintended effect of forewarning the Awami Leaguers, with the result that none of them except Sheikh Mujib was found at home when the soldiers arrived. He was arrested and flown to West Pakistan, where he was kept in a high-security prison. Even though the Shiekh's absence was a handicap for the League leaders, they were quickly able to get their act together and form a government in exile. On 10 April, the League leaders issued a proclamation of independence in which they announced:

We the elected representatives of the people of Bangla Desh, as honourbound by the mandate given to us by the people of Bangla Desh whose will is supreme, duly constituted ourselves into a Constituent Assembly, and having held mutual consultations, and in order to ensure for the people of Bangla Desh equality, human dignity and social justice, declare and constitute Bangla Desh to be a sovereign People's Republic and thereby confirm the decision of independence already made by Banga Bandhu Sheikh Mujib Rahman . . .

The Sheikh was declared president of the republic and in his absence the vice-president was to discharge the duties of the president. Tajuddin Ahmed, general secretary of the party, was chosen prime minister. A day after the proclamation Tajuddin announced from a clandestine radio station called Swadhin Bangla Desh Betar Kendra the formation of a liberation army around a nucleus of professional soldiers from the Bengal Regiment and East Pakistan Rifles who had rallied to the cause of the liberation struggle. He also announced the names of former army officers who were leading the struggle in different parts of the country. On 14 April the new government announced the appointment of Colonel M.A.G. Osmani, a former senior officer of the Pakistan army and adviser of the Sheikh, as commander-in-chief of its armed forces.

Soon after, the Bangladesh government appealed to India and other democratic countries for recognition and the establishment of diplomatic relations. Public opinion in India, inflamed by the atrocities, was in favour of recognizing the Bangladesh government. Most political parties also supported this demand, and it required all the skills of Mrs Gandhi's to resist it. She was widely criticized for not extending recognition but she had her reasons. It would certainly have further aggravated bad relations with Pakistan, and it could have created domestic complications. Some parties were articulating their support for recognition in terms of their party interests and ideological predilections. The CPM, which had a large following in West Bengal, was for immediate recognition but without military support. According to them this was to safeguard the 'people's war' character of the Bangladesh struggle. That Pakistan might retaliate by declaring war against India if it recognized the Bangladesh government did not seem to bother them. Their pro-China stance and their liaison with their counterparts in East Bengal were matters of deep concern for India. There were other, more extremist groups under the general rubric of the Communist Party (Marxist-Leninist), whose interest in immediate recognition was that they would gain support from like-minded persons across the border for their own revolutionary activity in India. Even the less revolutionary Left parties which were participating in elections and parliamentary institutions had developed an effective technique of enticing refugees into their vote banks. The arrival of new refugees held the prospect of more votes for them, particularly in West Bengal and Tripura. Thus there was every danger that the refugees would become a destabilizing factor in the social and political life of the eastern states.

Among the refugees several resistance groups functioned independently because of their incompatibility with one another. The personnel of the East Bengal Regiment and the East Pakistan Rifles had the professionally trained soldier's supercilious attitude towards the unkempt and 'indisciplined' guerillas. Then there were the armed political activists who were divided among themselves on finer points of politics and ideology. For Left-oriented students, the regular Awami League worker was too moderate and conservative to be a reliable comrade. And for the latter the former were under the influence of Moscow or Beijing and therefore a threat to Bengali nationalism. Each group had its own separate vision of the free Bangladesh for which they were struggling.

Among the Bangladesh leaders Maulana Abdul Hamid Khan Bhashani was the most colourful and unpredictable personality we had to look after. Before the crisis he had established himself as a powerful pro-China leader and was widely considered an India baiter. But even he had to escape from what he called Yahya Khan's 'inhuman repressions'. As he was a highly volatile person who was fond of making bombastic statements, we were anxious that he should stay away from the prying eyes of the media. His advanced age and delicate health also made it necessary that he should live in a quiet and relaxed place. He was therefore comfortably lodged in the peaceful hill resort of Ranikhet. But he would have none of it. Soon after his arrival there he started sending messages to the prime minister in which he extolled his own 'long cherished idealism' and expressed his desire to keep this idealism 'unpolluted'. According to him, this could be achieved only if he were given 'five acres of land and four tin sheds' in a village in the Dhubri area of Assam, where his son was buried. From such a base he would fight to achieve three goals. One, to bring into being an independent Bangladesh, two, to establish socialism in the new republic, and three, to work towards forming a confederation of Bangladesh with India. The Maulana's third goal scared Kao and myself—the main targets of his messages. It took a good deal of persuasion spread over two months to convince him that Dhubri was a disturbed area and that he would be better off staying safely where he was already nicely settled.

The provisional government of Bangladesh had created a command structure for the resistance force (called Mukti Fauj, later renamed Mukti Bahini) under Osmani, who, however, had not succeeded in establishing his authority beyond the regular army personnel: the political elements of the resistance movement proved too refractory for him. For that matter, Prime Minister Tajuddin's cabinet also harboured internal distrust. Some of his cabinet colleagues suspected Tajuddin of pro-communist leanings. His foreign minister Khondkar Mushtaq Ahmed was in contact with the US consulate in Calcutta without the knowledge of his colleagues. Their rivalries translated into an anxiety to maintain separate groups of their own for use in the post-liberation struggle for power.

This was not all. We also knew that none of the cabinet members of the provisional government were in the complete confidence of Sheikh Mujib. Just before he was arrested on 25 March he had told a close confidante that if he were killed or disappeared from the scene, his true successors, who would lead the movement, were five young men connected with the students' movement—he called them his Khalifas. These were Sheikh Fazlul Haq Moni (his nephew), Abdur

Razzak, Tufail Ahmed, Serajul Alam Khan and Shahjahan Siraj. The Khalifas hated Tajuddin as well as Khondkar Mushtaq. They were also wary of T.N. Kaul, P.N. Haksar and D.P. Dhar because of their pro-Moscow image. But they had staunch faith in Indira Gandhi, and also in R.N. Kao—whom they looked upon as a professional carrying out duties assigned to him by his prime minister.

The Khalifas formed a separate organization which they called Mujib Bahini. They were afraid that the leadership of the resistance movement might pass from the Awami League into the hands of the Mukti Bahini, which might turn sectarian under Leftist influence. Thus there was every danger of a clash between the two Bahinis. With the help of the Communist Party of India, the pro-Moscow communists organized a guerilla force of their own as a counterblast to the Mujib Bahini. The pro-China communists, who were in a state of confusion on account of China's support to the Pakistan military regime, splintered into several sub-groups. The group that attracted some notice was the one led by Mohammad Toaha. He stayed back with his group and claimed he was fighting against the Pakistan army as well as the Mukti Bahini. According to him the Awami League movement was part of the conspiracy of Soviet social imperialism and Indian expansionism.

This state of affairs was alarming. Clearly, there was an urgent need for these diverse groups to co-ordinate their activities if they were to succeed in their common and cherished goal of liberating Bangladesh. This was also in our own national interest since fissures in the resistance movement could cause it to spin out of control and create anarchy in a region of India which was already in a state of turmoil. The provisional government could not undertake the task of co-ordination without Indian assistance. After much reflection Mrs Gandhi assigned the task of helping the provisional government in these matters to D.P. Dhar who was then Indian ambassador to the Soviet Union. D.P. was recalled and appointed chairman of a policy planning committee under the auspices of the ministry of external affairs. This one-man committee was solely concerned with the Bangladesh crisis.

D.P.'s task was formidable but he was eminently qualified to undertake it. His winsome manner, his brilliant sense of humour, and his acute intelligence were all invaluable assets in his new job. He had the gift of flavouring his exposition of the same theme with subtle nuances in order to reassure and satisfy interlocutors of different shades of opinion. He also had the rare ability to listen to fools as well as knaves calmly, without losing his patience or showing signs of irritation. He could talk to soldiers, politicians, journalists and radicals of different hues in their own idiom. The five Khalifas, who at first refused even to meet him because they suspected him of being a communist, ended up as his admirers. Besides face-to-face meetings with various Bangladesh leaders, D.P. institutionalized his communication with the provisional government by stationing an officer in Calcutta for regular contact with the provisional government in Mujib Nagar.

The month of August proved fateful. Several events laid out the inexorable course of history, climaxing in the December war. On 5 August the Pakistan government published a white paper which made it clear that no peaceful settlement was likely. While presenting its version of the crisis, this white paper laid the blame entirely on the leadership of the Awami League which, according to it, had converted its mandate for autonomy into secession. It was full of wild charges against the Awami League and stories about its plans to break up Pakistan.

The white paper was expected to serve as a background for the declaration of 7 August, according to which 88 Awami League members of the National Assembly were allowed to retain their seats while the remaining 79 were to be given a chance to clear themselves of criminal charges against them. All those cleared of charges were assured that they would retain their seats in their individual capacity if they returned home. To add to the provocation, it was officially announced that Mujib would be tried by a special military court *in camera* and that the proceedings of the trial would be kept secret. Whether Yahya Khan was completely out of touch with reality or the victim of his own propaganda, we were not sure. What we were sure about was that the possibility of a peaceful solution had receded. In our judgement the attempt to produce a civilian administration with some semblance of local support was an exercise to mollify international public opinion. So far as Bangladeshis were concerned, their response was a sharp increase in assaults on the Pakistan military outposts at scores of places all over the province.

On 9 August India and the Soviet Union signed a Treaty of Peace and Friendship. The treaty had been under discussion on several occasions during the previous two years but never in a sustained or urgent manner. Several key persons in the decision-making process in the foreign office and the prime minister's secretariat had expressed their doubts on the desirability of India entering into such an arrangement with the USSR. The prime minister herself had serious reservations. She was concerned about India's image as a leader of the Non-aligned Movement. She also had some anxiety over the impact of such a treaty on domestic politics, particularly on account of Rightists who might fear that the country was being dragged into the Soviet camp—in the mid-term election campaign the Jana Sangh had denounced her as a Soviet agent. Nor was she unmindful of the fact that a closer relationship with the Soviet Union would encourage Leftists to further radicalize internal politics.

In the event the treaty received wide political support in the country, cutting across party lines. Perhaps this was due to the sense of insecurity and isolation that had gripped people at the time, for the press was full of forebodings about a US–China–Pakistan axis. In such a climate of opinion, the treaty was interpreted in India and abroad as India's response to the new configuration of power that seemed to be emerging. Mrs Gandhi's fears about the reaction of political parties did ultimately come true after the crisis was over, but that is another story.

What led her and her advisors to veer in favour of the treaty was an assessment of the consequences of Henry Kissinger's breakthrough visit to China. While the timing and substance of the visit had nothing to do with the crisis in the subcontinent, it nevertheless had an adverse effect on it from our point of view. In this context Indian misgivings were expressed by the imperturbable Sardar Swaran Singh, the foreign

minister, when he told parliament: 'While we welcome the rapprochement between Peking and Washington, we cannot look upon it with
equanimity if it means the domination of the two powers over this
region or a tacit understanding between them to this effect.' Because
of our strained relations with China, we had expected a reiteration of
the friendly assurances which Kissinger had conveyed during his visit
to Delhi. Only a week before his China parleys began he had told our
foreign secretary, T.N. Kaul: 'You know it would be silly for the US
to favour a situation in which 800 million Chinese and 600 million
people in this subcontinent form a group—a class dominated from
Peking—that would be inconceivable. That would be a price that
under no circumstances we would pay. Rapprochement with China
would be meaningless if that is the price one has to pay for it. It would
be surrender. About this, you should never have any doubts.' After
Nixon's announcement of his own proposed visit to China, Kissinger,
far from reiterating the assurances given to Kaul, chose to threaten
us with neutrality if China intervened in the ongoing Indo-Pakistan
crisis. That warning by Kissinger on 17 July was followed by the suggestion of the US under-secretary of state that India should control
guerilla activity on its side of the border and accept UN personnel to
handle refugee aid.

It was clear that the US government was reluctant to persuade
Yahya Khan to negotiate a political settlement with Sheikh Mujib. It
was disconcerting for us to find that the US had clandestine contacts
with Khondkar Mushtaq, the foreign minister of the Bangladesh government. Tajuddin, who knew about this, was afraid his colleague was
up to mischief. To get out of the clandestine trap, Mrs Gandhi thought
the Americans should be encouraged to approach the Awami League
leaders in Mujib Nagar. Accordingly, L.K. Jha was asked to make the
suggestion to the state department and to Kissinger. But the American
approach did not go beyond their own favourite, whom his cabinet
colleagues as well as Osmani distrusted. This confirmed Tajuddin's
fears. After some time Khondkar Mushtaq was relieved of his post,
though we knew that American clandestine contacts with him continued even after his exit. Incidentally, Tajuddin's fears about Khondkar

came true in August 1975 when he became president after the coup that resulted in the assassination of Sheikh Mujib, his family, and the top leadership of the Awami League.

Instead of helping to find a political solution that would be acceptable to the Awami League, the US government was, in our opinion, helping Yahya Khan to disrupt its leadership. And to provide further help to the Pakistan dictator, the Government of India was being pressed into curbing Bangladesh's freedom fighters. After all, Yahya was to be rewarded for services rendered by him to Nixon and Kissinger in their grand strategy for the detente with China. Mrs Gandhi, at that stage, thought enough was enough. We had to accept the fact that in the emerging geo-political pattern which Nixon and Kissinger were designing we were on the wrong side so far as they were concerned.

In fact, Kissinger said that to me quite candidly when he visited India again in 1974 to improve Indo–US relations. He told me if he were Mrs Gandhi's adviser in 1971, he would have told her to do exactly what she did do. In 1971 American Realpolitik was against us. So was time. As the monsoons receded refugees poured in in ever larger numbers. We desperately needed the crisis to end. The only way was open to us was to give effective military help to the provisional government and its military arm, the Mukti Bahini.

The provisional government of Bangladesh had been complaining bitterly that it was not getting enough arms from India. The arms which Bangladeshis had brought with them had been taken over by the Border Security Force to prevent their possible transfer to local extremists. After the formation of the Mukti Fauj these arms were returned. But these Chinese-made arms soon ran out of ammunition, which India could not replace. Without Indian help, which until then had been restricted to the provision of sanctuaries and logistic support, there was the danger that the Mukti fighters might deflect their activities away from their own freedom struggle and become a source of political turbulence in India, where they had widespread support. In fact the pressure to recognize the provisional government was becoming irresistible as the refugee influx continued unabated. Even elements within the Congress Party, over which Mrs Gandhi had gained

Henry Kissinger with Indira Gandhi, P.N. Dhar behind them, 1974

control only recently, were becoming restive and wanted her 'to do something' which would assure the people that India was not a passive victim. The party was also concerned about the impact the government's inaction might have on the elections due in several states in March the following year. Although the political parties had behaved with remarkable restraint, the threat to communal peace could not be ignored. The strong reinforcement of the Mukti Bahini served the dual purpose of stiffening the Bengali resistance movement, which now became the avowed policy, and relieving the pressure on the prime minister to recognize the provisional government of Bangladesh.

The treaty with the Soviet Union was meant to convey to the US government, the only government that could have decisively influenced Yahya Khan, that India was serious about a political solution of the East Bengal problem in a way that would enable the refugees to return home. Soon after signing the treaty this point was made most explicitly by the foreign ministers of India and the Soviet Union in a joint statement in which they said they 'considered it necessary that urgent steps be taken in East Pakistan for the achievement of a political solution.' The other country with influence in Pakistan was China. Besides political support, it had given military assistance to enable Pakistan's military solution to succeed in East Bengal. Having done that, China had advised Yahya Khan to find some political *via media* to tide over the crisis. It was our hope that the treaty would give additional reasons to China to pursue that advice. This was particularly necessary because Kissinger's China visit had created an atmosphere of jubilation in Pakistan and hardened Yahya Khan's attitude towards Mujib and the Awami League.

Behind the crowded events of August I had also a personal anxiety which kept nagging me. Haksar was to retire on 4 September and I was to take over from him. This was hardly a time when we could afford such a change. To replace Haksar was to replace a legend. He had rapport with the Russians, which I lacked. He was friendly with media people, from whom I shied away. For four years he had been at the centre of the concentric circles called the Indian administration, where I was a rank outsider if not an interloper. What worried me most was that he was not going to be available even for consultations because, as an IFS officer, he was entitled to spend his earned leave abroad. Indira Gandhi was more than willing to extend his tenure. I tried hard to persuade him to stay on but he was adamant about leaving for personal reasons.

By the end of August the situation had further deteriorated. The Pakistan government had summarily rejected the UN secretary-general's concern about Sheikh Mujib's trial, saying that 'it cannot accept the proposition that any judicial decision on the individual case of Sheikh Mujibur Rahman will have any repercussions outside the borders of Pakistan. No such repercussions are inevitable unless Pakistan's hostile neighbour, India, is encouraged to make them so.'[4]

---

[4] *Dawn*, Karachi, 16 August 1971.

Yahya Khan had prepared a plan for the new political arrangement that Dr A.M. Malik, the new civilian governor, was to implement. He took office on 3 September. The next day he announced what was called an 'amnesty' under which all 'miscreants' were to be pardoned, provided they had not been chargesheeted. Among these 'miscreants' were ninety Awami League leaders who were expected to co-operate with the new administration. They, however, managed to cross the border and joined the Mukti Bahini. Another component of the political plan that the governor had brought with him was to arrange by-elections to fill the vacant seats from East Bengal in the National Assembly. This exercise was undertaken by Major-General Farman Ali, adviser to the governor, who simply distributed the seats among loyal favourites.

Our response to these provocations was to continue the ongoing dual policy even more energetically. One part of the policy was to continue to mobilize international opinion in favour of a political settlement in East Bengal and persuade governments with influence in Pakistan to put pressure on Yahya Khan to abandon Sheikh Mujib's trial and come to a satisfactory settlement with the elected representatives. The second was to increase support to the provisional government of Bangladesh and the Mukti Bahini. Their enhanced fighting capacity was meant to convince Yahya Khan that his military solution was not working. The single objective of the two-pronged policy, though seemingly contradictory, was to encourage a political settlement and avoid an Indo-Pak war.

It was in furtherance of this policy that Indira Gandhi visited Moscow, Brussels, Vienna, London, Washington, Paris and Bonn. Each of these visits was an earnest of the Indian desire to leave nothing unexplored in an effort to ease the burdens imposed on India. Moscow was her first port of call. As the treaty with the USSR had been signed some weeks earlier, this visit gave her an opportunity to apprise the Soviet leaders of the deteriorating situation and the danger of war in the subcontinent. Being assured of Soviet understanding she visited the Western bloc leaders in late October and early November. On the eve of her journey on 23 October she broadcast a message to her countrymen and political parties. She advised them to stay calm and patient as the gravity of the situation demanded that 'we do not speak or act in anger or in haste.' About the purpose of her journey abroad, she said 'it seemed important in the present situation to meet the leaders of other countries for an exchange of views and put to them the reality of our situation.'

While Indira Gandhi was on her peace mission, a war psychosis was being built up in West Pakistan. Soon after the Indo-Soviet treaty, Yahya Khan told Columbia Broadcasting System on 11 August: 'The two countries are very close to war. Let me warn you, for the defence of my country, I will fight a war.' Maulana Mufti Mahmood, secretary general of the Jamiat-i-Islami, declared in Lahore on 29 August 1971 that 'it was in Pakistan's own interest to have direct armed confrontation to teach our neighbour the lesson they seemed to have forgotten so soon after the 1965 war.'[5] Taking the cue from his chief, his Sindhi chieftain advised the Pakistan government 'to get the nation ready for jehad against India.'[6] In response to the increasing successes of the Mukti Bahini, Yahya Khan declared that 'if the Indians imagine they will be able to take one morsel of my territory without provoking a war, they are making a serious mistake. Let me warn you and the world that it would mean war, out and out war . . . .'.[7]

These statements set the stage for similar jingoistic posturing by politicians, Islamists, retired generals and journalists. Sardar Qaiyum Khan, president of the so-called 'Azad Kashmir' government, threatened on 18 September that 'war with India would be the final one between two nations on the basis of religions.'[8] Not to be left behind in the race to hurl threats were the politicians. Bhutto, chairman of the Pakistan Peoples Party, assured the government that the 'PPP would extend wholehearted co-operation to crush Indian aggression.'[9] Khan Abdul Qayyum Khan, president of the Pakistan Muslim League, went to Dacca to announce that 'Muslims were united to frustrate the designs of India to disintegrate Pakistan. If India persisted in its designs,

[5] *The Pakistan Times*, 30 August 1971.
[6] *Jang*, Karachi, 29 September 1971.
[7] *Le Figaro*, Paris, 1 September 1971.
[8] *Dawn*, Karachi, 19 September 1971.
[9] *The Pakistan Times*, Lahore, 24 September 1971.

it would *cease to exist.*[10] The general council of Jamaitul-Ulema-e-Pakistan passed a resolution on 18 October appealing to the government of Pakistan to declare jehad against India.[11] To demonstrate that the threats of war were not just bellicose noise, Pakistan started moving troops all along the western border, including the ceasefire line in Jammu and Kashmir state, which was a violation of the ceasefire agreement. By the middle of October 1971 Pakistan had deployed most of its army along the Indo-Pak frontier in operational readiness.

It seemed clear to us that the war hysteria was being deliberately generated to avoid the search for a political solution to the problems Pakistan's rulers had created in East Bengal. Attention was being diverted from their civil war to confrontation with India. By the beginning of November, as the monsoons receded, the Mukti Bahini had intensified its operations and brought several areas inside Bangladesh under its control. The attempt of the Pakistan army to dislodge the Mukti Bahini from their positions led to clashes near the border; some of these developed into local battles. The one that attracted special notice took place on the night of 21/22 November, when Pakistani troops, supported by tanks and artillery, launched an attack on the Mukti Bahini base located near Jessore. The attack was a large-scale operation involving an infantry brigade, heavy artillery, and the air force. In the course of the attack Pakistanis crossed the frontier and attacked Indian villages in the Boyra area. Indian security forces brought down three Pakistani planes *over Indian territory* and captured their pilots, who had baled out. A day before the attack Yahya Khan had offered his 'hand of friendship' and made a plea to India 'to grasp it and let us begin a new era of good neighbourly relations'! Exactly a day later, i.e. on 23 November, Yahya Khan declared a national emergency. In the declaration he stated that he was satisfied that, 'a grave emergency exists in which Pakistan is threatened by external aggression.'

These statements by Yahya Khan were in keeping with his claim that Pakistan's problem lay not in East Pakistan but in India. In an attempt to prevent him from confusing world opinion Mrs Gandhi

[10] *The Pakistan Times*, Lahore, 9 October 1971.
[11] *Jang*, Karachi, 9 October 1991.

clarified the position immediately. Addressing Parliament on 24 November she said that 'the declaration [of emergency] is the climax of his [Yahya Khan's] effort to put the blame on us for a situation which he himself has created.' Referring to the Boyra incident she said that 'we regard this as a purely local action.' She added: 'It has never been our intention to escalate the situation or start a conflict. To this end, we have instructed our troops *not* to cross the borders except in self-defence.' She assured the house that 'even though Pakistan has declared an Emergency, we shall refrain from taking a similar step, unless further aggressive action by Pakistan compels us to do so in the interest of national security . . . The rulers of Pakistan must realize that the path of peace—peaceful negotiation and reconciliation—is more rewarding than that of war and the suppression of liberty and democracy.'

My extended reference to Mrs Gandhi's statement is necessary because the Pakistan government later twisted her phrase 'not to cross the border except in self-defence' and changed it to 'enter East Pakistan in self-defence' in order to project the Boyra incident as the real beginning of the December 1971 war. It was not convenient for them to acknowledge that the war began on 3 December, when Pakistan started hostilities on the western front with air strikes against military installations in north and western India and formally declared war against India. The truth about the Boyra incident was revealed by Siddiq Salik, public relations officer of the Pakistan army in Bangladesh in 1971. He says, 'in public, we termed the 21 November battle as an enemy attack supported with Migs, armour and artillery. In fact, it was an attempt on our part to throw back the enemy [Mukti Bahini] who had occupied the area since 13 November.'[12]

The 21 November incident led to an intensive discussion between me and D.P. Dhar, chairman of the Policy Planning Committee. He attributed the aggressive and provocative Pakistani military action to local commanders. His view was based on the intelligence reports we had received previously about the highly bellicose state of mind of junior officers in the Pakistan army. Exposed as they were to war

---

[12] *Witness to Surrender*, Oxford University Press, Karachi, 1977, p.119.

hysteria, they were straining at the leash. DP thought we should retaliate in a manner that would teach the young hotheads a lesson, even if it led to war, which at that stage seemed inevitable. I had a different assessment of the situation. I took Yahya Khan's war threats literally. To me the 21 November incident was a prelude to what was going to come.

I put the calculations of Yahya Khan and his military commanders for choosing the option of war in the following manner: Yahya Khan, having failed to set up a credible puppet civilian regime in East Bengal and being loath to come to a settlement with the Awami League—which he had banned and whose leader he had put on trial for treason—was left with no option but war. A war of attrition with the Mukti Bahini, with no hope of bringing it to a victorious end, would not serve his purpose. To lose to the Mukti Bahini posed dangers other than the ignominy of losing to a 'bunch of guerillas'. It could spark off autonomy movements in Sind and Baluchistan and threaten the entire political cohesion of West Pakistan. The loss of East Bengal in a general war with India was preferable to such a prospect. In such a war Pakistan could possibly gain sizeable territory in the state of Jammu and Kashmir, if not the whole of it, and bring India to a negotiating table with the chance that Kashmir could become compensation for the loss of East Bengal. There was also a possibility that Pakistan would win the war in East Bengal with Chinese help, which Bhutto claimed had been promised him when he had visited that country in early November. Even if the war were to go against Pakistan, there was every possibility that the major powers, especially the United States, would bring an Indo-Pakistan war to a speedy end through intervention by the United Nations or by exerting direct pressure upon India. I concluded by saying that if my assessment of Pakistani calculations seemed anywhere near the mark, then all we had to do was wait and let Yahya take the blame for starting the war. I reminded DP of Napoleon's immortal advice: 'never interrupt an enemy when he is making a mistake.' DP decided to accept this Napoleonic bit of advice.

After the 21 November incident there was no use hoping for a political settlement. Our contingency plans in case war broke out were put in high gear. India was ready to meet the war threat when Yahya

Khan told an American magazine before the Boyra incident that 'I have no reason to tell you that the war is not imminent because it is . . .'[13] and declared three days after the Boyra episode: 'In ten days time, I might not be here in Rawalpindi. I shall be fighting a war.'[14] And sure enough he kept his word.

The war came to an end on the eastern front on 16 December, when Lieutenant-General Niazi, commander-in-chief of Pakistani forces in Bangladesh, signed the instrument of surrender at Dacca. It ended on the western front a day later when Pakistan accepted the Indian offer of a ceasefire. India had no intention of continuing the war as it had achieved its war aims. Pakistan was in no position to continue even if it had wanted to. On the western front it had not met with the success it had hoped for. Acceptance of the ceasefire was therefore an act of prudence on Yahya Khan's part.

Henry Kissinger has his own story about how the war ended. In his memoirs, *White House Years*, he devotes a whole chapter to what he calls the Indo-Pakistan crisis of 1971. He gives a very detailed and ingenious account of his and Nixon's efforts to save West Pakistan from destruction which, according to him, was the Indian plan. To achieve this end, Kissinger says he had to arrange a series of secret meetings with Ambassador Huang Hua of China to co-ordinate their policies. He also had to send stern messages to Moscow to thwart Indian designs against West Pakistan. And to cap it all he had to order an aircraft carrier task-force to proceed through the Straits of Malacca into the Bay of Bengal to back up his warnings with a show of force.

Kissinger's account has the compelling appeal of a spy thriller, but for anyone who was intimately connected with the Indian side of the December war it reads like a complex exercise in scenario-building which has nothing to do with the facts. India's war aims, right from

[13] *Newsweek*, 8 November 1971.
[14] A.P., 25 November 1971.

3 December, were to liberate Bangladesh and prevent Pakistan from breaking through in the west, for which it conducted a lightning campaign in the east and a vigorous defence in the west. That India had no territorial claims on West Pakistan was made known to Kissinger and the state department by our ambassador and foreign minister. Kissinger admits that he did receive these assurances but complains that his Indian interlocutors were evasive about 'Azad' Kashmir. From this he concludes that India was going to take over that part of Kashmir and thereby bring about the collapse of Pakistan.

On 'Azad' Kashmir the Indian position was very clear. India did not recognize it as part of Pakistan; it was occupied by Pakistan in the war of 1948–9. The ceasefire line which was the result of that earlier conflict was no longer valid in the new circumstances. It was true that India had no intention of giving up some of the strategic points it had recaptured in 1971. It will be recalled that after the 1965 war India handed back to Pakistan some strategic passes in 'Azad' Kashmir, through which armed raiders had infiltrated. India had made that gesture at Tashkent to end the confrontation between the two countries. But that proved a vain hope, as Pakistan's attitude remained unchanged even after signing the agreement at Tashkent. India did not want to repeat that mistake.

It is possible that our ambassador, L.K. Jha, who according to Kissinger was evasive on the question of Indian intentions regarding 'Azad' Kashmir, was vague or not sufficiently briefed on the subject. But apart from L.K. Jha's supposedly evasive replies, Kissinger says his suspicion was backed up by the CIA, who were supposed to have had a mole in the Indian cabinet. The mole was later identified by an American journalist as none other than Morarji Desai—a gentleman who had left the government more than two years earlier, in July 1969, and was in fact in the opposition! Intelligence agencies do sometimes produce reports to support a policy on the basis of dubious sources and present them as authentic. Kissinger's pro-Pak tilt was well known; it is possible that someone in the CIA wanted to please him; perhaps even the CIA can sometimes succumb to that human weakness.

In his memoirs Kissinger describes Nixon's decision to send the naval task force to the Bay of Bengal as an act of great courage, quoting an observation of Bismarck: 'in foreign policy courage and success do not stand in a causal relationship; they are identical.' And success, according to him, was achieved on 16 December when Mrs Gandhi offered an unconditional ceasefire in the West. About her decision Kissinger says: 'there is no doubt in my mind that it was a reluctant decision resulting from Soviet pressure, which in turn grew out of American insistence, including the fleet movement . . .'[15] This judgement is unambiguously contradicted by Christopher van Hollen, deputy assistant secretary of state for the Near East and South Asia, the official who was monitoring developments in the subcontinent. In his opinion:

the United States did not need to remain mute to the Pakistan's army's repression in East Pakistan to protect the White House opening to China. Washington could have pressed President Yahya Khan harder to make political concessions in East Pakistan. India did not have a grand design to dismember East Pakistan; nor was the Soviet Union urging Indira Gandhi's government in that direction . . . Kissinger is wrong in concluding that Nixon's willingness to risk war with the Soviet Union, including the deployment of a US aircraft carrier to South Asia, saved West Pakistan and preserved the structure of world peace.[16]

Kissinger's assessment of the unilateral offer of ceasefire by India is so surrealistic that it reminds one of Thurber's 'Walter Mitty'. The facts as I know them are that while announcing the fall of Dacca on 16 December to a jubilant parliament Mrs Gandhi reiterated India's war aims: 'our objectives were limited—to assist the gallant people of Bangladesh and their Mukti Bahini to liberate their country from a reign of terror and to resist aggression on our own land.' This was followed by meetings with members of the cabinet committee on political affairs, leaders of the opposition parties, and the service chiefs, in quick succession. The purpose of these meetings was to brief them all about the offer of the unilateral ceasefire that she was going to make to Pakistan. She was particularly keen to avoid the possibility of opposition members indulging in any bellicose postures which would

[15] Henry Kissinger, *White House Years* (Little Brown and Company), p. 913.
[16] Christopher van Hollen, 'The Tilt Policy Revisited: Nixon-Kissinger Geopolitics and South Asia', *Asian Survey*, vol. XX, Number 4, University of California, p. 340.

have spoilt the impact of her offer. Consequently, on 17 December, while making the announcement of the offer, she said to a cheering Lok Sabha: 'we want to assure them [the people of Pakistan] that we have no enmity towards them . . . we should like to fashion relations with the people of Pakistan on the basis of friendship and understanding.'

Regarding the Indian reaction to the US fleet's movements, Indira Gandhi and her advisers were convinced it was a symbolic gesture meant for consumption by Pakistan, China and the Muslim states of the Middle East. In our opinion it was inconceivable that the American naval squadron was going into combat on behalf of Pakistan when the US was bogged down in Vietnam. Moreover, the fleet was under constant Soviet surveillance and the Government of India was well informed about its movement. In any case Dacca was expected to fall before the fleet could do anything about it. However, to strengthen public morale, Mrs Gandhi addressed a mammoth open-air meeting on 12 December in the Ramlila grounds of Delhi. To choose to address a million countrymen in open space when she could easily have broadcast to the nation on the radio was an act of courage since the congregation could have been a tempting air-raid target in those circumstances.

Before she spoke, her vast audience had been stirred by patriotic songs sung specially for the occasion by Lata Mangeshkar. Indira Gandhi herself was calm and composed. Her speech had no purple patches, no oratorical flourishes. Her criticism of US policies was indirect but conveyed her resolute defiance of Nixon's attempt at intimidation. Without naming the country but obviously referring to the United States, she said that

while threats were being voiced, it was mentioned that certain pacts with Pakistan were in existence. We had all along thought that these pacts were meant to contain communism. These were not meant to crush the democratic rights of poor, freedom-loving people. India was accused of not co-operating in the fight against communism and was told many times: 'We want to save you from communism.' Today, they tell us that the biggest country in the world is China and that no one should stand in the way of that country.

While she was addressing the Delhi public meeting, General Sam Manekshaw, chief of the army staff, was broadcasting a message from

All India Radio to General Niazi, commander of Pakistan's troops in Bangladesh, to lay down his arms. Niazi could take no comfort from the American fleet movement as his troops had started surrendering in various sectors under his command. So far as the fortunes of war were concerned, the American symbolic gesture only hastened the Indian army's march to Dacca, a march which was described by *The Sunday Times* 'as an achievement reminiscent of the German blitzkrieg across France in 1940.'[17]

The American decision to send a nuclear aircraft carrier task-force to the Bay of Bengal did however have an impact on Indian policy-makers. It strengthened those who wanted the country to possess its own deterrence against nuclear blackmail. That they had drawn the correct inference from the American action was confirmed by Kissinger himself later. In his memoirs, he candidly confesses that the task-force's movement was 'ostensibly for the evacuation of Americans but in reality to give emphasis to our warnings against an attack on West Pakistan.' The American decision led to an acceleration of the Indian nuclear programme and eventually to the testing of a nuclear device two and a half years later, in May 1974.

Regarding Kissinger's fears about 'Azad' Kashmir, India retained possession of 364 square miles of territory in the northern areas in Kashmir after the ceasefire line in Kashmir was converted into a line of control in terms of the Simla Agreement of 1972. Under the same agreement, 5000 square miles of territory in Sind and 386 square miles in the Sialkot–Shakargarh sector in Punjab, which India had captured, were returned to Pakistan. This was quite consistent with the Indian stand that it had no territorial claims on Pakistan.

The unilateral ceasefire episode was not an isolated event but of a piece with the general Indian strategy. Indian attitudes to the war were more accurately brought out in an editorial that appeared in *Le Figaro*, Paris, five days after the fall of Dacca. 'In India, the war is already well forgotten. For the observer who is very accustomed to this country, this is an immense surprise: no military parades, very few mass demonstrations. The editorials of the written and spoken press are of a

---

[17] *The Sunday Times*, London, 22 December 1971.

remarkable sobriety. More fuss is made in France or even in England over a five-nation rugby match . . . In all fields, a kind of restraint and prudence is to be discerned.' The editorial said in conclusion: 'This is rather an amazing lesson in democracy and it is also a mystery to see the little political weight of an army which numbers more than a million men and which has just won a war. India is decidedly a curious country.'

To give India's success a low profile was a deliberate act of policy on the part of Indira Gandhi and her advisers. They downplayed India's contribution to the Bangladesh freedom struggle to avoid hurting Bengali pride. They were also anxious to reassure India's small neighbours—whose apprehensions were being roused by hostile propaganda about the likely misuse of her military prowess by 'the new empress of India', as *The Economist* of London chose to call Mrs Gandhi. The Government of India therefore took steps to make sure that Indian troops left Bangladesh as soon as the government there had organized itself.

Indian troops in Bangladesh were under strict orders to observe a prescribed code of behaviour. A report by the British journalist Peter Hazelhurst throws some light on this subject.

Eleven days have passed since the Indian army occupied East Pakistan, and in that time it has become abundantly clear that Mrs Gandhi has fought what amounts to a war of liberation. . . . For the past 25 years, West Pakistan has been trying to convince the Bengalis that the Hindu infidels would pillage and rape East Bengal if Islamabad were not there to protect the Eastern Province . . . But today, lone and unarmed Indian soldiers stroll through the market places. The Bengalis beam at the sight of an Indian uniform and an atmosphere of confidence has replaced the pall of terror which has hovered over East Bengal for the last nine months. This is mainly due to the fact that the Indian army's performance as a temporary occupation force has surpassed its performance on the battlefield.[18]

India's unexpectedly successful management of the crisis has given birth to several myths, the most pernicious of which is that India had plans to dismember Pakistan from the very outset. The myth endows Mrs Gandhi not only with Machiavellian faculties of a high order but

[18] *The Times*, London, 30 December 1971.

also with exceptional prescience. For example, take the incident that took place on 30 January 1971. On that day two Kashmiris highjacked an Indian Airlines plane on a flight from Srinagar to Jammu and forced it to land in Lahore. On hearing the news Bhutto rushed to the airport, hailed the hijackers as freedom fighters, and congratulated them for their heroism. Soon afterwards the plane was set on fire, an act for which India banned Pakistan aircraft flights over Indian territory. Pakistan retaliated by taking a similar measure against India. Two months later, when it started its military build-up in the East, Pakistan alleged that the hijacking incident was the handiwork of Indian intelligence agencies to aggravate Pakistan's logistical problem and thereby help Bengali separatists! Evidently, India could not have succeeded in this diabolical plot without a helping hand from Bhutto.

Again, how could Mrs Gandhi or her advisers have divined that Kissinger would be so grateful to Yahya Khan for the help he received in organizing his secret mission to Beijing that he would sabotage the state department's sensible advice to the Pakistan government to seek a political *via media* with the Awami League? It would seem that Mrs Gandhi had foreseen the help she would receive not only from Bhutto but Kissinger as well in fulfilling her grand strategy against Pakistan!

Yet Pakistani detractors are not the only people to have created myths about her role in the separation of Bangladesh: her Indian admirers have done the same by glamorizing it. The truth is that there was nothing predetermined about the Indian strategy except its aim to send the refugees home—which India was determined to do at any cost. The denouement after the Pakistan army's crackdown was not inevitable. Several options were available to Pakistan and its allies and friends, especially the United States, to steer events towards a peaceful solution of the Bengali demand for autonomy. Instead, things were allowed to degenerate into a civil war between East and West Pakistan, which directly created conditions for an India–Pakistan conflict. In the absence of a serious effort to solve the basic problem, Pakistan's options narrowed down to war with India. Those same conditions reduced India's options too, so much so that if Pakistan had not declared war against India in December, India would definitely have done so.

CHAPTER NINE

Mrs Gandhi, Bhutto, and the Simla Agreement[1]

Soon after the end of the war in December 1971, Mrs Gandhi wrote to the secretary-general of the United Nations, indicating India's willingness to hold bilateral discussions with Pakistan at any time, at any place, without preconditions, to establish lasting peace between the two countries. A copy of the letter was sent to Pakistan through the Swiss embassy. This initiative was followed by her invitation to Pakistan to hold emissary-level talks to prepare the ground for a summit conference. Accordingly, Aziz Ahmed and D.P. Dhar, the emissaries appointed by the two governments, met at Murree in Pakistan in the last week of April 1972. After three days of hard bargaining the emissaries produced two documents: an *agenda* for the conference and an agreed set of *principles* that should guide the negotiations at the summit, which was proposed to be held at Simla in India in the last week of June.

The *principles* were meant to generate an appropriate ethos for the summit meeting between Prime Minister Indira Gandhi and President Zulfikar Ali Bhutto. Recognizing 'the need for establishment of durable peace' and 'ending the military conflict,' and the desirability of diverting 'resources towards development', the *principles* demanded a willingness to 'think afresh and cast aside the shackles of past policies'. In pursuance of this the Indian side took note of the traditional

---

[1] Sections of this chapter are based on my two-part article published in *The Times of India*, 4 April 1995.

Pakistani view that there could be no enduring peace unless the Kashmir problem was settled, and decided to persuade Pakistan to address the issue. At first Pakistan resisted discussion on this subject—as it had at Murree where Aziz Ahmed had taken the position that the time was not ripe to settle basic problems between the two countries. But D.P. Dhar had finally secured Bhutto's agreement to discuss Jammu and Kashmir and any other subject that he and Indira Gandhi thought fit to talk about. Eventually Jammu and Kashmir was formally discussed— partly in sessions between the principal aides of the two leaders, and fully in the meetings between the leaders themselves.

Pakistan's priorities were determined by events relating to the emergence of Bangladesh as a sovereign state. Bhutto was especially concerned with retrieving territories and prisoners of war taken by India during 1971. On Kashmir, Pakistan strongly felt that it would be more feasible to first try and settle other, less emotionally charged disputes step-by-step and take up the Kashmir question later. This approach, they believed, would generate a friendly atmosphere and a favourable public opinion for the acceptance of a solution to the problem, which would necessarily entail a compromise.

The overriding consideration for India was to put an end to its adversarial relations with Pakistan and forge an instrument that would help build a structure of durable peace in the subcontinent. In Pakistan too there were people who expressed a similar desire. Field Marshal Ayub Khan, who had led Pakistan in the 1965 war with India, wrote of the ceasefire line on 23 March in the leading Pakistan daily *Dawn*: 'Is it any rational line? What does it indicate? It is an outcome of war, what purpose does it serve? Does it serve any strategic or economic or any other interest?' He asserted that 'The ceasefire line in Jammu and Kashmir has been violated, changed and defiled on several occasions.' His opinion was that the old ceasefire line was dead: India could not afford to go from one ceasefire line to another. 'We should, therefore, extricate ourselves from the shackles of the past and seek a solution by fresh, bold and imaginative thinking.' India, though willing to take up the issues of occupied territories and prisoners of war, was keen in addition to solve long-term problems, Kashmir in particular. India had advocated a step-by-step approach in the past but this had not yielded the desired results. This time India was determined that the Simla Conference should not turn into a replica of the Tashkent Conference, which had addressed the immediate problems created by the war of 1965 without tackling the basic reasons that gave rise to it. To break this impasse Bhutto agreed to negotiate on long-term problems—his code name for Kashmir—provided that the solution, if arrived at, was implemented gradually, in a piecemeal manner, and in step with improvements in overall Indo-Pak relations.

To understand the political climate prevalent in the subcontinent in June–July 1972, when the Simla Conference was held, it is necessary to recall the events that preceded it—events that altered some basic perceptions that the Pakistan leadership had held dear. The emergence of Bangladesh as a sovereign state had starkly shown the inadequacy of religion as the sole basis of nationality. It also repudiated the two-nation theory and struck a deadly blow to Pakistan's claim, implicit as well as explicit, that it spoke on behalf of the Muslims of the subcontinent. Bhutto was acutely conscious of this fundamental change of context and he stated this frankly in his preliminary conversation with Indira Gandhi. He referred critically to his own views on these subjects, which he had articulated in extremely bellicose language earlier. He even lamented the tripartite division of the Muslim community in the subcontinent and hoped that, in the new circumstances, the community would become a strong force for peace and stability in the region. Furthermore, Bhutto said he was convinced by the events of 1971 that Pakistan could not acquire Kashmir via military intervention. In March 1972, a month before the meeting of emissaries in Murree, he told Indian journalists that a settlement of the Kashmir issue would emerge on the basis of a 'line of peace' and that the right of self-determination, in his view, was not to be exported from outside. 'Kashmir troubles me a lot,' Bhutto said. He did not want its dark shadow looming over Indo-Pak relations. He wanted his countrymen to

get over the trauma of the emergence of its eastern wing as a separate
independent state as quickly as possible and concentrate on making
the now smaller Pakistan a prosperous country. He told Indira Gandhi
in his meeting with her on 1 July: 'I have been saying in Pakistan: how
can we fight for rights of Kashmiris? I have prepared public opinion
for days ahead. But we cannot do it under compulsion.' Bhutto was
personally inclined to accept the status quo as a permanent solution of
the Kashmir problem. However, he had several constraints in this regard which he spelt out as follows:

(a) His political enemies at home, especially the army bosses, would denounce him for surrendering what many in Pakistan considered their
vital national interest. This would endanger the democratic set-up which
had emerged after fourteen years of army rule. In this context, Bhutto repeatedly talked about his fear of what he called the Lahore lobby, though
he never clearly explained what it was.

(b) He was anxious to obtain the support of all political elements in Pakistan
in favour of any agreement that might emerge at Simla. He made this
point at the beginning of the conference, while apologizing for bringing
with him an unusually large delegation, consisting of about eighty-four
members, who represented the entire political spectrum of Pakistan. He
wanted all members of the delegation to support and be committed to the
outcome of the conference. He said there should be no dissenters in his
delegation when he left Simla. He was probably thinking of his own
negative role *vis-à-vis* Ayub Khan after the Tashkent Declaration in 1966.

Bhutto was very keen on the support of Aziz Ahmed, who led the
Pakistan negotiating team. Ahmed was Pakistan's senior-most civil
servant and carried great weight in the ranks of its bureaucracy. He also
had the reputation of being a hardliner. Ahmed's support would secure Bhutto the support of Pakistan's officialdom, which constituted
a very powerful segment of the country's political elite.

Aziz Ahmed was against enlarging the agenda to include Kashmir.
But he yielded ground when the Indian side explained it was not insisting on an immediate and formal acceptance of the status quo,
which they believed could be looked upon as the imposition of harsh
terms by the victor in war. Haksar, who had assumed the leadership
of the Indian team when D.P. Dhar suddenly took ill, felt that such
a move might nurture a revanchist ideology in Pakistan. He reminded

The first session of the Simla negotiations between the two official delegations

his colleagues of the consequence of the Treaty of Versailles and persuaded them against doing anything which could be the basis of another war. The Indian side therefore put their proposal in a low key and
in an indirect manner by proposing that the name of the line dividing
India and Pakistan in Jammu and Kashmir be changed from the 'ceasefire line' to the 'line of control'. Aziz Ahmed objected to this. He pointed out, quite rightly, that the proposed change in terminology would
mean a change in the status of the line. He put forth this view vehemently and said he was not prepared to accept the change in nomenclature.

In the afternoon meeting on 2 July, which was to consider the third
and last Indian draft agreement, Aziz Ahmed said: 'This is our last
meeting . . . Pakistan cannot accept that the ceasefire line has ceased
to exist. That is the main reason why we are not accepting the Indian
draft.' For the Indian side this was a retreat from the statement made
by Bhutto in his previous day's meeting with Indira Gandhi in the presence of officials. In that meeting, after Aziz Ahmed's remark that 'We
have agreed to everything except Kashmir', Bhutto intervened and
said: 'I have, in a way, agreed to Kashmir being resolved by peaceful
means . . . As regards the Kashmir dispute, an agreement will emerge
in the foreseeable future. It will evolve into a settlement. Let there be
a line of peace; let people come and go; let us not fight over it.'

The transformation of the ceasefire line into the line of control was
the core of the Indian solution to the Kashmir problem. The *de facto*
line of control was meant to be graduated to the level of a *de jure*
border. Since no agreement was reached on this point, negotiations
were called off and the curtain came down on five days of hectic negotiations which had begun with great hopes throughout the subcontinent. This was the afternoon of 2 July. The Pakistan delegation was
scheduled to leave Simla the next morning.

Soon, word spread that the conference had failed. Media men rushed
off to announce the failure. In the midst of this enveloping gloom
Bhutto asked to see Mrs Gandhi and a meeting was fixed for 6 p.m.
at the Retreat, where she was staying. When Bhutto came to see Mrs
Gandhi, he met P.N. Haksar and myself briefly and said: 'You officials
give up too easily.' Mrs Gandhi and Bhutto then met for an hour while

Haksar and I waited in the adjoining room. Emerging from his *tête-à-tête* with Mrs Gandhi, Bhutto looked pleased and said, 'we have settled the matter and decided to give you some work to do before dinner.' After we saw Bhutto off, Mrs Gandhi briefed us on what had transpired.

At their meeting Mrs Gandhi told Bhutto she was sympathetic to his concerns and that she would hate to appear to be dictating terms to a defeated adversary. She agreed to the earliest possible withdrawal of troops from occupied territories in the interest of an overall agreement. On this question, India did not need the concurrence of Bangladesh as she did on the question of the return of prisoners of war who had surrendered to the Indo-Bangladesh joint command. At the same time she firmly reiterated the Indian desire for durable peace and stability in the subcontinent, which she thought was a precondition for economic and social development and the removal of poverty, the shared goals of the two countries—these had become the constant theme of Bhutto's speeches in his country. She had argued that this desirable state of affairs could be brought about only if India and Pakistan buried the hatchet and agreed on the settlement of the Kashmir issue along the lines suggested by the Indian side.

Mrs Gandhi elaborated the merits of the Indian proposal in the following terms: It was the only feasible solution. An important feature of the proposal was that neither country was gaining or losing territory on account of war. It did not involve transfers of population from one side to the other. Kashmiris as an ethnic community were left undivided on the Indian side. The line of control was therefore largely an ethnic and linguistic frontier. In fact in 1947, at the time of Partition, it was also an ideological frontier, being the limit of the political influence of Sheikh Mohammed Abdullah and his National Conference party. True, there were some anomalies in this otherwise neatly etched picture, but these, Mrs Gandhi pointed out, could be removed by mutual consent.

Bhutto responded with feeling and apparent sincerity. After long reflection he had come to the conclusion that the Indian proposal was the only feasible one. But he could not agree to incorporating it in the agreement for the reasons he had stated earlier. He would, however, work towards its implementation in practice and over time. Mrs Gandhi herself was worried that a formal withdrawal of the Indian claim on Pak-occupied Kashmir could create political trouble for her. She agreed that the solution should not be recorded in the agreement for the reasons advanced by Bhutto, but it should be implemented gradually, as he had suggested.

It was also agreed that the understanding would not be a written one. The insertion of secret clauses in the agreement was considered inconsistent with the desire to build a structure of durable peace. It was decided, however, that the agreement would be worded in a manner that would not create difficulties of implementation for Pakistan. This resulted in some last-minute negotiations which were carried on during the return banquet of the president of Pakistan on the eve of his departure for his country. Thus, some clauses included in the draft agreement had to be deleted to accommodate Bhutto.

The most important part of the agreement, sub-clause 4(ii), says: 'In Jammu and Kashmir, the line of control resulting from the ceasefire of December 17, 1971 shall be respected by both sides without prejudice to the recognized position of either side. Neither side shall seek to alter it unilaterally, irrespective of mutual differences and legal interpretations. Both sides further undertake to refrain from the threat or the use of force in violation of this line.' The phrase 'without prejudice to the recognized position of either side' was a concession to Bhutto to save him from domestic critics. The second and third sentences were assumed to prevent the abuse of this concession and to lay the foundation for a future settlement of the Kashmir issue.

This is how it was interpreted by observers who followed the negotiations closely. Peter Hazelhurst, *The Times* (London) correspondent, writing under the title 'Concessions at Simla Summit bring hope for deal on Kashmir', described the agreement 'as a historic breakthrough in the protracted efforts to resolve the differences between the estranged Asian neighbours during the past 25 years.' Interpreting sub-clause 4(ii) as given above he wrote:

Apparently this will mean that Pakistan has agreed to settle the Kashmir issue bilaterally with India and President Bhutto of Pakistan will not raise the dispute in the United Nations if he keeps to the spirit of the Agreement. This would appear to be an important concession to Mrs Gandhi, the Indian Prime Minister who has advocated bilateralism as the means of settling Kashmir and other disputes with Pakistan . . . The Agreement also stipulates that both parties have agreed to recognize the ceasefire line in Kashmir as it stood at the conclusion of the war in December, and convert it into a line of peace.[2]

Bhutto also knew that the Government of India had opened a dialogue with Sheikh Abdullah. He realized that India was in effect meeting the demand of separatist Kashmiris for representation at India-Pak negotiations on Kashmir via simultaneous but separate talks with Sheikh Abdullah. From his own sources and from reports in the Indian press he was aware of the probability of the Sheikh joining Indian mainstream politics. He knew that the ban on the Sheikh's entry into Kashmir was about to be removed. And when it was removed, three weeks after the Simla Conference, the Sheikh told his audience in Srinagar that the tragic events of Bangladesh had proved how correct Kashmiris were in rejecting union with theocratic Pakistan. The Sheikh's withdrawal of his demand for a plebiscite was expected to help Bhutto face the criticism of people at home.

Bhutto agreed not only to change the ceasefire line into a line of control, for which he had earlier proposed the term 'line of peace', he also agreed that the line would be gradually endowed with the 'characteristics of an international border' (his words). The transition was to take place in the following manner: After the resumption of traffic between India and Pakistan across the international border had gained momentum, the movement of traffic would be allowed at specified points across the line of control. At these points of entry, immigration control and customs clearance offices would be established. Furthermore, Pakistan-occupied Kashmir would be incorporated into Pakistan. To begin with, Bhutto's party would set up its branches there, and later the area would be taken over by the administration. India would make proforma

---

[2] *The Times*, London, 4 July 1972.

protests in a low key. (This is what actually happened in 1974, when Bhutto made POK constitutionally a province of Pakistan without much protest from India.) It was thought that with the gradual use of the line of control as the *de facto* frontier, public opinion on both sides would become reconciled to its permanence. In the meanwhile, the opening of trade and commerce and co-operation between India and Pakistan would result in easing tensions between the two countries. When Mrs Gandhi, after recounting their points of agreement, finally asked Bhutto: 'Is this the understanding on which we will proceed?' He replied, 'Absolutely; *aap mujh par bharosa keejiye* [you can rely on me].'

One of Bhutto's aides, who was also very close to the Americans, fully briefed James P. Sterba (the *New York Times* correspondent) on the understanding that his leader had reached with Mrs Gandhi. In his news analysis, which appeared within hours of the signing, Sterba, after referring to the inflexible positions of the two governments on the Kashmir problem, wrote: 'these positions have been drummed into the minds of the peoples of each side to the point where any compromise would be viewed largely as a "sell out" in both countries. And for years, such a sell out would have probably toppled the rulers who agreed to it.' Sterba added:

President Bhutto, Pakistan's first civilian leader in fourteen years, came to Simla ready to compromise. According to sources close to him, he was willing to forsake the Indian held two-thirds of Kashmir that contains four-fifths of the population and the prized valley called the 'Vale', and agree that a ceasefire line to be negotiated would gradually become the border between the two countries. The key word is '*gradually*' [emphasis added] . . . President Bhutto wants a softening of the ceasefire line with trade and travel across it and a secret agreement with Mrs Gandhi that a formally recognized border would emerge after a few years, during which he would condition his people to it without riots and an overthrow of his Government.[3]

This was the understanding between the leaders of the two countries and this was the Simla Solution of the Kashmir problem. The agreement that was signed at Simla in the first hour of 3 July 1972 was

[3] 'The Simla Agreement—Behind the Progress Reports There is the Possibility of a Secret Agreement', *The New York Times*, 3 July 1972.

the launching pad for an implementation of the Simla Solution. Some Pakistanis maintain that recent events in Kashmir have overtaken the agreement, while Indians insist that the dispute should be resolved through bilateral negotiations, as stipulated under it. This debate misses the crucial point that the Simla Agreement provided not only a mechanism for the solution of the Kashmir problem but also envisaged the solution itself.

The Simla Solution seemed the only way in which the political leadership of the two countries could resolve their conflicting claims over Kashmir. It is still the only way that remains open to them. To be sure, the aspirations of Valley Muslims need to be satisfied. The Indira–Abdullah Accord, which was an answer to this question, has come unstuck due partly to New Delhi's hamhandedness and largely due to the growth of Muslim fundamentalism in the Valley, as also because of the massive intervention of Pakistan, in flagrant violation of the Simla commitments. Had the Simla understanding been converted into the final solution of the problem, the Kashmir issue would have simply become an internal problem for India, namely one of altering the existing centre–state relations in a manner that would satisfy the Kashmiri demand for greater autonomy.

It was in the context of an utter disregard for the Simla commitments by Pakistan that I decided to make public the substance of the Simla understanding. I did this through a two-part article which was published in *The Times of India* in April 1995. Pakistani response to this came in an avalanche of statements and comments from the government, political leaders, columnists, and editorial writers questioning the veracity of what I had said. About the only person in authority who did not react was Pakistan's prime minister, Benazir Bhutto.

The expressions of disbelief in the existence of a verbal understanding between Indira Gandhi and Zulfikar Ali Bhutto were often accompanied by high praise of what Humayun Gauhar called Bhutto's

Signing the Simla Agreement, 3 July 1972

Aziz Ahmed (left), P.N. Haksar (centre),
P.N. Dhar (right)

diplomatic artistry. Writing on this subject in the *Political and Business Weekly* of 15 May 1995, Gauhar wrote:

If it took a private talk between Mr Bhutto and Mrs Gandhi in which he made certain commitments to her but which he was clever enough not to have written down in the Simla Agreement or on a separate piece of paper, then it was diplomatic artistry of the highest order. He would have known better than anyone else that such a private secret agreement, which is only verbal, was worthless. Face it Mr Dhar, even if we accept what you say, Mr Bhutto fooled your prime minister.

Gauhar explains the nature of Bhutto's artistry in Bhutto's own words. Three months before the Simla Conference Bhutto told Oriana Fallaci, the Italian journalist: 'Well, in politics you sometimes have to have light and flexible fingers . . . have you ever seen a bird sitting on its eggs in the nest? Well, a politician must have fairly light, fairly flexible fingers, to insinuate them under the bird and take away the eggs. One by one. Without the bird realizing it.'

Commenting on Pakistani rejoinders to my article, Alistair Lamb, the well-known author of several books on the Kashmir question (in which he has vigorously supported Pakistan's point of view), says: 'Pakistani refutations of P.N. Dhar's claims [that Z.A. Bhutto *did* privately agree with the Indian Prime Minister that this was exactly the way in which the Kashmir problem would be settled, with the line of control being allowed to evolve gradually into an international border] have not to date been particularly impressive or convincing though circumstances have removed over the years any significance they may ever have possessed. . . . Its essential veracity has been implied by Akram Zaki, former Pakistan Secretary General, Foreign Affairs'.[4] In India too my article was widely noted by the media and the predominant view was not very different from that of Humayun Gauhar, namely that India had lost on the negotiating table what its armed forces had gained in the battlefield.

Why did the Simla understanding not fructify? The agreement was certainly expected to start an era of peace and stability in Indo-Pak relations. The political leadership of both countries had found not only an effective mechanism for negotiation but also an actual solution to their conflicting claims over Kashmir. But events did not turn out as expected. Pakistan has flagrantly and massively violated the line of control, which Bhutto had called 'a line of peace', and unleashed a proxy war against India in Kashmir.

Why has the Simla Agreement proved so ineffective? Was India duped by Pakistan at Simla? Did Indian negotiators really lose at the conference table what its soldiers had gained on the battlefield? These questions have been raised but not discussed in depth and detail. Perhaps these questions can be fairly answered if we (a) describe the

[4] Alistair Lamb, *Unfinished Partition* (Hertingfordbury: Roxford Books), p. 296.

objectives, the broad assumptions of the two delegations and their negotiating styles; and (b) take note of developments after the Simla Agreement was signed, especially in the five-year period during which Indira Gandhi and Zulfikar Ali Bhutto, the architects of the agreement, continued to be at the helm of affairs in their respective countries.

The priorities of the Pakistani negotiators were of an immediate nature, namely to get back prisoners of war (POWs) and territories that they had lost to India in West Pakistan, and to delay the recognition of Bangladesh as an independent sovereign state until it suited them. India's major objective was to put an end to its adversarial relations with Pakistan, to build a structure of durable peace between the two countries, and to settle the Kashmir question. India also needed to settle problems resulting from the war, such as the repatriation of POWs, recognition of Bangladesh, restoration of communications, and trade, travel and diplomatic relations between the two countries. In terms of the concrete achievements of the agreement, Pakistan obviously succeeded. It got back what it wanted most, namely its lost territories, and after some delay its POWs. And along with China and several Muslim countries, it withheld recognition of Bangladesh till it was most advantageous.

Bhutto and Aziz Ahmed played what appeared to be very well coordinated roles in the negotiations at Simla. Bhutto presented the picture of a chastened patriot who had forgotten his declaration of a thousand years' war with India, a pragmatist who was now anxious to get his shrunken country back on its feet and lead it to prosperity and progress. In this endeavour he had, so he said, gone through an agonizing time and come to believe that the governments of the subcontinent had not served their people well. To him proof of this assessment was the continuing abysmal poverty of their people. Peace and stability in the region are the *sine qua non* of any solution to our peoples' problems, he asserted again and again. It was a statesman-like posture, and he gave the impression that he was anxious to wear a statesman's mantle too. He knew, he said, that the countries of the subcontinent needed to end their fractious history, which was not possible without mutual accommodation. But what stood in his way in this laudable attempt was that he represented a defeated country and, as such, any concession on his part would be interpreted as surrender and would make his countrymen feel even more insecure than they were immediately after their defeat. Ironically, the fact that Pakistan had lost the war in 1971 thus became a useful psychological lever in his hands at the negotiating table.

The born-again Bhutto practised his new style from the moment he landed in Simla, where he was received by Mrs Gandhi and her colleagues of the political affairs committee of the cabinet. She accompanied him in a car to Himachal Bhavan, where he was to stay. En route he saw people line up and clap their hands in welcome. He looked taken aback and asked Mrs Gandhi: 'Are these people jeering at me?' Anybody could see they were not, but he tried to make her vaguely uncomfortable. She had to reassure him by saying 'No, no, they are cheering you.'

Mrs Gandhi had anticipated Bhutto's mood and seemed very solicitous of his feelings. The day before he arrived she inspected the rooms which he was to occupy and spent a lot of time getting curtains, carpets, and furniture rearranged. She took me along for the final inspection and threw a tantrum when she saw a large portrait of herself in what was going to be Bhutto's sitting room. She ordered it removed as it was the last thing that would make him relax. She was mollified when she saw that the toiletries in the bathroom were all made in India. 'Let him see that the Indian economy is catering to civilian needs,' she said to me.

Aziz Ahmed was a contrast to Bhutto: his manner and posture were totally different from his chief's. He carried himself with an air of defiance, always keeping his hawklike nose at a particularly aggressive angle. While standing he would keep his left forearm horizontally behind his back, somewhat like Napoleon, except in reverse gear. He never let his stern visage loosen into a smile. On one occasion during a tea interval I said something funny which evoked laughter. One of his junior colleagues, I think it was Abdul Sattar (later Pakistan's high commissioner in Delhi), congratulated me on my achievement. He said he had never seen his boss laugh. Aziz Ahmed's speech was a flow of sharply worded direct sentences. Even when he tried to be pleasant he could not hide the hostile glint in his eyes. I had heard of his visceral hatred of Hindus from Kewal Singh, who had spoken to me of his dealings with Ahmed in 1965, when Kewal was India's high commissioner in Pakistan and Ahmed the head of the Pakistan foreign office. Kewal was awoken in the middle of a night in 1965, summoned to the foreign office, and abused for the war started by 'rabid Hindu leaders' when in actual fact that war had been planned by Aziz Ahmed and Bhutto, as was confirmed by Pakistani sources later. Kewal Singh has written about the harrowing experience of his encounter with Ahmed in his memoirs.

In negotiations Ahmed was belligerent, repetitive and rigid. He made contemptuous references to Sheikh Mujib. On the question of recognizing Bangladesh he adopted an arrogant air, as though dealing with a supplicant. He was nonchalant about the continued detention of Pakistani POWs and made some crude remarks in Punjabi about their wives not really missing their husbands. Whenever he was addressed in Urdu he replied in English. When Mrs Gandhi complained about his rigid attitude Bhutto agreed with her but pleaded helplessness in the matter. He said Aziz Ahmed's support was necessary for him to secure compliance from the civil service which was very important to sell any agreement with India among the people of Pakistan.

It seemed me to that Bhutto and Aziz Ahmed tried in a carefully calibrated manner to put the Indian team on the defensive. Strange as this may sound, the Indian team did not seem very comfortable with the fact of having won the war. I have tried to understand the psychology behind this attitude without success. Perhaps it was Indira Gandhi's view—namely that it would be unbecoming for us as victors to behave victoriously while hosting the summit—that infected our attitudes. Or perhaps our collective historical experience makes us feel more at home with setbacks.

Whatever it was, Bhutto took full advantage of our soft attitude. He would make public statements inconsistent with the spirit and letter of the agreement and then send private messages to Delhi to disregard them as his domestic compulsions. Even before the Indian army had vacated Pak territories, he made equivocal statements on Kashmir and Bangladesh and then sent Rafi Raza, his special assistant, to explain them away privately. The technique he used is best explained in Raza's own words:

The stage was set for Aziz Ahmed to visit Delhi for talks with P.N. Haksar. ZAB insisted I also go despite my concern about the two-man leadership creating awkward situations. He said it was essential to reach a settlement, and he could trust me to talk to the Indian Prime Minister on the lines he wanted. *I was to assure her that he meant what he told her at Simla, and he instructed me to give any undertaking to secure troop withdrawals and the return of Shakargarh.* He wanted to create a new, lasting basis for good relations in the subcontinent, and would in due course proceed with the recognition of Bangladesh. She should appreciate his limitations, particularly on war trials, and not misunderstand his recent statements. *I was to ensure there should be no opportunity for recording any discussion I might have with her.* He gave me a personal letter to the Indian Prime Minister stating that, although Aziz Ahmed was his Special Envoy, she should discuss political matters with me as his Special Assistant [emphasis added].[5]

Raza has a footnote (26) to his story: 'This private conversation cannot be repeated in full.' Obviously, it is too embarrassing to be made public. Similar messages from Bhutto, reiterating his Simla commitments, came in from time to time. I remember two: one through Farooq Abdullah in 1974, and the other through our ambassador K.S. Bajpai, after the resumption of diplomatic relations.

By sheer chance, I later came to know what Aziz Ahmed thought of India's negotiating stance. We were both attending the International Energy Conference at Paris in 1975. At the conference he was very cordial; there was no clash of interest between our two countries. When returning home we were booked on the same flight. In the long hours we had together we talked about several things, including the

---

[5] Rafi Raza, *Zulfikar Ali Bhutto and Pakistan 1967–77* (Karachi: Oxford University Press, 1997), p. 216.

Simla Conference. While on the subject of diplomats and their negotiating styles, I complimented him on the diplomatic skills he displayed in Paris and earlier at Simla. At the mention of Simla his expression
suddenly changed. With an undisguised sneer that distorted his face,
he said it was not Pakistan's skills but India's strong desire for positive
results that had made the summit a success. I would have taken this as
a compliment but for the sarcasm of his tone, which made a strong impression on my mind at the time. Three years later, in 1978, I happened to mention my conversation with Aziz Ahmed to my college friend
Yusuf Buch who was special assistant to Bhutto at the time of the Simla
Conference. Yusuf told me what Aziz Ahmed's real assessment had
been. He was of the view that even though all the bargaining chips were
stacked in India's favour, India's excessive anxiety to avoid the failure
of the talks at any cost became its major handicap. This weakness enabled Aziz Ahmed and Bhutto to secure a better bargain than what they
had hoped for. There was no element of self-congratulation in Aziz
Ahmed's assessment, but I believe there was much truth in what he told
Yusuf Buch.

Haksar gave the soft approach a strong intellectual justification by
references to comparable episodes in European history. His tendency
to lift an issue from its immediate context and generalize it in broader
terms of principle and historical experience was familiar to all of us.
G. Parthasarathy, who had known Haksar a long time, told me that
this was something Haksar had learnt from Jawaharlal Nehru. Be that
as it may, Haksar repeatedly referred to the baneful consequences of
the harsh terms the Treaty of Versailles had imposed on the vanquish-
ed. The more pertinent reason for the soft approach was to reassure our
other neighbours, especially Nepal and Sri Lanka, and dispel their
fears about the emergence of Indian hegemony which India-baiters in
those countries were bound to fuel.

To give substance to the objective of durable peace in the subcontinent the government decided that unresolved problems with our
neighbours must be resolved. One such problem between India and
Sri Lanka, dating from the colonial period, was to determine the
boundary in the 'historic waters from Palk Strait to Adam's Bridge'
and 'to clarify certain related issues' regarding navigation, fishing and

mineral exploitation in the area, and the status of the island of Kachchativu. These problems were discussed in Delhi in January 1974 between the two prime ministers when Mrs Bandaranaike visited India. Mrs Gandhi withdrew our claim to the island, which enabled her to clinch matters and an agreement was signed on 28 June 1974 by the prime ministers of India and Sri Lanka at New Delhi and Colombo respectively. The agreement was hailed as a historic landmark in their friendly relations, though some Indian critics felt it was an act of generosity to the cost of Tamilnadu.

Under King Mahendra's rule, relations between India and Nepal had been marred by mutual suspicion. The king had tried to play India against China and shown scant regard for India's security concerns. He was apprehensive of India's support to his political opponents, who stood for democracy and the replacement of absolute monarchy by a constitutional one. In 1972 he was succeeded by his young son, King Birendra. Mrs Gandhi visited Nepal in May 1973 to assure the new king of India's goodwill for his country. She told him that the degree of co-operation between the two countries depended entirely on him and his government. India would be willing to respond adequately to any initiative he might want to take.

Haksar's intellectualism did not convince all his colleagues and some were sceptical of his approach to Bhutto. They distrusted Bhutto and recalled his role at Tashkent, where he vociferously opposed a reference to the 'renunciation of force' clause in the proposed peace agreement. One of them remembered vividly that when Bhutto was asked how he felt about India by an interviewer on the 'Good Morning, America' programme of the ABC television network, he had replied 'implacable hatred'. Though Indira Gandhi had some reservations about Haksar's argument, she went along with him. Y.B. Chavan and Jagjivan Ram were unhappy about the return of POWs and territories to Pakistan without an adequate *quid pro quo*, but did not, as was their wont, articulate their misgivings clearly enough.

I shared their misgivings on the question of the territories but disagreed with them on the question of POWs. I favoured repatriating not only prisoners taken on the Western front but also those who had surrendered to the Indo-Bangladesh joint command. True, Sheikh

Mrs Bandaranaike being received at Delhi, 1974
(P.N. Dhar and D.P. Chattopadhyaya stand behind her)

An audience with the king of Nepal, 1973
(Kewal Singh is behind P.N. Dhar)

Mujib was unwilling to let the POWs go without Bangladesh being recognized as an independent state by Pakistan—he quite rightly refused to negotiate except on the basis of sovereign equality. He had also announced that some of the prisoners would be tried for war crimes. The opinion I gave Indira Gandhi was that we should persuade Mujib to abandon the project of a war-crimes trial but make the return of POWs to Pakistan conditional on the immediate recognition of Bangladesh as well as the creation of a mechanism for dividing the assets and liabilities of undivided Pakistan between the two countries. My argument for the speedy return of POWs was that the upkeep and security costs of about 100,000 prisoners were a heavy financial burden on us. Furthermore prisoners attempt escapes; these would cause shooting incidents which were likely to be interpreted in Pakistan as deliberate murder. Meanwhile Jagjivan Ram argued that delaying the return of POWs would deny Pakistan the services of three infantry divisions. This appealed to Indira Gandhi, though the validity of the argument was questionable. I recalled the opinion of Sam Mankeshaw that POWs generally do not make good fighting men immediately after their release; he thought this would be especially true of Pak POWs, whose camps Manekshaw had visited several times; he was sure they would be demobbed upon their return. In any case, Pakistan was not lacking in manpower to find replacements. And as it turned out, Pakistan did raise, by 1973, six divisions to replace the three divisions it lost in Bangladesh.

The prisoners' behaviour showed the extent to which they had been indoctrinated against India: some of the sick even refused medicine because they believed they were being poisoned. Manekshaw and his colleagues' visits made a good impression on them. They were overwhelmed by the fact that the Indian 'chief' had found time to come and comfort them. Humane treatment ultimately had a healthy effect on the prisoners and generated some good will which prolonged imprisonment would certainly have eroded. I was therefore for the return of POWs. But I was strongly opposed to the immediate return of the territories we had won. My point was that we ought to retain some leverage to induce Bhutto to implement the agreement in its entirety.

I made these points in a briefing session which Haksar and I had with Indira Gandhi. Before I could finish she grew impatient and flew into a rage. I was puzzled by her loss of temper. My hunch is that she was under pressure—this could only have been from the Soviets—to return the occupied territories. But this is only a hunch; I wasn't personally aware of any such pressure. Perhaps Haksar was. He signalled me to withdraw and I left the room. He told me soon after that he 'had quietened her down' and that she wanted to meet members of the political affairs committee of the cabinet.

At that meeting Indira Gandhi asked Haksar to brief her cabinet colleagues on the stage that negotiations had reached and explain the reasons for the possibility of our returning occupied territory. After his presentation, which struck H.Y. Sharada Prasad as 'a masterly exposition, notable for its incisiveness and grasp of political realities and historical and psychological insights', the members of the committee indicated their assent. My own impression is that her cabinet colleagues were persuaded to agree to the proposal because they felt she had already made up her mind, and that was that so far as they were concerned.

At this point, to clarify both my understanding of the Simla Agreement as well as my view of the desirability of India retaining war-won territories, I must return the narrative to certain other indirect and subtle pressures employed by Bhutto against us. In the Pakistan camp, besides the negotiating team there were several individuals like Wali Khan, leader of the Awami League, and Mazhar Ali, former editor of the *Pakistan Times*—such people had personal access to certain members of the Indian delegation. In this group I was surprised to find Aga Afzal, chief secretary of Pakistan's Punjab. He had no reason to be there except that he was a Kashmiri from Srinagar who was known to me and D.P. Dhar. When he and people like him met their Indian friends, they tended to play an identical role: they got busy carrying messages from one side to the other. Whether the role was assigned or self-assumed, one cannot say. The messages were mainly meant for Indira Gandhi and emanated mostly from Pakistanis who were known for their advocacy of peace, or from non-Punjabi Pakistanis who were against Punjabi military dominance in Pakistani politics. The central theme of the messages was the same, though the language in which they were couched varied: Bhutto should not leave Simla empty-handed; nothing should be done which would weaken his political leadership; India should not lose its chance to encourage the growth of democracy in Pakistan as this would be in India's long-term interest. These opinions, coming as they did from people who were otherwise critical of the Pakistani establishment, seemed to have some influence on the negotiating stance of the Indian delegation.

The end result was that India accepted Bhutto's plea that the solution of the Kashmir problem should be implemented in a piecemeal manner and in step with an improvement in overall Indo-Pak relations. To be sure, he did agree that 'neither side shall alter it [the line of control] unilaterally, irrespective of mutual differences and legal interpretation,' and undertook to 'refrain from the threat or the use of force in violation of this line' (para 4(ii) of the agreement). The tacit understanding, no doubt, was that gradually the line of control would emerge as an international border, and thus the Kashmir question would be settled. But this remained only a tacit understanding.

The fatal weakness of the understanding was that it was dependent upon a continued occupation of their positions of power by the two leaders who had signed the document. Not only that, there was also a presumption that Bhutto would stand by the verbal assurance he had given Indira Gandhi about implementing the understanding he had reached with her. The possibility that his political will might weaken, or that he might lose power, did not seem to bother the Indian side. If the return of occupied territories—which was India's only real bargaining chip—had been made dependent upon implementing the understanding, there might have been a chance of success. The domestic pressure in Pakistan to get back occupied territories could have been a lever for this purpose. But this did not happen. On the contrary, the very first step in the implementation process was the return of occupied territories, which was to take place within a period of thirty days after the agreement came into force. Indeed this was the only item for implementation that carried a deadline! I was not surprised when on his return home Bhutto in his address to the nation said: 'I had gone to India with two views, first to get our territory back and then to get our POWs back. I have done the first in five months—what Arabs could not get done in five years.'[6]

The withdrawal of troops from the occupied territories was completed by 30 December 1972 as scheduled. But after this Bhutto deliberately slowed down the process of normalization as envisaged in the Simla Agreement. He persisted in denying recognition to Bangladesh even though this delayed the return of POWs. To defreeze the situation, Bangladesh made a major concession. It decided to 'keep aside' the issue of recognition and signed an agreement with India on 17 April 1973 to the effect that the governments of the two countries would try to seek a solution to all humanitarian problems through the simultaneous repatriation of Pakistan POWs and civilian internees in India—the Bengalis in Pakistan and Pakistanis in Bangladesh (mostly Urdu-speaking Biharis who had collaborated with the Pakistan army in crushing the autonomy movement in East Pakistan). In pursuit of this initiative Haksar, Kewal Singh and I went to Islamabad in the last week of July 1973. We tried for a whole week to reach agreement but had to return empty-handed. Aziz Ahmed, who led the Pakistani delegation, was dead set against receiving any 'Biharis'. He was also opposed to letting Bangladesh hold back Pak POWs for a war-crimes trial, even though Bangladesh had reduced the number of such prisoners from more than a thousand to just 195.

It was only in the second round of negotiations in Delhi on 28 August 1973 that an agreement was reached. A large number of 'Biharis' were left behind in camps in Bangladesh, an inequity accepted because Sheikh Mujib was keen to rescue the Bengalis in Pakistan as soon as possible. Pakistan accorded recognition to Bangladesh much later, in February 1974. Two months after this the foreign ministers of India, Pakistan and Bangladesh met in New Delhi and decided that the 195 Pakistani POWs held for trial would also be repatriated to Pakistan. This enabled a three-way movement of prisoners and civil internees, a process completed by 30 April 1974.

In his desire to neutralize India's superiority in conventional warfare, Bhutto had embarked on a nuclear arms programme in 1972. The explosion of an atomic device by India on 18 May 1974 gave him

[6] *The Motherland,* 4 July 1972.

Foreign ministers of Bangladesh, India and Pakistan, signing
repatriation agreement on Pak POWs, New Delhi, April 1974

an excuse to postpone the resumption of communications, travel and
trade arrangements. This was accompanied by a barrage of anti-India
propaganda. The USA resumed its supply of arms to Pakistan in early
1975, thus vitiating the atmosphere further. These were not exactly
ideal circumstances for the 'durable peace' in which a second summit
on the final settlement of the state of Jammu and Kashmir, consistent
with the spirit of the Simla Agreement, could have taken place.

Even if the atmosphere had been more favourable, India would not
have been able to participate in a second summit because it was necessary to resolve the differences with Sheikh Abdullah before taking on
Bhutto again. The accord with Sheikh Abdullah was expected to help
both governments to implement the Simla understanding, i.e. to accept the line of control as the international border. Here, the Sheikh
made his position very clear. When asked in an interview if he still

Mrs Gandhi in Pokharan, with members
of the Atomic Energy Commission, November 1974

At Pokharan, November 1974: Gopi Kaul, Satish Dhawan, J.R.D. Tata, P.N. Dhar and M.G.K. Menon

wanted Pakistan to be a party to any settlement, he replied: 'That is no longer necessary. The problem of "Azad Kashmir" is there, but if we agree, we can jointly face Pakistan later. In case Pakistan fails to fall in line with our wishes, it will get isolated.'[7] Accordingly, negotiations with the Sheikh were carried on earnestly, but it took longer than expected to arrive at an accord with him. It must however be admitted that with regard to timing there was a certain degree of smugness in the Indian attitude, based on the comfortable feeling that until such time as a final solution was reached the line of control would be respected by Pakistan as the border.

In the event, the accord with Sheikh Abdullah was reached towards the end of 1974 and he took office as chief minister in January 1975, nearly two and a half years after the start of negotiations. The essence of the accord was acceptance of the finality of the state's accession to India and a fortification of the special status of the state as enshrined in Article 370 of the constitution of India. The Sheikh's colleague, Afzal Beg, protagonist of the Plebiscite Front, declared, as expected, that the Indira–Abdullah accord had rendered the demand for plebis-cite irrelevant—a stand which was endorsed by an overwhelming majority in the elections of 1977, which are universally recognized as the most free and fair elections ever held in that state. As fate would have it, these elections also resulted in the defeat of Indira Gandhi and her party.

For the record, it is necessary to mention that two attempts of sorts were made for a second summit meeting—one by Bhutto in 1974, the other by Sheikh Abdullah in 1976. The first was still-born and the second came too late to materialize. Bhutto's attempt came through the prime minister of Sri Lanka, Mrs Srimavo Bandaranaike. She wrote a letter to Mrs Gandhi on 14 October, after her return home

[7] Y.D. Gundevia, *The Testament of Sheikh Abdullah* (New Delhi: Palit & Palit, 1974), p. 151.

from a state visit to Pakistan, where among other things she had several meetings with Bhutto on Indo–Pak relations. Treating it as a very delicate matter, she took extreme care to keep the contents of the letter secret. She gave the letter, written in her own hand, to her high commissioner in Delhi, telling him the matter was private. Referring to her talks with Bhutto, she said in her letter:

At several of the meetings he [Bhutto] expressed his anxiety to rebuild friendship between India and Pakistan. He was anxious that talks started in Simla be resumed and stated that if further meeting could be arranged between you and him it will be useful. He requested me especially to be of assistance in the normalization of relations as well as exploring the possibility of arranging an early meeting [between] both of you. At this stage I pointedly asked him whether this was a request that should be conveyed to the Prime Minister of India. His reply was, 'indeed this is why I am making this request to you.' He further said that he made this request because he was aware of the 'close friendship' between us and 'the cordial relations between our two countries, India and Sri Lanka.'

Mrs Gandhi was touched by Mrs Banadaranaike's effort and gave considerable thought to her offer. She mentioned the main point of the letter to Chavan, the new foreign minister who, as usual, was noncommittal. The only other minister she consulted was Sardar Swaran Singh, who had moved to the ministry of defence. Sardar Sahib and I discussed the matter at some length. Both of us had serious doubts about the timing of the meeting. As I said earlier, we had thought of a second summit *after* reaching an accord with Sheikh Abdullah, but the talks with him were still continuing and had reached a decisive stage. Even otherwise, the environment for a successful summit was lacking. Had the Indo–Pak talks on trade and air links which were carried on at the official level, been successful, an atmosphere of friendly co-operation for the summit could have been generated. But Pakistan was being very difficult in these negotiations, particularly in matters relating to trade. What was worse, while Bhutto was talking of 're-building friendship with India' his government was engaged in working up opinion against India in the United Nations, where the general assembly was in session. Pakistan had found in India's nuclear explosion a plausible reason for whipping up anti-India sentiment. And

Bhutto was openly seeking arms from the United States, for the first time *against* India. In these circumstances his request for a meeting seemed to us no more than a ploy to please Mrs Bandaranaike.

The second attempt, by Sheikh Abdullah, was more specific. It related to the 'final' solution of the Kashmir problem as envisaged in the Simla Agreement. He was not pressing for an immediate meeting but for preparations towards a meeting with Bhutto at an appropriate time, which he hoped would be in the near future and for which he had several suggestions to offer. He wrote a carefully worded letter to Indira Gandhi on 24 May 1976. Even though nothing happened as a result of his effort, the letter is an important document in itself. It removes any ambiguity that some people continue to harbour about Sheikh Abdullah's views on the future of Kashmir as well as on what has been called the Simla understanding; hence the extensive quotation that follows:

I have been giving thought to some of the major elements of any such permanent solution [of the Kashmir problem] and have also conferred with my colleague, Beg Sahib, in the matter. I made a passing reference to them in my recent meeting with you. However, I should like to mention them in this letter in some further detail.

First of all, in any new talks with Pakistan about Jammu and Kashmir, we will have to draw Pakistan's attention to the fact that the recent Accord provides an altogether changed political context in which to seek such a solution. The Accord is the outcome of a long and protracted dialogue with the acknowledged representatives of the people of the State. If I may say so humbly, it has been my privilege to receive the support and the affections of the people of the State, as their leader, for over four decades. Beg Sahib, who headed the Plebiscite Front all these years, joined me in the dialogue and is one of the co-architects of the Accord; he has had an equally long record of service to the people of the State. But apart from these facts, it has been abundantly clear from the massive endorsement of the Accord at the hands of the people—which we have sought and received on numerous occasions, both during the long dialogue as well as after the Accord—that it has the overwhelming support of the people of the State. It was in recognition of this expression of the popular will that the Plebiscite Front accepted the position that the slogan of Plebiscite was no longer relevant, and converted itself into the National Conference.

Having based its stand on the principle of self-determination, Pakistan herself should recognize the importance and significance of this altogether changed political context in the State.

Secondly, we have to take into account the hard fact that perhaps a realistic settlement with Pakistan in regard to the future of Jammu and Kashmir will ultimately have to be found on the basis of a permanent border running roughly along the present Line of Actual Control. Presumably there is some degree of mental and other preparation in Pakistan to accept a solution along the same line. However, before we get involved in any negotiation on this point it seems to me very necessary that our Defence, Security as well as other experts should go into the matter quietly and discreetly and examine the Line of Actual Control with reference to the situation on the ground, and the essential strategic and other considerations that must be accommodated in any final adjustment of the Line. There may be instances where it may suit us to accommodate Pakistan for the sake of a more viable border; just as there will, no doubt, be instances in which we should insist upon adjustment in our favour to impart the Line the necessary degree of permanence and viability. All this will require detailed and careful staff work by those concerned. Perhaps a Cell could be created for the purpose so that this part of the work could be undertaken immediately and some proposals got ready. Particularly where any habitations may be involved in these proposals, we would also request for an opportunity to be consulted at the appropriate stage . . .

By the time internal preparations for the meeting got under way, the idea of holding general elections was gaining ground. The possibility of elections and ending the Emergency regime were so important that it put several important decisions, including a second summit meeting with Bhutto, on the back burner.

It is by no means certain that the second summit would have been successful. My reasons for this view are that after the Simla Conference was over, Indira Gandhi's political fortunes started to decline. The year 1972, when the agreement was signed, turned out to be a year of drought which further sapped the Indian economy—already under strain on account of the burden imposed by the war and the influx of refugees. The oil price hike imposed by OPEC in the following year threw the economy into disarray. There were acute shortages and a sharp increase in inflation. Prices rose by 24 per cent, the highest such increase in post-Independence India. Economic distress quickly turned into political turbulence, which was climaxed by the J.P. movement, leading to the political crisis of 1975, which Indira Gandhi tried to contain by declaring an internal Emergency in the country. These dire circumstances were hardly propitious for pursuing the unfinished part of the Simla Agreement, which had been denounced and called a black agreement by the Jan Sangh, the party most active in the J.P. movement.

Bhutto meanwhile had his own political difficulties. Like India, Pakistan was an oil-importing country and its economy had a similar balance-of-payments problem which was aggravated by the loss of export earnings from its erstwhile province of East Bengal. In these circumstances his politically attractive slogan of *roti, kapra aur makan* was in a shambles and resulted in frustrating the expectations he had aroused. His move to nationalize big business angered a powerful element in Pakistan politics without giving him any compensating political benefits. The improvement of relations with India, never a popular subject in Pakistan, lost whatever urgency it might have had a couple of years earlier.

The sudden fourfold increase in oil prices in 1973, less than a year after the Simla Conference, was not only a major economic event; it was also a most significant political development whose impact on Indo-Pak relations has hardly been noticed. The oil-producing countries suddenly acquired tremendous political clout; they became rich overnight, so rich indeed that some of them did not know what to do with their new-found wealth. This was particularly true of Saudi Arabia and the Gulf countries. Burgeoning oil revenues triggered an investment boom in West Asia, which created vast opportunities for trade and employment. Western bankers and investors were falling over one another, soliciting opportunities for the investment of oil revenues. The OPEC countries led the demand for a new international economic order in the United Nations, where their group dominated the counsels of the developing countries. Media commentators talked about a new 'Arab Century'. The term may have been a journalistic exaggeration, but oil revenues did invigorate Islam as a political force and triggered Islamic revivalism. Vast funds became available for the furtherance of what were called 'Islamic causes'. Little Gadaffi was so flush with money that he was prepared to finance the makers of an 'Islamic bomb'.

In this abruptly changed environment Bhutto saw new opportunities for Pakistan's economy and for a new geo-political strategy. These were sharply incompatible with the major premises on which the Simla understanding was based. Looking away from the subcontinent, Bhutto saw newly-emerging rich Muslim countries which would, besides compensating Pakistan for the loss of the Bangladesh trade, provide vast job opportunities for its nationals and significantly add to its foreign-exchange reserves. These new circumstances and opportunities obviated the need for better economic relations with India. Political and strategic co-operation with West Asian countries would, Bhutto felt, restore Pakistan's weight and stature *vis-à-vis* India.

The explosion of an atomic device by India in May 1974 provided him with added justification for accelerating his own nuclear arms programme and fuelled his ambition to win for Pakistan a leadership role in the Islamic world. Being a poor country it did not stand much chance against cash rich countries like Iran and Saudi Arabia. But Bhutto felt that Pakistan would emerge as a leader of the Islamic world if it was sole possessor of an 'Islamic bomb'. The Shah of Iran made disdainful remarks about Bhutto's 'ambitiousness' and his 'psychological kinks' to me during a mission to Iran in November 1976.

Islamic revivalism and fundamentalism created conditions which further undermined the Simla understanding on the Kashmir question. For Islamists, Kashmir could not be kept outside the list of Islamic causes despite the return of Sheikh Abdullah to the Indian mainstream and a free and fair election—which he won. The Jamat-i-Islami was able to set up about 600 *madrasas* in Kashmir with the help of Saudi and Gulf money. These new institutions were staffed with trained cadres of the Jamat from UP and Bihar, whose goal was to produce a new generation of Kashmiri Muslims who would forsake the more tolerant version of their forefathers' religion and minimize attachment to a Kashmir identity. Sure of the success of his efforts, the Amir of the Jamat-i-Islami of Kashmir told an Indian journalist in 1973: 'we will produce a generation of new Muslims in Kashmir in fifteen years.'

Bhutto himself came under pressure from the Jamat in Pakistan. Much against his inclination, he was forced to declare the Ahmeddiya community 'non-Muslim'. In these circumstances he was not going to prevent the flow of funds to Kashmir for the Islamic cause even if he so wished, which of course is very doubtful. With the arrival of Zia, Islamism became the official ideology of Pakistan, and gradually but steadily Indo-Pak relations returned to their old adversarial pattern.

Under Benazir, these relations deteriorated further. India and Pakistan would have been at war again but for the nuclear stand-off between them. Nothing could have been further from the minds of Indian negotiators at Simla than the present state of Indo-Pak relations. In that respect, it can be said that they failed to craft a viable and binding agreement which could be a basis for the durable peace they wanted.

But is that a fair judgement? Even if the Simla understanding had been implemented, would it have prevented Pakistan from doing in Kashmir what it has been doing there for the past eight years? A recognized international border in Punjab did not inhibit it from stoking the fires of insurgency there, or earlier in Mizoram. In retrospect, I am inclined to say that Simla has turned out to be another Tashkent, a temporary breathing space in the never-ending strife between the two major powers created by the partition of the subcontinent. The strife is deep-rooted because Pakistan has not been able to erase its birthmark, which makes it see itself as being in opposition to India and not as its neighbour. In the words of Josef Korbel, a member of the United Nations commission on India and Pakistan (and, incidentally, father of the current US secretary of state, Madeleine Albright), 'the real cause of all the bitterness and bloodshed, all the venomed speech, the recalcitrance and the suspicion that have characterized the Kashmir dispute is the uncompromising and perhaps uncompromisable struggle of two ways of life, two spiritual attitudes that find themselves locked

in deadly conflict, a conflict in which Kashmir has become both symbol and battleground.'[8]

I believe this conflict will continue until Pakistan decides to change
its ideological moorings, until it learns to live at least in a state of peaceful coexistence with India, if not one of friendship and co-operation.
That is the minimum necessary condition for building a structure of
durable peace in the subcontinent. Without this, development and
progress in relations between these countries cannot take place. The
Indian negotiators at Simla were aware of this truth but took a chance
with Bhutto. In retrospect, that gamble proved unrealistic.

[8] *Danger in Kashmir* (Princeton: Princeton University Press, 1965), p. 25.

CHAPTER TEN

The Emergency: How It Came About

The emergency that was declared in the early hours of 26 June 1975 was a severe setback in the political evolution of India. Under the new dispensation the rule of law was drastically abridged: citizens were deprived of their fundamental rights; freedom of the press was curbed through strict censorship; political dissent was suppressed through arrests and harsh police measures; and officialdom assumed arbitrary powers which it exercised without being accountable. In sum, these events changed the basic relationship between the citizen and the state and indeed threatened to change the character of the Indian state itself.

Existing accounts of the Emergency attribute all these developments to the flawed personality of Indira Gandhi. She was a forceful person, no doubt, but shifting circumstances and fickle public opinion enlarged both her virtues and her flaws. Her style of leadership also led to vast exaggerations of her role in shaping major events in the country over this period. After she defeated the entrenched leadership of her party in 1969, many thought she would transform Indian society through some personal magic. At the successful end of the war in 1971 she was hailed by Atal Behari Vajpayee as the incarnation of the goddess Durga. Only three years later Jayaprakash Narayan considered her the cause of everything that had gone wrong in Indian public life.

What made people react to Indira Gandhi in such contradictory ways is a fascinating subject for study but will not detain us here. Her personality certainly played a part in the Emergency, but the basic changes that took place at this time could not have been brought about by a single temperamental individual, however powerful. This is not to justify or whitewash her role in bringing about the tragedy that was the Emergency, nor to minimize its adverse consequences—which continue to bedevil our political life—but to insist that the Emergency had deeper causes than the villainy of one person or even one family. These we need to explore. We also need to examine the actions of those who have been elevated to the status of heroes in the post-Emergency period—in a manner that distorts the picture of an important phase in the history of Indian democracy.

My purpose here is (a) to discover the political and social causes of the Emergency, and (b) to take a critical look at the mythology that has been built around it. My argument is that the Emergency was a systemic failure and its causes must be sought in the political system as it had evolved, and in its response to adverse economic situations. The role of individuals also becomes clearer in my analysis when seen in the context of the system in which they were operating, rather than in terms of abstract ideas. Thus, to look for causes that led to the breakdown of the democratic system in 1975 we have to go beyond the events of the fortnight that began with the judgement of the Allahabad High Court which set aside Indira Gandhi's election in 1971 to the Lok Sabha on grounds of electoral malpractice. We need to explore the widening gap between the form and substance of democracy as it has operated in India. I argue that if by 'emergency' is meant an abridgement of the rule of law which is the governing principle of a democracy, then in India the democratic substance started deviating from the form long before 26 June 1975. The process was so gradual that it went unnoticed until the dramatic turn of events on 26 June 1975 forced it on the national consciousness.

Every political system needs a corresponding political culture in order to work. The formal structures of democratic institutions can easily be

Mrs Gandhi, before addressing secretaries to government, soon
after the declaration of 'Emergency'

imported and set up without much difficulty, but the culture that will
reflect their true spirit and ensure their smooth functioning has to
evolve internally. The transplantation of institutions from one environment to another involves a process of adaptation in which success is
not guaranteed. The hiatus between newly established institutions,
and inherited attitudes and behaviour, has been described succinctly
by the famous British statesman Lord Balfour:

Constitutions are easily copied, temperaments are not; it matters little what
other gifts a people may possess if they are wanting in those which, from this
point of view, are of most importance. If, for example, they have no capacity
for grading their loyalties as well as being moved by them; if they have no natural inclination to liberty and no natural respect for law; if they lack good humour and tolerate foul play; if they know not how to compromise or when; if
they have not that distrust of extreme conclusions which is sometimes misdes-
cribed as want of logic; if corruption does not repel them; and if their divisions

tend to be either too numerous or too profound, the successful working of British institutions may be difficult or impossible.[1]

This is perhaps an ethnocentric view, according to which democracy cannot prosper outside the Anglo-Saxon world. Of course democracy has prospered elsewhere, having taken strong root in countries like Germany and Japan which were earlier considered beyond redemption. While strict correlations between racial traits and democratic temper and behaviour are untenable, it must be admitted that the political culture of a country embodies and reflects its own values, beliefs and emotions, and that these may not be conducive to the proper functioning of the institutions it has imported. The Indian constitution-makers were not unaware of these problems. While introducing the draft constitution, B.R. Ambedkar told the constituent assembly candidly: 'Constitutional morality is not a natural instinct. It has to be cultivated. Democracy in India is only a top dressing on Indian soil, which is essentially undemocratic.'

Ambedkar was aware that the wholesale import into India of democratic institutions from what is called the Westminster model—which had evolved in its country of origin over several centuries—was going to be problematic. The British system of governance had emerged in a country that had passed through a renaissance, a reformation, and an industrial revolution which had produced a large and educated middle class. It was a polity whose electoral base was extended by gradual enlargement of the suffrage through successive reform bills spread over most of the nineteenth century, with 'freedom broaden[ing] slowly down from precedent to precedent.'

India, on the other hand, incorporated the full-blown British parliamentary system in a single step, after the brief and intermittent experience of running municipalities and provincial legislatures based on restricted franchise and limited powers under British surveillance. The Indian decision to work a parliamentary democracy was always going to be a huge challenge. Anthony Eden, writing about the Indian democratic experiment in his memoirs, says: 'Of all the experiments

[1] Introduction to *The English Constitution* (Oxford: World's Classics Edition), 1928.

in government which have been attempted since the beginning of time, I believe that this Indian venture in parliamentary government is the most exciting. A vast sub-continent is attempting to apply to its tens and hundreds of millions of people a system of free democracy which has been slowly evolved over the centuries in this little island.'

Independent India's founding fathers laid out a constitutional framework and a set of guiding principles of state policy on which society was to be organized in free India. This set of rules would have been ambitious even for more economically developed and socially homogeneous countries. Contrary to historical experience, India endeavored to initiate the process of capital accumulation necessary for its economic transformation on the basis of universal adult suffrage. A country with a low level of development and a meagre rate of savings was promised social justice as well as economic growth. A country with deep-seated religious traditions and mores adopted secularism as its state policy. A country where the individual is submerged in his family and his community adopted a libertarian philosophy which has operational meaning only where the individual is the decision-maker in private and public life. When all this and more of a similar nature is added up, it amounts to something very ambitious indeed.

The founding fathers were, generally speaking, unconscious of their ambitions. This is illustrated by the simple faith they had in the efficacy of what they advocated. For instance, Alladi Krishnaswami Ayyar, one of the framers of our constitution, said: 'The Assembly had adopted the principle of adult franchise with an abundant faith in the common man and the ultimate success of democratic rule, and in the full belief that the introduction of democratic government on the basis of adult suffrage will bring enlightenment and promote the well being, the standard of life, the comfort, and the decent living of the common man.'

India had little choice in the matter. The constitution of India was the end product of the freedom struggle, which was a mass movement spread over several decades. The masses who were mobilized to wrest independence from alien rulers expected participation in the governance of free India through universal adult franchise; they could not be denied, in Jawaharlal Nehru's phrase, the 'glow of freedom'. It must also be recognized that in the aftermath of Partition, Indian political leadership naturally gave a very high priority to the unity of the country which, it rightly felt, could be maintained only through the democratic political process. But the fact that constitutional parliamentary democracy was more or less inevitable and necessary for India did not mean that it would run smoothly. Democracy means the rule of law, but the freedom movement that determined the substance of India's constitution had also developed its own forms of protest and agitation—which were based on defiance of law and rejection of governmental authority. To switch over from the defiance of law to its acceptance has not proved as easy a task as was believed in the early days of independence. And yet the Indian political leadership went about it in a mechanical way and showed little awareness of the need for social discipline to achieve the objectives they had set for the country. Nehru described the entire enterprise rather sportingly as an 'adventure of democracy'. His ambivalence in the matter of social discipline is obvious in his reply to a question put to him in Sweden: 'Have you any trouble with the remains of the Satyagraha Technique you adopted to gain independence?' Nehru answered:

It is a very interesting but rather intricate question. First of all, a country which for a whole generation practised a certain technique of opposition to the government, it is not easy to shift over to make people think differently. It may be their own government, but people still have the habit of thinking of opposing the government. Because for a whole generation they thought so. Secondly, they are apt to adopt that technique, not rightly I think, but some variation of it, just to press on some complaint or something, which is sometimes apt to be a nuisance.

It is possible that Nehru and his colleagues thought that defiance of the law was a habit of the older generation and would not be passed on to their children, born in freedom. Looking at India, they had some reason for optimism: they were aware that the institutions and policies that had crystallized due to their labour had given India a working democracy, political stability, and a measure of economic success unknown at that time anywhere else in the Third World. Indeed India in the first decade of its independence was looked upon by many in the Western world as a new democratic model for economic development and social change and was presented to other developing countries as an alternative to the Chinese model. This seemingly easy success of the Indian enterprise under Nehru retarded the realization that in the long term a working democracy would have to depend on the continuing viability of its institutional infrastructure.

Against this background, it becomes easier to recognize the complacence of India's political leadership to the more serious challenges that democracy was later to face. Their laxness in relation to social indiscipline and disruptive political practice made it difficult for their successors to reverse the process. What is worse, these practices developed their own momentum and legitimacy. Montesquieu noted the nature of a political dynamic in his observation that, 'in the birth of societies, it is leaders of republics who create the institutions; afterwards it is the institutions that form the leaders of the republics.' The successors of the founders of our republic are creatures of the permissive political culture that they grew within.

Consequently, political culture in India has increasingly deviated from the norms of constitutional democracy over its evolution. Agitation, protest and the mobilization of public opinion on disputed issues have become more widespread than in the British period. Protests and disagreements are now conducted as if the government is not elected but imposed. Insurrectionary methods are preferred to democratic mechanisms for the management of conflict. Indeed, pre-independence methods of protest have been invested with much greater potential for disruption and turmoil. New weapons like *gherao, bandh, rail roko* and *rasta roko* have been added to the earlier arsenal. Any dialogue between the centre and the states—for example over a higher procurement price of foodgrains, or for the creation of a development project—are now less a matter of marshalling the relevant facts and arguments and more a demonstration of the ability to disrupt normal life and inflict damage on life and property. Former cabinet ministers lead protest processions in defiance of the law, get arrested, and are released as a matter of routine. This behaviour gives them political advantage even as they hold the law in contempt. A former president of the republic sat in a *dharna* in front of the Public Services Commission to protest against a minor policy matter. State governments sponsor *bandhs* to protest against the central government and the latter, in turn, dismisses state governments to gain an advantage for its own party. Demonstrations and the shouting of slogans are frequent even in parliament and state legislatures, where chosen representative of the people are expected to argue, debate and consider policies.

Part of the explanation for this phenomenon is that it is a carry-over from pre-independence techniques of protest against British rule. Ambedkar, one of the architects of the Indian constitution, as we saw earlier, had foreseen some of these possibilities. Winding up the debate on the draft constitution, he said:

if we wish to maintain democracy not merely in form, but also in fact, what should we do? The first thing in my judgement we must do is to hold fast to constitutional methods of achieving our social and economic objectives. . . . It means that we must abandon the method of civil disobedience, non-co-operation and satyagraha. When there was no way left for achieving economic and social objectives, there was a great deal of justification for unconstitutional methods. But where constitutional methods are open, there can be no justification for these unconstitutional methods. These methods are nothing but the Grammar of Anarchy and the sooner they are abandoned, the better for us.[2]

But Ambedkar's wise words fell on deaf ears. Some thought that he was merely attacking his old adversary, Gandhi, and nobody took his warning seriously. In the event the pre-independence methods of protest were not only allowed but also legitimized by the state's reluctance to enforce the laws enacted by it. The disobedience of law was given a political colour and interpretation. It not only carried no penalties, on the contrary it had an almost Gandhian moral aura.

The opportunities for disobedience of the law increased as the state widened its sphere of activities and, therefore, of its authority. Intellectuals, who were overwhelmingly of a radical orientation, supported

[2] Constituent Assembly Debates, Official Report, vol. XI. Reprinted by the Lok Sabha Secretariat, New Delhi, p. 978 (date of publication not given).

this tendency to disregard the law on political grounds and in fact made it a part of 'political correctness'. Gunnar Myrdal, a social democrat himself, analysed this problem in the early 1960s and was highly critical of the Indian state for its reluctance to enforce its own laws. He called it a 'soft state', which he defined as one 'where policies decided are often not enforced, if they are decided at all,' and where 'the authorities, even when framing policies, are reluctant to place obligations on people.' He bemoaned the fact that this reluctance is not only excused, it is also idealized.

Under successive regimes this soft state became softer. The leadership that took over from the founders of the republic did not have the political, moral or intellectual stature to evolve a political culture that was less permissive. Nehru had not made their task easier. He had set a precedent for the use of coercive and confrontationist tactics by permitting the overthrow of an elected government in Kerala in 1959. After his departure from the political scene, the use of such tactics to gain or retain power became more frequent and more blatant. Confrontation followed by concession gradually became the normal pattern of politics, especially of the so-called radical variety.

The field of operation for such politics widened further for two main reasons. One, the successive elections and five-year plans politicized the hitherto quiescent communities of backward castes, dalits and adivasis. Two, the breakdown of single-party dominance converted sectional and parochial interests, which were earlier encompassed within the Congress Party, into separate and independent political entities. While jockeying for power they formed shifting and unstable coalitions—as witnessed in several north Indian states between 1967 and 1972. The unbridled and unprincipled quest for power resulted in a series of revolving-door governments. As soon as a government was formed, those who were left out started agitations to bring it down. In Bihar, for instance, in the short period of fourteen months between March 1967 and May 1968, as many as four governments came and went out of office.

After the split in the Congress Party in 1969, the danger of political fragmentation and instability at the centre became evident as well. This was the time when doubts about the viability of a parliamentary system in India arose in many minds. A presidential system for a stable central government was mooted by several public men. Others felt that local issues should be separated from national issues for voters' attention and suggested that state elections be sequestered from those for the Lok Sabha. The mid-term elections of 1971 lent some credence to this latter suggestion, though there were other more powerful factors responsible for the result. The Congress success in the 1971 elections was on account of the radical and populist image projected by Indira Gandhi after the nationalization of banks. The result of the elections in the states in the following year was a gift of victory in the Bangladesh war; they were truly khaki elections. These results did deliver an effective government at the centre, but the magnitude of Congress victories had an unsettling effect on the parties and their political attitudes.

The party system was now tilted overwhelmingly in favour of the Congress, leaving opposition parties emasculated and splintered. The unchallenged leadership of Indira Gandhi gave her an exaggerated sense of power. She now began to feel that she could make the Congress Party an instrument of her own will. Having suffered at the hands of powerful bosses in the states earlier, she wanted party leaders in the states to be people entirely of her own choice who would carry out the party programme. Thus began the era of what were derisively called nominated chief ministers who owed their ascension to the wishes of her high command rather than to their own strength in the state legislative party. This had a demoralizing effect on the party. The impressive electoral victory of the Congress Party in 1971 had indeed a profound effect on its ideological outlook. The repetition of populist slogans became for Congressmen a substitute for policies, quite regardless of achievements on the ground. Congressmen began to depend on Indira Gandhi's charisma rather than on their own work in the constituencies. So long as her capacity as a vote-catcher remained unimpaired, they were satisfied with the world around them.

The attempt of the opposition parties to forge an alliance before the election on the plank of 'Indira Hatao' had failed. The possibility of their combining to cobble together a much needed viable opposition seemed remote because of the contradictory ideologies and the clash of personal interests among their leaders. With little hope of gaining power in normal circumstances, they looked for short cuts to achieve their goals. They waited for an opportunity to regain influence and striking power. Since the Indian economy, vulnerable as it is to shocks, can always provide opportunities for agitation and confrontation, they did not have long to wait.

Hardly had the government taken office in 1971 when it was faced with the Bangladesh crisis, which put the economy under heavy strain on account of the ten million refugees. This was followed by war with Pakistan and the termination of US aid. The economy deteriorated further because of the failure of the summer and winter rains in 1972–3, which resulted in a sharp decline in agricultural production; foodgrain output came down by 8 per cent. When OPEC raised oil prices fourfold overnight in 1973, a bad situation became a crisis: India's imports bill suddenly increased by a billion dollars. The oil price hike also caused an across-the-board increase in import prices, especially of food and fertilizers. The result of all these events, over which the government had no control, was an unprecedented bout of inflation. The price level rose by 23 per cent in 1973 and escalated to about 30 per cent by the middle of 1974.

The economy had become too fragile to withstand these setbacks without a reorientation of some basic policies. The preceding eight years—that is, the three years of plan holiday plus the Fourth Plan period—had shown no improvement in its performance; in fact the rate of growth of national income had decreased. So had industrial investment, particularly in the sectors producing basic and capital goods. Not only was economic growth not picking up, the basis of future growth was getting eroded. An economy which had been suffering from low growth had virtually nothing to cushion the sudden deterioration in the balance-of-payments situation caused by OPEC.

To save the country from financial bankruptcy, to sustain the imports of oil, fertilizers, and other essential items, and to prevent unacceptable shortages of food supplies, this crisis had to be met. But this could not be managed without the adoption of several unpopular measures. Besides going to the International Monetary Fund, the World Bank, and donor countries for more aid, India's rigid controls and licensing needed to be loosened to increase production and promote exports. Large business houses had to be permitted to expand production, which they had not been free to do before the crisis. To check inflation the government had to take steps not only to increase the supply of goods, but also to restrain the demand for them. For this purpose all wage increases and half of the additional dearness allowance of salaried employees were frozen and converted into compulsory deposits. These measures were criticized as anti-working class, even though a ceiling was imposed on all dividends paid·by private companies, and tax payers with an income of more than Rs 15,000 were required to put an additional four to eight per cent of their income into compulsory deposits.

All these steps went against the earlier policy pronouncements of the government, which aimed at less dependence on foreign aid, the decentralization of economic power, the promotion of distributive justice through nationalization, an expansion of the public sector, and a stricter regulation of the private sector. The government thus became vulnerable to criticism for ideological retreat. Mrs Gandhi found herself in a difficult situation as she was now subjected to contrary pulls from her professional advisers and her party colleagues. Her dilemma in this regard was highlighted dramatically when the government took over the wholesale trade in wheat and abandoned it precipitately when it ran into problems that had been anticipated. The proposal had been strongly opposed by B.S. Minhas, an economist member of the Planning Commission and her own office, but since it was even more strongly supported by the party leadership it had gone through. The fiasco of the wheat trade takeover brought out clearly the contradictions arising out of the dual role of a prime minister as head of an administration grappling with harsh economic realities on the ground, and as leader of a ruling party saddled with excessive ideological baggage. But for these difficulties, the crisis could have been turned into an opportunity for more basic reform of the economy. With politics in command the exercise for reform could not go beyond the management of immediate crisis.

The leftists in the ruling party had developed clever techniques to keep Mrs Gandhi committed to their ideological line. Manipulating the press was one such technique. The following episode will serve as an illustration. In late September 1973 when, on the initiative of the prime minister's office, a task force was being set up to suggest ways and means of handling the economic crisis, I submitted a note to Mrs Gandhi which spelt out the policies that the task force might consider. In view of the political sensitivity of some of the policies suggested, she showed it to some of her political colleagues. One of the more radical among them got a highly distorted and colourful version of it published in *The Times of India*. The authorship of the note was jointly attributed to me, to L.K. Jha (governor of Kashmir), and to B.K. Nehru (high commissioner in London). Since Jha and Nehru were supposed to be pro-American, their collaboration was expected to discredit the note. 'The Jha–Nehru–Dhar paper argues that the benefits India could reap in the form of investment, technology and exports, justifies inviting multinational giants to enter the Indian market in selected fields. This would involve a reversal of the existing policy, which inhibits the inflow of foreign capital,' the newspaper reported in bold letters. This embarrassed Mrs Gandhi so much that she decided to contradict the story herself.

In an insidious move to inhibit me from making suggestions which were not to the liking of leftists, *The Patriot* made the following comment at the suggestion of the same person who had briefed *The Times of India* earlier:

The recent attempt to implicate Prime Minister's secretary P.N. Dhar's name with the moves to influence the government to reverse its economic policies is regarded in informed circles as deliberate mischief.

Stories were circulated that Mr Dhar had joined former Indian envoys to the United States, L.K. Jha and B.K. Nehru in submitting a note to the Union Cabinet pleading for liberalization of policies towards multinational corporations and Indian big business.

While the official contradiction already issued by the government has revealed that this story was a complete fabrication, informed sources regard the timing of this tirade as significant.

These sources do not consider it a mere coincidence that the canard about Mr Dhar should have been spread at a time when he was engaged in negotiating an important agreement with the Soviet leaders in Moscow and was scheduled to hold high-level talks about strengthening of economic ties between the two countries.

The reference to my visit to Moscow was a highly exaggerated description of my mission, which was no more than the negotiation of terms on which the Soviets were to give us a loan of two million tonnes of wheat.

In these circumstances, economic policies hovered between past political commitments and new economic compulsions, between meeting the demands of radical ideologues on the one hand and a pragmatic response to the realities on the other. It was in this atmosphere of ideological incoherence that the government had to manage the most serious economic crisis faced by any Indian government.

The unprecedented increase in prices and the severe shortage of essential goods were a bitter disappointment to the people, since the

With M. Kuzmin, first minister of foreign trade, after signing
an agreement on wheat and corn with the USSR,
October 1973

recent elections had roused expectations for a better life. These were propitious circumstances for political opponents to assail the government. The assaults came thick and fast, causing widespread political turmoil. For three years the country was rocked by violence, student agitations, strikes, *gheraos*, *bandhs*, civil strife, calls for revolt and finally for revolution. It was altogether the most challenging period in the governance of the country. From this stormy period I highlight two episodes which triggered the chain of events that led to the Emergency of 1975—namely the railway strike of 1974 and the political movement of 1974–5 associated with Jayaprakash Narayan (JP).

Before describing the nature of the railway strike of 1974, a few observations on the trade union movement in India are necessary by way of background. This movement began as an offshoot of the broader freedom struggle and has ever since remained part of the country's political system, not as an independent factor but as a splintered appendage of political parties. All major political parties have their trade unions and their political rivalries are reflected in trade-union rivalries. Leadership of the trade unions has continued to be provided by professional politicians from the urban middle class. With the diversification of political parties and the emergence of competitive populism, the leadership of the trade unions has followed a similar pattern. About 20 to 30 per cent of industrial disputes in the 25 years between 1950 and 1975 were due to inter-union rivalries. To keep their following intact, even moderate trade-union leaders had to maintain a certain level of militancy and give calls for strikes, leading to a kind of competition over militancy among rival leaders.

Another political dimension of the trade-union movement in India is the role of government in trade-union matters. To secure industrial peace in the interests of the war effort, the British government had, during World War II, assigned to itself the power to intervene in industrial disputes as a conciliator or arbiter. After independence the government tried to introduce legislation which would reduce government intervention in industrial disputes and let labour and management resolve their conflicts through a system of collective bargaining, as is the practice in industrial countries. The trade unions opposed the government's efforts. The Congress Party's own trade-union associate, the Indian National Trade Union Congress, was also against such legislation. Union leaders favoured government intervention because they knew they could secure from the government and its agencies (e.g. the labour department) more than what they could from management.

The government is not only the largest employer in the country, it also looks upon itself as custodian of the interests of labour. It has therefore tried to be a model employer. In this attempt it has enacted legislation which is extraordinary in its disregard for the economic viability of the business enterprises it owns. P.C. Mahalanobis, who formulated the early strategy for India's economic development, saw the deleterious effects of such laws and warned against them: 'Our labour laws are probably the most highly protective of labour interest—in the narrowest sense—in the whole world. There is practically no link between output and remuneration and hiring and firing are highly restricted. It is extremely difficult to maintain our economic level of productivity, or to improve productivity.' Labour legislation, which worried Mahalanobis, has implicitly condoned coercive union practices, especially among the better-paid white-collar workers, where the militant leadership of unions has prevented the emergence of a stable system of industrial relations. This, in turn, has directly hit increases in productivity. Indirectly, it has induced employers in industry and agriculture to substitute capital for labour wherever they can, and thereby retarded the growth of employment—the most effective instrument of poverty alleviation. As against unionized labour, there is a very large and increasing pool of exploited workers in the so-called informal sector which is neglected by the union leadership as well as by the state. The interests of unionized labour have thus become a special interest, above the interests of the working class as a whole.

The advocates of this special interest project every labour agitation as a consequence of economic distress, and the public often perceives these agitations as such. With that psychological and political advantage on their side, labour leaders believed that if sufficient pressure were mounted and threatening attitudes adopted, their demands would be met, which is often what happened. Many such demands were conceded by the government from time to time, especially to white-collar employees of nationalized banks and the Life Insurance Corporation. Over-generous wage settlements distorted the general wage structure of the country and became the goal of less favoured employees in other enterprises. With such a history of government policies, the railway strike of 1974 was an event waiting to happen.

The Indian Railway system is the country's largest public-sector undertaking. It employed about 1.4 million people in 1974, i.e. ten per cent of the total employed in the public sector and seven per cent in the entire organized sector. Apart from its size, the railways form the arteries of the body economic. Therefore, anything happening in the railways, either by way of wage increases or work stoppages, is bound to have serious repercussions on the whole economy. In 1974–5 the average earnings per employee in the railways were double the income of the average standard family of three. Although the real incomes of organized workers, particularly in the public sector, were better protected against inflation than those of other fixed-income earners, railwaymen had a grievance when they compared themselves with employees in some public-sector undertakings who were more generously treated. Besides, the prevailing atmosphere of political turbulence and industrial strife had not left them unaffected. Apart from these general reasons, there were several specific reasons that turned the railway strike into a political storm.

During the days of political fragmentation following the 1967 general elections, competition among political parties extended to the trade unions. In the railways, besides the two recognized national unions—

the All India Railwaymen's Federation (AIRF) affiliated to the Socialist Party, and the National Federation of Indian Railwaymen (NFIR)
dominated by the Congress—about 200 separate unions of different
categories of railwaymen had cropped up through the efforts of the
CPI, the CPM, and the Jan Sangh. The competition for influence
among railwaymen took the form of rivals organizing strikes in their
respective zones, and by particular categories of workers, to weaken the
two recognized national unions.

This was a new phase of militant unionism in the railways—a phase
of go-slows, work-to-rule, wild-cat strikes, and disregard of legal norms:
strike leaders often operated underground. The deterioration of the
economic situation and a sharp increase in prices in 1973 and 1974 added to the militancy. The first major event of this new phase of militancy took place in August 1973 when the loco running staff, having
organized a union of their own (All India Loco Running Association),
went on an illegal wild-cat strike. This was a psychological moment for
the aggressive union in its confrontation with the government. L.N.
Mishra, the railways minister, encouraged by Raghunatha Reddy, the
labour minister, caved in and accepted the demands of the loco men.
Mishra wanted to buy peace at any cost and Reddy, a Left radical,
wanted to extend the control of his like-minded radical colleagues
within the unions.

The consequences of surrender to the loco men were far reaching.
The national unions of railwaymen responded to the new situation
created by the success of the loco men by radicalizing their own leadership. Peter Alvares, the moderate leader of the AIRF, was replaced
by George Fernandes in November 1973. Before taking over the leadership, Fernandes had declared openly, in October, in an address to the
National Railwaymen's Union, that his aim was to organize a strike
which 'could change the whole history of India and bring down Indira
Gandhi's government at any time by paralyzing railway transport to
a dead stop.'

The change of leadership proved a turning point in the affairs of the
railway's trade unions. Fernandes proved a forceful personality, an indefatigable organizer, a demagogue who could inflame audiences with

his fist-in-the-air oratory, and a political adventurer in need of a constituency. The circumstances—an adverse economic situation and an organized force of two million restive workers—suited his purpose admirably. He set to work energetically. In March 1974, at a meeting of the recognized and unrecognized unions and associations of railwaymen, a central forum called the National Coordination Committee for Railwaymen's Struggle (NCCRS) was created and Fernandes made its convenor. Having secured a commanding position over the railway trade unions, he and his colleagues set out to launch the first national political challenge by a trade union to the central government since independence.

The NCCRS formulated a charter of demands which, among other things, included the revaluation and regradation of jobs in the railways, and pending that, immediate parity in wages with those of workers in central undertakings such as HMT, BHEL and HSL; bonus at the rate of one month's wages for the years 1971–2 and 1972–3; the decasualization of all casual employees—estimated to number three lakhs—and their confirmation in service, with all benefits given to them retrospectively. Acceptance of these demands by the railways board would have cost Rs 450 crore. Further, the government would have had to accept similar demands by central government employees who had given calls for a strike, and that concession would have cost an additional 900 crores. Similar demands from other sectors would then have followed as there was going to be a 'Bharat Bandh', a solidarity strike in sympathy with the railwaymen.

With railway finances in a parlous state and the government incurring large deficits, there was no way it could cope with such demands without adding fuel to the raging inflation. The opposition parties seized upon the situation as yet another opportunity to weaken the government. Two weeks before the strike began on 8 May, they were attacking the government for its failure to check the rise in prices—and when the strike started they were urging it to concede the railwaymen's demands even though they knew that this would raise the rate of inflation from 2.5 per cent a month to 2.5 per cent a week. Encouraged by political support, George Fernandes thundered that there would be no peace in the railways without a negotiated settlement, which however he was trying hard to prevent. In a speech meant to mobilize railwaymen for the strike he said:

Realize the strength which you possess. Seven days strike of the Indian Railways—every thermal station in the country would close down. A ten days' strike of the Indian Railways—every steel mill in India would close down and the industries in the country would come to a halt for the next twelve months. If once the steel mill furnace is switched off, it takes nine months to refire. A fifteen days' strike in the Indian Railways—the country will starve.[3]

This was a threat of sabotage and the government knew it was not an idle threat. There was information on the railwaymen's plans to derail essential goods-train services, including foodgrain supplies to deficit areas. Mughalsarai, the largest railway marshalling yard in Asia, was to be converted into a graveyard of trains. It was clear to the government that the strike was politically motivated and was planned to paralyse the country. With its back to the wall, the government had to defend the state and assert its right to govern.

It had to resist the strike, which it did successfully. The strike was called off after twenty days, on the morning of 28 May 1974. The government's demonstration of its will to resist demoralized the workers and led to dissensions among the constituents of the National Coordination Committee. The CPI-dominated AITUC gave a call for the withdrawal of the strike. This, along with the appeal of President Giri, a former trade-union leader of railwaymen, to call off the strike gave the leaders a face-saving opportunity to formally end a movement which had already started fizzling out. The government had succeeded, but the effort required was colossal and not without financial and political costs. The government had to adopt harsh measures to handle the situation. It had to invoke the Defence of India Rules, which were formally still in operation under the Emergency proclamation of the 1971 war, to declare the strike illegal. It had to mobilize the territorial army to maintain the safety of railway tracks; it had to arrest under the Maintenance of Internal Security Act leaders and workers who were likely to go underground; it had to maintain

[3] *The Hindu* (Madras), 30 March 1974.

skeleton passenger services and essential services with help from the security forces.

The uncharacteristic firmness of the government surprised everybody. Radicals at home and liberals abroad criticized the government for breaking the strike, the former because they were in sympathy with the political character of the strike and the latter because of their misperception that it was a normal dispute between workers and management—of the kind with which they were familiar in their own countries. Perhaps the most pertinent comment on the strike was made by *The Times of India* in its lead editorial on 20 May under the title 'Firmness Pays':

Tactics adopted by the motley group of political parties were well beyond the ambit of legitimate trade-union activity. In fact their main aim was to wreck the economy and paralyse the administration. This is why they pitched their demands so high and displayed so little interest in negotiating a settlement. They had, perhaps, calculated that by raising false hopes among railwaymen and mobilizing many key categories of staff, they would be able to bring all rail services to a halt and create economic chaos. Indeed in the past, some of them had succeeded in holding the authorities to ransom by lightning strikes, go-slows, *gheraos* or even sabotage in certain areas.

This was the role of the trade-union leadership that led the railway strike during the troubled days of 1974. At the same time, it would be unfair to lay the entire blame at their door. Permissive legislation, indulgent interpretations of the law by the judiciary, and politicking by ruling parties in trade-union affairs were all responsible for turning unionized labour, which is a small fraction of the country's total workforce, into the Frankenstein that it became. And though the government in 1974 faced up to the militant leadership of the railway unions, it was not because of any basic change in its thinking about the appropriate role of trade unions in a democracy; it was because the government had no choice in the matter. With the economy in such dire straits, it simply could not afford to appease the strikers, which it would otherwise have done, regardless of how much they might have deviated from trade-union norms.

The strike may have been a failure from the railwaymen's point of view; it was a success for the opposition parties. It gave them an opportunity to continue, despite their deep ideological differences, to weaken the government. The strike turned out to be a dress rehearsal for similar joint action when new opportunities were unfolded by the Nav Nirman in Gujarat, and by JP's Sampurna Kranti.

According to JP, it was the success of the Nav Nirman movement, led by the Gujarat students, that inspired him to launch his movement. It is therefore necessary to examine the nature and achievements of that movement first.

Earlier, I have outlined the difficult food situation in the country in the wake of the 1972 drought. In Gujarat the situation became much worse because the drought was followed by a poor kharif crop which resulted in a sharp increase in the prices of wheat, jawar, bajra and other essential commodities. Students were the first organized group to protest against rising food prices, the spark being lit by students of L.D. Engineering College, Ahmedabad, when they protested against increased mess charges. This was the small beginning of a movement which brought down the Gujarat government and much else in the country.

Sensing an opportunity for political gains by exploiting genuine hardship, opposition parties, particularly the Bharatiya Jan Sangh (BJS) and the Congress(O), supported the students' agitation against the government's failure to hold the price line and encouraged them to form a 'Nav Nirman Samiti' to spearhead the movement. At the same time, these parties cynically organized opposition to the procurement levy of foodgrains, which would have increased supplies available to the government for distribution. As the student agitations spread to other towns in Gujarat, they became more violent, leading to police firings in which 85 people were killed. The BJS, Congress(O), CPI(M), SP and others now gave calls for *bandhs* and organized *dharnas*. With the increase in the tempo of the agitations, the demands of the opposition leaders also escalated, culminating in a demand for the resignation of the ministry.

There were charges of corruption against Chimanbhai Patel, the chief minister. Among his other failures, it was alleged that he had made money by allowing the price of groundnut oil (the most popular cooking oil in the state) to rise. There may have been some truth in the allegation. But the demand was not for legal action against the chief minister; it was for the resignation of the Congress government which had a majority of 140 in a house of 168. As the disturbances continued unabated, the government resigned and president's rule was imposed on 9 February 1974. Since the president's proclamation had kept the state assembly under suspension the demand now was for dissolution of the house. JP visited Ahmedabad two days after the imposition of president's rule. He complimented students and youth on their role in bringing down the Congress ministry and encouraged them in their efforts to get the assembly dissolved. To achieve that objective the agitation was continued with renewed vigour, resulting in 95 deaths and injuries to 933 innocent people, besides loss to public and private property. Several Congress members of the assembly were *gheraoed* to force them to resign. Several did, but the number was not large enough to clinch the issue.

The opposition parties were determined to get the house dissolved, especially because they had lost the state elections in UP and Orissa in February. They needed to retrieve lost ground in Gujarat, where they felt their electoral chances were better. With that end in view, Morarji Desai undertook an indefinite fast, starting from 11 March. His fast added a new urgency to the need to accept the students' demand for dissolution of the assembly. The central government, fearful of the consequences of Morarji Desai's fast, dissolved the assembly on 15 March. Morarji ended his fast soon after, in the traditional Gandhian style. Congratulations poured in for the success of the students' efforts from many quarters, and the Nav Nirman movement became a model for similar agitations in other parts of the country. Nobody shed a tear for the demise of the rule of law and constitutional means of changing governments. And JP was *inspired* by these happenings!

Jayaprakash Narayan was many personalities rolled into one. It is not possible to give him a definite political or ideological label. In the course of his fifty-year-long political career he could at various times have been described as a Marxist, a socialist, a Gandhian, an anarchist, and a populist; as an underground revolutionary trying to organize a guerilla force for violence and sabotage; as an inspirer of mass movements designed to topple elected governments; as a visionary like Robert Owen and William Morris; as a *brahmachari* in the married state and a *sanyasi* passionately involved in public affairs. His role in the Quit India movement cast him in a heroic mould and his rejection of Nehru's offer of a cabinet post gave him a high moral stature in a country where renunciation of power is held in high esteem. His transformation from an enthusiastic follower of Marx into the legatee of Gandhian political morality was a personal odyssey and a moral struggle to find the right aims and the right means to achieve them. In this quest he was drawn to Vinoba Bhave's Sarvodaya movement. He called it the politics of the people, or *lokniti*, as distinct from *rajniti* (politics of party and power). He found in *bhoodan* (distribution of land to the landless) 'the gem of total agrarian revolution'. From *bhoodan* the movement would proceed to *gramdan* (communization of land) and culminate in *gram swaraj* (village self-government). He worked zealously for this new agrarian economic order, but the movement did not seem to gather momentum. It did not provide an effective solution to the problem of land hunger in rural India. The *bhoodan* movement was certainly a worthy exercise in idealism but it did not go very far in solving the problems it was supposed to. It was a good gesture towards the rural poor, but it was just a gesture. Once he realized the limitations of the movement, JP's interest in it waned.

In the meanwhile his disappointment with the Indian political system was deepening. He was convinced that unless something was done about the political malaise, reasonable economic progress was not possible. He felt it was the duty of non-party people like him to prevent increasing distortions in the political system of the country. In an endeavour to set things right, he mobilized Gandhian workers to go out on a campaign for voters' education in 1971 and 1972, but this was not effective. The electorate gave Indira Gandhi a thumping majority at the centre and returned her party to power in the states, from where it had been dislodged in 1967. All these developments dismayed JP because they did not fit with his scheme of things. Gandhian concepts as he understood them had already failed to be relevant within the vicissitudes of Indian democracy. JP was now groping in the dark. Then he suddenly saw, he says, a way out. Writing in *Everyman's Weekly* on 3 August 1974, he ruminated: 'I wasted two years trying to bring about a politics of consensus. It came to nothing . . . Then I saw students in Gujarat bring about a political change with the backing of the people . . . and I knew that this was the way out.' He was so buoyed by the success of the Gujarat students that, after initiating a similar movement in Bihar, he thought he had found a panacea for India's ailments. Never a realist, always a believer in grand gestures, he was going to make the grandest possible gesture of his life: he was going to give a call for '*Sampurna Kranti*'. This was his term for a comprehensive social revolution that was to include all aspects of life—social, economic, political, cultural, ideological, educational and moral. Nothing less. And how was it going to be achieved? The comprehensive social revolution was to be ushered in by people led by '*Yuva Shakti*', youth power.

Such a call by any other leader would have been dismissed as grandiloquent and quixotic. But the moral and political stature of Jayaprakash Narayan lent a degree of credibility to his call, and disgruntled political elements who had tasted blood in Gujarat were quick to see another opportunity to gain power through this short cut. They took advantage of JP's advocacy of extra-constitutional methods of agitation in Gandhian moral terms with the expectation that some of its morality would accrue to them. Even Atal Behari Vajpayee, a moderate leader and an accomplished parliamentarian with a democratic disposition, felt inclined to say in a paper which he read at the Bharatiya Jana Sangh conference in Hyderabad in September 1974: 'The established leadership has been using the parliamentary method only as a cover for protecting their evil designs. The response cannot be confined to the parliamentary level. This war has to be fought in the streets, in the chambers and legislatures, in the corridors of power, in all sensitive power centres of the establishment.'

The Socialist Party was, as expected, much more belligerent. Its leadership adopted a resolution at their Calicut conference in December 1974 which said: 'since the capacity of the parliamentary system to achieve reform and renewal from within is getting severely limited, extra-constitutional action and popular initiative become absolutely necessary.' In this race for me-too-ism, the CPI(M) could not allow itself to be left behind. Its distinguished ideologue E.M.S. Namboodiripad wrote in the party's official organ: 'The CPI(M) and other left parties are conscious that the problems facing the country cannot be solved through election and work in the parliamentary forum alone. Precisely because of this, they do not accept the position that every issue must be solved only through constitutional means.'[4] All these parties worked hard to convert JP's call into a confrontationist movement which eventually ended in the Emergency.

The forced resignation of the Gujarat government gave a signal to Bihar's students, who were dissatisfied with the high prices, the inadequate supplies of foodgrains to their messes, and the growing problem of unemployment. The Akhil Bharatiya Vidyarthi Parishad (ABVP), which had played an important role in the Nav Nirman movement, took the initiative in organizing the students for a Gujarat-like struggle. As a result the ABVP, the Samajwadi Yuva Jan Sabha (SYJS) which owed allegiance to SSP, and the Chhatra Sangharsh Samiti (CSS) got together and forced what was called the Bihar Rajya Sangharsh Samiti to spearhead the agitation.

The demands that the students presented to the chief minister were: increase scholarships, remove minimum marks restrictions for those who sat for medical examinations, and improve supplies of wheat and rice to hostels. The chief minister's response satisfied the students and they promised him co-operation in apprehending black marketeers, profiteers and hoarders. This did not suit those politicians whose aim was to overthrow the state government; they were not confident of achieving that objective by themselves. Jayaprakash Narayan, impressed by the Nav Nirman movement in Gujarat, agreed to lead the movement when he was approached in early April 1974. He was given the impression that the opposition MLAs and some Congress MLAs were

[4] *People's Democracy*, 12 June 1975.

ready to resign their seats, and that the Gujarat success could be repeated in Bihar.

This led to a demand for the dismissal of the government and the dissolution of the assembly. The MLAs' response to demands for their resignation, however, was very disappointing to the leaders of the movement. Despite a visit by Morarji Desai for this purpose, not even his own party Congress(O) MLAs offered to resign. MLAs from other political parties showed even greater reluctance. After serious efforts at persuasion and intimidation, only 42 MLAs out of a total of 318 resigned. Some Harijan and Adivasi MLAs who had been forced to sign resignation papers backtracked after they were set free. Since the resignation campaign had not succeeded, students were again brought into the battle. They were asked to boycott colleges and not appear for their examinations. Most students did not respond—despite a campaign of coercion and intimidation during which a student was shot dead.

To revive the movement, which seemed to be losing steam, JP sought to widen its base and forge new organizational instruments to carry it forward. He tried to bring in to the movement farm workers, landless labourers and other poor sections of society and highlight their demands for land to the landless, as well as rationalization of land revenue and fair wages to agricultural workers. The CPI(M) was expected to extend its support to the movement by launching supplementary and convergent agitations. To provide a stiffer organizational support to the movement, the Chhatra Sangharsh Samiti (CSS), and the Jan Sangharsh Samiti (JSS) were formed. It was the task of these bodies to raise funds and volunteers for the movement. The momentum of the agitation was to be maintained by well-sequenced calls for *bandhs*. Accordingly, a series of *bandhs* was organized, climaxing in a Bihar Bandh which unleashed widespread violence and disruption. Notwithstanding the violence associated with the *bandh*, JP gave a call for a *gherao* of the assembly and the residences of MLAs. He himself led a procession to the secretariat where he staged a *dharna*. The government continued in office, unmoved.

Since the movement was not yielding results as fast as its counterpart had done in Gujarat (that movement lasted only ten weeks), the Bihar leaders, including JP, were getting desperate. And the more desperate they got, the more drastic became the steps they took. JP called a conference of opposition parties and independent public figures in November in Delhi, where they decided to organize a *gherao* of parliament by one million people. Subsequently, the idea of a *gherao* was given up in favour of a massive demonstration outside parliament and similar demonstrations in the states. By December the CSS and the JSS were asked to form Janata Sarkars and Janata Adalats in villages as organs parallel to those of the government. On 26 January 1975 rival Republic Day celebrations were held at different places in the state. In February a march to the All India Radio station was organized. In March JP gave a call to students to revive the no-tax campaign. In May a three-month programme to form Janata Sarkars was announced.

Despite all this turbulence, which resulted in over 500 casualties, of which 70 proved fatal, the Bihar movement was not getting anywhere. JP therefore decided to lift his Bihar struggle to an all-India plane. He joined forces with opposition parties and tried to galvanize the political infrastructure in other states. Parties everywhere had independently been stirred to action by the success of the Gujarat movement. The BLD had, even earlier, called upon its followers to prepare for the launch of a people's struggle. The Socialist Party, enthused by the Bihar experience, exhorted other Leftist parties not to let the opportunity of mass struggle slip by. The CPI(M) reached for a common understanding with JP. In Orissa, JP's Sarvodaya colleagues took the initiative to rope in students and other anti-Congress parties like the BLD, SP, SUCI, and Congress(O). In Madhya Pradesh the BJS, the SP, the BLD and others had joined hands to support a Bihar-type agitation. In Bangalore student fronts of the BJS, SP and Congress(O) got together to form a Karnataka Nav Nirman Samiti. In Uttar Pradesh JP himself helped in the organization of a Jan/Chhatra/Yuva Sangharsh Committee with a comprehensive programme of agitation. Other such alliances with similar objectives were set up between the opposition parties which commanded local influence in Punjab, Rajasthan, Delhi and Haryana.

While the turbulence unleashed by the movement was going on, JP went on making statement after statement which made it impossible for the government to find a *via media*. Inaugurating an all-India youth conference at Allahabad in June 1974 he let it be known that 'though he himself would not take part in any armed insurrection or rebellion, he would not restrain revolutionaries from taking to the gun'.[5] He was reported to have said in Patna that 'he had never taken up arms against the government, nor did he want violence, but if the people wanted it from him, he would do that at an appropriate time'.[6] Again, in Patna: 'A violent people's revolution can be successful only if the army and the police rebel, as happened during the Russian revolution. But this is not the situation here as yet'.[7] Addressing a meeting in Bihar to exhort people to celebrate Republic Day separately, he told them: 'A revolution will not come either through elections or from Parliament or Assembly, but a revolution, peaceful or bloody, will always be of the people and by the people'.[8] Obviously, JP had little faith in gradual reforms such as are possible under a democratic system. He seemed to want all or nothing.

He thus made it impossible for the government to negotiate, although it had strong reasons to seek some kind of a settlement with him and bring the conflict to an end. There was a very vocal group of anti-communist socialists in the Congress Parliamentary Party led by Chandra Shekhar and Mohan Dharia who were pressing hard for a dialogue with JP. The other reason was the government's desire to get JP's support for policies to fight inflation. Since some of these policies, especially those affecting the working class, were going to be unpopular, it was thought that it would be helpful if a leader of the eminence of JP, who was so exercised about the price rise, would support the anti-inflation policies of government.

With that aim in view I made an attempt through Sugata Dasgupta, director of the Gandhian Institute of Studies, Varanasi, to solicit JP's support. But JP did not respond, nor did he spell out in any concrete manner how he would battle against rising prices or eliminate corruption—the two major aims with which he had started his movement. He took no notice of the government's hard-headed package of

[5] *Times of India*, 22 June 1974.
[6] *Motherland*, quoting a UNI report, 31 August 1974.
[7] *Everyman's Weekly*, 26 October 1974.
[8] *The Statesman*, 12 January 1975.

economic policies which actually brought down inflation, a fact which was widely noted both in the country and abroad. Even the stern action which the government took against hoarders and smugglers left him unimpressed. Instead, he announced, months after the evident success of these policies, that 'none of the evils against which the movement is aimed can be removed without radical change in the whole society. The objective may appear to be limited in character, but they may not be achieved without an all-round revolution—political, economic, social, educational, moral and cultural'.[9] His ideology of the revolution offered no outline of the alternative social order beyond rhetoric and slogans like 'communitarian society' and 'partyless democracy'. The programmes of the movement did not lay down concrete objectives beyond those meant to mobilize people's agitations. What the country needed, according to JP, was 'permanent institutions of peoples' power.' Evidently these did not include existing institutions in the country.

Perhaps the most accurate assessment of JP's total revolution can be made in his own words, the words he once used about Gandhism. He called it 'a compound of timid economic analysis, good intentions and ineffective moralizing.' He called this 'a dangerous doctrine' because 'it hushes up the real issues and sets out to remove the real evils of society by pious wishes.'[10] But the political groups which provided the workers and cadres for JP's movement had a concrete and well-defined objective, namely to overthrow the Congress government and seize power, which they could not do on their own. JP thus provided the umbrella of leadership to a medley of disparate groups ranging from the RSS and Jana Sangh all the way to Anand Margis and Naxalites, the Congress(O), the SP and the SSP. The common objective that held these parties together was a demand for the dissolution of the assembly; everything else was supposed to follow from that.

Some of the dangerous implications of JP's movement were seen by discerning observers. *The Pioneer* of 6 June 1974 bluntly pointed out:

[9] *Everyman's Weekly*, 12 December 1974.
[10] Bimal Prasad (ed.), *A Revolutionary's Quest: Selected Writings of Jayaprakash Narayan* (Delhi: Oxford University Press, 1980), p. 56.

Sarvodaya leader, Jayaprakash Narayan is really playing with explosives. The movement that he is leading to oust the [Bihar] Ministry, *gherao* the legislatures, to spread disaffection among the ranks of the police force against the government and to plunge the state into a 'no tax' campaign may trigger off violence on an epochal scale much earlier than apprehended. Ostensibly he is purging the government of all that is evil. But the methods he is choosing are frankly coercive and undemocratic.

The Hindu said on 11 June 1974:

. . . the real question is whether a duly elected legislature should be dissolved just because a student's agitation, however eminently led, demands it. Mr Narayan, who had so far chosen to remain outside the mainstream of politics and thus shirked the responsibility to shape it and the country's affairs on what he deems to be sound lines, now seeks to enter the house through the wrong door and even bring it down on the heads of every body. . . . It is also clear that what inhibits the government's firmer handling of the situation created by him is Mr Narayan's undoubted stature as a Gandhian and an upright man. Should he virtually exploit such public standing to usher in what are disorder and disrespect for law and order and the democratic set-up as a whole?

Comments of this kind had no effect on JP. He had worked himself up into the mood of a self-righteous, moral crusader immune to criticism. His intransigence and the government's reluctance to be firm with him had far-reaching consequences for Indian politics. The two together made the democratic process increasingly vulnerable to extra-constitutional assaults and brought it under the shadow of a parallel process of organized coercion. Allowing such regular use of coercion practically legitimized it. Extra-constitutional and disruptive methods of protest used by extremist political groups, whose ideology is based on a rejection of democratic procedures, became the preferred technique of mainstream political parties and groups.

JP's movement did not leave the Congress Party unscathed. Its effect was that Indira Gandhi and her party became impervious to charges of corruption against partymen; she accepted their self-serving opinion that attacks on them were really attacks on her. She became susceptible to the CPI assessment of the political situation, according to which JP was unwittingly heading an externally supported fascist movement. They used to compare the praise showered on JP in the

US in 1974 with the total indifference shown to him in 1971 when he visited that country to campaign for the Bangladesh freedom movement. The change in the US attitude was, according to them, a reflection of the change in JP's role. In 1974 he was campaigning against Indira Gandhi, whom the Nixon administration wanted to punish for her defiance in 1971 and for the explosion of a nuclear device later. In this context, the hectic activity of Peter Burleigh a US consular officer, who was constantly in touch with the agitators, was looked upon as proof of American involvement with them.

Indira Gandhi herself had apprehensions of foreign involvement in the affairs of the country on the pattern of what had happened in Chile. It was widely known that Salvador Allende's ascent to power in Chile had upset Nixon, who was not prepared to 'lose' Chile if he could help it. According to the syndicated columnist Jack Anderson, the International Telephone and Telegraph Company (an American multinational) and the CIA had organized Allende's overthrow in September 1973. Indira Gandhi believed every word that Jack Anderson wrote on Chilean affairs. Since she herself was known to be high on Nixon's hate-list, she had become apprehensive of what she called 'the foreign hand'. Intelligence reports about plots to overthrow Mujib's government in Bangladesh added to her fears. Congressmen friendly to the CPI sowed suspicions in Indira Gandhi's mind against those of her colleagues who were advocating a compromise with JP. The result was mistrust among Congressmen and increased factionalism in the party at a time when it needed to stand united to confront the economic and political crisis.

I had known JP since 1961, when I published a monograph on the economics of small industries. It was an empirical study whose conclusions had cast doubt on some of the assumptions on which the government's support to these industries was based. The issues I had raised provoked JP so much that he came to my house with my friend L.C.

Jain to talk about it. Although I could not convince him of my viewpoint, he gave me the impression that he would like to keep in touch with me. Some time later he told me he was keen that I visit the Gandhian Institute of Studies at Varanasi, which was one of his many concerns. It so happened that, about the same time, the UGC asked me to review the working of the institute as part of their normal procedure for the grant of finance to such institutions. JP invited me to discuss my report with him. This led to several discussions on the relevance of the ongoing research in social sciences in the country, during which he talked about his own ideas on such research. In 1968 he sent a Sarvodaya team to Kashmir to report on the political situation there and asked me to join the team. Again, we were together at a conference organized by the Society of Friends at Nuwara Eliya in Sri Lanka in 1968, primarily to get Indians and Pakistanis together to discuss their problems (though participants from Iran, Afghanistan and Nepal were also invited to give it a broader regional cover).

Such being the background of my association with JP, I believed I could help throw a bridge between him and Indira Gandhi. I roped in Radhakrishnan of the Gandhi Peace Foundation and Sugata Dasgupta, Director, Gandhian Institute of Studies, Varanasi, to help me in this endeavour. At my request, they both tried to find out what he expected Indira Gandhi to do regarding electoral reform, corruption in high places, land reforms, and so on. I had hoped that some concrete suggestions would emerge on which there could be an agreement between JP and the prime minister. However, nothing came of these efforts except, as a by-product, the discovery of the real reason for JP's displeasure with her. This happened when Dasgupta, in his exasperation at my persistent questioning, said, 'Frankly speaking, these policy questions are secondary matters. My advice to you is, *un ko kuch maan deejiye* [he should be shown some reverence].' I could not let this cryptic remark pass without seeking elaboration.

According to Dasgupta and Radhakrishnan, JP expected that, after she became prime minister, Indira Gandhi would establish with him the same sort of relationship that her father had with Mahatma Gandhi. JP was sentimental about many things and had some sort of affection for her. Nehru had been like an older brother for JP, and his wife

Prabha Devi was a friend and source of solace for Kamala Nehru. Indira Gandhi had not only neglected her filial obligations, she had done something worse; she had, according to JP, come under the influence of Moscow through her liaison with the CPI after the 1969 split in the Congress Party. That had enraged him and that was the reason why he had tried to help organize a consolidated opposition of non-communist parties against her at the time of the 1971 elections. Indira Gandhi, on her part, had some respect for JP as a human being, but not a great deal for his ideas, which she thought were woolly and often irresponsible. According to Indira Gandhi, JP was a theoretician of chaos, and politics for him was the art of the impossible. With such perceptions about each other, it would have been difficult for JP and Indira Gandhi to develop a common political understanding. The fact that both were endowed with fierce egos made this virtually impossible. JP's self-righteousness and Indira Gandhi's paranoia reinforced each other, and destiny seemed to have no alternative in mind for them but to collide.

Towards the end of 1974 the Bihar movement was showing clear signs of fatigue. The cadres were losing their enthusiasm as the state government, unlike that of Gujarat, had withstood their onslaught. The grassroots organization that JP had expected would sprout from his call for 'jana-shakti to sustain the movement' failed to materialize. In the meanwhile, the economic situation had improved in the wake of the government's anti-inflation policies adopted in July. Prices had begun to fall by October and food supplies had increased because of imports, a moderate agricultural recovery in 1973–4, and 'dehoarding' by traders fearful of police raids. The visibly earnest efforts of the government to get a grip over the economic situation was resulting in some favourable public opinion. Had nothing intervened, the process of a return to normalcy would have gained speed.

But that was not to be. In early January 1975 L.N. Mishra, the railway minister, was assassinated in Samastipur, Bihar. This was followed by an attempt on the life of the chief justice of India. Both had been targets of virulent propaganda; the former as the Congress Party's fund-raiser and the latter as a favourite of Indira Gandhi (JP called him her stooge), because he had superseded three of his colleagues when he was elevated to the post of chief justice of the supreme court. These incidents convinced Indira Gandhi that there was a conspiracy against her and the government. JP's warning, in an interview with Karanjia, the editor of the weekly *Blitz*—'if Mrs Gandhi does not take steps to change radically the system and persists in standing in the way of revolutionary struggle, she cannot complain if, in its onward march, the movement pushes her aside with so much else'—only added to her anxiety about the possibility of greater violence in the country.

Gujarat, where the economic and law-and-order situation had greatly improved under president's rule, came alive once again with Morarji Desai's announcement of an indefinite fast on 7 April, this time for the restoration of people's rights to elect their representatives. The blow for the restoration of democracy, after the forced dissolution of the state assembly by a similar method, was later to be called by him 'the start [of] the battle I had been dreaming of since 1969.'[11] The government had scheduled the elections in September but Desai wanted them before the end of May. JP strongly supported Desai, criticizing the government's promise to hold the elections in September 'as a cleverly designed political rape'. The government, once again, gave in and to save Desai's life agreed to hold the elections on 10 June in the blazing heat of summer, an unusual time for holding elections in India. Desai ended his fast after his victory and the elections were duly held on 10 June.

The results were announced on 12 June. The Janata Morcha, a four-party alliance of the Congress(O), the Jana Sangh, the BLD and the Socialist Party, formed earlier with Desai as leader, won the elections. The result of the Gujarat elections was a big setback to the prime minister's political standing because she had vigorously campaigned for her party in the state. But an even bigger blow had been struck against

[11] Interview with Oriana Fallaci, published in *The New Republic*, July 1975.

her moral authority earlier in the morning of the same day by Justice Jagmohan Sinha of the Allahabad high court. He had set aside her election to the Lok Sabha on grounds of electoral malpractices in his judgement on an election petition filed four years earlier by Raj Narain. 12 June thus proved a red letter day for the opposition parties, especially for JP, for whom Indira Gandhi was by now the source of everything that had gone wrong in the country.

Justice Sinha had done for them what the opposition were not able to do for all their striving. For Indira Gandhi it was the worst setback of her political life. It became a testing time for her and JP, the two principal antagonists in the political strife of India; the test was how they would react to the judgement. It was also a·defining moment for Indian democracy and the rule of law. For the opposition parties, the judgement was the fulfilment of a mission and Justice Sinha became their most-talked-about hero overnight. He was hailed as a Solomon. They disregarded the part of the judgement that stayed his order for twenty days to enable Indira Gandhi to appeal to the supreme court.

The opposition could not wait. They lost no time in mounting a campaign—both open and secret—to force Indira Gandhi to resign the office of prime minister. The national executives of the BJS, the BLD, the SSP, the Congress(O), and leaders of the Akali Dal got together to form a ten-member National Programme Committee to formulate a programme of action. The programme was drafted by Nanaji Deshmukh of the BJS and included, among other things, suggestions such as processions and demonstrations by students and youth in various areas of Delhi, the gherao of industrialists and businessmen supporting the prime minister, gate meetings outside mills and factories in and around Delhi, lunch-hour meetings of central government employees, demonstrations outside the prime minister's residence by various sections of the people—including teachers, doctors, lawyers, students, *jhuggi-jhompri* dwellers, businessmen, housewives, scooter and taxi drivers, construction workers—and the beating of *thalis* from rooftops at night.

JP participated in these preparations and went far beyond. At a rally held on the Ramlila grounds in Delhi under the auspices of the Jan Morcha, with Morarji Desai as chairman, he said: 'Friends, the civil disobedience will be of varied types. A time may come when, if these people do not listen, it may be necessary to derecognize the government. They have no moral, legal or constitutional right to govern; therefore we would de-recognize them; we would not co-operate with them; not a paisa of tax shall be given to them.' In the same speech he asked the army, the police and government servants not to obey orders which they considered wrong and challenged the government to try him for treason. After this inflammatory speech Morarji Desai asked the approval of the audience for the programme of agitation which had been chalked out by the programme committee. All this was happening on the evening of 25 June. Early next morning Indira Gandhi announced her response to the activities of the opposition leaders on All India Radio. It was the declaration of a National Emergency.

What led Indira Gandhi to take such a drastic step? Did she have to pick up the gauntlet thrown down by JP on the Ramlila grounds? There is no simple answer. Her problem was much more complex than JP's, for whom what was happening in the country was like a medieval morality play in which all the angels were on his side. He had no dilemmas, his mind was full of certitudes. He was more attuned to the rhetoric of revolution than to the complexities of administering a difficult country. Indira Gandhi's situation, on the other hand, was agonizing for her. Not only was her own political future at stake, her party was under severe strain by the infighting and factionalism. Above all, she was the prime minister and she had to worry about the consequences of her exit on the governance of the country. Her mind was a jumble of all these personal and public concerns, which were not easy to disentangle.

First, her personal interest. She was aware that if she resigned even before the supreme court could rule on her appeal, she would impress some sections of public opinion and could probably come back to power if the court decided in her favour. Had the opposition leaders, particularly JP, left the onus of the decision entirely to her, it is not improbable that she would have resigned. But they were keen to exploit the situation, exercise their newly gained strength, and demonstrate that they had *forced* her to resign. Even before she could file her appeal, to which she was entitled, a delegation of opposition leaders from the Congress(O), JS, BLD, SP and Akali Dal called on the president and presented a memorandum to him saying that 'a grave constitutional crisis had arisen as a result of Mrs Gandhi continuing to occupy the office of the prime minister despite a clear and categorical judicial verdict.' They pressed for her resignation. In their public utterances she was mercilessly demonized. This exhibition of personal animus brought out the fighter in her and strengthened her resolve to defend herself. She was also worried about the goings on in the party. Though the Congress Parliamentary Party had reiterated its 'fullest faith and confidence' in her leadership, she was unsure about her pro-tem successor's attitude. Would he let her come back? He might rattle some skulls in the cupboard, especially the ones in that of her son Sanjay, to keep her out of office. Such were her personal worries.

As regards her public concerns, Indira Gandhi was almost certain that her party would split if she resigned even temporarily. She was unsure about the intentions of Jagjivan Ram and so-called young Turks like Chandra Shekhar, who had not forgiven her for not compromising with JP. Her worst fears were about the opposition coming to power; it was a spectre that haunted her because she believed it would be a disaster for the country. She agonized over all these considerations.

Those who would lose power and influence by her exit were quick to soothe her perplexed mind by organizing demonstrations of support and loyalty in front of her house. Sanjay and his supporters and various Congress party workers were prominent in this campaign. The ideologues urged her to stand firm against 'right reaction' and refuse to resign. The CPI passed a resolution to that effect only a day after the Allahabad judgement. Legally minded people dismissed Justice Sinha as a stickler for the letter of the law. They maintained that while what had been proved (according to the high court) might constitute technical violations of an 'impractical' and 'stringent' election law, there was no logic in unseating a prime minister for minor technical irregularities. The judgement rested on such technicalities as whether the services of a gazetted officer had been utilized before his actual date of resignation from government service, and whether the erection of rostrums by state governments for the security of the prime minister, according to long-standing practice, could invalidate an election.

Judges are human beings and not necessarily like the blindfolded lady holding the scales of justice in one hand and the sword of law in the other. They suggested that Justice Sinha may have been swayed in his opinions by the prevailing political atmosphere. They found it difficult to understand why he gave so much importance to the exact date of resignation of Yashpal Kapoor, the official who had become her election agent, particularly as the resignation did take place and he had not drawn his salary from the date of his resignation letter. Some made dark references to Justice Sinha's caste, which was the same as JP's. In fact a fortnight earlier Indira Gandhi had been told that the judgement would go against her because Justice Sinha was under strong pressure to make it so. She did not do anything about it except mention it to R.N. Kao, the head of RAW. Others maintained, somewhat facetiously, that the country was paying for the mistake of having enacted such a detailed and self-righteous election statute.

In the midst of this cacophony Indira Gandhi withdrew into her lonely self. At the moment of her supreme political crisis she distrusted everybody except her younger son, Sanjay. He disliked those of his mother's colleagues and aides who had opposed his Maruti car project, or had otherwise not taken him seriously. It so happened that these were the people who he rightly thought would advise his mother to quit office. He knew he would get into serious trouble if his mother were not around to protect him. For all her childhood insecurities, Indira Gandhi had compensated, one should say over-compensated, her sons, particularly Sanjay, with love and care. She was blind to his shortcomings. Her concern for Sanjay's future well-being was not an inconsiderable factor in her fateful decision.

All these cogitations and counsels came to an end on 24 June when Justice Krishna Iyer of the supreme court, before whom she had moved her appeal for absolute stay order against the Allahabad high court judgement, granted her only a conditional stay, which meant that she could continue as prime minister but not function as a full voting member of the Lok Sabha. This was the fateful moment of decision for her. Feeling diminished in her authority by Justice Iyer's verdict to cope with the threatened disorder that was looming large—the opposition parties announced their plans of countrywide satyagraha—she pressed the panic button and her contingency plan for the declaration of an internal emergency came into operation.

When the fateful moment arrived, JP did not let the law take its own course. Whether it was his mistrust of Indira Gandhi's motives, or his own lack of faith in the democratic method, or his ambition to go down in history as a political messiah of the Indian people is beside the point. Similarly, Indira Gandhi showed more faith in the repression of political opponents and dissidents in her party than in her own ability to engage them constructively or fight them politically. Whether she opted for the Emergency to save herself from loss of power or as shock treatment to bring the country back to sanity is also beside the point. The fact remains that both JP and Indira Gandhi, between whom the politics of India was then polarized, failed democracy and betrayed their lack of faith in the rule of law.

The terms of reference of the Shah Commission of Inquiry set up by the Janata Government were restricted to 'inquire into the facts and circumstances relating to specific instances of subversion of lawful processes and practices, abuse of authority, misuse of power, excesses and/or malpractices committed *during the period when the Proclamation of Emergency made on June 25, 1975 was in force or in the days immediately preceding the Proclamation.*' The limitation of the period for which the enquiry was to be conducted effectively prevented the commission from scrutinizing what led to the Emergency. Consequently, the commission conducted an extensive probe into the 'excesses' committed during the Emergency. Its detailed reports reveal cases of transgressions of law, the settling of personal scores by people in authority, unhealthy relationships between political bosses and civil servants, the highhandedness of police officers, and so on. The most important aspect of these excesses was not that they happened for the first time, but that they occurred on a large scale and to people who were hitherto shielded from such unpleasant experiences. As the commission pointed out, similar things had happened in several states earlier, when there was no Emergency. In this context they referred to reports by commissions of enquiry into the conduct of Pratap Singh Kairon (chief minister of Punjab), Bakshi Ghulam Mohammad of Jammu and Kashmir, Mahamaya Prasad (chief minister of Bihar), Govind Nair and T.V. Thomas (ministers in Kerala), and so on.[12] While emphasizing the enormity of what had happened during the Emergency, the Shah Commission thought it fit to refer to 'excesses' which had become a part of the normal way in which the Indian political and administrative system had been functioning even before the Emergency.

How then do we assess the phenomenon of the Emergency? Was it an aggravation of the tendency to disregard the law which had become a part of Indian political culture? In which case, was it the logical climax of this culture? Or was it an aberration caused by Indira Gandhi's personality, twisted by her sense of insecurity? Whatever the final assessment that historians may make about Indira Gandhi, one conclusion is clear from the events preceding and following the Emergency declaration: it was not a contest between a revolutionary leader leading the hosts towards a new social and political order and a wily politician anxious to impose her personal dictatorship on the country. The actual outcome, on both sides of the barricades, was much less spectacular. JP proved an ineffectual revolutionary and Indira Gandhi a half-hearted dictator.

After the arrest of JP and other opposition leaders, the movement they led simply collapsed. The political situation quickly stabilized and subversive activities suddenly came to an end. There was no mass upsurge, no spontaneous demonstration. The opposition parties'

[12] Third and Final Report of Shah Commission, Paras 24–8.

attempts to whip up an agitation failed to generate support. The collapse of the movement puzzled many people at home and abroad. *The New York Times* wondered how the movement could just 'melt away'. *The Guardian* of London wrote: 'India's State of Emergency is almost three months old now, and rapidly becoming the Mystery of the Missing Opposition'; it lamented the absence of 'the angry voice' against the Emergency. C.G.K. Reddy went around the city of Delhi and was disappointed not to find 'at least a few of the lakhs of people who had gathered only the previous evening to hear JP, determined to bring down the prime minister and who would now organize themselves to resist what was virtually a dictatorship.' JP himself agonized over the question, 'where have my calculations gone wrong?'

The obvious explanation was that the JP movement was not as widespread as the media had made out. It had no grassroots organization of its own to carry out the leader's behests in his absence. The hard core of the movement was confined to the Jan Sangh and its RSS cadres. The students who provided the vanguard had lost their enthusiasm even before the Emergency began. The poor did not see JP offering any workable solutions to their problems. The organized working class was never a part of the movement. The underclass which provides recruits for noisy demonstrations withdrew from the scene when the organizers of the rent-a-crowd were no longer around with money and transport for the exercise. When people felt really oppressed, as they did during slum clearance and compulsory sterilization programmes, they demonstrated spontaneously and forcefully and their 'voice of anger', which *The Guardian* missed in the first phase of the Emergency regime, became loud and clear. But that was the result of the Sanjay phenomenon, a by-product of the Emergency, to which I will return later.

The first impact of the Emergency was in the urban areas, on people mostly of the middle class. These were impressed by the immediate gains of the Emergency: no strikes, no *bandhs*, industrial peace, quiet on the campuses, suppression of smugglers and hoarders, stable prices, spurt in economic activity. The twenty-point programme, announced five days after the declaration of Emergency, held out hope for the alleviation of poverty for the rural poor. The programme included implementation (so far avoided) of land-ceiling legislation, a big increase in the allotment of house sites for the landless, a moratorium on rural debts to give relief to small farmers, village artisans and landless farmers, and the abolition of bonded labour. The adoption of these measures was possible only under the new regime as the issues they addressed came under the jurisdiction of the states, many of which had ignored them in the past. All these measures, put together, provided the Emergency with some legitimate political and social purpose. But not for long.

As weeks passed into months, the realities of Indian political and social life began to reassert themselves. Before the Emergency, Indira Gandhi used to say she did not have the power to implement policies she thought India needed for its regeneration. But when she did acquire all the power she needed, she did not know what to do with it. When the PMO sought to broaden the anti-inflation policies initiated in 1974 into a more liberal economic regime, critical voices were raised against what was deemed a subversion of the Nehruvian ideology by the pragmatists. This criticism came not only from the CPI but also from the so-called progressive elements within the Congress Party. Since both these groups were staunch supporters of the Emergency, Indira Gandhi withdrew her support to her secretariat. She herself was unimpressed by the prospects of the liberalization policies which were to put India on a high-growth path, and which would ultimately eliminate poverty and make India truly an economically self-reliant power. Her economic horizons did not go beyond the medium term. The sad fact was that she did not have an outline of a socio-economic framework for the realization of which her power could be used. Nor did Sanjay and the hand-picked group which surrounded him.

She was more satisfied with what had already been achieved in the economic field. After gaining effective control over runaway inflation, she was particularly satisfied with the success of the twenty-point programme in the area of rural development, where some of the immediate gains were, no doubt, impressive. The implementation of the land ceiling legislation, for example, yielded by December 1976 1.7 million acres for distribution among the landless as against 62,000 acres between 1972 and 1975. Similar results were achieved in the allocation of house sites; over three million sites were allotted in the first year of the Emergency. But these results suffered from a fatal weakness. They were achieved by official fiat; there was no durable institutional mechanism that would carry these and other elements of agrarian reform forward.

At the national level the Congress Party did talk about radical land reforms but at the local level the party organs were opposed to them. The lower rungs of the party continued to be dominated by agrarian interests which would have been hurt by such reforms. Thus the economic power structure that had evolved since independence remained undisturbed by the Emergency and the economic policies that had led India into a low-growth syndrome remained essentially unaltered.

The era of industrial peace which prevailed for more than a year seemed to be nearing its end by September 1976. Union leaders were feeling restive about the continuation of restrictions on bonus and dearness-allowance payments which were required to be put in compulsory deposits, under the anti-inflation programmes of 1974. White collar employees, particularly in banks and insurance companies, were agitated. The government tried to mollify union leaders by making changes in labour laws which made the lay-off of labour in sick businesses even more difficult than before. There was, therefore, no hope of making labour markets more flexible despite the recent experience of the railway strike.

The Emergency made no difference to factionalism in the Congress Party. In many states party leaders faced a serious challenge from rival factions which functioned virtually as an open opposition. The emergence of Sanjay and his Youth Congress marginalized the Congress Party leadership which had already been emasculated. The Congress president, Dev Kant Barooah, was more a sycophant than a leader. He could not go beyond laboured witticisms which made him seem some sort of an amiable court jester. Reshaping the party into an instrument of economic and political change was beyond his capacity. Indira Gandhi herself showed no interest in reforming and rejuvenating her party, not even for the implementation of the twenty-point programme by which she set so much store. Under these circumstances, we had a regime in which concentration of power was divorced from the guiding hand of an ideologically motivated party with a well articulated and concrete programme. In the field of administration the system returned to its normal rhythm after a brief period of brisk activity. The policeman and the babu returned to their petty tyrannies. The only field in which there was demonstrable activity, particularly in Delhi, Haryana and western UP, was in family planning and slum clearance. Schemes in these two areas were given emphasis in order to please Sanjay Gandhi, who had become an alternative power centre in Delhi.

Sanjay was not an office bearer of the party, nor did he have a formal position in government, yet he was able to influence both. This he managed only partly by using his mother's name. He could not have gone far on this track had he not succeeded in establishing an independent power base of his own in the shape of the Youth Congress. Ironically, like JP, he too gave a call for 'youth power', and such young men as are ever ready for action joined him—as they had joined JP's movement. Again, like JP, he ridiculed 'isms', attacked the communists, and outlined his own programme of social regeneration by laying emphasis on literacy, banning dowry, family planning, and protection of the environment *via* tree plantation. This was his five-point programme, which paralleled the twenty-point programme of the government. Of his five points, he pursued family planning and slum clearance schemes most relentlessly.

Both these programmes were being implemented with conspicuous insensitivity and hamhandedness. Officials, policemen and teachers were all dragooned and intimidated to achieve targets. Although the practical achievements of these programmes were very meagre, their adverse impact on peoples' minds was disproportionately strong. As the stories of victimization passed from mouth to mouth, the numbers of alleged victims multiplied a thousand-fold and the nature of the alleged oppressions gained in brutality. The impact of these rumours was similar to those in 1857, when it was said that the British government was trying to convert Hindu and Muslim sepoys to Christianity by making them use cartridges greased with the fat of cows and pigs. Compulsory sterilization, often misconstrued as castration, created so much revulsion against the regime that the Congress Party was routed in the 1977 elections in the northern states, where the impact of the new family-planning policies had already alienated people.

Notwithstanding the economic gains of the period, the Emergency regime did not succeed in bringing about the much-needed reform in economic policies. Nor did it bring about changes in political practice that would have made the restoration of democracy possible on a more viable basis. The group that had gained closest proximity to the prime minister during the Emergency was more interested in the exercise of power for personal aggrandisement than for larger political and social ends. Without a clear sense of direction in which to take the country, they converted the regime into a personal despotism of rule by sycophants.

CHAPTER ELEVEN

The Merger of Sikkim

At the time that the Indian government was preoccupied with the political turmoil of 1974–5, a storm was brewing in Sikkim which presented a serious threat to the country's security. Being a small princely state tucked away in the mountain fastnesses of India's northern frontiers, not much was known about Sikkim at the time. To understand the nature and dimensions of the situation that arose, it is necessary to refer to some basic features of Sikkimese society, its politics, and the history of its relationship with India.

Sandwiched between Nepal in the west and Bhutan in the east, and bordering Tibet (which had been absorbed by a resurgent China in 1950), this heterogeneous state was convulsed by a mass upsurge which began in April 1973. The status of this little domain and the nature of its governance had become the subject of political struggle amongst different sections of its people. The state being a protectorate of India, the government of India had to respect its autonomy with regard to its internal affairs, and at the same time ensure that Indian rights over and responsibilities for the defence and territorial integrity of Sikkim remained unimpaired.

The racial diversity of Sikkim's population had fractured its politics along ethnic lines, while its location on the southern slopes of the Himalaya had put it within the defence perimeter of India and given it a geo-political importance totally out of proportion to its size and resources. Sikkim was a sparsely populated state. In the early 1970s its population was no more than 200,000 and Gangtok, its capital, had just about 25,000 people. Even this small population was divided into three main ethnic groups. The Lepchas, believed to be the original inhabitants, are a hospitable and gentle people. They did not resist the incursions of the more virile and tough Tibetans who were driven out of their own habitat by physically harsh conditions and religious strife among rival sects. These Tibetan immigrants found in the empty spaces of Sikkim enough land to settle on and pasture for their herds of yaks. In the absence of resistance from the natives, they continued to arrive till they outnumbered the Lepchas who not only conceded land and pasture to the Bhutias—as the Tibetan immigrants were called—but also recognized them as high born while considering themselves lowly. On account of their passivity, the Lepchas retreated into remote valleys, making it easy for Bhutias to dominate the religious and cultural life of Sikkim. Certain lamas brought the two communities together under the spiritual and temporal rule of a Bhutia nobleman who founded the Namgyal dynasty in 1642.

The demographic and ethnic picture of Sikkim underwent further and more drastic change after the Anglo-Gorkha wars of 1814–16. As is well known, the British were greatly impressed by the Gorkhas, whom they found to be not only brave soldiers but also good farmers. The Lepchas, on the other hand, seemed averse to hard labour, while the Bhutias either lived as graziers in high altitudes or were engaged in trade. To lay the foundation of Sikkim's agrarian economy, the British encouraged immigration by the Nepalese. They also expected Nepalese immigrants to counterbalance the pro-Tibetan Bhutias. And so the Nepalese began to settle as cultivators in the middle altitudes and gradually became the largest segment of Sikkim's population. This change in the basic demographic structure of Sikkimese society had inevitable political consequences.

Indian independence broke the spell of the middle ages under which the Sikkimese had lived until then. Fresh winds began blowing in the Himalayan highlands, stirring people to reach out to the twentieth century. There were also some dramatic events on the other side of the Himalaya. The seizure of Tibet by the Chinese in 1950 suddenly brought Sikkim into the vortex of international politics. The Chinese communists, as heirs to the Chinese empire, made no secret of their ambition to be the dominant power in Asia. This made Sikkim, along

with the rest of the Himalayan region, an area of geo-strategic importance overnight. The Tibetan revolt against the Chinese and the consequent flight of the Dalai Lama to India in 1959, and the Sino-Indian
border conflict—a series of events in quick succession—placed Sikkim
in the centre of an area of tension.

The event that had the most profound impact on Sikkim was the
Sino-Indian war of 1962, even though its border with Tibet remained
calm during the hostilities. The Maharaja of Sikkim declared a state
of emergency to coincide with a similar declaration by India. Trade
with Tibet came to a sudden stop and the peaceful border became a live
frontier, with Indian and Chinese soldiers in eyeball-to-eyeball confrontation at Nathu La, the traditional gateway to Tibet. The ruling
clique of Sikkim began to see in the new circumstances an opportunity
for their own aggrandisement by trying to play their big neighbours
against each other. This was perhaps in imitation of the policy of
neutrality that Nepal was projecting with regard to China and India.

Around this time rapid changes were taking place in the ruler's own
household. Maharaja Tashi Namgyal had lost interest in official matters after his estrangement with his wife and had assigned the task of
governance to his son, Maharajkumar Palden Thondup Namgyal.
The maharajkumar showed talent in administrative matters and with
the help of his diwan, N.K. Rustomji, had gained considerable experience by the time his father died in December 1963. The Government
of India looked to him to maintain stability in Sikkim and safeguard
the special interests of India as the protecting power. But events did
not turn out that way.

In March 1963 the maharajkumar married an American, Miss Hope
Cooke. Two years later, when he and his American wife were crowned,
they assumed the title of Chogyal and Gyalmo, i.e. king and queen,
instead of the traditional maharaja and maharani. Although the assumption of these new titles was clearly an attempt to raise the status
of the state, the Government of India extended recognition to the new
titles as a gesture of good will. Even before this, the new ruler had been
trying to wrest concessions of a more substantial nature from India.
For instance, he wanted to double the strength of the Sikkim Guards,

a paramilitary unit which had been formed with Indian help. The Government of India agreed in the interest of good relations, but some doubts arose about the Chogyal's intentions when a 'national anthem' was played at the annual presentation of colours to the Guards. The Chogyal was evidently assembling the symbols of a nation state before making a bid for the real thing.

For this purpose the arrival of the Gyalmo, i.e. the former Miss Hope Cooke, turned out to be an important event. Besides fanning her husband's ambition to dizzy heights, her own fantasies introduced a new and unsettling element in Sikkimese politics. She wrote an article in the *Bulletin of the Institute of Tibetology* contesting the legality of the transfer of Darjeeling to the British and claimed Sikkim's sovereignty over that area. In 1966, at her initiative, some officials formed a group called the 'Study Forum' with the ostensible purpose of improving the administration. The quest for administrative reform turned out to be a smokescreen for reorienting Sikkim's politics in an anti-Indian direction. The forum tried to hijack politics from the political parties and establish itself as the mouthpiece of the Chogyal in his effort to gain more and more concessions from the Government of India. It ended up as a vehicle of anti-India propaganda to gain popular support but proved ineffective—as we shall see later.

India's military reverses in the 1962 border war with China had lowered her prestige in the minds of the ruling groups in the Himalayan kingdoms. China's easy success had lent some credibility to their anti-India propaganda. India had become a soft state in everybody's eyes. In these altered circumstances, the ruling group in Sikkim saw an opportunity to upgrade their autonomous status to that of independent nationhood. India's demonstrated weakness in relation to China inflamed their ambition, which was further fuelled by China's ambiguity over the recognition of India's treaty rights in the Himalayan states. Even before 1962, China had been equivocal on that question: this was made clear during Chou-Enlai's visit to India in 1960. At a press conference in Delhi he had said: 'China fully recognizes India's special relationship with Sikkim and Bhutan.' However, in the official version that appeared in *Peking Review*, the term 'special relationship' was changed to 'proper relationship', with the obvious intention of creating confusion. After 1962, China undermined India's position with much less restraint. To demonstrate its anti-Indian posture in the Indo-Pak war of 1965, China chose the Sikkim–Tibet border to stage an incident by claiming that India had set up military projects to promote aggression on the Chinese side of the border. Again, for the consumption of the potential anti-Indian element around the Chogyal, Marshall Chen Yi, China's foreign minister, asserted that the Sikkim–Tibet border did not come 'within the scope of the Sino-Indian border question.'

China's repeated attempts to create tension on the Sikkim–Tibet border was interpreted by some friends of the Chogyal as a signal to contest the special treaty relationship between Sikkim and India. India could therefore no longer afford to take risks in the matter of its security. The defence of Sikkim was a strategic compulsion for India as it provides the shortest route from Tibet to the Gangetic plains. Its passes can be crossed even in winter without much difficulty. Nathu La is the only place on the boundary with Tibet favourable to India from the point of view of defence. For all these reasons the defence of Sikkim was too important to be trifled with.

In view of China's belligerent stance on the border, and especially after the attack on Indian troops at Nathu La in 1967, the Government of India had to make sure that the autonomy of Sikkim remained within the limits defined by the treaty, i.e. freedom in internal matters without the international identity which the Chogyal was seeking. To his dismay the Chogyal found that, barring some officials and a few Bhutia landholders, the majority of his people were not interested in his grandiloquent ambitions, their main interest being the state of internal development. All they wanted was transfer of power to their elected representatives and faster economic progress.

The movement for greater political freedom was led by the Sikkim National Congress (SNC) and the Sikkim Janta Congress (SJC). Both these parties had their support base among the Sikkimese of Nepali origin, from whom the Chogyal and his establishment were alienated. The fact that the leader of the SNC was Kazi Lhendup Dorji, a nobleman from the Bhutia community to which the Chogyal belonged, added to his discomfiture. The person who drove the Kazi to lead the movement for democratization and for liberation from feudal oppression was his wife, Elisa Maria Langford Rae, a Belgian woman. 'Kazina' Dorji was appalled by the poverty of the Sikkimese, regardless of their ethnic origin. She worked hard to mobilize public opinion against the regime. She viewed the royal pretensions of the Gyalmo with disdain and used her talents for organization and publicity most effectively in behalf of the SNC. She continued her work for the party even when driven out of Sikkim—she had to take shelter temporarily in Kalimpong. She also proved an astute politician. To extend her husband's support base she adopted Nar Bahadur Khatiwada, a young, bright and popular Nepali political worker, as her son. Nar Bahadur turned out to be a great asset in her efforts to gather support for her husband's leadership.

The year 1973, which began with the fifth general elections in Sikkim, proved a watershed in its political evolution. The results of the election, which was held in January of that year, led to a train of events which continued to rock Sikkim for the next two years. The election results, which favoured the Sikkim National Party (SNP), the party of the Chogyal, led to a crisis. The SNC and the SJP, the two major parties, charged that the presiding officer had aided and abetted the SNP, which was known to be a pro-palace party, in rigging the elections. The two parties joined forces and formed a Joint Action Council (JAC) on 31 March to conduct a full-scale movement against the existing electoral system. That system was based on the principle of 'communal parity' supposedly to give a balanced representation to different communities. Under the parity formula a successful candidate had to get a minimum of 15 per cent votes from a community other than his own. This was resented by the Sikkimese of Nepali origin who were already dissatisfied with the composition of the council, which consisted of six Nepalese, six Bhutia/Lepcha members, and five members nominated by the Chogyal at his discretion. Besides changes in the electoral system, the two parties wanted administrative and political reforms. The sheet anchor of their movement was the JAC resolution which demanded a repoll on the basis of one-man one-vote, with adequate safeguards for the Lepcha–Bhutia minorities. Their additional demands included a democratic form of government, a written constitution incorporating fundamental rights, the establishment of an independent judiciary, the codification of laws, and finally a revision of the Indo–Sikkim Treaty 'in such a manner that a perpetual and steady friendship could be assured between India and Sikkim.'

The Chogyal's response to the JAC-led movement was negative rather than conciliatory. His confrontational attitudes polarized Sikkimese politics. Instead of opening a dialogue with the opposition leaders, he arrested and held K.C. Pradhan, leader of the SJC, for sedition, an action which provoked fierce protest from the people. The JAC backed demonstrations throughout the state. As a mark of protest two executive councillors whom the Chogyal had nominated to the newly elected council refused to join it.

The protest movement assumed a menacing form on 4 April, the day on which special festivities had been arranged to celebrate the Chogyal's fiftieth birthday. The police opened fire on a demonstrating crowd, resulting in several casualties. This infuriated the volunteers of the JAC, who then attacked and took control of many police stations. The next day, warrants of arrest were issued against Dorji and other JAC leaders. In response, demonstrators began to pour into the capital. The Chogyal had not anticipated the strength of the opposition against him. The truth dawned on him only when he learnt that about 15,000 volunteers of the JAC were marching on Gangtok with plans to besiege the palace and force him to abdicate.

Part of the reason for the new vigour of the pro-democracy movement was the belief of its leaders that India was not going to let them down, as it had done earlier. In the past, every time their movement had gathered strength, the Government of India had intervened and helped the Chogyal suppress it. This was done as a matter of obligation under the treaty. That experience had made the Sikkimese leaders distrustful of our ministry of external affairs. Mrs Gandhi herself had come to believe—not without reason, I must say—that some of our problems in Sikkim had been aggravated by our own officials. She was tired of the fruitless discussions which the MEA was holding with the Chogyal to persuade him to be more responsive to the political aspirations of his people and more friendly in his relations with India. These interminable discussions, which resolved nothing, had only made the Chogyal more intransigent. I too had begun to accept the assessments of Sikkimese affairs which emanated from the Research and Analysis Wing (RAW) of the cabinet secretariat in preference to the confusing and often conflicting reports that came to us from the MEA and its diplomatic sources. RAW's agents had extensive contacts in Sikkim and were familiar with the feelings of its people. Through them the Sikkimese leaders came to believe their movement had at long last gained the full support and sympathy of the Government of India.

Our diplomats and the intelligence people continued with their differences, but to me the former seemed more suave while the latter were better informed and more effective on the ground. With the appointment of Kewal Singh as foreign secretary the differences between the two sets of officials lost their operational significance. Kewal was a shrewd officer who knew that the prime minister was dissatisfied with the way his predecessors had handled the Chogyal. He had no interests of his own to defend and had no difficulty co-operating with R.N. Kao, the head of RAW. With Kewal as foreign secretary and Kao as head of the intelligence and PMO as the clearing house of policy, Indira Gandhi was able to stay in constant touch with the situation in Sikkim.

Kao had an exceptionally able second-in-command to help him implement the new policy, P.N. Bannerji, a joint director of RAW who was stationed in Calcutta. Bannerji was a good judge of men and events and was gifted with a keen analytical mind. With his unassuming manner, friendly disposition, and sincerity of purpose he won the trust and loyalty of the people with whom he worked. Speaking about Bannerji's personal qualities, Kao once told me that Sheikh Mujibur Rehman's wife used to confide to him her problems with her husband, as she would a brother. Bannerji was supported by P.K. Sen, Vinayak Bhattacharya and P.K. Ghosh—a team of excellent officers. Under Kao's overall guidance, the RAW team helped the pro-democracy leaders build up their organization and make their weight felt in the politics of Sikkim. This process had started several months before the storm broke in April 1973.

I had been in close touch with our political officer, K.S. Bajpai, an

R.N. Kao and P.N. Dhar

astute diplomat and keen observer of changing circumstances. His messages about the fast-moving situation were alarming. From intelligence reports too it seemed as though the administration was about to collapse. These reports were confirmed by Avtar Singh, secretary in the ministry of external affairs, who had flown to Gangtok on 5 April. Most of Sikkim, according to his report on the evening of the same day, had slipped out of the Chogyal's control. When Avtar Singh, accompanied by Bajpai and the officer commanding the Indian troops in Sikkim, called on the Chogyal, they found him in a desperate state.

Some of his officials were suggesting that the Tibetan refugees be armed to suppress the revolt, without realizing that such a measure would lead to communal riots and other unpredictable consequences. It was obvious that the situation could not be brought under control without Indian assistance. The Chogyal, after consultations with his own officials and Avtar Singh and his colleagues, formally asked for Indian help to restore law and order in his state. He sent a letter to this effect to the political officer on 7 April, late in the evening. Within just a week the political scene had undergone a dramatic change and the Chogyal now found it impossible to hold his people back. The Chogyal's request for the restoration of law and order was immediately followed by a telegram addressed to Mrs Gandhi by the leaders of the JAC, appealing to her 'for help in saving the innocent people of Sikkim from the ruthless repression unleashed by the Durbar to perpetuate its feudal privilege against the demand for democratic rights . . .' The telegram also made reference to 'misuse of funds India generously provides' and concluded with a renewed appeal 'to intervene to save lives and secure democratic rights of the people of Sikkim.'

With the hostile Chinese poised on the border, we could not afford to let the situation deteriorate further. In anticipation of the need for help to the Sikkim durbar to restore law and order, we had to take preliminary steps. Kewal Singh and I met the prime minister on 6 April to brief her on the situation and seek her instructions. The meeting lasted only about half an hour. Kewal was surprised to find that she had already made up her mind before listening to what he had to say. He guessed that the leaders of the anti-Chogyal movement had kept her informed through RAW. She was brief and told us that she would accept the Chogyal's request for help as soon as it came. Since she was leaving for Lucknow the next morning, a meeting of the political affairs committee of the cabinet was convened the same afternoon so that the decision could be endorsed in anticipation.

On 8 April we initiated swift action on the request from Gangtok. The brunt of the task fell on Kewal, who had to work round the clock without respite. The army units stationed in Sikkim were asked to help restore order, which they did without difficulty. The administration was taken over on 9 April. B.S. Das, who had served as head of the diplomatic mission in neighbouring Bhutan, was appointed chief executive. Surendrapal Singh, minister of state in the ministry of external affairs, made a comprehensive statement in the Lok Sabha the next day, giving an account of the situation in Sikkim and the circumstances in which India had assumed the administration of the state. His statement had an immediate impact on the leaders of the JAC, specially the promise held out by him that 'India would now make every effort to ensure that the interests of the people are served and safeguarded and that Sikkim marches on the road to political stability, security and economic prosperity.' The JAC suspended their protest movement on 9 April. Kazi Lhendup Dorji, its president, told the press that the decision to call off the agitation was taken in view of the Government of India's promise to meet 'the legitimate demands' of the people of Sikkim. K.S. Bajpai, who was in touch with the leaders, had also assured them of Delhi's full support.

To honour the commitment made by the Government of India, Kewal Singh, accompanied by the political officer, met the Chogyal and persuaded him to agree to political and administrative reforms. Chastened by the political opposition he was having to face, the Chogyal agreed to call an all-party conference to produce a set of agreed reforms. He did not appreciate the readiness with which the Government of India had come to his rescue, though he did speak against the propaganda launched by the New China News Agency against India's 'intervention' in the state. He refuted their allegation that the movement in Sikkim was directed by India or any of its agencies. Regardless of this, we were not bothered about the Chinese propaganda, not even if they really believed it. If that were the case, India's indifference to their accusations would at least give China the message that India was no longer worried about its hostility.

After four days of negotiations, an agreement on a democratic set-up for the state was reached on 8 May between the three political parties and the Chogyal in the presence of Kewal Singh. India's role in the negotiations was meant to be that of a facilitator—to bring the Chogyal and his political opponents together and help them hammer out an agreement. But given the attitude of the Chogyal, Kewal Singh and Bajpai had to use all their diplomatic skills to make it happen. The agreement ran into eleven articles with several sub-clauses covering electoral reform, improvements in administration, and expansion of the powers of the assembly which was to be elected in April 1974.

The most contentious issue related to the modalities of the election which, it was agreed, should be worked out by the election commission of India. Besides the delimitation of constituencies, the commission had to review the parity formula under which the elections were earlier held. This was an onerous task as the Chogyal believed that safeguards for the minority community to which he belonged could be provided only by the existing formula—a scheme to which both SNC and SJC were bitterly opposed. The deadlock was resolved by a compromise scheme suggested by the commission, according to which the assembly's 32 seats were to be composed as follows: 15 for the Bhutia/Lepcha candidates; 15 for the Nepali candidates; one for the monastic community (the Sangh), and one for the Scheduled Castes. In communal terms, the Sangh seat was a Bhutia seat and the Scheduled Caste one was a Nepali seat. Thus the composition of the assembly favoured the Chogyal and the minorities. To meet the demands of the majority community, the basis of election was changed to one-man one-vote as applied in the Indian system of reserved constituencies. According to this, the candidate had to be from the community for which the seat was reserved but the electorate included all communities: whoever got the largest number of votes cast was the winner. The old system, under which a candidate had to obtain at least 50 per cent votes from his own community and 15 per cent from the other community to win, was abandoned. The agreement also expanded the list of the subjects on which the new assembly could propose laws and adopt resolutions from eight to fourteen. The additional items included important matters pertaining to the problems of development and governance.

The elections of 1974 were to be held on the basis of the new formula. In preparation for the elections, the SJC merged with the SNC, with Kazi Lhendup Dorji as leader. The reinforced Sikkim National Congress won all the seats that it contested except one. These included constituencies in which the minority communities dominated. The elections were free and fair. There was no interference whatsoever from outside, unless the efforts of RAW to boost the morale of the Congress leaders is considered interference—as Morarji Desai alleged after he became prime minister in 1977. Be that as it may, the landslide victory of the Congress, which captured 29 out of 32 seats, vastly increased the prestige of the Kazi. These results proved that the new electoral formula had helped him throw bridges across the ethnic divide. He interpreted the overwhelming mandate he got from the electorate as the desire of the Sikkimese people for a more representative government. As the undisputed leader of the people he began to raise the demand for a new constitution and a new political dispensation. He thus set the political agenda for the immediate future.

I had hoped that after the elections peace and stability would return to Sikkim and, with one distraction less, we would be able to turn to other pressing matters. This proved wishful thinking. The demand for a new constitution created a situation in which it was no longer possible for India to stay neutral between the Chogyal, whose ambition was to remain the focal point of power, and the Kazi, who represented the popular will. India's earlier policy of shielding the Chogyal from his people's demands was not workable any more. The elections had released forces which could be harnessed constructively only through democratic channels. The Chogyal, blinded by personal ambition, could not read the writing on the wall, though his wife did. Having witnessed the fury of the anti-Chogyal demonstrations, she had concluded that the party was over. She left for the USA in the summer of 1973 and never returned to Sikkim. She divorced the Chogyal in 1975. He, however, pitched himself against the aspirations of the majority of his people, against whom he had developed an atavistic dread. In these circumstances the Government of India had to choose between the Chogyal and authentic representatives of the Sikkimese people. It was not difficult for India to support democratic leaders. Apart from being the right choice on its merits, this was in India's national interest. But to implement it, India had first to recover from the overhang of past support to the Chogyal and his father.

The reversal of the traditional policy of support to the Chogyal took many people by surprise. Whereas we could not prepare public opi-nion for the change because of the obvious dangers, the Chogyal was lobbying with various journalists and politicians, making subtle use of the power of weakness, the moral leverage one can get by appearing to be the victim of a bully. It was not therefore surprising that at the time of Sikkim's merger some people believed it was a takeover job by India. This is far from the truth, and a consequence of general ignorance of the history of this princely state. I will therefore digress to outline Sikkim's political relations with India from Nehru's time in order to suggest that there was a substantial justification for India's intervention.

After the withdrawal of the British in August 1947, various political groups in Sikkim had joined together and formed the Sikkim State Congress (SSC) on 7 December and demanded accession of the state to India. They had also passed a resolution demanding the abolition of landlordism and the removal of feudal privileges, which they believed possible if they joined the mainstream. Their plea for accession had the support of Sardar Vallabbhai Patel and Sir B.N. Rau, the constitutional adviser, but it was rejected by Jawaharlal Nehru. The Government of India therefore signed a Standstill Agreement in February 1948 to give the Sikkim durbar time to think the matter over and sort out the problems that would arise if the demands of the SSC were met. As it happened, they did not need much time to ponder. The maharaj-kumar (later the Chogyal) organized a group of landlords and formed a new political party called the Sikkim National Party (SNP) which dutifully passed resolutions opposing the formation of a representative government and accession to India.

Undaunted by the opposition of the durbar, the SSC continued to mobilize public support in favour of their stand. In December 1948 its leaders came to Delhi to meet Nehru, who assured them that the voice of the people would be regarded as the supreme authority in shaping the destiny of Sikkim. After this meeting the leaders expected the durbar to be more receptive to their demands. But there was no positive reaction for more than a year. They therefore decided to demonstrate their determination to fight for their legitimate rights. At the annual conference of the SSC, Tashi Tshering, its leader, launched a 'no-rent' campaign asking people not to pay land revenue and taxes until their demands were met.

The state government responded with repression. Barring Tashi Tshering, all the leaders of the movement were arrested and a curfew imposed on Gangtok. The arrest of the leaders brought people out on the streets in defiance of the curfew. Fearing disorder the government did not execute a warrant for the arrest of Tashi Tshering and thought it prudent to make some concessions to the SSC. On the advice of the Indian political officer, the maharaja agreed to form a 'popular ministry' with Tashi Tshering as chief minister. But the formation of such a ministry did not solve the problem for it could not implement any of the promises they had made to the people—such as the abolition of landlordism, forced labour, and house tax. In desperation, Tashi threatened to quit the ministry and resume his agitation against the durbar. The Government of India sent Dr B.V. Keskar, deputy minister in the ministry of external affairs, to Gangtok to try and prevent a breakdown. He did not succeed in his mission and the ministry was dismissed.

The Government of India did not want a political vacuum in the state. Its policy continued to support a stable regime in Sikkim and to achieve this objective it sought more involvement from the Sikkimese people with their government. This could not be achieved without first revamping the administration, which was in a mess. To undertake this task, J.S. Lall of the Indian Civil Service was appointed diwan in August 1949. He had not proceeded very far in his work when China announced, in October, that it was sending its army to 'liberate' Tibet. This was a new development which was bound to affect Sikkim both directly and in the wider context of Sino–Indian relations. Against this new background, the Government of India initiated consultations with the maharajkumar and representatives of Sikkim's political parties in March 1950. Among the items for discussion were the necessary administrative arrangements (including the association of popular representatives with the state government) and future relations between Sikkim and India.

On 20 March 1950 there was a provisional agreement as a result of which an advisory council, consisting of two nominees each of the SSC and the SNP with the diwan as president, was to be set up in order to associate the people's representatives with the administration. The relations between the state and India were to be defined in a treaty which was negotiated later in the year and signed on 5 December 1950, the date from which it came into operation. Under the treaty it was agreed that India would continue to be responsible for Sikkim's external relations, defence and communications. As regards internal matters, the state was to continue to enjoy autonomy, subject to the ultimate responsibility of the Government of India for the maintenance of good administration and law and order.

Some elements in the SSC were disappointed with this agreement. They felt that in the absence of a full-fledged representative government, the grant of internal autonomy would only strengthen the maharaja. They suspected that the Government of India was tilting in his favour. The SSC therefore continued to press the maharaja and the diwan for a truly representative government. The SNP however was opposed to further democratization. As a party of landlords and lamas it had vested interests in the status quo. As pressure for change mounted from the SSC, the SNP tried to undermine it by denouncing it as a party of the Nepalese, thereby creating tension between the two major segments of the Sikkimese population. In these circumstances there was every danger of ethnic disharmony degenerating into communal disorder.

The search for communal peace became the major concern of the Sikkim durbar. It sought to balance the majority and the minorities in power-sharing. After discussions between the representatives of the two political parties and the maharaja, a solution was evolved in the form of the parity formula which gave heavy weightage to the minorities. Under this parity formula the seats in the proposed state council were to be divided equally between the Lepcha/Bhutias, who constituted 25 per cent of the population on the one hand, and the Nepalese, who constituted the remaining 75 per cent on the other. Besides the elected members, the maharaja was to nominate five members of his choice to the council. Although Tashi Tshering, the father of the Sikkimese freedom movement, condemned the formula as 'unjust and communal', his colleagues in the party accepted it and the election was held on that basis in August 1953. The results of the election confirmed the fracture of Sikkimese politics along ethnic lines. The SNP won all the Bhutia/Lepcha seats and the SSC the Nepalese ones. Since the nominated members were expected to go with the SNP, it was obvious that the SSC was reduced to a minority in the council. In ethnic terms, the Nepalese majority had become a political minority. Such an arrangement was not likely to be stable.

The parity formula failed to provide a satisfactory solution to the problem of power-sharing between the ethnic communities. The council's functioning was marred by dissension among the councillors and between them and the diwan. The unproductive life of the council was scheduled to end in 1956 but was extended to December 1957. In the meanwhile some principal actors on the political scene had also changed. Tashi Tshering had died and Kazi Dorji, his successor in the party leadership, had resigned from the council as well as from the party. J.S. Lall was replaced by N.K. Rustomji as the new diwan.

Before the second election was held in November 1958, the maharaja announced a small increase in the size of the council and some amendment in the mode of election which left the balance between the two ethnically divided political formations unaltered. The results of the elections, once again, were along predictable lines. The SSC won all the Nepalese seats while the five Lepcha/Bhutia seats and the Sangha seat were captured by the SNP. The results convinced C.D. Rai, a Nepalese leader, that the only way to make the maharaja yield to their legitimate political demands was to widen their political base and form a really strong composite party. Accordingly he joined forces with Kazi Lhendup Dorji (who had left the party earlier and formed a separate party) and Sonam Tshering who had broken away from the SNP. A new political formation called the Sikkim National Congress (SNC) came into existence as an opposition party in May 1960.

The SNC leadership outlined the political future of Sikkim in moderate terms. They supported the continuation of the Chogyal as head of state—but as a constitutional monarch. They also accepted the concept of a council based on 'communal parity' but wanted its members to be elected by a joint electorate. Furthermore, they wanted an independent judiciary with a high court. All these were eminently reasonable demands that took care of the specific problems of Sikkim, namely the existence of the institution of a Chogyal and the ethnic divide. But having learnt from experience that the mere passing of resolutions did not impress the durbar, they decided to launch a satyagraha to enforce their demands. They had also submitted a memorandum of their demands to the Indian prime minister. The Indian political officer advised the Congress leaders against satyagraha, and informed them that the prime minister had received their memorandum and would be glad to meet them. Accordingly, the leaders of the SNC met Nehru in August 1960 in Delhi. After the talks they gave up their plan of launching a satyagraha and waited for things to happen. But nothing did. Once again it seemed to the Sikkimese leaders that the Government of India was tilting in favour of the durbar.

The flight of the Dalai Lama with 60,000 Tibetan refugees to India had palpably increased tension between India and China. India's need for peace in Sikkim was understandable from the Indian point of view. But the Sikkimese had a legitimate grievance, for they had to pay the price for it by way of postponing their demands. Not only that, they had also to face the calculated hostility of the durbar, designed to erode Congress influence. Just around that time, an interim election for the council had to be held because the election tribunal had set aside the election of five candidates. In spite of being the second largest party in the council, the SNC was denied any seat in the council on fine technical detail. Again, in July 1961, the durbar promulgated a Sikkim subjects regulation providing the rules regarding citizenship to residents of Sikkim. These regulations discriminated against Nepalese residents, who were the backbone of the SNC. Taking advantage of the 1962 India–China war, the durbar postponed elections to the council, whose life had ended in May of that year. The council was replaced by an advisory consultative committee of thirty-one which was packed with pro-palace members.

In these circumstances, it became difficult for the SNC to play the role of an effective opposition party. Its lack of success weakened its leadership in the eyes of its followers. Notwithstanding its weakened position, the SNC did well in the third general elections which were held as scheduled in March 1967. Led by Kazi Lhendup Dorji the SNC emerged as the largest single party in the council. But electoral success brought no benefits to the Congress. After the elections were over, the durbar tried to divert attention from domestic political problems by rousing anti-India passions. On the Chogyal's suggestion, three pro-palace executive councillors were made to issue a statement demanding revision of the 1950 treaty and the abolition of the status of Sikkim as a protectorate of India. The statement created quite a stir in both Gangtok and Delhi.

After Delhi lodged a strong protest, the Chogyal dissociated himself from the authors of the statement and stated publicly that they had gone beyond their jurisdiction. Yet the anti-India activities continued under his inspiration. When Sikkim went to the polls for the fourth time in April 1970, anti-India feelings had assumed a high pitch. The SNP, the pro-palace party, started demanding revision of the treaty openly and accused India of being an imperialist power. Even the SSC, which had demanded a merger with India in 1949, was prevailed upon to support the SNP demands. What encouraged the Chogyal in his anti-India posture was his growing belief that India was too frightened of China to take a stand against him. He was also encouraged by several Indian officials whom he pampered. Some of them are believed to have held out prospects of a United Nations membership for Sikkim, and the Chogyal thus believed that Delhi was too weak to resist his demands. In 1970 the Government of India was indeed a weak minority government, preoccupied with its own problems of day-to-day existence.

The foregoing digression on Indo–Sikkimese relations after Independence provides the background for India's policy in 1973. The stormy events that followed the elections of that year had convinced Indira Gandhi that our Sikkim policy needed drastic revision. She was highly critical of the policy of drift that had enabled the Chogyal to reduce the effectiveness of Indian presence in the state. The political officer and the diwan, the two key Indian officials around whom the administration of Sikkim revolved, had gradually lost their function. The former had become some sort of an ambassador to the Chogyal's court and the latter a kind of chief secretary who was accountable to him. This transformation had come about gradually, without being much noticed in Delhi. Even when it was noticed, it was either ignored or justified for one reason or another. The ministry in charge of Sikkimese affairs, it was obvious, had been either weak or indulgent in handling the Chogyal. As a consequence he had succeeded in frustrating the aspirations of his people and also posed a threat to Indian security in a very sensitive and strategic area.

To divert the attention of his people from their demand for a more representative government, the Chogyal had for nèarly a decade taken recourse to generating anti-India feelings. He and his wife had tried to create something like Sikkimese nationalism. For this purpose the Gyalmo had reconstructed her own personality: she changed her dress and manners, and even the tone and tenor of her voice in order to sound like an authentic Tibetan princess. The Lepcha dialect, which was understood by a minuscule minority, became the official state language. Since these efforts at nation-building proved counterproductive, the Chogyal and his consort concentrated their efforts on uniting their subjects against the enemy, India, which could be held responsible for all their ills. Subtle anti-Indian references began to appear in school textbooks. However, their effort to produce a new generation of nationalist Sikkimese youth suffered from a fatal flaw. Instead of becoming a symbol of unity for his ethnically divided people, the Chogyal became a partisan of Bhutia/Lepcha minorities. In the process he antagonized the powerful Nepalese middle class. His concept of nationalism excluded the majority of his people, with the result that he found no takers for his ideas beyond a small though articulate group of Bhutia officers.

It was not difficult to see the fundamental contradiction in the Chogyal's position. He could not sustain his anti-India stand when the majority of his people were disgruntled and alienated from him.

Mrs Gandhi decided to take direct interest in revising the government's policy on Sikkim. She told me in very clear terms that her father had made a mistake by not heeding the Sikkimese demand for accession to India in 1947. She said she had never asked him about his decision in the matter, but her guess was that he had assumed that the Chinese would leave Tibet's autonomy undisturbed and, in anticipation of this, he had perhaps thought it fit to do nothing in Sikkim that would provoke them. She had no hesitation in admitting that in retrospect Sardar Patel's instinctive reaction seemed correct. The short point that emerged was that we should undo our earlier mistake and support the people of Sikkim in their struggle against the Chogyal which they had launched in 1973.

I must add that Mrs Gandhi did not take this decision without feeling sorry for the Chogyal. She had inherited her father's favourable opinion of him. Nehru had looked upon him as a young man of promise, a potentially dynamic leader who would lead Sikkim out of its medieval thraldom. The Chogyal's father, the maharaja, had requested Nehru to help his son to grow up to shoulder the responsibilities that would fall to his lot in the future. According to R.N. Kao, Nehru, with his interest in tribal affairs, accepted the suggestion and invited the maharajkumar to spend several months in Delhi. During that period the maharajkumar stayed in Teen Murti House, where he was treated as a member of the family. Indira Gandhi came to know him well and developed a personal regard for him. She had met him earlier in his own habitat, in 1952, and again in 1958, when she had accompanied her father on his visits to Sikkim. She had been interested in Sikkimese culture since then and had become a votary of the special cultural identity of Sikkim, particularly of its Lepcha/Bhutia component. She attended the maharajkumar's coronation ceremonies as his personal guest and was impressed by the speech he made on the occasion. In that speech he had recalled with sincere affection his memory of Jawaharlal Nehru and referred to India's assistance in very laudatory terms. He had also tried to retain an element of personal warmth in his relationship with Mrs Gandhi. While welcoming her on her first official visit as prime minister he had said, 'We are happy and feel greatly honoured to welcome you today, not only as the prime minister of our great neighbouring country and our protecting power but more so as a very dear friend of Sikkim.'

Mrs Gandhi's disappointment with the Chogyal began when she found him too weak to resist the Gyalmo's blatant anti-Indian moves. She had presumed that, in view of the coolness in Indo–American relations which began with the Bangladesh crisis in 1971, the Chogyal would take care to be sensitive to Indian concerns. Instead he felt encouraged by the Sino–American detente after President Nixon's visit to China in 1972. With the help of the Gyalmo, whose American connections were widely talked about in Gangtok, he had tried to develop an active anti-India lobby.

Now, to return to the political situation in Sikkim: the dramatic results of the elections of April 1974 had clearly registered the desire of the Sikkimese for a fully representative government. Kazi Lhendup Dorji, who had emerged as the undisputed leader, was forcefully arguing for a new constitution which would be in consonance with the aspirations of the people. The Government of India, having overcome its excessive regard for the sensitivities of the Chogyal, was now more supportive of these demands. On 11 May 1974, when the newly elected assembly met to pass the motion of thanks to the Chogyal for his address, it also passed a resolution which called for the speedy development of the constitutional framework envisaged in the 1973 agreement signed by the Chogyal, the Government of India, and the leaders of the political parties. The resolution moved by Kazi Lhendup Dorji, who had been elected leader of the house, spelt out the people's demands:

The Assembly accordingly resolved and hereby requests the Government of India to depute immediately a constitutional adviser for (i) giving a legal and constitutional framework for the objective of this resolution; (ii) defining the powers of the Chogyal, the Chief Executive, the Executive Council and the Assembly; and (iii) recommending to the Government of India specific proposals for further strengthening Indo–Sikkim relationship and for Sikkim's participation in the political and economic institutions of India as desired by the resolution.

In response to the assembly's demand, the Government of India sent

G.K. Rajagopalan, a constitutional expert, to Gangtok with a draft constitution. The members of the assembly made it very clear to Rajagopalan that they wanted a constitution in which all powers would vest in representatives of the people. They were dissatisfied with the expert's draft. After discussions with the Kazi and his colleagues and consultations with Delhi, the draft was amended to the satisfaction of the assembly. The amended draft became the basis of the constitution bill which was to be considered by the Assembly on 20 June.

The Chogyal, for his part, had challenged the very legality of the assembly's resolution. Having realized the grave implications of the resolution and the draft constitution bill that emerged from it, he decided to use all the means available to him to prevent its adoption. He tried to create dissension amongst leaders of the Congress and succeeded in persuading two of them to oppose the draft constitution. He mobilized Sikkimese officials, most of them from his own community, to oppose the section which sought 'participation and representation for the people of Sikkim in the political institutions of India', which he maintained was in violation of the treaty. When the assembly was to meet on 20 June, demonstrations were organized to prevent members from entering the chamber: the police had to use tear gas to disperse the demonstrators. The assembly finally met in the evening and passed the constitution bill with some amendments.

Having lost the first round, the Chogyal rushed to Delhi to persuade the Government of India to reverse the political process that had become irreversible. After meeting the foreign minister he called on the prime minister on 30 June. I was very impressed by his calm and dignified manner and the way he presented his case. Very courteously he told Mrs Gandhi that the constitution bill was in violation of the treaty. He also hinted in a subtle manner that the way things were likely to develop in Sikkim would not be in India's interest. He called the politicians of Sikkim a bunch of unreliable people whom India should not trust and described himself as the best friend of India in Sikkim. His defence of the treaty—considering how hard he had worked against it in the past—did not seem to embarrass him. The irony of the situation was not lost on Mrs Gandhi, who spoke to me about it with relish afterwards. But to the Chogyal she was brief, almost curt. She said the politicians he was running down were the chosen representatives of the people and advised him not to go against their wishes. He wanted the discussion to continue but Mrs Gandhi fell silent and looked aloof. She had perfected the use of silence as a negative response. After an oppressive moment in which nothing was said, the Chogyal stood up to leave. Mrs Gandhi bade him farewell with folded hands and an enigmatic smile, still without saying anything.

The protocol officer was waiting outside the room to see him off. I was about to say goodbye to him when, instead of going towards the lift, he said he wanted to speak to me and accompanied me to my room. He stayed with me for nearly an hour, repeating his point of view again and again. He wanted me to convey what he told me to the prime minister. I promised to do that but told him it would not be realistic for him to hope that she would go against the wishes of the assembly. Although I felt relieved when he finally got into the car and left, I was very impressed by the way he had conducted himself. He had every reason to be tense and agitated but he showed no such signs. Throughout that afternoon he was self-possessed, calm and dignified. His performance would have been the envy of an accomplished diplomat. He was lucid in his presentation and polished in his manner. He would have been very persuasive had his past behaviour not destroyed his credibility. Had he acted like the King of Bhutan, who resisted the temptation of taking advantage of India's weakened position *vis-à-vis* China, the Chogyal would not only have done good to himself, he would have been an asset to India. His overweening ambition, the tragic flaw in his character, overwhelmed his intelligence, which he possessed in ample measure, and finally destroyed him.

Having failed to persuade the prime minister to help him, the Chogyal decided not to stand in the way of the assembly any longer. He realized there was no point in further delaying its session for a final consideration of the constitution bill. He also indicated that he would give his assent to the bill after the third reading. He did want to address the house to give his comments on it, but the mistrust he had generated in the minds of the members was so great that they refused to allow him that courtesy. Instead, his speech was read out to the house by the chief executive. This speech was his swan song. In it he referred to what he

P.N. Dhar bidding farewell to the Chogyal, 30 June 1974
(Courtesy *The Times of India*)

called the lacunae and anomalies in the bill. He laid emphasis 'on the three basic principles' which he said he had also conveyed to the prime minister. These were: 'the maximum participation of the people of Sikkim, respecting the legitimate rights and responsibilities of the Government of India in Sikkim and ensuring the separate and internal autonomy of Sikkim guaranteed under the 1950 Indo-Sikkim treaty.' If he had expressed these views in 1973, the future of Sikkim, and his own future, would have been very different.

The house heard the speech in solemn silence and passed the bill unanimously as it had emerged from the previous session, without change. Things had gone too far for members to pay attention to what the Chogyal had to say; they had lost faith in his bonafides. It was a sad moment for him but he accepted the decision of the assembly calmly and gave his assent to the bill on 4 July, a day on which his American wife might well have been celebrating the Independence Day of her own country, to which she had returned after her failed attempt at being queen of her Himalayan Shangrila.

The Kazi hailed 4 July 1974 as a 'red letter day' and 'the dawn of a new era' for Sikkim. The new constitution was promulgated a day later and he was sworn in as chief minister. For him it was the beginning of new challenges. On 24 July he formally asked Delhi to take action on clause 30 of the constitution relating to Sikkim's 'association with Government of India'. Under that clause the Government of Sikkim could request the Government of India to (a) include the planned development of Sikkim within the ambit of the Planning Commission of India while that commission was preparing plans for the economic and social development of India and to appropriately associate officials from Sikkim in such work; (b) provide facilities for students of Sikkim in institutions of higher learning and for the employment of people from Sikkim in the public services of India (including the all-India services), at par with those available to the citizens of India; (c) seek participation and representation for the people of Sikkim in the political institutions of India. While Delhi was still considering the matter, the Kazi sent a reminder asking for a response to his request. This was followed a day later by a letter from S.K. Rai, general secretary of the Sikkim Congress Party, requesting the Government of India to take 'early decision on the request made by the Government of Sikkim regarding closer ties and representation in Parliament.' The Chogyal also sent a letter to the prime minister through B.S. Das, the chief executive, suggesting a continuation of the separate identity of the state. Once again Delhi was faced with the old but by now familiar problem of 'the palace versus the people'.

But the problem had ceased being a dilemma for Delhi. The Chogyal had proved an undependable ally and the Government of India, having had enough of him, had decided to opt for the people. It decided to respond positively to the chief minister's request, which was a direct consequence of the new Sikkim constitution, and grant Sikkim the status of an associate state. The Constitution of India had accordingly to be amended to implement the decision. The draft amendment bill, which was circulated among parliament members on 31 August, provided, among other things, for associate status for Sikkim and the election of two members by its assembly—one to the Rajya Sabha and another to the Lok Sabha.

Under the new dispensation, we believed that Sikkim would continue to possess a distinct personality of its own, so dear both to the Chogyal and to the prime minister, and a special relationship with the Government of India different from that with all other states. The bill also safeguarded the position of the Chogyal as head of state. But the Chogyal did not see it that way and continued to express his unhappiness through letters and telegrams to the prime minister, to the annoyance of the Kazi and his colleagues. In parliament the bill met with opposition from the Congress(O) and the CPM. The former called it a 'disparate marriage between a Republic and a Monarchy'. Their main point was that the Indian constitution was being amended beyond the scope envisaged by the founders of the constitution. The CPM were concerned primarily with the Chinese reaction which, according to them, would be adverse.

Sardar Swaran Singh, who piloted the bill, answered the opposition effectively. To Congress(O) members he said: 'Our constitution is a dynamic and living constitution.' He recalled that 'there were for instance Part A and Part B states, Raj Pramukhs and Upraj Pramukhs. They are gone and we have now, more or less, a unified and integrated picture of the country. This could be achieved just by amending the constitution to meet the wishes of the people.' He assured the CPM that the merger was not a hostile act against any third party. The Lok Sabha passed the bill as the thirty-sixth amendment of the constitution with an overwhelming majority on 4 September 1974, followed by the Rajya Sabha on 7 September. Predictably, there was bitter criticism from China and Pakistan. There was also a students' demonstration against India in Kathmandu and the Nepalese foreign minister made some critical remarks, which he later toned down after a representation from the Indian ambassador. The rest of the world did not much notice the event. There were some adverse newspaper comments, with *The Statesman* taking the lead. In Sikkim the news was received with great jubilation by an overwhelming majority of the people. In India there was a warm welcome to Sikkim, except by the CPM, who passed a resolution against the constitutional changes.

In the prime minister's office we took the criticism in our stride; it had not gone beyond predictable limits. Our hopes were that the Chogyal would at long last realize that the odds had gone against his extravagant ambitions, and that he would reconcile himself to being constitutional head of his state and let Sikkim settle down to a stable internal and external position. But this proved wrong. He continued skirmishing with his chief minister and did not allow a working relationship to develop. Our advice to the chief minister was to be patient and wait for better counsel to prevail. But the Chogyal proved incorrigible. Matters came to a head in February/March 1975, when the Chogyal was invited to the coronation of the king of Nepal. In view of Nepalese criticism of the constitutional changes, his ministry was against the visit. The Chogyal disregarded their advice and went to Kathmandu. What he did there was most objectionable: he went out of his way to meet the Pakistan ambassador and the Chinese vice-premier, Chin-hsi Liu. According to intelligence reports he sought help from both. Fishing in troubled waters, they promised support if he were to raise the matter at the United Nations. The Chogyal also approached Senator Charles Percy of the United States but was cold-shouldered by him. He then went public in a press conference on 1 March 1975 where he said: 'We want to achieve separate identity, want to preserve our identity and international status. We have informed the Government of India both orally and in writing about this.' When asked if he would approach the United Nations he replied: 'We will leave no stone unturned.' The Gyalmo was meanwhile active in the United States, cultivating India baiters. So was his sister, a lady who bore the wonderfully refreshing name of Princess Coocoola, at the other end of the world; her frequent visits to Hong Kong had roused the worst fears of our intelligence establishment.

What upset the Chogyal's ministers most was a statement he made in Kathmandu wherein he said there was no responsible democratic government in Sikkim. He also alleged that a bomb or handgrenade had been thrown at his car while he was leaving his state for Nepal. Since the car was discovered to possess no more than a small aperture in its windscreen, the story seemed dubious and was looked upon in Sikkim as an attempt by the Chogyal to defame his ministry. The Chogyal's shenanigans in Nepal, and the so-called assassination attempt, provoked the general secretaries of the Sikkim Congress and the Sikkim Youth Congress to issue a joint statement in which they threatened that 'instead of welcoming him to Sikkim, people would greet him with full-throated anti-Chogyal demonstrations.' When he returned home, the Chogyal was alarmed to find demonstrators demanding that he quit the state. When he entered Sikkim there was a clash between his palace guards and demonstrators at Rangpo; this was ominously reminiscent of the 1973 demonstrations.

Sensing the people's anti-Chogyal mood, the Kazi introduced a resolution in the Assembly on 10 April which demanded that the institution of Chogyal be abolished and Sikkim be declared a constituent state of India. A copy of the resolution was sent to Delhi. For the Kazi and his colleagues this was the final stage of a long-drawn-out struggle against the Chogyal. The resolution of the assembly asking for merger with India was put to the vote through a special referendum on 14 April 1975. The resolution was approved by an overwhelming majority. All three ethnic groups voted for the merger, though for separate reasons. For the Nepalese, the Chogyal was an oppressor. Their leaders were convinced that the Chogyal would never function as a constitutional head. Merger with India would give them the benefits of a full-fledged democracy, which meant access to political power and expanding economic opportunities. For the Bhutias the balance of power in the state had already shifted away from the Chogyal, the defender of their interests and privileges. They felt threatened in a Nepali dominated but closed political system, which is how they defined Sikkim as an associate state of India. According to their reckoning their religious and other minority interests would be safer in Sikkim as an Indian state. The long domination of the Lepchas by the Bhutias had brought the two communities nearer each other in religious and cultural spheres, but had not released the Lepchas from the abject poverty in which they were trapped. They too saw in a merger hopes of economic betterment. Thus for the first time the three main communities found in the merger a common solution to their fears and ethnic rivalries, however paradoxical this may seem.

The referendum in Sikkim was followed by due parliamentary process in Delhi. Accordingly the constitutional (38th amendment) bill was moved in the Lok Sabha on 23 April 1975 by Y.B. Chavan, who had succeeded Sardar Swaran Singh as foreign minister. The passage of the bill, making Sikkim the twenty-second state of the Indian Union, was quick and smooth. It was passed the same day with 299 members in favour and 11 against. The Rajya Sabha passed it on 26 April and the president signed it on 15 May. On 16 May 1975 Palden Thondup Namgyal ceased to be the Chogyal and the rule of the Namgyal dynasty, which had been on the throne of Sikkim for 333 years, came to an end.

For the Chogyal it was a personal tragedy, a fate brought about by his relentless pursuit of personal ambition in disregard of the interests of his people and their aspirations—an end common to backward-looking monarchs in an era of expanding democratic movements. For India it was a question of retrieval from a situation that had been deteriorating for a whole decade. The way Sikkim was handled after the debacle of the Indian army in 1962 had encouraged the Chogyal to erode the effectiveness of Indian presence in the state, which was vital to the Indian defense system. For Mrs Gandhi it was a case of undoing what she believed had been Nehru's mistake.

The credit for the Sikkim affair certainly goes to Mrs Gandhi's resolute leadership. She did not allow the domestic political turmoil unleashed by the Nav. Nirman and JP movements to ruffle her calm. During the two years beginning with the anti-Chogyal agitation of April 1973 and ending with its merger in 1975, she kept the formulation and execution of the policy on Sikkim firmly under her own control. She has been justly admired for her management of the Bangladesh crisis, but the qualities of leadership required in resolving the Sikkim crisis were no less exacting. This is not to say that the two crises were similar in their magnitude or consequences. To be sure, the emergence of Bangladesh changed the political map of the subcontinent, while the merger of Sikkim with India only closed a gap, albeit a dangerous gap, in India's northern defences. But the circumstances attending the two events were less favourable in the latter case.

At the time of the Bangladesh crisis in 1971, Indira Gandhi had several advantages: she was the undisputed leader of the country; her popularity was at its zenith; her policies had the widest possible support in the country; public opinion around the world supported India for shouldering the burden of the refugees; and Pakistan was almost universally criticized for what its army had done to the hapless Bengalis. By 1974–5, Indira Gandhi's image in the country had suffered considerable damage. India was in the midst of an economic slump, the negative effects of which were further aggravated by widespread strikes and agitations. Jayaprakash Narayan, who commanded countrywide respect at the time, had launched a movement for Indira Gandhi's ouster. There were other difficulties in her way. To most, Sikkim was just a small and inoffensive principality nestling somewhere in the Himalaya, being bullied by its big and aggressive neighbour. The dangerous games the Chogyal was playing were not known outside India. Needless to say, the fact that Sikkim was a protectorate of India only strengthened the image of India as an imperialist power. To add to this, India's neighbours were suspicious of her intentions. Their leaders, having denied democracy to their own people, had not only no sympathy for the movement for democracy in Sikkim but were actually afraid of its spread-effects. Pakistan and China did not lose this opportunity to spout venom. Against this background, it was Indira Gandhi's extraordinary faith in the rightness of India's objectives and her unflinching will to succeed that steered the country through the Sikkim crisis.

CHAPTER TWELVE

My Experience
of the 'Emergency'

On the fateful day of 12 June 1975 I was roused from my bed early in the morning by a call to say that D.P. Dhar had died. DP was our ambassador in Moscow and had come for official consultations to Delhi, where he took ill and was admitted to the Govind Ballabh Pant hospital. I was devastated by the news. DP and I had known each other since our college days in Srinagar. I had seen him just the previous evening; he was to get a pacemaker the next day. He showed no anxiety about himself but was much bothered about the political situation in the country. When I'd left him he'd held my hand a long time and given me a long, silent look. That look haunted me for a long time.

I got ready as quickly as I could and rushed to the hospital. Upon arrival I found Indira Gandhi already there, giving instructions about the funeral and various other arrangements. Leaving the hospital, I tried to reach DP's wife in Moscow. It took my office a long time to contact the embassy and when at last I got the connection and was speaking to DP's wife, Sharada Prasad rushed into my room and in an agitated voice shouted: 'The Allahabad judgement has come and the prime minister has been unseated.' It took me some time to absorb the meaning of what Sharada Prasad was saying as my heart was hewn and my mind crowded out with memories of DP.

Realizing the enormity of Sharada Prasad's news, I went to the prime minister's house (PMH) and saw that some ministers and the Congress president had already arrived and divided themselves into two groups. One group was considering the legal aspects of the judgement and the other its political implications. The former group centred around the law minister and the latter around the Congress president, Dev Kant Barooah. Indira Gandhi was oscillating between one group and the other, uncommunicative and withdrawn. I sat for a little while with each group to get a feel of the situation and later went to my office; the prime minister was keen that the work of government should go on as usual. She asked me to see her every morning at her house as she felt she might not get to the office for the next few days.

Over the first two days after the Allahabad judgment, my meetings with her were taken up entirely with the usual office work. It was only on the third day that I had occasion to discuss with her the problems posed by the judgment. I told her I had received several letters from people expressing views on how to meet the crisis. The bulk were from the usual busybodies, but I had kept the few that were worth reading separately for her to go through. She took the entire lot, saying she would go through them all. Over the ensuing discussion I said that everyone who had read the judgment thought the charges trivial. I reported the views of Fali S. Nariman, the additional solicitor general, who had examined Justice Sinha's judgement in depth. According to Nariman the judgment was based on extremely weak arguments which would not stand careful scrutiny at the supreme court. She was pleased to hear this and added she had been told that *The Times* of London had described the charges as comparable to the violation of traffic rules. I said the opposition had, however, succeeded in making these charges a part of their agitation against corruption; in view of that, it would be better to await the verdict of the supreme court, which, I hoped, would go in her favour. I cautioned against letting the Congress Party launch a counter-agitation against the judgment.

I was referring to the public demonstrations that the Congress Party was organizing in her support and in criticism of the judgment. I said that to argue that the judge's verdict would be rejected by the people, as some Congressmen were saying it would be, was not very different from JP's rhetoric about the Lok Adalat. In my opinion, I said, the best answer to the opposition's clamour for her resignation was to say that she would await the supreme court's verdict on her appeal, to which she was entitled, and abide by it. Until then she must ride the storm. She made no comment except about the demonstrations in front of her house. She said she didn't like all the shouting and the noise, '*magar log nahi mantay*' (but the people don't listen). Her response bothered me a little but I did not think too much about it.

The next day we talked about official matters; nothing more was said about the political crisis. On the 17th, when I met her, she looked agitated and before I could sit down she spoke with anger and said things were going wrong in the office. When I asked what was bothering her, she said I was deliberately sitting on certain home ministry files relating to appointments.

Indira Gandhi had spoken heatedly to me on a few occasions in the past, but never before had she impugned my motives. Since she was vague about the nature of the files, I was not able to respond to her accusation immediately. Even if she had been more specific I might not have been able to answer her because I took very little direct interest in the routine appointment of officers, having left these matters in the hands of a very competent joint secretary. When I looked into the matter I found that 'the files' were one specific file, and this file was no more than a minute by the prime minister saying that certain appointments should be routed through the minister of state in the home ministry who, at the time, was Om Mehta. In the rush of work the file had already gone to the ministry in a routine manner, though after a delay of two days. Had I seen the file I would have realized that it was an attempt to bypass a senior minister, Brahmananda Reddy, and I would certainly not have sent it to the ministry without bringing it to the notice of the prime minister.

It was known to me that Om Mehta was in contact with R.K. Dhawan, who worked as additional private secretary at the PMH. For a moment I thought that the man behind the prime minister's minute must be Dhawan, who was said to be establishing a network of his own to gain personal power. But the way the prime minister spoke to me that morning convinced me there was more to it than Dhawan's manoeuvrings: she obviously had some serious grievance against me. I wondered whether she was irked by my views on the Congress demonstrations. Whatever it was, I came to the conclusion that my position had become untenable and that I should quit. I sent this note to her on the same day, punctiliously written in the required bureaucratese:

This morning PM told me that I was said to be sitting on the file in which she had given instructions regarding routing of proposals for certain appointments through M.O.S. (O.M.). Papers relating to this matter are placed below for P.M's perusal. It will be clear from the notings that necessary action has been taken in accordance with P.M's wishes.

P.M. has known me for a number of years now. I am neither hypersensitive nor demonstrative. I would not have said much about this matter but it seems to me that doubts have arisen in P.M's mind about me. It is crucial that at a time like this P.M. should have a competent and trustworthy Secretary to serve her. I therefore feel that I should quit.

After P.M. has seen this I will put up papers formally.

Before I sent the note I showed it to Sharada Prasad, for whom I had great regard. I was much relieved to find that he supported my decision. I got back the note two days later, though it was initialled by the PM the same day. I did not see her during those two days. When she called me on the third day, she said I did not look well and made solicitous enquiries about my health. Without referring to my letter she said it was a terribly testing time for her and her friends. She had full faith in me but sometimes I was too academic and too detached, she added. As she said this her eyes moistened. I was totally unprepared for this kind of reaction on her part. All I could say was that I was sorry. After an uncomfortable silence of a minute, which felt like an eternity, I left her room feeling I had behaved like a cad by sending her that resignation note.

In the meanwhile things were dangerously heating up in the country. The opposition leaders were casting off all restraint in their campaign to oust the prime minister. Though she was awaiting the judgment of the supreme court on her appeal against the high court judgment, her party continued to organize demonstrations of loyalty in front of her house. She seldom came to the office and was closeted at home most of the time with Dev Kant Barooah, Rajni Patel and S.S. Ray. On 25 June the supreme court gave its conditional stay order on her appeal. That night at 11 p.m. I was called by the prime minister to her house. The atmosphere in the house was tense. Ray and Barooah were there. Ray looked grim while Barooah wore a huge grin and was trying to look relaxed as usual. Mrs Gandhi told me tersely: 'The situation in the country is very bad. We have decided to declare internal emergency. There is going to be a cabinet meeting early in the morning tomorrow after which I am going to broadcast the decision on AIR.' Having said this, she handed me the draft of the proposed speech. Just at that time Sharada Prasad, who had also been summoned, walked in. I went over the draft with Sharada and suggested the addition of the following line in the concluding paragraph of the draft: 'I am sure that internal conditions will speedily improve to enable us to dispense with this proclamation as soon as possible.'

Sharada and I left the house together in despair. After a while he asked me gloomily what would happen at the cabinet meeting. I said mechanically that it would be a routine affair. He fell into a deep silence. All this time I had been cursing myself for not having carried out my decision to resign earlier, when the opportunity for it had arisen.

After 26 June the prime minister resumed her old pattern of work. The only difference was that her pace of work became feverish and she was more businesslike in her manner with officials as well as politicians. She called a special meeting of all secretaries from all ministries and exhorted them to tone up the administrative machinery, cut delays in decisionmaking, and produce tangible results. This was the first time ever that all secretaries had been called for a meeting with the prime minister. Most of them appeared genuinely enthusiastic in their response to the prime minister's call for hard work and discipline. Some, who could not get an opportunity to speak, met me after the meeting and promised to do their best in the new circumstances. In this context the person who made an unforgettable impression on me was an ICS officer who had recently retired and was looking for a job. He said he was dreaming about an opportunity like the one created by the Emergency and his hands were itching to make use of it; all the while he rubbed his hands energetically.

In her own secretariat, however, there was no great enthusiasm, though her staff worked as disciplined officers. They were all aware that a rival mini-secretariat was emerging in the PMH. None of my colleagues made any effort to establish a special relationship with the

PMH, as certain officers from other ministries were doing. The most significant fact was that the PMH was also distancing itself from the PMS. This could not have happened without Mrs Gandhi's explicit instructions. My colleague G. Ramachandran, with his wry sense of humour, used to say that she knew that the PMO was the water works while the PMH was the sewage system, and that though both were needed for public hygiene, they should be kept separate.

These developments were extremely disturbing for me. I was torn by conflicting considerations and could not decide what I should do in the circumstances. I knew that my friend and former colleague P.N. Haksar, who had taken charge of the Planning Commission as deputy chairman a few months earlier, would be in similar mental turmoil. When I consulted him about my dilemma he told me that, as far as he was concerned, he had decided not to resign and had been meaning to tell me this. 'We must stay in the system and try to reverse the process, or at least prevent further degeneration. Outside the system you will count for nothing, although it will certainly bolster your ego to resign.' Several other friends and colleagues who were upset at the declaration of an Emergency gave similar advice. One of them was Syed Mir Qasim. He had become a cabinet minister after resigning the chief ministership of Jammu and Kashmir. I had worked very closely with him during the negotiations which culminated in the Indira Gandhi–Sheikh Abdullah accord in January 1975. He reminded me of the fact that, at the beginning of the negotiations, he had given me his letter of resignation and asked me to use it whenever required in the interest of the accord. He said his purpose in bringing this up was to impress upon me that resignations must serve some purpose. If I stayed on, I might help improve the situation. His view was that if I left the government I would weaken those who wanted the system back to normal.

Having decided to stay on, I had to chalk out my own work priorities. I thought that under the new circumstances it was possible to broaden the scope of economic reforms which had been started in a small and tentative way the previous year to meet the challenge of the oil crisis. I was encouraged by Indira Gandhi's desire to do something in the economic arena which would be as memorable as her handling of the Bangladesh crisis. She had shown great political courage the previous year by accepting unpopular measures to combat inflation. In the circumstances created by the Emergency, with the opposition locked up, I presumed she would find it politically more feasible to revise some of the economic policies which had outgrown their original purpose or were actually counterproductive.

The areas crying for reform were obvious. For example, the policy of import substitution had gone beyond the requirements of protecting infant and strategic industries; the public sector, which was necessary in the early stages of development, had been extended beyond its proper sphere and become a hospital for sick industries; controls which had proliferated had become dysfunctional; labour legislation was preventing improvement in productivity and inducing employers to substitute capital for labour. But even as these policies had become less and less relevant to the solution of India's basic problems of poverty and backwardness, they were upheld by radicals in the Congress Party and outside as harbingers of the socialist society we were supposed to be building. In actual fact, the so-called radicals were merely continuing to provide an ideological justification for the structures of privilege and protection that past excesses of policy had created. I used to quote to them Lenin's famous observation: 'our faults today are the continuation of our merits of yesterday.' But as I said earlier, in actual practice substantive economic reforms did not go beyond the twenty-point programme and some limited gains of a short-term nature.

The second priority which I set for myself was to explore the possibility of a reconciliation between Indira Gandhi and JP. Although my earlier effort in 1974, at the time of economic crisis, had not proved successful, I believed that a post-Emergency reconciliation was imperative. The stakes for both of them were too high to be disregarded. My hope was that the reconciliation would end the Emergency without India going back to the kind of lawlessness which brought it on, or at least provided the major reason for its promulgation.

The first opportunity in this endeavour came in late August 1975, when the prime minister received a message from JP in which he expressed grave concern about the Bihar floods and asked for a month's release on parole so that he might mobilize people's help and organize popular relief in co-operation with the central and state government. The PM did not want to respond directly; she was still feeling the sting of the letter JP had sent her a month earlier in which he had bitterly criticized her. What had hurt her most was his remark that 'nine years is not a short period of time for the people who are gifted with a sixth sense, to have found you out.' She looked upon JP's suggestion as a political ploy. She told me JP was probably trying to upstage the government. I disagreed with that interpretation and told her that in my opinion JP was offering an olive branch. In the meanwhile JP sent another message in which he emphasized that he would not exploit the period of freedom for political purposes. Finally, it was decided that some knowledgeable person should go and reassure JP that all possible arrangements were being made to help the victims of the floods in Bihar.

So I asked B.B. Vohra, additional secretary in the ministry of food and agriculture, who had specialized in water management problems and had been to Bihar and participated in flood-relief work there, to visit JP in Chandigarh and apprise him of relief arrangements undertaken by the government. He did this on 4 September. After listening to Vohra's account of the steps the state and the central government had taken on the floods, JP reiterated his plea for release. He wanted to be free to mobilize popular support for relief work because he felt that government action would not suffice by itself. He also asked Vohra to convey a message to the Government of India, which Vohra jotted down. The highlights of what JP told him were:

A great deal of work needs to be done . . . I am very keen to serve my people . . . confident that I shall be able to rally popular support . . . Even though I am not in touch with them I am confident that all opposition leaders in Bihar will listen to me . . . It would be wrong . . . absolutely improper and morally wrong . . . for me to take political advantage of the present situation in Bihar . . . I have no intention of making even a mention of political matters . . . The British government released political workers in 1934 [the reference was to the release of Rajendra Prasad and others at the time of the Bihar earthquake that year]; the present tragedy calls for a review of the situation for similar means . . . If I am released the whole agitation can be called off . . . a proper atmosphere would have been created.—B.B. Vohra, 5/9/75.

JP had also asked Vohra to tell me verbally that 'this was a good time to review the entire policy that had been followed in the name of the Emergency.' These messages convinced me that JP's stance had changed from one of belligerence and confrontation, and that he was now ready to negotiate. Indira Gandhi did not agree with my view. She thought I was too optimistic, but she was not discouraging either. In spite of her strong reservations, she agreed that it would be desirable to establish some contact with JP but was not sure who could be entrusted with that delicate job. She mentioned the names of two well-known politicians who had earlier undertaken similar missions but failed. When she gave me details of those efforts I felt that those gentlemen had been more interested in augmenting their own political capital than in closing the gulf between her and JP. In view of the earlier experience, she felt there was now a need for a low-profile person who was not an active politician and who JP would trust. The only person who I thought fulfilled these conditions was Sugata Dasgupta, whom JP had appointed as director of the Gandhian Institute of Studies at Varanasi. I had known Dasgupta for some time and had faith in his integrity and competence. After securing Indira Gandhi's approval I talked to him; Dasgupta was very happy to undertake the mission. He was to meet JP on 25 September 1975, but just before his departure for Chandigarh we received a letter from JP addressed to Sheikh Mohammed Abdullah with the request that it be transmitted to the addressee. The letter shed some more light on the way JP's mind was working. After complaining bitterly against the prime minister's reluctance to settle across the table the issues posed by his movement, he concluded his letter with the following statement:

However, in spite of all that has happened and is happening, I am prepared, in the interests of the country, to seek the path of conciliation. I shall, therefore, be much obliged if you kindly see me as soon as possible so that I could discuss this matter with you. I being the villain of the piece, the arch conspirator, the culprit number one, a return to true normalcy, not the false one established by oppression and terror, can only be brought about with my cooperation. I am herewith offering you my full co-operation.

Since JP was now in a mood to explore the possibility of a reconciliation with Indira Gandhi, I thought Sugata Dasgupta's visit was well timed.

Dasgupta had a cordial meeting with JP. He came back with the impression that JP was keen on being released and was looking for a respectable manner of withdrawing the movement. He told Dasgupta that the proposal for people to take up relief work would have given him a suitable opportunity to abandon the movement. Since that had not happened, JP suggested that if the government were to announce the dates for a general election, or electoral or educational reforms, he would withdraw the movement. JP, it appeared to Dasgupta, was troubled by the feeling that people were blaming him for the Emergency—apparently Justice Tarkunde had told him so. JP complained that the prime minister was holding him responsible for all of India's ailments and had called him and his colleagues assassins. When Dasgupta told him that there was a rumour that, on the appointed day of the satyagraha, lakhs of people would surround her house and drag her out to sign her resignation letter, JP immediately intervened in an agitated manner and said: 'But this could not have taken place as this was far from my mind. I have always been non-violent.' Towards the end of the interview JP said that if nothing happened and nobody took note of what he was saying, he might go on a fast at the end of October.

Dasgupta's report encouraged me and I thought we had an opportunity to clinch outstanding issues with JP. But I made the mistake of sending the report to the prime minister in its original form, without comment, and without highlighting the main points. As a result, her reaction was less positive than I had expected. Her written comments to me on the report were:

1. It is not 'rumour' that my house was to be surrounded. It is what Oriana Fallaci reported Morarji as saying.
2. I have not blamed JP for 'all' or any ills; (a) only for blaming all ills on the

Congress and me personally; (b) for giving respectability to the RSS, JS, Marxists and Naxalites; (c) for giving a clean chit to corrupt elements while talking about corruption. And making political use of corruption; (d) offering shelter to the corrupt in the Congress and (e) for inciting students, government servants, police . . . defence services.

3. I have never called him an assassin.
4. I have said that other parties and groups are taking advantage of him.
5. THERE CAN BE NO QUESTION OF CONDITIONS. [These words were in capital letters.]
6. If he fasts, I think we should deport him to the UK or USA. Let his 'friends' look after him.

The outburst of polemics was followed by a directive:

This does not mean that we should not negotiate. If there is the remotest possibility of success we should make every effort. However, I must state that I do not trust his word. But this is just a thought to keep at the back of your mind.

Sugata met JP again on 9 October. This time the results were less reassuring. The deputy commissioner had been asked not to be present at the meeting even though this was required by the rules. In his effort to let Sugata meet JP alone and at the same time keep that a secret from his staff, the deputy commissioner had planned to go with him to JP's room and then move into an anteroom which had been set up the previous day. JP, not knowing the purpose of the new arrangement, had got the impression that some dignitaries were coming to see him: it could either be Sheikh Abdullah responding to his call, or perhaps the committee for the review of the Maintenance of Internal Security Act was going to interview him by way of a prelude to his release, as was speculated by the press. He was therefore full of expectation.

He could not hide his disappointment when, instead of dignitaries, he saw Sugata, who had nothing more exciting to tell him than that the government was considering raising the number of interviews he had requested and expanding the definition of the 'family' to allow his nephews and such like to meet him. He had, however, the unpleasant job of telling him that whereas his non-political letters would be sent to their addresses promptly, the political letters would be returned to him. Saying this, he returned the letter JP had written Sheikh Abdullah. To soften the impact of the bad news, Sugata also informed him that he had learnt that JP's brother-in-law had sent the Sheikh messages along the lines of his own letter. This information mollified JP somewhat. Sugata added that since the Sheikh knew that JP was keen on his intervention in his dispute with the government, he should let the matter rest and wait for the Sheikh's reaction. JP accepted Sugata's advice and next day, when Sugata met him again, JP handed back the letter to him, asking him to keep it or let 'Dhar keep it', since he had kept a copy for himself. After repeating, once again, that there was no question of his reviving the movement, JP outlined his plan of action to him: 'If elections are announced and I am freed, I will try to support the opposition. Of course, I would not take part in the elections or have anything to do with them after they are over. But I would try to so arrange matters that there is one candidate from each constituency. The BLD, the JS and Congress(O) should give up their identities and merge.' Sugata further reported that JP thought the Socialists would not join him in his task; that the JS, as a party with its present image, had no future and that the names of the parties should be done away with and a new party should emerge. He also told Sugata:

I know that the results of elections will be difficult to predict. If the group I support loses, then I would be quite prepared to leave politics. I stand for elections and surely for this type of democracy. I would make it quite clear to the people that I have full faith in this democracy and I will be prepared to go all out for it. I shall seek no office but I shall try to see that such an alliance wins the election. If they lose and Congress wins, all this should be accepted with grace.

Sugata had hastened to ask whether the ensuing elections should be under the existing electoral laws—or would he insist that the laws be changed forthwith? 'No,' JP said, 'the changes could be made by the next parliament and elections need not wait for that.' Sugata then asked whether there should not be an understanding between the opposition and the prime minister on there being no violence. JP replied that the immediate understanding should be that the movement was withdrawn and all parties would fight the election accepting it as the only way of sorting out their differences. He felt it should be sorted out through the ballot but that one could discuss matters before and after it.

Besides outlining his election strategy to Sugata, JP made other observations, two of which I found interesting. One was about his disillusionment with Congress dissidents who he had thought would leave the party but who were now condemning him in public. The other related to Sanjay Gandhi's interview with a Delhi journalist which JP had liked. He was, it seems, pleasantly surprised at the views expressed by the young man! In his interview Sanjay had severely criticized the Soviet Union and the Communist Party and made critical comments on the economic policies of the government.

From Sugata's reports it was clear that JP was chafing at his continued imprisonment. Moreover, it seemed to me that in the absence of a higher level of contact, he had probably come to the conclusion that the prime minister was not interested in serious negotiations. He conveyed it by his emphasis on the elections as the only way out of the impasse. In his frustration he asked Sugata rhetorically: 'What should I do if the elections are not announced and democracy goes?' Answering this himself, he said: 'in that case I would prefer to remain in jail and read and write. In such a scheme of things it will not be possible for me even to oppose the government because people like me can function only in a democracy.'

In normal circumstances the general elections should have been held in January/February 1976. Had they been held then, there is no doubt that the Congress Party would have won. People felt gratified at the positive results of the Emergency regime, notably the revival of the economy, price stability, relief from strikes and hartals, and a general atmosphere of discipline and peace. Indira Gandhi feared that the 'Emergency gains', as these positive results were called, would be dissipated in the atmosphere that general elections were bound to generate. Sanjay Gandhi and his advisors wanted to postpone elections as long as possible because they needed time to further their own plans. Sanjay had ambitions of becoming an independent power centre and a leader in his own right. His five-point programme and his attempt to forge the Youth Congress—an auxiliary body of the Congress Party—into a parallel if not a rival organization of the parent body pointed in that direction. To impress his cronies that he had a mind of his own, he was frequently irreverent about his grandfather and mother. Indira Gandhi was much impressed by Sanjay's organizational abilities but aware of his limitations. She would say: 'Sanjay is a doer, not a thinker.' Actually his mother was not the only one impressed by his drive and ability to get things done; I remember vividly J.R.D. Tata telling me how impressed he was by Sanjay's pragmatism. He called on me one day, soon after he had met Sanjay, and was overflowing with praise for the young man. JRD had met me occasionally and discussed economic affairs, but on that occasion he was only full of Sanjay.

Indira Gandhi believed that, given more time, the gains of the Emergency would multiply. In the event, the general elections due in early 1976 were postponed by a year. Though disappointed at the decision about the elections, I hoped that their postponement would provide more time to negotiate with JP and enable us to evolve a consensus on the fundamentals of how democracy was to operate in the country. But this hope was to turn sour.

In early November 1975, before the decision to postpone the election was taken, we got reports that JP was suffering from a serious kidney ailment. Consequently, he was released on parole on 11 or 12 November. I had asked Sugata to be in Chandigarh in case JP needed anything for which he might not want to approach the local officials. I was glad to learn from Sugata that JP felt he was looked after very well and had no cause to complain about the hospital. He asked Sugata to tell me that the situation should be normalized and he should be released. After being released, he said, he would want to go to Delhi or Bombay for more complete treatment—nobody should think that he would be precipitate, given his state of health. He also felt there was no purpose in carrying on the movement; he would concentrate on the elections when they came. JP was also sure that 'Indiraji will win the elections, and it is wrong to think that I will remove her by undemocratic methods. I am no threat to the government.' When Sugata asked him how he would feel if the elections were postponed for valid reasons, JP reacted positively by saying that although he would like the elections to be on schedule he would not misunderstand postponement if there were valid reasons. I was much relieved by that observation because I was afraid that the postponement, against which he had laid much emphasis, might put him off completely.

When JP was transferred from Chandigarh to the All-India Institute of Medical Sciences in Delhi, I went to see him, partly to make sure he was well looked after. He was tired and sounded weak but was very pleased to see me. He thanked me graciously for keeping in touch with him and assured me he was willing to play a constructive role. He added, however, that since he had been identified with the opposition he had to consult their representatives as well. His only complaint was that our talks were dragging on without concrete result. I told him we needed time for the walls of distrust between him and the prime minister to come down. He said he would feel more comfortable if I kept in direct touch with him and avoided intermediaries. I promised to do my best.

To keep up the momentum of these talks with JP, I thought we needed someone with a political background and a flair for negotiations, someone who was also involved in JP's movement and had wide contacts with opposition leaders. I asked Radhakrishna, secretary of the Gandhi Peace Foundation, who was on parole, to take over from Sugata. Radhakrishna went into action wholeheartedly. He stayed with JP for several days at a time and kept in touch with some opposition leaders. After discussions with JP he wrote to me on 14 March 1976, saying that JP should not be identified with the rest of the opposition but should be utilized to bring about a changed role and a working relationship between the ruling party and the opposition. 'My anxiety is that JP is daily becoming sceptical whether there will be response from your side at all,' Radhakrishna wrote and urged me to meet JP. He thought the meeting would clear the decks for a face-to-face meeting between JP and the prime minister. Radhakrishna emphasized that JP was 'eager to find an honourable solution to the present impasse. Even his plea for early elections was aimed at defusing the situation.'

I was keen to meet JP myself but felt I should have something to offer which would serve as a basis for reconciliation between the ruling party and the opposition. Mrs Gandhi was not forthcoming with anything specific. I told her that without something concrete, my visit to JP would look like yet another probing mission which, in my opinion, was unnecessary at a stage when JP had laid his cards on the table. In response, she noted on Radhakrishna's letter: 'To keep contact is good but if you go, the publicity will not be good and some will take advantage of it.' My reading of her reaction was that she was influenced by strong opposition not only from Sanjay but also from Barooah, Rajni Patel and pro-CPI elements in the Congress Party who were opposed to negotiating with JP: that was seen as an American ploy to weaken the prime minister.

In the meanwhile, sometime in May, an incident occurred which roused Indira Gandhi's ire against Radhakrishna. An appeal had been made by him to people abroad and at home for funds to buy and maintain a dialyser for JP. At Radhakrishna's suggestion, and with my full support, Indira Gandhi made a handsome contribution from the prime minister's relief fund for this purpose. Radhakrishna sent an acknowledgement of the donation after receiving JP's concurrence. However, Mrs Gandhi's donation had, according to Radhakrishna, 'stirred a number of hardliners' in JP's camp and he was made to return the money. This incident came as a godsend to the opponents of negotiations. It was contended that if JP could not resist the hardliners in reaction to a gesture of good will, he would be powerless against them in more serious matters. The incident was a setback to our efforts but Radhakrishna took it in his stride and continued to work with zest, as before.

Sometime in the first week of July I got a telegram from JP requesting me to meet him. This was the handiwork of Radhakrishna. Feeling he had lost credibility with Indira Gandhi, he had got JP to send the telegram direct. Somehow, Radhakrishna had worked himself up to the belief that my meeting with JP would break the logjam. I was much less certain because I observed that the prime minister was becoming sceptical about the usefulness of these negotiations. However, she found it difficult to disregard JP's direct request to me. She raised no difficulties about my visit to Bombay, but at the same time she had nothing to say on substantive issues between JP and the government.

I met JP in Bombay on 16 July at 47 Quest End, Cuffe Parade,

I met JP in Bombay on 16 July at 47 Quest End, Cuffe Parade, where he was staying. He had his dialysis in the morning and looked relaxed and in much better shape than when I had met him in Delhi earlier. After a few preliminary remarks about his health he came to business right away. He began by saying that the only reason he had asked me to take the trouble to come down to Bombay was that he wanted his thoughts to be conveyed to the prime minister accurately. He felt his health had improved and he had regained some vitality and believed he would like to use his improved physical state for the good of the country. He seemed to be genuinely sad when he said that he should be held partly responsible for bringing the country to this pass. He never thought that his attempts to remove corruption from government and politics would lead to the abolition of civil liberties. He had learnt his lesson and believed that most opposition groups had learnt their lesson as well, and those who had not were not worth much. At this point I intervened and told him that the prime minister felt that the opposition were taking advantage of him. The Jan Sangh and the RSS had trained cadres and a well-defined ideology from which they were not going to be swayed, I said. JP replied that he knew some people thought they had made a fool of him, but the fact was 'they have met me, including the Poona group and surrendered to me.' I was astonished at his naivete and expressed my scepticism about their demonstration of deference to him. I told him that at best it could be a tactical move on their part. JP then went on to give me his vision of the Bihar movement, and his involvement in it, which according to him started—a typical example of the selective memory of politicians—with the police firing on students in Gaya. He made no reference to his demand for the Bihar ministry's resignation. He wanted only electoral and educational reforms and the removal of corruption, he said. 'I have no rancour for P.M. and no ego except to help P.M. in restoring democracy,' he added with great deliberation.

I briefed him on external relations and economic policies. He said there was now a greater balance in those areas and added that 'there should be a similar balance in the internal political life of the country.' And to achieve that balance he wanted to know what guarantees and assurances were required by the prime minister. 'I will give whatever

I can and what I cannot I will say why I cannot.' And for that purpose he should be allowed to meet the relevant political leaders. He hoped our meeting would be 'a first step on the path of peace and for a disciplined democracy.' At this point I told him about the reports the government had about underground political activity. He said he was unable to ask them to call them off until he was able to hold out some hope to them.

The meeting had lasted an hour and a half when someone came in to show JP his plans for the next week. I discovered he was already planning to go to Patna via Nagpur, where he wanted to meet Vinoba Bhave. Bhave was on a hunger strike to persuade the government to ban cow slaughter. This, I thought, would give me a chance to raise the question of the use of fast-unto-death as a political weapon. But JP bypassed it by saying that this cow business was an irrelevant issue. It would unnecessarily create problems in the north-eastern states.

Having come to Bombay with misgivings about the outcome of the meeting with JP, I became hopeful at the way things had gone. However, I was flummoxed when he said that he would like to know the prime minister's reaction to his views as soon as he reached Patna, which gave me hardly four days! JP was obviously impatient, and I could not blame him. I had no choice but to tell him that it would take more time than that for me to report to the prime minister, get her response to the basic issues of educational and electoral reforms that he had raised, and get back to him.

While Indira Gandhi was fully informed about the attempts made to bring about a reconciliation between the government and the opposition, she was steadily yielding ground to Sanjay in his strivings for power. By early 1976 Sanjay and the group around him at the PMH had expanded to include Bansi Lal, who had been shifted from Haryana to become defence minister; Om Mehta, minister of state in the home ministry; and Kishen Chand, the new lieutenant governor of Delhi.

With the informal assistance of obliging officers, the PMH had started functioning like a well-oiled extra-constitutional authority, even aspiring for greater control over the decision-making process of the government. They did not like the idea that the PMS was outside their range of influence. After Nirmal Mukerjee's departure from the home ministry, they had gained significant control over that ministry. The head of the Delhi administration was now at their beck and call.

But this was not enough for the PMH. They had tasted power and were thirsting for more. At first they adopted the tactic of approaching individual officers in the PMS, telling them what to do in matters which interested Sanjay. This was done through R.K. Dhawan, the additional private secretary posted at the PMH, who had access to his colleagues in the PMS. He would convey what he wanted as though he was passing on instructions from the prime minister. The officer concerned would invariably report to me about this and explain the implications of Dhawan's suggestions, and seek my instructions. Most often Dhawan's demands were of a kind which could not be entertained. This was resented and the PMH started complaining to the prime minister about the unhelpful attitude of her own secretariat which, according to them, stood in sharp contrast with the co-operation they received from senior officers in other departments and ministries. What was most galling for them was that no officer of the PMS ever went to meet Sanjay or Dhawan to take instruction on any matter, big or small.

In these circumstances, the PMH adopted the byzantine technique of poisoning the ears of the prime minister against senior officers of her secretariat. The first victim of this campaign was B.N. Tandon, a joint secretary, a very able and painstaking officer who used to handle matters relating to the ministry of home affairs and the Delhi administration. Files sent by him, particularly those which dealt with appointments, started getting delayed at the PMH. We learnt that the reason for this delay was to make sure that the candidates recommended would be suitable for their purposes. The criteria of merit and integrity were being replaced by a new emphasis on loyalty. Since the ministry which initiated the proposals had already been taken under their de facto control, the PMH wanted the PMS to be a mere post office for these files. Tandon's careful notings on these files were being found irksome.

In the PMS the established procedure was that matters which required a decision from the prime minister were put up to her after a thorough examination, with suggestions, where necessary, regarding the alternatives. The work of the secretariat was divided by subject and ministry among senior officers. Excepting the most important matters, which went up to the prime minister through the principal secretary/secretary, senior officers sent papers direct to her while keeping the principal secretary/secretary informed. The success of the arrangement was essentially due to the fact that the senior officers worked as a team. Mrs Gandhi's disposal of files was quick; papers submitted to her were returned with her orders within a day. Papers sent to her during the day were disposed of before she left the office the same evening, and those sent to her house were received back the next morning. But under the new dispensation, files pertaining to personnel began to pile up at the PMH. After a month or so of this development, I complained to the prime minister that while we were expecting other ministries to quicken the pace of decisionmaking, our own office was becoming a bottleneck. She did not reply and turned the conversation to some other subject. Next morning she sent me the following note marked personal and secret.

I was astonished when you told me yesterday that files were pending with me. Immediately on my return home I checked on the position. I find that only six or seven cases are pending from before and there is reason for each one as they have to be gone into further. All the other cases were given to me only on the 25th. Two cases were received on the 20th when I was away on tour. On the 21st I had no time to look at these particular files.

A note from you regarding the appointment of Additional Secretaries is pending. But perhaps you remember I had noted earlier that these proposals should be kept pending until the panel is approved because I wanted to know why certain persons have not been included and also because I wanted to get an integrated picture of the entire panel.

sd/-
Indira Gandhi
27.4.76

Despite this defensive note to me, Mrs Gandhi had conveyed her annoyance at the delays to people at the PMH. This had enraged Sanjay. I learnt this from N.K. Seshan, her private secretary, who was present when Sanjay was fulminating against me, telling his mother that what was wrong with her secretariat was her secretary and not its officials. He also told her that what the secretariat needed was a loyal administrator with experience of law and order, someone who personally knew senior civil servants. Seshan worked mostly in the PMS but was also required to be at the PMH: he was my only colleague who functioned at both places. Being a man of exceptional integrity, he was unhappy at what he saw was happening at the PMH. One day, after a heated argument that he had with Dhawan, he came to me with his letter of resignation. The only reason he stayed on was because I told him that by resigning he would please Dhawan. I did not forward his letter to the prime minister but told her about the incident. Dhawan did not like it and saw to it that Seshan's visits to the PMH were drastically reduced.

A few days after I had received Mrs Gandhi's note on delayed files, H.C. Sarin, a retired member of the Indian Civil Service, paid a casual visit to my office. He said he had come to see the prime minister but thought he would say 'hello' to me as well. He was carrying a bundle of papers which, he said, contained his suggestions about a fresh set of slogans that would popularize the Emergency regime and explain its rationale. He also mentioned that he was the author of slogans that had appeared soon after the declaration of Emergency. The only thing I remember about the slogans was their emphasis on the need for discipline. While on the subject he said, 'You know, P.N., the impression about you is that you have lots of brains but what you do not have is the *danda* in your hand that your job requires.' This was said in a bantering tone and we both laughed.

I did not think much of Sarin's remark until it came back to me in a rather unusual way. One day my friend G. Parthasarathy, who had joined the ministry of external affairs as chairman of the policy planning committee, came to see me, as he would from time to time. I don't remember how the conversation started but it got round to an expression of concern for my health. He told me that, for some time past, every time he came to see me he found me under strain. I said in my kind of job I could not help being under stress. He said I should leave my present job and immediately added that I could have any other job I liked because, he was sure, the prime minister would want me to stay around. I laughed at his remark but he returned to the subject with an insistence which did not come naturally. He had taken Talleyrand's advice to diplomats—that they should not be overzealous—to heart, not only in professional matters but as a philosophy of life. His excessive concern for my health made me suspicious. From the way he talked I felt he was conveying a message. When he said my job was no longer suitable for me, I asked him who he would like as a replacement. He answered without hesitation: 'a man like H.C. Sarin.' At that point I do not know what happened to me. I almost shouted at him and said that I was not leaving my job unless I was dismissed. G.P., who was a gentle and soft-spoken man, was a little flustered at my agitation and for the first time since I had known him he raised his voice and said: 'What is the matter with you? I was just worrying about your health.' 'Don't worry about my health, I'm fine,' I replied. That ended the conversation.

Reflecting on G.P.'s advice, I was convinced there was more to it than his concern for my health. I thought that perhaps the prime minister had asked him to speak to me. Perhaps she was not interested in negotiations with JP and did not want to say so. She had given me no such indication directly. The only contentious issue between us at that time was on B.N. Tandon's account. She invariably had some complaint or grievance against him. A few months earlier another joint secretary had been added to the staff in view of the Emergency. P.N. Behl, this new joint secretary, was supposed to relieve Tandon of some of his work and replace him after he moved out of the secretariat. Behl did not fit in the secretariat and was most uncomfortable. After a while we were told he had fallen ill. I was not able to find out the nature of his illness. My colleagues believed he simply could not stand the pressure of work. Mrs Gandhi was embarrassed by Behl's non-performance because he was her choice, or more correctly Sanjay's choice, and I had played no part in his appointment.

Though Behl's appointment had not proved a great success for the

PMH, their litany against the secretary and his colleagues continued unabated. Seshan always knew exactly what was going on because the junior staff at PMH found relief from the tense atmosphere by unburdening themselves to him. A week or ten days after GP'had spoken to me, Seshan told me he had learnt that Sanjay wanted to get rid of me because he believed I was sending secret messages to jailed opposition leaders. The leader with whom I was supposed to be conspiring was Morarji Desai. It so happened that a few days earlier Arvind Buch, a trade union leader of Ahmedabad and an admirer of Desai, came to see me to enquire after Desai's health. I assured him there was nothing to worry about, but if he wished he could go and see him at the Tavdu irrigation guesthouse in Gurgaon, where Desai was being held: Buch was delighted at this unexpected offer and wrote a letter of thanks to me after his visit to Gurgaon. That was all there was to the conspiracy with Desai. The incident, however, got me worried: if a casual visit to Desai could cause so much concern in Sanjay, what would he not do to sabotage negotiations with JP? My departure, whether voluntary or enforced, would help him in that effort. I needed to check where the PM stood in this matter.

At our usual meeting the next morning I found her in a plaintive mood. This time it was not only against Tandon but against the entire office. 'Nothing gets done until I take the initiative,' she said angrily. This remark had become her refrain to rationalize the activities of her son and his cohorts. With what Seshan had told me at the back of my mind, I seized a chance to talk about myself. I told her that I had been working in the PMS for nearly six years, a long enough time for anyone to get stale. Under the prevailing circumstances, the office needed someone with greater administrative experience, I added. She cooled down and said I had been working too hard and needed relief, but that I could not go. She asked me if I had anyone in view who could help out. I mentioned H.C. Sarin. She remarked that he was very competent but immediately changed the subject. I followed up this conversation with a formal note about Sarin's appointment without mentioning the designation of the job: I left that to her. Sarin, having learnt about the proposal from V.C. Shukla—a daily visitor to Sanjay in the PMH—came to see me and said he would like to be an adviser rather than my replacement, but added that basically he had agreed to shoulder any responsibility. In the event, nothing happened; the PM did not respond to my note. When I raised the matter again she merely said, '*Theek nahin hai*' (It isn't okay).

Sometime in June 1976, when my seniormost colleague G. Ramachandran, an additional secretary, was due for promotion, I got another chance to talk to the prime minister about myself. I told her my contract was to end in November the following year, by which time I would have spent seven years in the secretariat, too long a period for anyone to stay in a job like mine. I reminded her that when I joined the secretariat I had worked as an understudy to her secretary, P.N. Haksar, for nine months. I suggested it was time we thought of a similar arrangement for my successor. Mrs Gandhi reacted with alacrity. She said it was an excellent idea and that I should come up with a name; in the meanwhile she would think about it. Within two or three days, before I had begun my search, she told me she had heard very good reports about A.T. Bambavale, an IAS officer from the ministry of finance, who was at that time on deputation with the Asian Development Bank at Manila. She asked me for my opinion of him. When I told her I did not know much about him, she repeated that she had heard excellent reports and that we should try and get him.

Bombavale joined us a month later. Even though I was told that his candidature was sponsored by Sanjay and Dhawan, he did not give the impression of being their man. He was very correct and proper in his behaviour and quickly fitted into the ethos of the secretariat and gave no cause for complaint. He did not pry into matters that were not his concern. He was keen to earn the good will and co-operation of his colleagues in the secretariat, in preparation of taking over from me after my departure in November. Whether he disappointed his sponsors I do not know. Perhaps they were wanting me to go before they took charge of the PMS.

April 1976 was a difficult month for me, and not only because of my emerging conflict with the PMH on the question of appointments. It was in that month that the new family planning programme was adopted. The programme was a mix of incentives and disincentives and proved a turning point in Sanjay's political ascendancy. Since family planning was one of the five points of his programme, he un-officially took over its implementation in states like Haryana, UP and Bihar, where the chief ministers were anxious to do his bidding. Delhi was, of course, his private fief. In their anxiety to reach impressive targets, the programme degenerated into a campaign for compulsory sterilization on a scale which sent shock waves all around North India.

The family planning programme further aggravated the conflict between the PMS and Sanjay. I started getting complaints about forced sterilization from diverse sources, including some that were official. Although most were reluctant to speak out in writing, some were pre-pared to take the risk. One such was Prem Sagar Gupta of the CPI who gave a factual report which I sent to the prime minister. It came back to me with a note from her saying that all the allegations made in the report were found baseless and that we should not listen to motivated stories. The promptness with which the report was returned gave me the impression that her note must have been based on verbal assurance given to her by Sanjay or one of his cronies, without enquiry.

She was so convinced about the veracity of what they told her that on 4 October 1976 she wrote a letter to C. Rajeswara Rao, the general secretary of the CPI, the only non-Congress party which had sup-ported the Emergency, in which she complained against 'the manner in which your party is working against us in some districts . . . Last time also I specifically told you about the CPI's opposition to our family planning programme. This is now reaching limits which can-not coexist with cooperation with us.' The prime minister's letter did not deter the CPI from bringing to the government's notice cases where coercive methods had been used while implementing the new family planning policy. On 25 October 1976 Rajeswara Rao sent to Dr Karan Singh, minister of health and family planning, an eighteen-page report which gave details of the excesses committed when enforc-ing sterilization. A copy of the report was sent to me, which I passed on to the prime minister. A day later another memorandum contain-ing similar facts about the happenings in the Muzaffarnagar district was sent by some MPs and MLAs to the prime minister, the president, the chief minister of UP, and to Shahnawaz Khan and Khurshid Alam

Khan. Mrs Gandhi's reaction to all these complaints was that it was an orchestration of anti-Sanjay propaganda.

I was not able to fathom the reasons for Sanjay's disregard of criticism against his family planning programme. One might have been able to explain it had he been just a power-drunk technocrat impervious to the political consequences of his actions. He was not that; in fact he had revealed his political ambitions soon after the declaration of Emergency. Just two months after that event, Sanjay gave an interview to Uma Vasudev, a Delhi journalist, in which he outlined a political credo which caused his mother great embarrassment. The way she handled that episode threw some light on the nature of the relationship between mother and son.

On the evening of Sunday, the 27th of July 1976, I received an urgent message that the prime minister wanted to see me at once. The message could not have been more ill timed. I was at my brother's place in Greater Kailash for a rare family get-together. I had to abandon the dinner and rush off to see the prime minister. It must have taken me no more than half an hour to reach her. Even so, Mrs Gandhi was impatient and had scribbled a longish note for me. 'Sanjay has done something terrible and I am upset,' she said, while handing me the note. It was about the interview—in which Sanjay had attacked the USSR, CPI, and the previous economic policies, besides holding forth on a variety of other issues. The interview was a calculated attempt to please the Americans. To get the largest possible publicity for this interview, elaborate arrangements had been made and the attention of several important people drawn to it. Mrs Gandhi was greatly concerned about the adverse reaction of the CPI and the Russians, who had supported the Emergency. She suggested I do something by way of damage control. This was not very difficult at that time because of press censorship rules. She could easily have asked Vidya Charan Shukla, her minister for information and broadcasting, to do what was required. But she did not. Perhaps she was afraid that Shukla, who was taking his orders from Sanjay, might betray her. It was much safer to ask me to do her bidding because Sanjay would believe that I had acted on my own. It was apparent to me by this that Mrs Gandhi was, in

The first two pages of a handwritten note from Indira Gandhi to P.N. Dhar
on Sanjay Gandhi's interview

The second two pages of a handwritten note from Indira Gandhi to P.N. Dhar on Sanjay Gandhi's interview

The final two pages of a handwritten note from Indira Gandhi to P.N. Dhar on Sanjay Gandhi's interview

some ways, afraid of her son, at least to the extent of fearing his displeasure.

To my mind the interview was not an indiscreet act of a headstrong youth or an inept advisor, as Mrs Gandhi had suggested to me. It was a daring attempt to bypass the prime minister. More disconcertingly, it demonstrated that she had very little control over him. In fact it was being said that he had made irreverent remarks about his grandfather and described his mother's cabinet with the epithet 'ignorant buffoons.' I had also heard reports about his admiration for Ferdinand Marcos of the Philippines: one of the few books that adorned Sanjay's shelf was *The Democratic Revolution in the Philippines* by Marcos. Copies of this book had been presented by the author to Mrs Gandhi and her entourage during Marcos' visit to Delhi. It was this book, I was told, that had fired Sanjay's imagination and made him look upon Marcos as his role model.

In his quest for power Sanjay was also trying to establish contact with foreign missions in Delhi. One of his cronies was reported to regularly meet a US embassy official in a very suspicious manner. He would park his car at Safdarjang Road, the residence of the prime minister, and walk across to the Delhi Gymkhana Club to meet him. It seemed to me that Sanjay was getting impatient for the driver's seat. His success in bringing about the Emergency with ease and without opposition had given him a great deal of self-confidence. In the Youth Congress he had a political organization under his direct control. He was now reaching out to establish contacts outside the country on his own. The interview, it seemed to me, was a clear first sign of this.

Indira Gandhi wanted her son to succeed her, but not so soon. She would have liked him to curb his adventurism, to learn more about India and the world, to give up the company of his lumpen friends and advisors; in short, to serve a period of apprenticeship and be maturer for the eventual job. He did not, of course, pay much attention to her opinions. He thought his mother a ditherer who would act only when pushed by a person with stronger convictions, or when the circumstances left no alternative. He believed he knew the kind of leadership India needed, and he was going to provide it. What was alarming was Mrs Gandhi's ambivalent attitude to her son's recklessness. I was not sure whether she was simply unwilling or plainly unable to restrain him. With all her known strengths, there were points of vulnerability: Sanjay seemed to know them better than anyone else and exploited them most cynically. All one can say is that Mrs Gandhi's problem with Sanjay was psychologically complex and far from being a simple case of a widowed mother's difficulties with an impetuous son.

Given his ambitions, Sanjay had perhaps calculated that the Emergency would last long enough for people to forget their adverse reactions to the family planning excesses, and that the middle class, which was his constituency, would welcome the longer-term beneficial results of a reduced growth in population. It was therefore obvious that any attempt to restore normality in the country would meet with his implacable opposition. He favoured an indefinite postponement of the elections, whereas negotiations with JP were about agreement on the reforms that would bring in a more orderly democratic system. The agreement was to be followed up with a free and fair election. All this was anathema to Sanjay. He had by now become the main hope of all those who had developed a vested interest in the Emergency. Radhakrishna, my main contact with JP and other opposition leaders, became his *bete noir*. Sanjay thwarted me in my attempts to secure Radhakrishna's unconditional release. I had to work hard to get him freed on parole from time to time. Mrs Gandhi used to receive reports about the subversive activities of the Gandhi Peace Foundation and the dangerous role of Radhakrishna. These reports were no doubt inspired by Sanjay to discredit him and paralyse my efforts. Despite these handicaps, Radhakrishna continued to work for reconciliation till the time Mrs Gandhi announced the general elections. His last report to me was dated 12 January 1977, based on a visit to JP in Patna.

According to Radhakrishna, reports about JP's contacts with the government had reached the opposition leaders in jail. They were curious to know what was going on and, being politicians, they wanted to be part of the act. But barring Morarji Desai, most were in a demoralized state. Biju Patnaik and Karunanidhi tried to initiate talks among opposition leaders on how to break the deadlock. Patnaik circulated a note on the subject but could not go far as neither of them had the confidence of the opposition parties. JP had no use for their efforts.

Towards the end of 1976, some of the representatives of the four non-communist opposition parties did meet to prepare for a dialogue with the government in order to restore normal democratic political processes in the country. But JP was anxious to keep these efforts under his own control to prevent confusion among the opposition parties. Soon after the four-party meeting, Radhakrishna spent the weekend of 8–9 January with him. In his talks, which turned out to be the last before the announcement of elections, JP emphasized the need for direct talks between the prime minister and himself, without intermediaries. He told Radhakrishna: 'if someone [had] to prepare some grounds, an agenda or atmosphere, someone like P.N. Dhar or Achyut Patwardhan could be useful. P.N. Dhar could go to Patna and have a quiet and unnoticed meeting.' JP himself was 'prepared to go to Delhi if matters required his meeting with P.N. Dhar.'

On substantive matters, JP spoke to Radhakrishna at some length. The main points he made were:

(1) A postmortem of the past would be disastrous to meaningful dialogue. The opposition's readiness and commitment to ideals, principles and methods were clear and unequivocal as recorded in the document recently released by them.

(2) A meaningful dialogue could begin only after all political prisoners had been released unconditionally and civil liberties and press freedoms restored. The withdrawal of the agitation and the dissolution of the Sangharsh Samiti could follow simultaneously.

(3) The question whether with the restoration of normality there would be a 'return' to conditions prior to the Emergency, namely agitational tactics by opposition parties, disturbances on campuses and disorder in trade unions, was of primary importance. This was perhaps where the gains of the Emergency would be sought to be consolidated. While these matters needed to be discussed thoroughly, JP's own attitude was that he had never accepted political tactics such as *gherao* etc., nor did he consider that trade-union activities, as they were, were satisfactory. On the contrary, he had been advocating a better and broader sense of social responsibility among trade unions. At the root of campus troubles were an indifferent education and unresponsive authorities. But these were questions that could be fully discussed and a consensus reached.

(4) He was, however, deeply concerned about the issue he had raised at the time of the Bihar movement. Lifting the Emergency might normalize

political life, but there was a need for free and fair elections without the use of large sums of money. He was also concerned about the urgent need of educational reconstruction, involving youth in national development, and the eradication of corruption by establishing the institutions of Lok Ayukta and Lok Pal with adequate powers.

Radhakrishna's report was full of promise but it was doomed because Indira Gandhi had lost interest in a settlement with JP and, through him, with the opposition. I found it hard to say this to Radhakrishna. It was painful for me to see her no longer seeking a national reconciliation, which alone would have secured a consensus on how democracy could function meaningfully in the country. Now that negotiations with JP had ended in nothing, I did not know where to look for a way out of the deadlock.

As the negotiations with JP were getting downgraded the efforts to reform the constitution were gathering momentum. After the passage of the thirty-eighth and thirty-ninth amendments, which made the declaration of an emergency non-justiciable and protected the 1971 election of Mrs Gandhi, many in the Congress Party and outside began to make suggestions about changes in the constitution. According to them, these would make it possible to restore normality in the country. Opinions on the subject varied from reform of the existing parliamentary procedures through changeover from the parliamentary to a presidential form of democracy, to a thinly veiled and crudely constructed arrangement for absolute power in the hands of a chief executive.

This demand for reform had its own history, which pre-dated the declaration of an Emergency. It began in 1967 when, in their judgement on the Golak Nath case, the supreme court decided by a majority of six to five that the fundamental rights, including the right to property, were part of the basic structure of the constitution. In such matters the constitution could not be amended under the ordinary amendatory process provided in the existing constitution under article 368.

Agitations for reversal of the judgement were, however, confined to radical elements in the Congress Party and carried on by the Congress Forum for Socialist Action. The legal difficulties into which legislations on bank nationalization and the abolition of the privy purses of the princes had run gave further support and impetus to the effort of radicals for a comprehensive revision of the constitution. These revisions, they contended, were necessary to promote economic and social revolution in the country.

After the elections of 1971 the radicals in the Congress Party, who were reinforced by the inclusion of several ex-communists, acquired a position of dominance in the higher counsels of the party. They used their freshly gained influence to agitate for the restoration of parliament's power to amend the fundamental rights denied by the supreme court in 1967. Mrs Gandhi, who was convinced that her spectacular electoral success was due to her radical call for the abolition of poverty, endorsed the radical demand. The result was the passage of the twenty-fourth, twenty-fifth and twenty-sixth amendments of the constitution in quick succession, within just one year, from August 1971 to September 1972. The amendments, in the opinion of Mohan Kumaramangalam, a leading spokesman of the forum, 'made a single whole' based on the concept of the sovereignty of the people as expressed through their representatives in parliament.

These amendments did not go unchallenged. In 1973, in a writ petition which became famous as the Keshavananda Bharati case, a special bench of thirteen judges of the supreme court found itself divided on the fundamental question of the scope of the amending powers of parliament. The majority of the judges tried to partly accommodate the opinion of the dissenting minority. While excluding the right to property from the 'basic structure' of the constitution, they agreed on subjecting any legislation undertaken in the name of the directive principles to judicial review. Although the judgement did not affect the validity of the legislation on bank nationalization, of princely privy purses, or the special retirement and pension privileges of members of the Indian Civil Service, the government considered it a setback for its progressive legislation. Under the influence of radicals, the government now retaliated by superseding the three most senior judges who had not been sympathetic to its cause while appointing the next chief justice. After the Emergency, the demand for comprehensive constitutional reform was no longer confined among the radicals: it was articulated by Congressmen in general who were outraged by the severity of the judgement of the Allahabad high court.

Besides the radicals, there were eminent non-party individuals who could be described as conservatives—such as J.R.D. Tata and G.D. Birla, the industrialists; Nani Palkhivala, the jurist; and B.P. Sinha, the former chief justice of the supreme court. Having seen the consequences of political instability after the 1967 elections, they advocated a presidential form of democracy. The Westminster model had, according to them, led to political fragmentation, unstable governments, competitive populism, and low economic growth—all of which made the country almost ungovernable.

During the Emergency B.K. Nehru, our high commissioner in London, made a very thoughtful and detailed contribution to this subject. He was one of those who had supported the Emergency because he was convinced that the Westminster model had not worked in India. A few months after the declaration of Emergency he wrote a letter to Mrs Gandhi in which he argued forcefully and persuasively in favour of a presidential form of democracy. I myself felt that B.K. Nehru's ideas, over which he had worked for several years, needed careful consideration. On his visit to Delhi towards the end of 1975 I had occasion to discuss these with him in greater depth. The objectives of his proposals were to (a) provide a stable government both at the centre and in the states, (b) improve the quality of men and women who govern the country, (c) ensure that the executive government is strong enough to address itself to solving the major problems of the country even though the measures required for their solution may, for the time being, be unpopular, (d) re-establish the rule of law, (e) ensure that the elected representatives of the people who make the laws actually represent the people, (f) ensure that local problems are settled and local development takes place according to the wishes of the local people, and finally (g) reduce corruption.

To realize these multiple objectives he proposed a complete separation of the legislative from the executive function of government by making it impossible for any member of the legislature to hold an office of profit under the government, including a ministership; a fixed term of office for the president and governors, without any possibility of their removal during the term—except by impeachment on grounds of moral delinquency; the president and the governors to be elected by a college of electors who themselves represented the people. This college of electors was to consist not only of members of parliament and state legislatures, but also members of all local bodies, down to panchayat levels. Such an electorate would be broad enough to ensure a wide reflection of the wishes of the people, and at the same time small enough not to require much expenditure. To ensure the all-India character of the presidency, it was proposed that the president should not only get an overall majority of the votes cast throughout the country but also a specified percentage of votes from all the zones into which the country would be divided for this purpose.

For election to the legislatures, the primary body in B.K. Nehru's proposals was the village panchayat or the town area or the municipal committee. The next tier would be the district board, which would be elected not directly but by a college of electors consisting of all the primary local bodies in the district. For the state legislatures the college of electors would be district boards of the state, and for the central parliament the members of the state legislature would form the college of electors. The mode of all these elections was to be proportional representation on the basis of the single transferable vote.

Finally, according to B.K. Nehru the reason why India was increasingly becoming a lawless country was that those to whom the law had been entrusted for enforcement were not allowed to exercise their powers. The autonomy of the services was therefore vital for the establishment of rule of law. He proposed that the position of civil servants should be specifically and clearly defined in the constitution.

The more I reflected on my own brief experience of the different aspects of the governance of the country, the more convinced I became of the relevance of these proposals to our needs. Some of the proposals, like the revitalization of the local bodies and making them the basis of the country's system of self-governance, would, I believed, also meet some of the important demands of Jayaprakash Narayan. I spoke to

Mrs Gandhi on this subject at length. She showed interest and told B.K. Nehru to discuss his ideas with her political colleagues, without associating her name with them. He told me he found considerable support for his ideas. But the leftist parties, particularly the two communist parties, were against the presidential system. Their opposition was based on the simple fact that under the parliamentary system they had greater scope for growth and influence than under a presidential one.

Mrs Gandhi passed on B.K. Nehru's letter to Barooah, Rajni Patel, and S.S. Ray for their opinion. This group, whom my colleagues in the secretariat called the 'triumvirate', had emerged as her chief advisers on legal and constitutional matters. As a result of their discussions, Rajni Patel produced a paper on constitutional reform entitled 'A Fresh Look At Our Constitution, Some Suggestions'. The paper had been drafted by A.R. Antulay, but the authorship was kept a secret. When Mrs Gandhi gave me a copy of this paper, she told me that it was a confidential document which Patel had prepared for the four of them. The paper laid heavy emphasis on the weak position of the prime minister under the existing constitutional arrangements and went on to make suggestions for the institution of the elected president who, 'being elected by a popular direct mandate should, in the nature of things, enjoy more authority and powers than even USA President.' It had made no provision for checks and balances between the executive, judiciary, and legislature. Its bald and unenlightening introduction and five annexures dealt mostly with measures to enhance the powers of the executive, and curb the judiciary, and suppress the opposition by banning what it called 'communal and fascist anti-national and anti-social organizations.' It made a mockery of the presidential form of democracy and twisted the constitution in an unambiguously authoritarian direction. This document, which was supposed to be confidential, was leaked out by Barooah as a trial balloon. It was badly received. Many people were alarmed at its extremist formulations. Mrs Gandhi was anxious not to be associated with it, having been reluctant to associate herself even with B.K. Nehru's proposal because she feared people might think her support for the presidential system was for personal reasons.

The worst part of the Antulay exercise was that his document gave ideas to Sanjay Gandhi, whose minions highjacked the idea of constitutional reform and organized a campaign for convening a new constituent assembly. They had no thoughts on what the constituent assembly should do beyond a single point programme of continuing the Emergency in one form or another. Things were now getting out of control.

Barooah, having realized he had made a mistake, wanted to divert attention from the Antulay document. He did it successfully at the annual session of the Congress Party, which was held at Kamagata Maru Nagar, near Chandigarh, in November 1975. He got a resolution passed there which asked for a committee to be set up 'for a thorough re-examination of the Constitution to make adequate alteration to it so that it may continue as living document.' As a sequel to the resolution, a committee of Congressmen under the chairmanship of Sardar Swaran Singh was set up. The committee became the new centre of attention for all those interested in constitutional reform. Antulay's document was dismissed by the law minister as 'unauthentic'. He attributed it to 'mischievous people who want to create a scare'! That was the end of it.

Mrs Gandhi was against the presidential system, which she feared would endanger the unity of the country. In other respects her views on constitutional changes were very ambivalent. In August 1975, a couple of months after the declaration of the Emergency, she said, 'I am not thinking in terms of a constituent assembly or a new constitution. We cannot but be a democracy, a secular democracy, and a democracy striving steadily to enlarge its socialist contents. But we can and we should have a look at the provisions and procedures. Many of these provisions and procedures have in effect worked against the Constitution.' In her conversations with me she laid emphasis on improving the existing procedures, which in my opinion were needed anyway—whether or not the constitution was amended in a more significant manner.

I mentioned the prime minister's concerns about the working of parliament to S.L. Shakhder, secretary-general of the Lok Sabha. I was glad to find that he himself was concerned about what he called 'a steady decline in the quality and tenor of parliamentary performance'. He felt that 'parliament was not devoting adequate time and attention to its allotted functions under the constitution. Instead it was spending a lot of time on extraneous matters. Taking advantage of various procedural devices—or, sometimes, merely under their cover—members often divert the attention of the parliament from important items entered in the Order Papers, and delay legislation or other business requiring urgent attention of parliament.'

With this assessment as his background, Shakhder suggested that parliament should function through a system of committees, which was at the time being thought of in the UK as well. The committee system, he felt, 'would ensure constant and continuous scrutiny of government activities under parliamentary surveillance'. In place of the existing consultative committees, which he thought 'were hardly serving any purpose', he proposed the composition and the working of the joint committees of both houses of parliament to be formed under broad subject headlines. According to his proposals the work of the parliament was to be conducted mainly through these committees. The committees would be an extension of the parliamentary mechanism to ensure executive accountability. He had also suggestions on other matters, like calling attention notices, zero hour, privilege notices, adjournment motions and no-confidence motions.

Shakhder's suggestions, though limited in their scope, were nevertheless eminently sensible. But before they could even be considered they were overtaken by events leading to the establishment of the Swaran Singh Committee. The committee as constituted consisted of Congress Party members only, most of whom, though knowledgeable, were no experts. This caused worry to people like P.B. Gajendragadkar, chairman of the law commission and formerly chief justice of India, who was otherwise sympathetic to the objectives of the committee. He wanted matters relating to constitutional change to be examined by experts before they were considered by the political leadership. But the party-dominated committee had several advantages for Barooah and his triumvirate colleagues. It served the twin purpose of absorbing the energies of the radicals and at the same time reassured the conservatives that, under the chairmanship of Sardar Swaran Singh, the reforms would not go too far.

The committee's deliberations, however, did not fully satisfy the triumvirate. They felt its recommendation would need to be further strengthened and decided to pursue this with the technical assistance of H.R. Gokhale, the law minister, and his staff. The impression they gave was that their exercise was a kind of technical back-up for the committee's work. They spelt out the purpose of the entire exercise in a note to Mrs Gandhi which said:

The Emergency has helped to convert a soft and politically permissive state into an effective democratic state. The gains of the Emergency have to be consolidated and structural changes in the constitution have to be effected to ensure that the government is not prevented through obstruction or subversion from carrying out the mandate of the majority. 1. To remove as much as possible the fetters that at present stand in the way of the proper functioning of the prime minister and the government. 2. To prevent as much as possible judicial interference of essential legislative and executive acts.

The triumvirate, having secured Mrs Gandhi's agreement on the objectives as formulated by them proceeded to work out the required changes in the constitution on their own. They directed H.R. Gokhale and his staff, who did the actual work. The law minister was unhappy at the additional changes he was asked to incorporate in his draft bill, which went beyond what the Swaran Singh Committee had envisaged. But he felt powerless and did not protest to the triumvirate or complain to Mrs Gandhi. Barooah, on the other hand, gave her the impression that the party found Swaran Singh's recommendations inadequate. So far as she was concerned, she did not go into the details of the proposed changes in the constitution, nor did she make her own enquiries about the wishes of the party. In these circumstances, the triumvirate found it easy to have things their way.

In all the discussions on the constitutional changes, Sanjay Gandhi had been kept out. His mother had no doubt that he had little to contribute on the subject. The triumvirate had their own reasons for keeping him out. They looked upon him as a threat to their newly acquired power. S.S. Ray, who was most actively involved in the exercise,

was tired of Sanjay's rudeness and wanted to keep him at a safe distance. But Sanjay and his mentors, such as Bansi Lal, were equally
contemptuous of the triumvirate, whom they considered political
lightweights. They were not willing to leave the field of constitutional
reform to them or to Swaran Singh. They went into action and got the
UP, Punjab and Haryana state assemblies to pass resolutions demanding the setting up of a constituent assembly. Sanjay had kept his mother
ignorant about the initiative that he and his clique were taking, though
Bansi Lal had vaguely mentioned the idea of converting the existing
parliament into a constituent assembly to Mrs Gandhi; but she had
not taken it seriously.

The state assembly resolutions shocked Mrs Gandhi, particularly
because the movement was disguised by its sponsors as a groundswell
by Congress legislative parties in the northern states. Many Congressmen opposed to Sanjay were perturbed by this development. The CPI
condemned it publicly as a disastrous move and an attempt to scuttle
the forty-second amendment bill, which had already been introduced
in parliament several weeks earlier. Privately, Rajeswara Rao, general
secretary of the party, wrote to Mrs Gandhi on 23 October 1976,
saying, 'A great responsibility rests on your shoulders at the critical
moment. We hope you will oppose this suicidal move without any
hesitation.' She decided to stop the movement for the constituent
assembly before it could gather further support and let the debate on
the amendment bill scheduled on 25 October proceed without diversion.

As the family planning programme gathered momentum, stories about
the excesses committed in its implementation proliferated. There were
exaggerations, no doubt, but the hard core of truth that these stories
contained was very disturbing. The perpetrators of the excesses, however, took advantage of the fact that in several cases the allegations were
found groundless and thereby argued that these were stories put out

by the anti-family planning propaganda. In any case, even if the guilty had been identified, they would have escaped punishment because they were under Sanjay's protective umbrella. For us in the PMS, it was a no-win situation. Or was it?

In the beginning, Indira Gandhi had been an enthusiastic supporter of the family planning programme: she would brook no criticism of it. But when the facts about coercive measures began to sink in, she developed reservations. Her blind spot for Sanjay, however, inhibited her from taking a firm stand against it. She defended the programme publicly, though she was feeling uneasy about its human and political implications. Without being more explicit about her concerns, she would vent her feelings by blaming officers for what she called their 'overzealousness'.

Despite her support to Sanjay, I got several indications from Mrs Gandhi that she was very concerned at the situation as it had developed. She felt things were getting out of control and that something had to be done. She told me somewhat accusingly that we had 'fallen in a rut'. She was also becoming apprehensive of the arbitrary power wielded by some of Sanjay's supporters, such as Bansi Lal, whom she seemed unwilling to curb lest she annoy Sanjay. Keeping all these things in view, I prepared three notes: one on the deteriorating administration, a second on the stalemate in negotiations with JP, and a third on the lack of unanimity about the proposed changes in the constitution. In the third note I had underlined her own strong reservations on changing the Westminster model in any drastic manner. The conclusion which I drew from these notes was that the only way to get out of the rut was to hold elections.

I gave her the notes to read during our long journeys on the ten-day African tour which started on 8 October. The tour was a goodwill visit to a few friendly countries with whom we had no problems to settle. Since no serious negotiations were to be undertaken, the tour was going to be a relaxed affair. Taking her away from the daily grind of time-consuming routine, which filled a good part of her day at home, such journeys provided the prime minister leisure and quiet for calm reflection. It was in that hope that I gave her my notes. But I was also apprehensive that nothing might come of my effort because she had included Sanjay and Bansi Lal in her party. If she showed them my notes, they were bound to oppose all I had said. But if I was sure of anything, it was that my notes were bound to increase her worries about the situation in the country and that they might, on further reflection, lead her to take some positive steps. I therefore pinned all my hopes on the African safari.

Being a fast reader, she went through all I had given her within a couple of hours of our getting into the plane. I had imagined she would be shocked by what I had given her to read. But, no, she was her cool self and complained against Brahmananda Reddy, the home minister, to whom she said she had spoken about the police excesses. This was unfair as he was completely sidelined by his junior colleague, Om Mehta, a confidante of Dhawan and Sanjay—and with her own tacit agreement. I let that remark about Reddy pass and told her that the police excesses were the product of the Emergency, and that we could not restrain the police without addressing the source of their newly acquired power. She said, 'yes, something should be done,' but did not elaborate; something minor intervened to end the conversation.

I returned to the subject later. The point I made was that either she should make a serious effort at national reconciliation or go in for elections. She said my talks with Radhakrishna were not yielding results. I protested and said he was being most helpful; only I had nothing to offer that would enable him to carry the talks further. She kept mum at that. The only positive signal I got was that she would mull over the suggestion about elections. The fact that she had not shown my papers to Bansi Lal was also encouraging.

On our return journey to Delhi Bansi Lal came and sat next to me and talked about the need for setting up a new constituent assembly. The main purpose of the assembly, he told me, would be to make Behnji (referring to Mrs Gandhi) president for life. He added that he had mooted the idea to her and she had suggested he should discuss it with me. This was the first time during the tour that Bansi Lal had spoken to me on a serious matter. I was taken aback but told him that his idea needed careful thinking and did not encourage him to speak further on the subject. He then embarked on a tirade against R.K. Dhawan and criticized the PM for raising him to a position which he did not deserve. I was not sure whether he was trying to please me to gather my support for his atrocious idea or whether there was a rift between him and Dhawan.

When I reported my conversation with Bansi Lal to Mrs Gandhi, she said he had buttonholed her in the plane, and in order to get rid of him she had asked him to talk to me. She repeated what she had told me, and some others earlier, that unless we were clear about the work of the constituent assembly it would be a risky undertaking; it would open a Pandora's box. I felt greatly relieved to find that she was keeping Bansi Lal at arm's length, and so I was hopeful about the possibility of the date of the election being brought forward.

But I had not counted on the indefatigable efforts of Bansi Lal's friends to pursue their independent line of action. On 20 October 1976, i.e. three days after her return from the African tour, Mrs Gandhi was confronted with a resolution passed by the members of the Bihar Congress Legislature Party and Provincial Congress Committee. The resolution demanded that the forty-second amendment bill be referred to the parliamentary drafting committee for scrutiny instead of being debated in the house. The assemblies of Punjab, Haryana, and UP followed suit by passing resolutions for the convening of a constituent assembly. Other assemblies were expected to reinforce this demand. Neither Bansi Lal nor any of his supporters behind this move had given serious thought to the work of the constituent assembly which they were demanding. But they were quite sure of one thing, and that was that if the assembly was convened it would be a very convenient way of postponing elections. For some of them it was more a tactic to continue the Emergency regime than a genuine effort to produce a new constitution.

These developments were ominous. And when on 5 November 1976 the life of the fifth Lok Sabha was extended till February 1978, I thought the game was up. But something for the better happened only two days later, and I felt encouraged again. As a routine matter I showed Mrs Gandhi a report which I had just received and which gave details of the extreme coercion to which some simple village schoolteachers had been subjected because they had not fulfilled the sterilization quota assigned to them. She fell silent after reading it. This was the first time she did not dismiss such allegations as false—as had become her habit. She appeared saddened by the report. After a long pause she asked me in a tired voice how long I thought the Emergency should continue. This was for me the most propitious moment to say what I was wanting to say for some time. I said that in my judgement the positive phase of the Emergency was already over, and that it needed to be brought to an end as early as possible. 'And go back to anarchy and lawlessness?' she countered sharply. 'It need not be so', I said, 'particularly if we conclude our negotiations with JP; he seems to have realized his mistakes and has offered to help in developing a consensus with the opposition parties on issues which will make our politics less disruptive and our democracy less disorderly.'

'I do not believe he means business. In any case the opposition parties are not going to listen to him; they have their own agenda,' she replied.

That meeting, somehow, became a crucial one. It turned out to be the first of a series on the appropriateness of holding elections which had only recently been postponed a second time by another year. She was uncomfortable about the second postponement. She had justified the first postponement of elections due in February 1976 on the grounds that it would 'put the 20-point programme in jeopardy'. But she had promised that 'after it is implemented and the people have benefited we would certainly hold elections.' She thought the second postponement gave out the wrong signal—that she was afraid to face the people. It hurt her self-respect and her pride in her own leadership. She was nostalgic about the way people reacted to her in the 1971 election campaign and she longed to hear again the applause of the multitudes. She wanted to regain her ability to reach the people at an emotional level. She was also now less disdainful of critical foreign comments, particularly from the USA and the UK. In fact when I showed her certain hostile cartoons from the foreign press—these had been sent to me anonymously—she was quite receptive, though I could tell she was upset.

Events again took a turn for the worse. The Gauhati session of the Congress held on 20, 21 and 22 November 1976 established Sanjay

'Lock Him Up!'

A cartoon against the 'Emergency'

Gandhi as undisputed leader of the Youth Congress, which overshadowed the parent body. It was said he had walked away with the Congress president's clothes. Mrs Gandhi herself was very impressed by Sanjay's performance and had said, apparently with satisfaction, 'our thunder has been stolen'. All these developments were contrary to the indications I had received all through my recent discussions with Mrs Gandhi. I was most disappointed. But my colleague, V. Ramachandran, who I had taken into confidence in this matter, sustained my morale. He said the path to the elections had to follow a zig-zag course. In his terminology, while I was on the zig during the tour, I was on the zag now. Every evening after that he used to ask me whether I was on zig or zag.

But this tension did not last long. After Mrs Gandhi's return from Gauhati I was pleasantly surprised to see that, contrary to the general

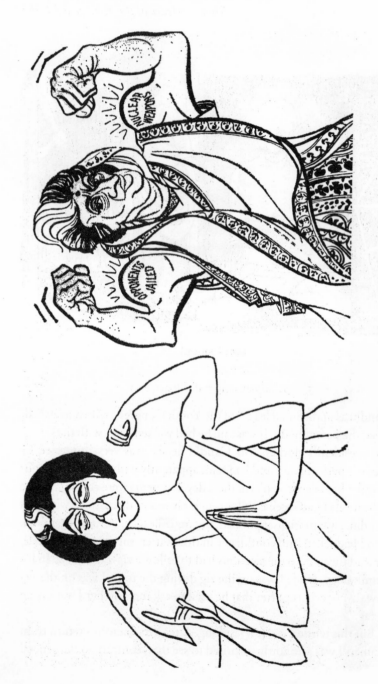

A cartoon against the 'Emergency' in a Dutch paper

A cartoon against the 'Emergency' in a Washington paper

impression, she was not carried away by the euphoria generated at the Congress session. I was intrigued by the discrepancy between her private feelings and her public reaction at Sanjay's performance there. Was she herself becoming afraid of him? Was that possible? She had no reason to give a wrong impression. Or was I indulging in wishful thinking? These thoughts crossed my mind. She told me Sanjay was not mature enough to see through some of the people on whom he relied. She was worried that the Youth·Congress might have put off some of her good party workers. She was critical of his wife, Menaka, and thought her influence on him was not healthy. '*Us kay tou abhi say par nikalnay lagen hain*' (She's begun growing wings already) was her caustic comment on Menaka Gandhi.

Being aware of her obsessive love for Sanjay, I would normally have attributed all this to temporary annoyance. But it was more than a passing mood this time. I knew how carefully she had kept Sanjay out of all discussions on constitutional reforms. I also knew how much she had resented the passage of the constituent assembly resolutions by the three assemblies without her knowledge but with Sanjay's approval. Was Sanjay proving too wild even for her?

This being her state of mind, I felt encouraged to raise the question of elections once again. She said she was thinking about them but did not want to be pushed. I did not want her to think that the election question was my hobby horse. I wanted other people to speak to her, but it was not easy to find many such people. I talked to K.C. Pant, who was fed up with the situation as he was dogged by Bansi Lal's intelligence agents from Haryana. He supported me in my efforts but he himself had lost access to her. I spoke to Haksar, who was to meet her after a long spell of silence. He talked to her about his problems in the Planning Commission but told me he did not get a chance to talk politics, nor was he encouraged to do so. I spoke to B.K. Nehru, whose thoughtful ideas on constitutional reform had been shelved. He agreed with me that the forty-second amendment was odious and bode ill for the country, and that fresh elections were the only way out of the *cul-de-sac*, even if there was no agreement or understanding with the opposition on the changes in the constitution or the rules of the political game. In his conversation with Indira Gandhi he advised her to hold elections soon.

Odd as it might seem, some Congressmen who believed that their party would lose in the elections also supported the idea of holding them. They were so disgusted with Sanjay and his associates that they did not hesitate to tell his mother the opposite of what they believed would be the outcome of the elections. They were not prominent leaders, but they were known to be in touch with the grassroots.

Indira Gandhi was now veering round to taking a decision on elections, but she needed some prodding on their timing. I submitted her a confidential note saying that if she decided to hold elections, we would have to act fast as March was the most convenient time for such an event, and it was already December. The chief election commissioner had to be given enough prior notice, and several other decisions had to be taken, such as the release of political prisoners and the lifting of press censorship.

I do not know what she did with my note, but her having taken the decision became apparent when she started asking questions about the economic trends, the price situation, the attitude of trade union leaders, factionalism in the party, the names of candidates likely to win, and so on. All this she did at great speed, but in a very casual manner. In this exercise she sought help only from Om Mehta, the minister of state in the ministry of home affairs, and D.P. Chattopadhyaya, the commerce minister. Both these men were political lightweights, but she trusted them. She kept Sanjay out of this exercise and she conducted the discussions in a very noncommittal manner, giving the impression that all this was just tentative thinking on her part. I thought it smacked of more than her usual sense of caution and not wanting to let anyone know her mind.

Something had happened to her. She was brooding most of the time. She went through the entire series of decisions without the usual tensions that used to characterize her decisionmaking style, almost as if she were unconcerned about the results. It seemed as if she was driven by a fate to which she had surrendered. The only thing on which she showed keen personal interest was the formal date of announcement of the decision. I had suggested the first of January, but she chose a later date. On the first of January I invited Swaminathan, the chief election commissioner, to tea at home and took him into confidence about the forthcoming elections for which he had to prepare. He was delighted and complained that I had only served the 'great news' to him with a single cup of tea. In the evening I received a bottle of whisky from him.

The Emergency ended as suddenly as it had begun. On 18 January 1977 Indira Gandhi announced that the fifth Lok Sabha was dissolved and that the elections would be held two months later. The opposition leaders, the press, and the people at large were as stunned by this announcement as they had been a year and half earlier, when she had declared the Emergency. Despite official reassurances that normality would be restored as soon as possible, people were sceptical. The fact that the Lok Sabha elections were postponed twice had further damaged the government's credibility.

The sudden decision to hold the elections, which ended in a disastrous defeat for Indira Gandhi, has become a subject for much speculation. Before the elections were actually held it was feared by many that they would be rigged and rushed through with the press gagged and with the opposition leaders either in jail or with very little time to organize themselves to canvass support for their candidates. But when the opposition leaders were released and censorship lifted and there seemed no official interference in the electioneering of the opposition or with the electoral process, these fears were dispelled and gave place to the expectation that the elections would be free and fair. And after the anti-Congress opposition combination looked as though it would carry most states, the decision to hold the election appeared even more puzzling, especially to those who, like Morarji Desai, were convinced that Indira Gandhi was determined to retain power 'anyhow, anyway'. Some intellectuals believed she had acted under US pressure! Others, particularly foreign observers, made the ridiculous suggestion that since Bhutto had announced elections in Pakistan, Indira Gandhi had to do the same in India—a case of compulsive sibling rivalry between the two countries!

It was only after her defeat in the elections that it was realized that

Indira Gandhi's decision was not prompted by extraneous considerations. The belief grew that she had opted for elections because she had felt sure of winning. If things did not happen the way she expected, it was simply a case of her misperception of ground realities—a common failing in authoritarian leaders, it was said. Accordingly, it is assumed that in the absence of a free press she was dependent for information only on sycophants from her own party and officialdom. To be sure, there was much sycophancy, but Indira Gandhi was too mistrustful a person to have swallowed the flatterer's opinion entirely. It is said that the intelligence agencies fed her with stories which gave her an entirely false picture of the political situation in the country. Their reports did tone down the negative parts here and there, but it is not true that they did not reflect the current and crosscurrents of public opinion. Actually, Indira Gandhi knew more about the situation in the country during the Emergency than she was prepared to admit. That being so, was her decision to hold elections a calculated risk—or was it something else? There may never be a conclusive answer, but I believe she was not comfortable with the Emergency, and she wanted to get out of it, somehow, anyhow.

CHAPTER THIRTEEN

Change of Players and the Last Curtain

The decision to hold elections was too sudden and unexpected for any quick estimates of the outcome. Media reports on the emerging trends of likely voter behaviour became available only gradually, after the censorship was lifted. To be sure, there were some official reports, mainly from the intelligence agencies, but they were based on spotty, fragmentary, unreliable data. These agencies were not professionally equipped for the task. In any case it was not easy for them to hazard a credible guess in the circumstances that prevailed.

Yet we did not have to wait long to see which way the wind was blowing. Within a few days of the announcement of elections, four opposition parties with influence in the northern states—the Jan Sangh, the BLD, the Congress(O) and the Socialist Party—combined to form the Janata Party under the leadership of Morarji Desai, with JP as its patron saint. This was the result of JP's untiring efforts. Unlike his experience in 1971, he succeeded in 1977 because the Emergency had made Mrs Gandhi the common enemy of all the opposition parties, their only shared aim being her ouster. The Emergency had at long last made their earlier slogan, 'Indira Hatao', meaningful for voters. It was now easy for JP to deny the advantage of a fragmented opposition to the Congress Party. In the earlier elections, the opposition parties had, by cancelling one another's vote, made it possible for the Congress to secure a majority of seats even though the votes cast in its favour were always less than 50 per cent.

The formation of an electoral alliance of opposition parties caused no surprise, but what nobody expected was that Jagjivan Ram, the influential Harijan leader, would resign from the cabinet and the Congress Party. He was the longest serving and most experienced member of the cabinet. He was Nehru's colleague in the interim government of 1946 and had continued to be a member of the cabinet with only a brief interruption since then. He combined vast administrative experience with shrewd political sense. Being a cool and calculating politician, he had kept his ambitions under control and was biding his time to strike. And when he did strike it was a signal for others to follow. Everyone, including Mrs Gandhi, knew it was not an impulsive act but the first step of a well-thought-out plan. His defection had a shattering effect on the morale of the party in the northern states. In his letter of resignation, besides denouncing the Emergency, he attacked Mrs Gandhi for destroying intra-party democracy. His letter was therefore bound to encourage dissidence within the party.

The most important of these dissidents was H.N. Bahuguna, former chief minister of UP. He had been bitterly against Mrs Gandhi ever since November 1975, when he was made to resign. He was an emerging leader with a dynamic personality and authentic secular credentials, which made him popular among Muslim voters. He demonstrated his organizational capabilities to great advantage when he worked as general-secretary of the Congress under Jagjivan Ram as party president. But Mrs Gandhi had looked upon him as an ambitious opportunist and turned against him. During the remaining months of the Emergency he tried hard to clear 'the misunderstandings' with her, but she did not give him a chance, particularly because his successor, N.D. Tiwari, had earned the patronage of Sanjay. Bahuguna felt humiliated. He had his opportunity now; he left the party along with other prominent Congressmen and joined Jagjivan Ram, forming a new party called Congress for Democracy. The new party, by aligning with the Janata Party, significantly improved the electoral prospects of the opposition. Most notable among these was the imam of the Jama Masjid of Delhi who successfully projected the family planning policies of the Congress government as anti-Muslim.

With the new alignment of political forces it became easier to evaluate the emerging voting pattern; or so I thought. According to my assessment, which I made around the middle of February 1977, the Congress Party was likely to emerge as the largest single party, but not with enough seats to be able to form a government on its own. Taking into account their setback I had calculated that it would get about 220 to 230 seats in a house of 542. From the national viewpoint I thought that was no bad prospect. An unambiguous Congress victory would have further strengthened the very elements that had a vested interest in the Emergency. If, on the other hand, the Congress Party was forced to solicit support from other parties, it would have to negotiate with them and the outcome, hopefully, would be an agreement on the rules of the political game. Such an agreement would narrow the gulf between the government and the opposition and give democracy a better chance to evolve in a positive direction.

During the last phase of her election campaign Mrs Gandhi was in Patna, where she sent for me. Her summons were so urgent that I had to seek the help of RAW for a plane to reach her. She was in an agitated state when I met her. Candidates who were not doing well were complaining to her that the officers of the election commission were openly helping Janata candidates. She had been convinced by a senior Bihar leader about the partisan behaviour of these officers. This, of course, was not true, but it took me a whole hour to make her reject allegations against the election commission. During the meeting I also had an opportunity to give her my own assessment of the election results. I told her that to be able to form a stable government her party would need the support of the Janata, and that this would call for negotiations with JP, who had emerged as the mentor of the Janata. She agreed with my assessment of her party's performance but dismissed the possibility of an understanding with the Janata. 'I know them better than you do. Morarji would never allow that, now that he is the leader of a much larger party than the rump of Congress(O). JP will be cast away after having served his purpose,' she said.

On my return to Delhi I saw that Congressmen returning from the campaign were very pessimistic. But neither I nor any of them was prepared for what actually happened. In the entire Hindi belt, the traditional stronghold of the Congress Party, it was left with just two seats, while the Janata swept the polls. The Congress suddenly became a regional party of the south, where it won all but a handful of seats. Instead of my estimate of 230 seats, it got only 153. The Janata and its allies had gained an absolute majority. My estimates were haywire. The results humbled me completely. I felt too silly to face Mrs Gandhi. When I met her on the day of her defeat she looked stunned. I had no words to comfort her. Several people in my presence said she had been misled and that it was a mistake to hold the elections. She seemed not to hear what they were saying. More than the defeat of her party in the north, she found it difficult to believe that, of all people, Raj Narain had defeated her convincingly in her own constituency which she had nurtured so assiduously.

With the defeat of the Congress Party, Delhi was abuzz with ugly rumours which reached Mrs Gandhi as soon as they were set afloat. The city had become a vast whispering gallery; it echoed with stories about Indira Gandhi's alleged crimes and thinly veiled hints that the Janata Party had prepared plans to destroy her and Sanjay. She was not worried about herself but only about Sanjay. In this she found herself quite isolated. Rajiv had no sympathy for his brother. He came to see me, very concerned about his mother and full of anger against his brother. He said he had been a helpless observer of his brother's doings. A couple of times he had tried to tell his mother what was going on under her own roof but he was dismissed as being naive. He did not press his point because he was afraid he would be suspected of being jealous of his brother's success. He told his mother in my presence, 'you have been brought to this pass by Sanjay and Dhawan.' She said nothing in reply but looked forlorn. She spoke to me and Kao about Sanjay's safety. All we could do was to strengthen the security at her residence.

Mrs Gandhi's last day in office began with a meeting of the council of ministers where she read out the letter of resignation she was going to give to B.D. Jatti, the acting president, and the public statement to be issued later. The grim silence with which the members heard her was broken by B.P. Maurya. In his usual flamboyant manner he suggested that the letter should include a paragraph thanking the people of India for their love and affection for the outgoing prime minister, which he spelt out in extravagant terms. I felt embarrassed by what Maurya said, not because the letter drafted by Sharada Prasad and me had been found wanting, but because of the sheer absurdity of the idea in view of the magnitude of her defeat. Many will have shared this view, yet nobody reacted to Maurya's suggestion one way or the other. Mrs Gandhi mumbled something not quite audible but which sounded like a rejection of what Maurya was saying. I repeated her objections to such additions more explicitly but he continued to deliver his oration in high praise of Mrs Gandhi, punctuating it with dirty looks at me.

With a few minor changes the statement was retyped, and soon Mrs Gandhi got into the car to go and see the acting president. I accompanied her. We did not exchange a word till we reached the acting president's residence. Jatti, his wife, and a couple of family members were standing in the drawing room, awaiting Mrs Gandhi. They welcomed her ceremoniously with an *arti*. Jatti looked shaken and sat next to her on the sofa, his hands folded. Mrs Gandhi looked cool and composed. Just when Jatti opened his mouth to say something, his wife broke into sobs. This made everybody rather uncomfortable, to put it mildly. Luckily, at that very moment servants came in with trays of tea and snacks and Mrs Jatti's sobs were fortunately drowned in the clatter. While sipping tea everybody looked tense, not knowing how to behave. After a few moments of discomfiture Mrs Gandhi gave her letter of resignation to the acting president, who neither opened the letter nor said anything to Mrs Gandhi by way of response. As soon as Mrs Gandhi got up to leave I realized that the acting president had not asked the prime minister to continue in office until the new government was formed. I walked over to him to remind him about the constitutional requirements, whereupon he nervously said, 'yes, yes' half a dozen times to me, and then addressed the prime minister as I had suggested.

Upon tendering her resignation Mrs Gandhi did not return to South Block but went home. In the afternoon she invited the secretaries to government and her own staff to tea, to bid them farewell. They were with her for more than an hour, during which she behaved like a thoughtful hostess without showing any trace of anxiety about the days to come, though all sorts of rumours were afloat about the steps that the new government was going to take against her.

The electoral victory of the Janata Party marked the first major break in the nature of the political regime. And given the heterogeneous character of the new ruling party, the civil service was full of apprehensions. For Pande and me, a period of uncertainty, almost suspense, followed Morarji Desai's election as leader of the Janata Party in parliament on 24 March. Just as we were speculating about the modalities of his actual induction into the office of the prime minister, we were pre-empted by a message that Morarji was already in Parliament House and wished to see us. When we arrived there, things seemed dramatically different. This was only to be expected. We were so used to seeing N.K. Seshan handling the desk of the private secretary to the prime minister that it was a minor shock to find Ram Lal Parekh of the Gujarat Vidya Peeth installed in his place in the outer office. We were told that Morarji was already in the prime minister's room. Obviously we were not going to get a chance to welcome him formally, as we had anticipated. Pande seemed somewhat surprised that the leader of the Janata Party was already ensconced in the prime minister's office without any procedural preliminaries. As for me, I felt like an alien. Parekh announced our arrival and we were ushered in at once. Morarji was not at the desk but on a chair placed in an alcove in the room. He was dressed in snow-white khadi and wore a prominent tilak on his forehead. We greeted him and he acknowledged our namaste with a nod. Pointing to the prime minister's desk, he said in a clear, firm voice, 'I will not sit in that chair until I am sworn into office.' Pande need not have worried about correct procedures. Their sanctity seemed to be in no danger, at least from the new prime minister.

In answer to Pande's question about the date and timing of the swearing-in ceremony, Morarji said he would be sworn in alone and proceeded to ask us if there were administrative matters which needed his immediate attention. After going through a few such matters, over which he took quick and in our view correct decisions, I told him that Pande's extended term was coming to an end. Morarji then asked me who the new cabinet secretary should be. I handed him a note in which Pande and I had listed the eligible candidates and suggested the name of Nirmal Mukerjee for approval. He went over the draft quickly and said, 'Yes, it is a good name. Please go ahead.'

When Pande left and I was alone with Morarji, I asked him when he would like to meet my colleagues from the prime minister's secretariat. I had hardly finished my sentence when he broke in loudly, 'PM's secretariat is too big, it must be slashed.' At this point I took out the list of officers from my folder and gave it to him. He scanned it and said, 'Is that all?' Obviously, he did not expect the list to be so short. Even so, he continued with an air of dissatisfaction: 'Why did Mrs Gandhi have so many PAs? I can work with less than half of them.' I explained that her work had to be organized in two shifts. He glanced at the list again, and stopped at Salman Haider's name. 'Why should we have an officer from the foreign service?' I explained the rationale: 'the officer keeps a record of the PM's meetings with foreign dignitaries; co-ordinates with the ministry on routine matters and helps the PM's secretary to maintain liaison with the foreign secretary.' Interrupting me he asked: 'Why should PM's secretary have a special liaison with the foreign secretary?' Again, I explained the reason: 'The PM is intimately connected with foreign affairs; the PM provides, in consultation with the foreign minister, the necessary guidelines for policy.' 'No, no, this must be ended,' he exclaimed. 'And why do we need an information advisor? I don't need his advice. I will tell him what he has to do.' At this stage I ceased explaining.

I then brought up my own case and told him I was on contract with the Government of India until November 1977 and that I had requested his predecessor to allow me to take the leave I was due. This would enable me to demit office in early April. Besides, it was only natural that he would want his own man as his secretary; I would therefore like to be relieved of my responsibilities as soon as possible. 'I haven't thought about this matter at all. I never think of things before time. In

pause he asked me in an unexpectedly friendly tone 'Why are you in such a hurry? I have had good reports about you.' This was said in a rhetorical manner, requiring no reply.

I was strictly formal with Morarji for the few days that I worked for him. I attended the oath-taking ceremony, which I had never done before. At that function he gave me Mrs Gandhi's letter of congratulations, which I had drafted for her earlier, and asked me to give him a draft reply, adding, 'please make it warm and cordial.' After being sworn in he asked if I had a car to take me to his press conference; this I had no plans to attend, but now had to. At the conference many journalists noted that I 'was seen furiously taking notes of the instructions PM was giving about new policy directions.' What I was actually doing was drafting the PM's reply to Mrs Gandhi's letter. The only thing I remember about the conference was that I saw a new face among the officials sitting behind Morarji. I asked Sharada Prasad who he was and to my astonishment learnt that he was no other than Kanti, Morarji's son, who had no official position. Shades of Sanjay, and so soon, I wondered.

The next day, 25 March, was the first official day of the new prime minister in South Block. Soon after his arrival he sent for me and told me he had called on Mrs Gandhi at 1 Safdarjung Road as a matter of courtesy and had noticed that there was too much security there. 'What is she afraid of? It is not good for her to be surrounded by so many policemen.' When I explained that the security for her had been beefed up because of the hostile atmosphere against her and Sanjay, he disagreed, saying: 'No, it is her vanity.' Having referred to Mrs Gandhi's vanity, he gave me his views on women who wielded power. According to him all such women, Cleopatra downwards, had been vain and had brought much trouble to the world. Of the string of other names he mentioned I remember Catherine the Great of Russia and Razia Sultana of the Delhi Sultanate, in particular. He dwelt on the subject of women for quite a while. By the time he finished his next visitor had arrived and therefore no official business could be transacted.

Radhakrishna telephoned me the same day to ask if I would like to see JP, who was in Delhi and staying with him: he said JP had asked about me. After office hours I drove straight to Radhakrishna's place. He was waiting for me outside the house and took me through a circuitous route to JP's room. This, he explained, was to avoid other people-mostly favour seekers who had collected there—to see JP.

JP was lying on a bed, exhausted, but his face radiated satisfaction. After asking me how I was and what my future plans were he said, 'I hope the Janata government will have the wisdom to use your talents.' I thanked him for his kind thought and told him I had had enough of government and was looking forward to going back to the Institute of Economic Growth. He then asked for my views on economic policy. I told him I was as unrepentant about the soundness of the government's recent economic policies as I was when I had met him in June 1976. My only regret was that these policies were just the beginning and did not go far enough. I said the new government had been left with several assets, such as adequate foreign-exchange reserves, sizeable food stocks, and a stable price level. It could take off from there and introduce economic reforms which would generate a higher economic growth and better income distribution. Having said this, I expressed my reservations about the ability of the Janata Party to evolve a coherent set of such policies. Before JP could react to what I had said, Radhakrishna came in and announced that Morarji, who was addressing a public meeting in the Ramlila Grounds round the corner, had suddenly decided to come and see JP. This abruptly ended our conversation. I was not able to meet JP again.

I met Morarji on all of the seven days I served as his secretary. In these meetings he did most of the talking, which was in contrast with his predecessor—Mrs Gandhi was a very good listener, an unusual trait in Indians, particularly those in authority. She listened carefully, attending to what was being said, took notes of the important points made, and sent them to the relevant people for comments, elaboration, verification, and so on. She was sensitive to the tone and manner of her interlocutor, which enabled her to judge the motive behind what she was being told. Morarji was the very opposite in every way. He was a poor listener. He was as loquacious as she was taciturn. He seemed to have answers to all questions and solutions for all problems. He was never tentative in his responses, which he delivered with a magisterial ring in his voice. He seldom tried to establish a rapport with his listener. He talked to individuals as though addressing a public meeting. The thing that struck me most about Morarji was that he had no doubts whatsoever about absolutely everything he said or believed. He was sure he could do no wrong and that morally he was always right. I found his lack of doubt quite frightening, all the more because people who had known him told me he had mellowed considerably.

On administrative matters he was quick in his responses and could clear files without delay. The old PCS officer was still alive in him so far as normal administrative work was concerned. I must also add that in these matters I found him far from rigid; in fact he was quite flexible if one stood one's ground and had cogent arguments. On certain policy matters he was inflexible. Sometimes he could be simplistic, and on occasion exasperating. In one of my meetings I had to show him a top secret intelligence report indicating the existence of a large espionage network in which the agencies of two countries were involved. One of the agencies belonged to a country whose government was otherwise very friendly. As soon as he finished reading the report he asked me to draft an indignant letter to the head of the friendly state, telling him he did not like what was going on. When he saw the look of surprise on my face he added, 'I can write to the other gentleman also.' Having said that he remarked, 'I hope we are not doing any such thing ourselves.' This led to a discussion on the functions and working of RAW. He did not show much interest in what I was saying about that organization and cut in to ask 'what does RAW do here at home?' When I told him that internal intelligence work was handled by the Intelligence Bureau, he looked unconvinced and shot another question at me: 'why are there so many RAW men posted in India?' When I completed what I thought was a full explanation for the deployment of RAW personnel in the country, he dismissed it with a shrug. 'They were reporting to her about us and her own colleagues. You may not know that. Probably Dhawan has the file,' he said.

Another subject on which Morarji had a long discussion with me was the role of the prime minister's secretariat in the governance of the country. He told me privately and at length what he had said publicly about the extraordinary powers wielded by the secretariat under Mrs Gandhi. Her office had usurped the work of other ministries. He did not like that. He emphasized the need to cut down the secretariat and make its functions consistent with the working of a democratic government. After noting my lack of response he specifically asked my opinion. I said my hesitation in venturing an opinion on the subject was due to my feeling that my association with the previous regime did not exactly qualify me for an objective assessment. I then began by quoting to him the opinion of Asquith, the British prime minister who had said that 'the office of the prime minister is what its holder chooses and is able to make it.' I suggested that he should wait and see for himself how the secretariat functioned before restructuring it. I told him that as his government settled in, he would know what he needed from the secretariat and what he did not; and which of its functions were relevant from his point of view and which were not.

I agreed with him that the PMS should not take on the work of other ministries but pointed out that it should nevertheless be equipped to know how the government as a whole was functioning, where things were going wrong, or were likely to go wrong, or where the policy of the government was not properly implemented. The PMS could not perform that role unless it had enough able officers to stay in touch with the rest of the administration. I expressed my views on this at some length. In brief, I said that it was not true that in parliamentary democracies the prime minister was merely the chairman of the council of ministers (a notion being popularized by some Janata Party leaders and some journalists). The prime minister, as its leader, had to take ultimate responsibility. He was the chief executive. There could be circumstances, such as in a coalition government (I did not mention the Janata Party by name) where the prime minister was like a chairman, but even in such situations the prime minister could not give up his leadership role even if it were limited to that of co-ordinating the work of the ministries. Without such a provision the government's policies would have no coherent frame of reference and become subject not only to normal political pulls and pressures but even passing moods and ad hoc ministerial groupings. Thus, in my opinion, an adequate and competent secretariat, or office-as Morarji had decided to rename it—was necessary for the proper and legitimate functioning of the prime minister, particularly in a country like India, where the prime minister was the executive head of the central government, which had to operate as a co-operative federal system.

I ended my presentation by saying that I was only talking about the PMS and not the PMH. I emphasized the distinction between the secretariat and the personal staff who worked at the house of the prime minister or a minister. The personal staff at the house was meant to assist the PM or the minister with official work. If such staff were used for other than official purposes, or by family members, it was something that could not be prevented by rules; it all depended on the style of functioning of the person concerned. I had already heard whispers about Kanti Desai using his father's name to peddle influence. Morarji heard me without interruption, which surprised me, but his last words on the subject were a reiteration of the litany that the PM's secretariat was too powerful and must be cut down to size.

After another discussion with Morarji about my relinquishing office, it was decided that I could leave on 31 March. I paid him a farewell call in the afternoon that day and was with him for half an hour. The meeting was most cordial. He asked me not to hesitate to call on him if I had anything to say on matters of public interest. I thanked him for the kindness and courtesy with which he had treated me, and with that the curtain came down on my six and a half years of active association with the Government of India.

I was succeeded by V. Shankar, a retired member of the Indian Civil Service who had made a name for himself as Sardar Patel's private secretary. After he took over from me, he called on me formally at my house in the old tradition of the civil service. He was most courteous and understanding during the changeover. When Raj Narain, who was allotted the government house that I was occupying, started harassing me to vacate it forthwith, Shankar stopped him by complaining to Morarji about it on my behalf. He told me later that it was Raj Narain's personal astrologer who had recommended an early date of entry into a government house. Since that was not possible, the demands of the stars were met by changing the number of the house from 9 to 8 Race Course Road: apparently 9 was an unlucky number for Raj Narain.

After the appointment of several commissions of enquiry into the wrongdoings of the Emergency regime, it became fashionable and rewarding to be a victim of its excesses. One such victim was Dr R.K. Caroli, the cardiologist. When the Janata Party came to power, he alleged that he had been approached by the health minister's private secretary with the proposal that he (Dr Carolli) should advise Jagjivan Ram, who had complained of pains in the chest, to be hospitalized in order to prevent him campaigning in the election. For that service, Carolli said, he was promised a suitable reward on behalf of the prime minister's secretary. Carolli further asserted that he stood by his professional ethics and bravely resisted the overtures of the health minister's secretary. I learnt about this preposterous allegation when I was in New York. I wrote to Shankar and told him it was a cock-and-bull story so far as I was concerned and requested him to show my letter to Morarji. Shankar wrote back saying that Morarji had asked him to tell me he did not believe for a minute in my complicity in the alleged conspiracy. In the event, Carolli's story was, on investigation, found spurious.

Morarji was not the only politician who treated me generously. Atal Behari Vajpayee, the foreign minister, came to my rescue when in 1978 my appointment to a senior post in the United Nations secretariat led to a furore in parliament. Raj Narain and several other members raised questions about the appropriateness of letting a person who had worked with the former prime minister join the UN. Raj Narain also wanted to know whether I was a bourgeois or proletarian economist. He suspected—rightly in my opinion that I belonged to the former category, for which as a good socialist he harboured a strong antipathy. Vajpayee defended me in a manner that lifted the morale of civil servants in general: they were apprehending a witchhunt under the new political dispensation. Answering the questions put to him on my account, Vajpayee said, 'the United Nations wanted an eminent economist, and by all standards Professor P.N. Dhar is an eminent economist, and while selecting people we do not make such types of distinction which the honourable member would like us to make.' He added that 'Professor Dhar was himself not keen on the UN appointment and he was not going abegging [*sic*] for a job . . .'.

Among other interventions, Dr Karan Singh made a statement which, though not strictly relevant to the questions raised, proved a silencer for the irrepressible Raj Narain. He said, 'I would like to say with full confidence on the floor of the House that when there was a big debate going on in the innermost councils as to whether elections should be held in the country or not, Professor Dhar played a very important part in the decision that elections should be held and we should go back to the people.' I was relieved to read the proceedings of the parliament debate and impressed by the fair and firm stand taken by Vajpayee. It could not have been easy for him in the prevailing atmosphere, where many members had genuine grievances against the Emergency regime and all those associated with it.

I could not meet Mrs Gandhi during the week I was serving the Janata government. When I called on her later I found her somewhat withdrawn. At first I attributed it to the trauma of defeat. But even when she called me to discuss certain personal matters I found her unnaturally formal with me. I got the feeling that something was rankling in her mind. Could it be my advice on the elections? I had heard that some people had told her I was in league with Janata leaders before the elections, but I was sure she would not believe that sort of rubbish. I did not have to wait too long to know the truth. It came in the form of a letter from her a few weeks later, wherein she made an oblique reference to an incident which I had mentioned to Pupul Jayakar in response to her curiosity about Morarji's style.

I had told Pupul that when I introduced my colleagues to Morarji I naturally began with Bambavale, the seniormost member who had been slated to succeed me if the government had not changed. Before I could even mention his name, Morarji told me I was introducing a person whom he already knew very well, as he was the son of a very good friend. While mentioning this simple matter to Pupul Jayakar, I could not help making a lighthearted comment: here was someone whom Sanjay had selected as his trusted man, but who really turned out to be a darling of Morarji. I do not know what slant Pupul had given in telling the tale to Mrs Gandhi, but her reaction was most puzzling. She wrote to me, saying:

Nothing has hurt me so much as the estrangement between us. You cannot have forgotten the confidence I reposed in you. I wanted you to have the total background picture. How could you think for a moment that someone else could take your place, especially a complete stranger, whom I had brought in in the mistaken belief that he would be able to take some of the administrative burden off your shoulders? This is yet another example of the efficiency of the propaganda and rumour machine that has worked as successfully to isolate me from those whom I regarded as my friends. Anyway, wherever you and Sheila are, you know that my good wishes will be with you.

The letter completely flummoxed me. I showed it to Pupul Jayakar to check what she had told Indira Gandhi about the Bambavale story. She admitted she had mentioned it just to amuse her and added that Indira Gandhi had taken it in grim silence. I continued to be baffled by her amnesia about the fact that she was the one who had appointed Bambavale to replace me. Although I met her several times afterwards, I did not succeed in unravelling the mystery. It was only after several months that I learnt from the grapevine the real reason behind her farewell letter. Sanjay had persuaded her to believe that she had been pushed by me to hold the elections against her own judgement, and that it was all part of a conspiracy against her. She was obviously in a mental state in which she would believe anything, however far-fetched, so long as it absolved her of responsibility for what had happened.

It was only after she returned to power in 1980 that she became her normal self so far as I was concerned. She was genuinely hurt when I was not able to call on her in Belgrade, where she had come to attend the funeral of Marshal Tito. I was there with the secretary-general as part of the UN delegation. The Yugoslavs kept us so busy that there was no time for anything else. But Mrs Gandhi took it amiss and complained to several friends about my misdemeanour. She also made a pointed reference to it in a letter acknowledging the condolence message my wife and I had sent her after Sanjay's tragic death. This was her way of saying that things were normal between us again.

I met her for what turned out to be the last time in April 1984 when I was on home leave from the UN. She was extremely cordial and friendly. I had just returned from Srinagar, where I had gone to see my sister, so the conversation turned naturally to Kashmir. After a few preliminaries about goings-on in the UN, she started complaining rather angrily about Farooq Abdullah. Her criticism of Farooq was so bitter that I felt compelled to say she should not take drastic steps, such as dismissal of his government. I reminded her of the heavy price the country had to pay for the dismissal of Farooq's father in 1953. I also reminded her that she herself had disagreed with her father on that occasion and had written to him about it from England, or wherever she was at that time. She made no response to what I said and continued with her litany of complaints against Farooq, one of which was that the Congress Party office had been attacked and destroyed. I was amazed at this particular allegation because I had passed the building only the day before and found it intact. I said so. Unfortunately, at that point her telephone rang. She excused herself and told me she would send for me again. But this did not happen. When my leave was over I returned to New York. After some time I learnt from newspapers that Farooq Abdullah's government had been dismissed. In retrospect I felt that when I met her she had already made up her mind about Farooq and that she would not have changed her decision even if I had met her again. Nevertheless, I felt very bad about not having had the opportunity, for I was full of foreboding of things to come. Farooq's dismissal was bad enough but his replacement by Gul Shah, I knew, was going to be a disaster. Then came the tragedy of operation of Bluestar, and finally the assassination of Indira Gandhi.

I was awoken by an unfamiliar voice on the telephone from London in the middle of the night of 30–31 October 1984, giving me the terrible news. The disembodied voice did not identify itself nor did I get a chance to find out who it belonged to. It ended as abruptly as it began its single dreadful sentence. My wife thought it was a prankster and she immediately telephoned my brother in Delhi, who confirmed Mrs Gandhi had been shot by her Sikh guards and been removed to the All India Institute of Medical Sciences. He was hopeful about her survival. But the mysterious voice had firmly announced her death to me, which was soon confirmed by all the American news services.

New Yorkers learnt about the assassination of India's prime minister before Indians did in Delhi. From early morning I started getting telephone calls from friends and colleagues in the UN, sharing their sense of shock at the ghastly event and anguish for the future of the country. The Indian members of the UN staff organized a condolence meeting where I was asked to be the main speaker. I tried my best to rise to the occasion but got choked halfway and had to stop. The audience was very understanding. They got up, observed two minutes' silence, and dispersed.

The secretary-general was very kind to me. He asked me and his chef-de-cabinet, Virendra Dayal, to accompany him to Delhi. We reached there on 2 November. Soon after our arrival we went to Teen Murti House, where Mrs Gandhi's body lay in state. A large crowd was milling around the gate, seeking entrance for a last glimpse. The house was enveloped in immense sadness. The wreath-laying ceremony took a few minutes, after which the secretary-general left. I was in a daze and lingered a little longer. When I left I found the city exploding in violence. I went around in a UN car, which was allowed to enter curfew-bound areas, and saw frenzied mobs looking for Sikhs to kill. Indira Gandhi would have been horrified beyond belief to see what her death was doing to her beloved country. A day before her death she had told her countrymen in Orissa, 'when my life goes I can say that every drop of blood that is in me will give life to India and strengthen it.'

On 3 November, foreign delegations were taken to the open ground next to Shantivana where Indira Gandhi was to be cremated. I felt strange sitting among foreigners to witness Rajiv Gandhi perform the last rites before the pyre was lit. This feeling of strangeness became unbearable when, next day, I accompanied the secretary-general on his visit to 1 Safdarjung Road to convey his condolences to Rajiv Gandhi, the new prime minister. We were received in the room where his mother used to meet her visitors. My heart went out to Rajiv when I saw him, looking sad but serene. I wanted to give him a hug but hesitated for considerations of protocol. I did not follow what the secretary-general said to Rajiv as my mind was surging with my own memories and associations with that room.

After saying goodbye to Rajiv that evening, my mind continued to dwell on the days I had worked for Mrs Gandhi. I had had the privilege of being a witness to the courage and conviction with which she had led the country through a very difficult period. If one compared the circumstances in which she became prime minister and the problems she had to grapple with, one could say that in some respects she was a better prime minister than her father. Jawaharlal was the hero of the freedom movement and the darling of the people when he took on the reins of his country. He was revered by the Indian intelligentsia and respected internationally as a statesman and leader of the non-aligned world. He enjoyed the loyalty of his colleagues, who were men of great distinction and ability in their own right. The Congress Party enjoyed the prestige due to it as the vanguard of the freedom movement. The opposition parties were weak or non-existent. Indians were full of self-confidence and hope of a better future.

What Indira Gandhi inherited was a country humbled by China and harassed by Pakistan, an economy wrecked by drought and threat of famine. The Congress was a demoralized party dominated by a cabal of chief ministers with no vision beyond that of holding on to power. People were getting disillusioned with politicians and losing faith in government. Mrs Gandhi had demonstrated no great qualities of leadership before she assumed the office of prime minister. Her only asset was that she was Nehru's daughter.

She certainly lacked his intellectual calibre and ideological commitments but she more than compensated these inadequacies by greater courage and decisiveness. I doubt that her father would have handled the Bangladesh crisis of 1971, the economic crisis of 1974, the problem of Sikkim, and the nuclear dilemma with the firmness she showed. Like all human beings, great leaders have their flaws. So had Mrs Gandhi. In fact, she had more than her share. She had now passed into history which would deliver its verdict in time. These thoughts stayed with me all the way back to New York in November 1984.

They are still with me.

Democracy Under Stress: India Since 1977

L et me reiterate what I said in the preface to this book. I have tried here, by using episodes from my own career as an entry point, to highlight some of the major dilemmas that India, a large, diverse and poor country, has faced in its attempt at self-govern-ance. Perhaps the most central dilemma I have outlined is that while on the one hand the experiment of authoritarian rule during the twenty-one months of the Emergency established beyond doubt that India has to be self-governing to be governable, on the other the return of Westminster-style democracy has yielded unstable governments that make governance increasingly difficult.

How has democracy fared in the post-Emergency period? In this concluding chapter, I attempt to evaluate the direction that demo-cracy has taken in India since 1977.

When the Janata Party came to power, many who had been im-pressed by Jayaprakash Narayan's exhortations and his influence on the new government expected a more genuinely democratic order to emerge under the new dispensation. JP had promised an alternative model of governance. Before the new government took office, JP solemnly administered an oath to all the Janata members of parliament at Gandhiji's samadhi that they would abide by democratic values and stand united in defending them.

But what happened after this naive, if well meant, demonstration of pieties over 'value-based politics'? The party was not able to elect a leader as prime minister. Instead, JP and Acharya Kripalani had to use their moral authority to impose Morarji Desai as their nominee for the post. Their nominee was accepted by the party but that did not end the internal struggle for power. When it settled down to the business of governance, the Janata government looked very much like the Samyukta Vidhayak Dal governments that had plagued Bihar, UP and Madhya Pradesh during 1967–71. In some respects it was worse, because it was buffeted less by ideological conflicts than by the clashing personal ambitions of its leading lights.

In the ensuing naked struggle for power, there were no holds barred. Who could have imagined that Raj Narain, sworn enemy of Indira Gandhi, would seek the help of her son, who was supposed to be the evil genius of the Emergency, so that Chowdhry Charan Singh might dislodge his colleague Morarji Desai from prime ministership? But this is exactly what Raj Narain, who called himself the Hanuman of Charan Singh, did. Nor was this an isolated event. Other 'evil geniuses' of the Emergency and 'heroes' of the anti-Emergency movement became colleagues and joined hands, from time to time, to help each other in their power games. Witness V.C. Shukla, much arraigned by the Shah Commission for the rigours of press censorship under the Emergency, as the minister of external affairs under the prime ministership of Chandra Shekhar, a devotee of JP. More spectacular was the metamorphosis of Chimanbhai Patel, whose 'most corrupt regime' gave rise to the Nav Nirman movement in Gujarat, which in turn had inspired JP to launch his Sampurna Kranti; after being expelled from the Congress Party, he formed a group called Kisan Mazdoor Lok Paksh which became a constituent of the Janata Morcha and later of the Janata Dal itself!

All this was the sad outcome of JP's valiant strivings. He had reason to be in despair, a feeling which he shared with his closest confidants in the Sarvodaya movement. He realized that, in his anxiety to gather support for his revolution, he had relied upon people who merely used him for their own purposes. He had been carried away by the dubious success of the Nav Nirman movement. He mistook the passing idealism of students for long-term political commitment. In his enthusiasm for the movement he disregarded the fact that the support of political parties for the students was only directed towards bringing the government down, nothing more.

Although a poor judge of Indian politics and politicians, JP sometimes had flashes of deep insight. In his convocation address to the Banaras Hindu University in February 1970 he was remarkably prescient:

Politics has become the greatest question mark of this decade. Some of the trends are obvious. Political disintegration is likely to spread, selfish splitting of the parties rather than their ideological polarization will continue; devaluation of ideologies may continue; frequent change of party loyalties for personal or parochial benefits, buying and selling of legislators, inner-party indiscipline, opportunistic alliances among parties and instability of governments—all these are expected to continue.

The bitter truth is that what JP apprehended early in 1970 as the likely political scenario came true after his great success of 1977.

Neither Indira Gandhi's efforts to put 'democracy back on the rails' through the enforced discipline of the Emergency, nor the outpourings of JP's revolutionary rhetoric, have made any difference to the working of democracy in India. Indeed the Emergency as well as the JP movement further weakened the institutions essential for genuine democracy. Both these events reduced respect for the rule of law: the Emergency by an authoritarian disregard for legal norms and the JP movement by rationalizing and glamorizing the defiance of all authority.

Indira Gandhi's return to power in 1980 proved that the Janata Party was not a viable alternative to the Congress. Since it also demonstrated that her party could not produce an alternative leadership, it is not surprising that she came to consider herself indispensable to both party and country. Her three years in the political wilderness after her defeat in 1977 could have been an opportunity for her to reflect on what ailed India. Instead, even had she been temperamentally inclined towards self-reflection, all her energies had to be focussed on grappling with numerous inquiry commissions that were set up. None of these, including the Shah Commission, came up with any serious analysis of what was wrong with Indian politics and how it might be set right. Nor did anyone else. Indira Gandhi's own camp was ideologically too passive to inspire her. Thus her predominant area of concern shrank towards ensuring political stability and she was led to believe that this could be guaranteed only if the Congress was in power.

As a result, the Congress Party began to concentrate almost exclusively on strengthening short-term electoral prospects, regardless of the means adopted. In several cases these proved calamitous. The party's support to Jarnail Singh Bhindranwale to outplay the Akalis in Punjab went out of control and encouraged the secessionist movement in the state, which led to the army assault on the Golden Temple and ultimately Indira Gandhi's assassination by her Sikh security guards. Similar short-term gains were pursued in Kashmir, where Farooq Abdullah's government was dismissed and replaced by that of Ghulam Mohammad Shah, who sought political support from the secessionist Jamat-i-Islam to stay in power. To secure that support he had to recruit Jamaiti cadres in the Kashmir armed police. In both cases stability was sought with the assistance of avowed destabilizers.

Rajiv Gandhi tried at first to reverse this trend. In his presidential address to the centenary session of the Congress in December 1985, he voiced his worries about unwholesome developments in his party. He wanted to restore the Nehruvian political culture of his grandfather's Congress, but he could not prevail against party managers who were only concerned with cultivating vote banks. Once again, the result was a cynical pursuit of short-term electoral gains. The supreme court judgement on Shah Bano, the Muslim divorcee whom the court had granted alimony, was upturned by a constitutional amendment to please Muslim clerics. To compound the folly, the locks of the disputed Babri Masjid were opened to please a Hindu constituency, with disastrous consequences for communal peace and social harmony. The political environment today accepts the use of such reckless and dangerous methods to garner electoral support, even though it is obviously contrary to the basic norms of a secular democracy and against the national interest.

Beneath the turbulence on the political surface, marked by the rise and fall of political parties and personalities, ran a deeper current of dissonance—dissonance between the rapid politicization of the masses and the imperatives of orderly government in a society undergoing profound and far-reaching changes. Such developments make democracy vulnerable to oscillation between extremes of social disorder and civil strife on the one side, and demands for authoritarian measures to maintain political and social stability on the other.

The end of the Emergency was the beginning of a new phase of democracy, generating new challenges. This phase was marked by the entry of north India's dominant peasant communities on the political scene in a big way. The number of their representatives has steadily increased since the first general elections. In the sixth Lok Sabha, they constituted about 40 per cent of its membership. It was on the strength of rural votes that the Janata Party swept the polls in the northern states in 1977. With their new found strength, they were quick to seek rewards for their support to the new government.

The expansion of economic opportunities and educational facilities in the wake of the Green Revolution gave rise to a powerful lobby whose political clout grew from strength to strength through successive elections. After the Janata government assumed office, the rural lobby mobilized the upwardly mobile sections of these dominant peasant communities to demand job reservations in government and quasi-government services, and preferential treatment for admission to educational, technical and professional institutions. The demand for reservations was based on the plea that their low status in the caste hierarchy had resulted in their social and educational backwardness. In terms of caste disabilities, it was claimed that they were not far removed from the Dalits—which of course was not true. But in 1977 they were in a very advantageous position to bargain for these benefits as their influence in the ruling party had significantly increased. Their most important and articulate leader, Chowdhry Charan Singh, being the home minister in the Janata government, was in a position to oblige. On his initiative a mammoth kisan rally was held in Delhi to demonstrate their political strength. Against the backdrop of this political mobilization, the government set up a commission under the chairmanship of B.P. Mandal in January 1979 to consider the demand for reservations of the 'intermediate castes', also called 'other backward classes' (OBCs).

In 1955 Kaka Kalelkar, chairman of the first backward classes commission, raised a basic objection against reservations. He said: 'National solidarity demands that in a democratic set-up government recognise only two ends—individual at the one end and the nation as a whole at the other—and that nothing should be allowed to organise itself in between the two ends to the detriment of the individual and the solidarity of the nation.' This was a sweeping statement, unrealistic for an hierarchically layered and diverse society. In 1980 Mandal, in contradistinction to Kalelkar, went to the other extreme and made membership of specific castes and communities the basis for granting reservations, which he recommended for a very large number of such entities.

The roots of individualism, the basis of liberal democracy, have always been weak in India. Mandal weakened them further by attaching overriding importance to the familiar identities of caste and subcaste, leaving no space for the concept of the autonomous individual. The constitution and the law may continue to pronounce in behalf of individual rights, but Mandal erased the individual from public discourse. The primordial bonds of *jati* supplanted the individual as the primary building block of the political constitution of society. The concepts of equality and social justice, which developed in the course of freeing the individual from oppressive arrangements of various kinds, were put into a communitarian mould. The struggle to free Indians from caste and create a modern civil society has been made even more difficult than it already was.

The Janata government fell before it could take action on the Mandal report. It was left to V.P. Singh, in 1990, to implement Mandal's recommendations in an effort to outbid his coalition partner, Devi Lal, in securing OBC support. Since then the transformation of castes into political categories has gathered much momentum. While caste restrictions are certainly melting down in other fields, in the area of politics caste identifications have intensified. Mandal has tried to give it ideological respectability by presenting caste-based reservations as a step towards social justice, regardless of the fact that it is the affluent section of the backward castes or the 'creamy layer'—in the language of the supreme court—that benefits from these reservations.

The Mandal Commission zeroed in on their favourite recommendation by the simple device of accepting the validity of objections raised by critics, and then playing them down as motivated or inconsequential. Thus the arguments that the recruitment of a few thousand OBCs against reserved vacancies will not have a perceptible impact on the general condition of OBCs, or that reservations will impair the quality and efficiency of services, or that the benefits of reservations will be skimmed off by sections which are already better off and leave the backward section high and dry—these were all accepted by the commission as 'based on fairly sound reasoning' but then dismissed as 'arguments advanced by the ruling elite which is keen on preserving its privileges.'

The commission's main emphasis is not upon the general upliftment of the backward classes: it did not make a case for the universal application of justice and rights. It candidly stated that 'the chief merit of reservation is not that it will introduce egalitarianism among OBCs. But reservation will certainly erode the hold of higher castes on the services and enable OBCs in general to have a sense of participation in running the affairs of their country.'[1] Mandal desired that the OBCs get their share of higher education and jobs which the older middle class, largely made up of the higher castes, had managed to secure for themselves through a highly subsidized educational system. In this, Mandal was as insensitive to the dehumanizing poverty prevalent in the country as was the older middle class.

The arithmetic of electoral politics being what it is, reservations have been accepted by most parties as an indispensable device to secure the support of powerful vote banks. This is how Mandal succeeded in

[1] *Report of the Backward Classes Commission, First Part 1980* (Government of India, 1980), p. 57.

trivializing the vision of social justice held before the poor of this country.

The struggle to gain middle-class benefits is a normal historical process, but the use of the caste ladder for that purpose has had wider political consequences. Caste leaders have used the electoral process to emphasize caste consciousness and manipulated inter-caste tensions and rivalries to gain and retain power. They have succeeded in creating an ideological milieu which favours competition in backwardness. The pursuit of excellence is denounced as elitist. The message of the Mandal ideologues seems to be that to move forward you have to be labelled 'backward', which you can be if you are identified as a member of a backward caste. Inevitably, therefore, more and more castes want to be included in the new privileged category of backward castes, thus giving rise to new challenges and conflicts.

Given the nature and extent of its poverty and the resultant vulnerabilities, India's overriding national interest is to accelerate its economic growth, eliminate want, and promote greater social cohesion. Indeed these were the goals of economic development initiated under the regime of five-year plans. But the economic policies India followed for nearly four decades yielded a rate of growth which was too low for it to achieve these objectives. By the mid 1970s the low-growth economy came under severe strain as a result of high inflation caused by crop failures and a steep increase in oil prices. A decade later this became politically unacceptable: the government's budget was not yielding any surplus for development. In fact the three non-plan items of expenditure, namely defence, interest on past debt, and subsidies, added up to more than the central government's net tax revenue. On the political front, the aspirations of the emerging middle class for higher earnings were running into the barrier of slow growth, and the poor—who in the mean time had become sufficiently politicized—were demanding the better life promised them. These demands could be met only if the economy grew much faster.

When an effort was made by Rajiv Gandhi to accelerate growth, it was found impossible without a drastic revision of the old policies. He did succeed in raising the rate of economic growth in the 1980s, but it could not be sustained in the absence of a basic reform of economic policies. Rajiv Gandhi was not able to change the mindset of his colleagues or overcome the opposition of powerful groups that had benefited most from planned economic development and the democratic process as it had worked out in the country.

The beneficiaries of earlier policies were mainly rich and middle farmers, medium and small industrialists, traders, the labour aristocracy, government employees, and business groups operating in sheltered markets or trading in scarce commodities. Even though these form a small part of the total population, they are large in absolute numbers—125 to 150 million out of the country's total population of 950 million. It is not possible to subsume these groups under a standard category called 'middle class'. They are separate economic and social formations, their political linkages are weak and often fragmented, and they have some common characteristics. They have all moved up in the scale of income and status. In the income-distribution table, most of them occupy middle brackets. Though only about one-seventh of the total population, together they constitute a potential market the size of France and Great Britain combined. Politically they are aggressive and skilful, and therefore influential far beyond their numbers. They have successfully espoused programmes and policies which further their interests in ideologically attractive terms—such as social justice.

With the passage of time, and alongside economic development, there has been a significant increase in the numbers, economic strength, and political power of these groups. The rich and middle farmers have triggered off the Green Revolution, which has sharply reduced India's chronic food deficits and provided the country with food security. But they have achieved this by securing ever-increasing procurement prices for their produce and expanding subsidies for their inputs—concessions which have become permanent features of India's agricultural policy.

Similarly, small industrialists and businessmen have broadened the social and regional base of entrepreneurship in the country. There has been a phenomenal growth in the number of units, investments, and output in the modern small-scale sector. Their contribution to industrial output is about half the total output, and they provide two-thirds of India's industrial employment. This is an impressive achievement, but the economic and social costs of this achievement have been equally great. Modern small industry has been concentrated in a few metropolitan areas and large towns; its role in industrializing the countryside or expanding employment has been limited. The progress it has achieved has been the result of large-scale state assistance, which has gone far beyond the legitimate requirements of development.

Besides the provision of industrial estates, technical aid, hire purchase and marketing facilities (which are necessary for their development), assistance to these industries includes large subsidies by way of excise duty concessions, concessional credit, and sales-tax exemptions. Entire industries have been reserved as 'small industries', whose number has been increasing from time to time. For example, the Janata government increased the number of products reserved for the small-scale sector from 128 in 1977 to 836 in 1979. Many of these industries, such as toys, garments, sports and household goods, had tremendous export potential which India lost to South Korea and Taiwan and later to China. The transition of government policies from promotion to protection has created a vested interest in smallness. The ultimate success of small enterprises is to cease to be small, except where it has an inherent advantage—and ironically the policy environment has encouraged small enterprises to stay small. Small industries continue to be ideologically attractive and their support is widely sought at election time, especially at the state level.

Again, the public sector has an essential role as an engine of growth. This is true especially in the early stages of industrialization, when capital is scarce and enterprise shy of entering sectors with long gestation periods. In India the public sector lost its basic rationale when it went beyond its proper sphere, and its extension became an end in itself. In the process, the public sector absorbed about half the total industrial investment, regardless of costs and returns.

As a model employer, the government provides job security and indexation of wages to the labour force it employs. Since profitability has not been the governing consideration of these businesses, the work-force employed is much larger than is warranted by technical or economic considerations. Job Security and militant trade unionism have caused a decline in the work ethic, resulting in loss of production and a deterioration in the quality of services. But no political party seems prepared to withstand the public sector's extravagant demands for fear of being dubbed reactionary.

The rapid proliferation in government employment has taken place in the wake of increased governmental supervisory and regulatory activity, especially in the economic and social spheres. Alongside the increase in numbers has been a vast expansion in the reach of the authority of higher levels among civil servants. The power to grant or reject favours, the power to say yes or no can make or mar a business, and thereby opens up opportunities for corruption among bureaucrats. The unionization and politicization of services have resulted in over-manning within the lower ranks of the bureaucracy and a decline in their discipline. In these circumstances it was natural for the bureaucracy to develop vested interests in policies that made the Indian economy one of the most rigidly regulated in the world. No wonder that the Indian bureaucracy has been so strongly opposed to liberalization, and to the privatization of the public sector.

In sum, economic development, which has given rise to these special interest groups, has provided them with a political clout which they use unabashedly for their own sectional interests. The wider deprivations of the urban poor, landless rural labourers, and marginal farmers, all of whom swell the ranks of the left-out millions, are not a part of their consciousness. The irony is that these exclusive interests of so-called 'middle income groups' have received the support not only of conservative parties but also of parties which are avowedly socialist in their proclaimed ideologies. This is in the nature of a tribute that these parties pay to keep a hold on the special interest groups in Indian politics.

As is usual in India, policies are reviewed and changed only when the country is overtaken by a crisis. It was only in July 1991, when the economy was hit by a severe balance of payments crisis and the country was on the verge of defaulting on its obligations to foreign creditors, that an economic reform process was started with the assistance of the

International Monetary Fund. Even so, it is only politically less risky measures—such as reduction and rationalization of taxation, delicensing of industry, and freer trade policies—that have been adopted. This is not to say that these are not important; indeed they mark a decisive break with some of the old policies that held the economy back. But what remains to be done is even more crucial to the success of our reforms. To impart dynamism to the economy it is necessary to cut down subsidies to people who are not poor, drastically reform the public sector, revamp the financial sector, and review labour legislation in order to create a healthy and stable industrial relations system. But all these are areas in which vested interests, the beneficiaries of old policies, are bound to be hurt and are therefore politically difficult to manage.

But poverty cannot be eliminated without accelerating economic growth and substantially increasing investment in health and education. To achieve that purpose, resources have to be mobilized. The past policies of raising rates of taxation to higher and higher levels proved counterproductive in terms of revenue yield. Tax revenues can only be increased by broadening the tax base, i.e. by taxing those currently outside the net for one reason or another, such as traders and big farmers. Large resources for development can become available by cutting down subsidies and drastically restructuring public sector units running at a loss. In a paper issued by the Government of India in May 1997 it was revealed that all subsidies, explicit and implicit, put together amount to more than 15 per cent of the country's gross domestic product, which is very near the government's tax revenue. Even after excluding subsidies, which can be justified on some economic or social grounds, the percentage remains around 10 per cent, most of which benefit people who are not poor. Once the politicized poor are able to see through this charade of 'social justice' perpetuated by entrenched interest groups, it may become easier to release resources for a more buoyant economy.

Another arena of conflict is the relationship between majorities and the country's numerous minorities—religious, ethnic and linguistic. Religious minorities constitute the core of what is called the 'minority problem'. Just as the federal constitution was expected to provide a co-operative framework between the centre and the states, the establishment of a secular state was expected to eliminate or minimize religious strife and establish communal harmony. The constitution-makers explored various constitutions while framing the one they thought would suit India best, but in establishing the basis for a secular state they were not guided by the sorts of secular states that exist today. If by secularism is meant a process which lessens the hold of religion on political culture and social institutions within a society, then it must be said this was not a part of their thinking: all that they meant by secularism was equality for all religions in the eyes of the state. Such a definition was certainly consistent with the dominant Indian traditions. The constitution guaranteed religious freedom to all its citizens: the state was required to be neutral in religious matters. The neutral state, it was hoped, would allay the misgivings of religious minorities, especially Muslims, who had grave fears about their prospects in a free India. The disappearance of the British from India was believed to have removed the main prop which sustained communal politics. There seems to have been no anxiety on account of the possible re-emergence of religion as a political ideology, and if there was any it did not take the form of measures to discourage such an eventuality.

For about a decade after Independence communalism, especially Muslim communalism, did indeed seem to be on the decline. The trauma of Partition had left Indian Muslims unsure of their place in Indian society. The movement for Pakistan drew its main support from provinces which remained in India. The elite that had mobilized the Muslims of India on the basis of the two-nation theory, left for Pakistan, leaving the rest to fend for themselves. Under the new dispensation, instinct led them to look for safety, which they sought by supporting the ruling Congress Party. Their support for that party was based less on its professed non-communal character than on the fact that it was the ruling party. As the memory of the Partition receded, traditional Muslim leaders gradually resumed their hold on their co-religionists. The electoral process gave the Muslims, as it gave other minorities, opportunities to trade votes for communal advantage.

Economic development helped fill the depleted ranks of the Muslim middle class. Since Mughal times, Muslims have been engaged in handicrafts and allied small-scale industries. With the active support of the government under the five-year plans, there has been a vast expansion of these activities, and consequently in the emergence of a new Muslim middle class. The prosperity brought about by the Green Revolution in western Uttar Pradesh and the opening of job opportunities in West Asia since 1973 have expanded this class further. Other smaller professional groups have helped add up to a substantial Muslim middle class. Both size and growing economic strength have given this class of the Muslim community some much needed self-confidence.

It used to be said, particularly in the early days of Independence, that once Muslims regained their self-confidence they would review their past political fears in terms of new opportunities and break out of their narrower communal shell to participate in political processes more as Indians than as Muslims. The past, however, has continued to hold most Indians in its thrall. A large part of the national struggle against British imperialism consisted in working out a *modus vivendi* between Islam and Indian citizenship. Gandhi made an effort on the basis of religious tolerance and interreligious understanding. Nehru believed co-operation at the level of class interest would break down communal barriers. Maulana Azad and the Jamait-ul-Ulema-i-Hind worked for a political coalition between Hindus and Muslims to fight a common foe. All these efforts collapsed when India was split into two sovereign states.

After Independence, the problem for Muslims was to work out a relationship with the state which was neither exclusively theirs nor one from which they were excluded. The way the Muslims function and fare in India will provide a precedent for their co-religionists situated in similar circumstances elsewhere. This is the challenge for the new Muslim middle class and its political leadership, though currently their leaders continue to think in the political idiom with which they were familiar in pre-Independence days. Students of the political history of India are puzzled by the fact that the movement for the creation of Pakistan was supported mainly and enthusiastically by the Muslims of Uttar Pradesh and Bihar, and less by other Muslim minority provinces; this seemed to disregard the consequences of the success of their effort to their own future. Several explanations have been suggested for this seemingly irrational or, if you like, self-sacrificing behaviour. It is even more puzzling that there has been no great change in their attitude since then. Maulana Wahidudin Khan, editor of *Al-Risala* and director of Delhi's Islamic Centre, has analysed this mind-set of the Muslim leadership very candidly. In his opinion:

As a result of the passitivity of Maulana Azad and other like-minded public figures, the Muslims of the post-partitition era continued to think along the lines laid down by Jinnah and supported by Mohammad Iqbal. New leaders who thought differently did emerge later, but, being lesser in stature, they were unable to rid Muslim thinking of the Jinnah–Iqbal dominance, established in pre-Independence days . . . Prone to highlighting their problems while glossing over their opportunities, Muslims came to know and use no other language but that of demands. . . . To my way of thinking, the present Muslim leadership, both religious and liberal, is, on almost all counts, an extension of Jinnah's style of leadership.[2]

At one time a hope for change did appear. This was in 1958, when a convention of Muslim legislators (members of the union and state legislatures) unanimously supported the position of the Government of India on the Kashmir question. On that occasion, the nawab of Chattari referred to the special interest of Indian Muslims in Kashmir: 'it is the only constituent state in the Indian Union where Muslims are in a majority. As such they feel that the progress and prosperity of Kashmir is a visible symbol of the secular democracy which is flourishing in India and a guarantee of the maintenance of this composite culture which has been India's special contribution to the civilization of the world.' But this hope for change disappeared rather soon and has not been revived even by developments such as the reluctance of Pakistan to receive the Urdu-speaking people of Bangladesh (or Biharis as they are called) who fought for Pakistan, and the difficulties faced by Muslim migrants from India who continue to be called 'muhajirs' fifty

[2] 'Time to leave Jinnah behind', *The Observer*, Delhi, 19 June 1999.

years after their migration. On the contrary it is the maulvis from UP and Bihar who, recruited by the Jamat-i-Islami, have succeeded to a large extent in subverting the traditional tolerant Islam of Kashmir.

The shift in Muslim opinion on Kashmir since 1958 can be seen from writings that appear in the Urdu press, which largely moulds Muslim public opinion. At the height of the Pakistan-supported insurgency in Kashmir, a New Delhi monthly, *Afkar-i-Milli*, said in an editorial: 'We have always shown Islamic solidarity with Muslim causes everywhere, be it the Khilafat movement in the case of Ottoman Empire, or against American–Israeli collusion over Palestine, and in support of Afghan people's Jihad against the Red Army in Soviet-occupied Afghanistan. Why then are Muslim leaders tight-lipped on Kashmir.'[3]

In fairness it must be said that the existence of Pakistan as an Islamic state and the rise of fundamentalism in several Muslim countries have made it even more difficult for Indian Muslims to adjust to secularism than it might have been. Exposed as they now are to the increasing influence of Islamists from the Muslim world, it is difficult for the Indian Muslim to reconcile his Islamic identity with his Indian inheritance. Indeed, being placed in a non-Muslim environment has only made Indian Muslims even more jealous guardians of their Islamic heritage. This explains their exaggerated preoccupation not only with their normal religious symbols and rituals but even with their studiously distinct dress and appearance. A kind of ghetto psychology has, over the years, taken hold of the Indian Muslim mind, a sense of being beleaguered.

Hindu reaction to Muslim anxieties has been of two opposite kinds: either it has been marked by distrust, lack of sensitivity, and reluctance to accept legitimate dissent, or marked by an exaggerated emphasis upon the rhetoric of secular non-interference in anything that can even remotely be connected with the Muslims, which has in practice meant a wrong-headed deference to the views and opinions of reactionary mullahs. The first reaction is largely responsible for the deterioration in Hindu–Muslim relations. Militant Hindu communalism has been

---

[3] Quoted by Omar Khalid, 'Kashmir and Muslim Politics in India', in *Perspectives in Kashmir*, edited by Raju G.C. Thomas (Boulder: West View Press, 1992), p. 278.

a constant factor in Indian politics, but until the late 1970s it was a minor factor. Since then it has grown in strength and respectability. The insurgency in Punjab and Kashmir has cast doubt in the minds of many middle-class Hindus about the viability of a composite Indian nationalism, which Gandhi and Nehru had tried to build. They have become increasingly receptive to the idea of defining Indian nationalism in Hindu terms, which is what Hindutva is all about. Its advocates are trying to forge a national identity for Hindus; they are trying to correct 'the historic failure' of Hindu society to evolve itself as a political community. But Hinduism does not lend itself to a restatement in fundamental terms, which is what the advocates of Hindutva are trying to do in imitation of Islam. Hindutva reached a sort of peak in the elections of 1998. India's experience of the Vajpayee administration has demonstrated that India is too diverse for Hindu nationalism to be a practical proposition. It is also becoming clear that Hinduism will lose what is best within it, and India will diminish in stature if Hindutva efforts succeed. The only option available to India is to revitalize composite nationalism—but that cannot be an exclusively Hindu concern.

The second Hindu reaction, namely an excessive deference to mullahs, has marginalized liberal Muslims and made them even less influential in the affairs of their community than they might have been. The government has not supported liberal Muslims when they have fallen foul of fundamentalists. The way Arif Mohammad Khan (who stoutly defended the supreme court's judgement on Shah Bano in parliament) was let down by his prime minister or the indifference government showed to the fate of Mushirul Hasan when he was being hounded out of Jamia Millia Islamia because he had questioned the wisdom of banning Salman Rushdie's *Satanic Verses*, could not have heartened liberal Muslims. It is therefore not surprising that they have failed to gather worthwhile support among their co-religionists. There are, of course, a few outstanding individuals who want their brethren to come out of the shadows of the past and make a constructive contribution to the future, but unfortunately they are too few to be effective. The government's anxiety to appear sympathetic—in the manner of a benevolent medieval monarch—has further added to the confusion about what secularism really means. Treating the visits of government dignitaries to temples and shrines as public functions at the tax payers' cost, the subsidization of pilgrimages, the continued use of quasi-religious concepts like 'Hindu undivided family' for tax advantage—all these have not enhanced the image of the Indian state as uninvolved in the religious affairs of its citizens.

In practice, the concept of secularism has undergone several other distortions. For example, Jawaharlal Nehru's observation that major-ity communalism is more dangerous than minority communalism, which was made in the immediate context of the Partition to curb anti-Muslim feelings, was raised to the status of a permanent doctrine, with the result that secularism was never used to fight minority communal-ism. Indeed, the acceptance of Muslim communal demands became a test of secularism. The approval of clerics like the imam of Delhi's Jama Masjid was actively sought by political leaders for some of their policies which they thought would affect Muslims. Perhaps the root of the trouble lies in the constitution: the respect for all religions enshrined in the constitution has turned out to include respect for all varieties of fanaticism and obscurantism.

Unsurprisingly therefore, with the passage of time the influence of religion on the society, culture, and politics of non-Muslims has in-creased, belying the hope of modernists like Nehru that this influence would decline with education. The state is now helpless to curb evil social practices—such as the denial of a maintenance allowance to a Muslim divorcee, or the inhumanity of dragging a Hindu widow to commit sati—lest it be accused of interference in religious matters. The democratic government of India is reduced to the position of the colonial British government, which gave up further attempts at social reform after 1857 because it believed that the Mutiny was the result of injured religious sentiment. The laissez-faire policy towards what fana-tics call 'religion', combined with permissive democracy, has put secu-larism·upon its head.

In matters of religion and secularism, other countries of the subcon-tinent are part of the Indian domestic scene. Nothing is easier than to inflame religious animosities in the countries of the subcontinent. They are quick to take the worst view of happenings in their neigh-bourhood. The continued adversarial relations between India and

Pakistan have further complicated the problems of Indian Muslims. As Wilfred Cantwell Smith observed:

Rather than coming firmly to terms with the realization that the position of India's Muslims depends primarily on two things, their aspiration towards Indianness and India's aspiration towards secularism, Pakistan has tended to deride that secularism. Pakistani Muslims have had so heavy a psychological investment in the conviction that Indian Muslims are mistreated, that at times one cannot but detect a morbid welcoming of adverse news and a resistance to awareness of Indo-Muslim welfare . . .[4]

Similar views are being expressed by some liberal Pakistani writers. In a perceptive article on Indo-Pak ties, Iqbal Khan says:

when reporting or commenting on anti-Muslim riots in India, our editors and reporters can barely hide their glee at what they perceive as the 'failure' of Indian secularism: phrases like 'India's so-called secularism' or 'the world's largest democratic and secular state is once again consumed by the flames of anti-Muslim riots' are meant to tell the public that the Indian state is hypocritical about its constitutional commitments to secularism. But if secularism is not having much success in India today, is this to be regretted or celebrated?[5]

Thus, in its pursuit of secularism at home, India has to contend with the ideologically based anti-secular policies of its neighbours. This asymmetrical situation, which has existed since Partition in 1947, is now becoming unsustainable because of the Hindu backlash. It needs to be noted here that the real danger of religious fundamentalism does not lie in its emphasis on doctrinal purity or in its disapproval of the Western way of life; it lies rather in its quest for political power and in its desire to capture the state. India has not only to strengthen secularism at home but also to stand up for it in the neighbourhood. This raises a whole set of challenges for India's domestic and foreign policies.

---

[4] W.C. Smith, *Islam in Modern History* (Princeton: Princeton University Press), 1975, p. 268.

[5] *Frontier Post* (Pakistan), reproduced in *The Times of India,* 13 February 1991.

Groups and classes are known to seek political power as they climb the economic ladder and acquire a sense of self-awareness and importance. The temptation to pull levers in order to expand economic opportunities and areas of influence is natural. To gain greater support and acceptance, emerging groups present their demands as the demands of the majority, the underprivileged and the poor. They articulate their positions in such ideological terms as would appeal to larger constituencies, and thus appear irresistible.

In western democracies which reached their present stage of maturity over a long period of time, new social groups emerging as a result of technological change and economic growth were enfranchised and brought into the political mainstream by a gradual process. As the social base of democracy in these countries got extended by stages, political parties provided the mechanism for orderly change. Political ambition and dissent were channelized through the party system; emerging groups were incorporated in the power structure through the electoral process which acted as a mediator for rival claims. Thus group conflicts were contained within a political framework based on a general consensus. However, on occasion, even this long-drawn-out process was not immune from social and political upheavals.

In India the development of democracy was compressed into just a few decades. The British government had introduced the representation of Indians to provincial and central legislatures on the basis of a very restricted franchise—limited by qualifications of education and property. Soon after Independence India established its political system on the basis of universal adult franchise and full-fledged democracy which was patterned after the most sophisticated model available, namely the Westminster model, which had taken two centuries to mature in its original home. This was an act of faith in their people on the part of the founding fathers of Indian democracy. As the democratic system evolved, the results seemed to vindicate their faith, at least in its first phase under the leadership of Jawaharlal Nehru. It is true that the democratic process was not always tidy or smooth even at that time, often resulting in large-scale turbulence, but it worked nevertheless.

During its first phase the democratic system successfully incorporated over six hundred princely states of various sizes and types into a coherent administrative framework and federal political system. The system was again tested severely during the turbulent days of the reorganization of states on a linguistic basis. But democracy survived the turmoil and India was not balkanized, as some people had feared. These and similar events made Indians take it for granted that it would be able to handle the centrifugal forces successfully. This self-image was endorsed by many keen foreign observers. Indeed, *The Economist* (London) saw in Indian diversity an asset for its unification. It was their view that 'a country with half a dozen religions, up to twenty languages, a many-layered caste system has infinite practice at not disintegrating. India's diversity is so extreme that like rubber-jointedness it is a means of staying in one piece.'

Today Indians are less self-confident about the viability of their political system as a mode of governance. The old fears about India's disintegration have been revived by separatist movements in Punjab, Kashmir and Assam, by the recrudescence of violent communal hostility fuelled by religious revivalism and fundamentalism, and by the sharpening of caste conflicts. Today the spectre of chaos haunts the country; it is a fear with a deep resonance in its historical memory.

Is India now nearing the end of yet another of those brief phases of political unity which have punctuated her chaotic history from time to time? To put this question in another form, has Indian democracy ceased to be resilient enough to cope with the demands of new and emerging groups? Can the challenge to the authority of the state be met without recourse to authoritarianism? Can the democratic government maintain order without oppression? Can change take place without upheaval? To answer these questions one has to examine the nature and condition of our political parties and the socio-political outlook of the emerging groups.

The Congress Party, the party of the freedom struggle, played a creative role in the formative period of the Indian state after independence. It was then led by an outstandingly charismatic leader and other stalwarts of the independence movement with their experience of forging unity out of diversity by working across ethnic, regional and linguistic lines. Under Jawaharlal's leadership, the Congress Party provided the main element of the political infrastructure for Indian democracy. The Congress Party, by virtue of holding power at the centre as well as in the states, mediated regional and social conflicts through its party mechanisms and its control over the central and state administrations. Speaking about the centre–state equation of his time, C. Rajagopalachari called it 'a question of relationship between the state branches of the Congress Party and its central organization.'

This was evidently an exceptional set of circumstances which could not have continued indefinitely. The Congress monopoly of power collapsed in 1967. Even when it regained greater electoral support after 1967, the party did not recapture its mediating role. The domineering central leadership and the absence of party elections denied it the opportunity of self-renewal. Eventually, it got reduced to a mere electoral machine, drawing strength more from the popularity of the leader than from the grassroots support of its members. But though enfeebled, the party still has many assets. It has a psychological and organizational presence in all parts of the country which it has built over more than a century, first through political struggle and, later, through the exercise of power. In the political market, it can still command a premium of good will. Under a younger and more dynamic leadership it can revive and assume a dominant role again.

Be that as it may, no party can stay in power in a democracy for all time. Nor can democracy endure if it is always dependent on charismatic leaders. The test of a true democracy is that it can be run even by mediocrities. What is grievous about the decline of the Congress Party is that its decline has not been counterbalanced by the emergence of an alternative national party or parties. The non-Congress parties are either regional in outlook and inspiration or have become so owing to their limited electoral support despite their national pretensions. The Communist Party (Marxist) has a national outlook in theory but its political support is confined to local power bases in West Bengal, Tripura and Kerala. The BJP has wider political support. The results of the 1998 general elections demonstrated the possibility of the party extending its influence in the southern and eastern regions of the country also if it moderates its espousal of Hindu nationalism which had confined its influence to northern and western states. But whether it succeeds in becoming a party of Indian nationalism remains to be seen.

It is often said that we need not bemoan the emergence of regional parties. Since these parties have demonstrated their ability to combine with multi-regional parties to share power at the centre, it is a development to be welcomed as it will strengthen the federal structure. Also, at the central government end of the federal system, it is being increasingly realized that no prime minister, not even one with a passion for centralizing power, can do without the support of the state governments or without a pluralist support for his power structure. These are potentially healthy developments for a co-operative federal system. But the potential for strife is also ever-present. A clear indication of the danger was visible during the formation of the BJP-led coalition government in March 1998. Regional party leaders like Jayalalitha, Mamata Bannerji and Naveen Patnaik demanded special dispensations for their respective states as a price for their support. The demands may be at the cost of other states and result in inter-state strife or at the cost of the centre, giving rise to competitive regional chauvinism and the aggravation of centre–state relations.

In other respects too, the strain on centre–state relations can increase for two opposite reasons. The continuing process of national integration in the political, economic and social spheres creates the need for a coherent national agenda, while the growing economic demands of backward communities and backward regions generate pressure for more resources and greater political access at the state level. The strains arising out of these opposite trends cannot be resolved without an adequate response from political parties and political institutions.

The ongoing economic reforms are also bound to affect centre–state and inter-state relations in significant ways. The gradual retreat of the government in the allocation of resources in favour of the private sector and the substitution of central planning by the market mechanism can accentuate regional differences. With reduced resources at its command, the centre may not be able to help the poorer states. In that case some states are likely to grow at a faster rate than others, and thereby generate tensions which can weaken the bond of interdependence which is the essence of a co-operative federal system. This pessimistic outcome is not inevitable. Other and better outcomes are certainly possible, depending on the attitude of political parties to economic reforms.

The economic reforms could lead to healthy competition between the states to foster growth-oriented policies which attract capital and enterprise. The so-called poor states like Bihar and Orissa are rich in resources; all they need is growth-oriented policies, which may materialize once they find that the centre is not to be blamed for their mistakes. The national economy which provides a common market to all the states is a great common asset from which no major regional party would like to secede. Even political aspirations for secession can get muted by the economic advantages of membership of a larger group. Besides, the prospect of power sharing at the federal centre can be a great incentive for better centre–state relations. Above all there is something which one might call the idea or concept of India which, with all its vagueness, is tangible and durable enough to give the country a centre of gravity.

The DMK stood for a separate state at one time but gave up the demand in 1962, when the country was facing an external threat to its national integrity. The Akalis are betwixt and between a separate state and a more autonomous state of the union where they can rule on a more enduring basis. Separatism in Kashmir is more a 'Muslim problem' than a regional one. Both in Punjab and in Kashmir, religious ideologies are sometimes dressed up as regional grievances to secure the support of secular-minded political elements and the liberal intelligentsia.

Whether the separate interests of regional parties can mesh into a coherent national framework smoothly and without much turbulence remains to be seen. In the immediate future the political parties are likely to continue to coalesce and break-up till a more rational and stable party system, based on harmonization of different interests through a process of give and take, emerges. In the meanwhile it is only the strength of national sentiment and parties with a national outlook that can contain parochial and sectional interests.

The only non-Congress party which at one time seemed to have the potential of becoming a national party, both in its territorial sweep and social bases, was the Janata Party of 1977. But it turned out to be a false promise. Its only achievement was its election victory in 1977. Its disintegration began soon after. The Janata Dal, like its predecessor the Janata Party, was a conglomerate which brought together a variety of political interests under the umbrella of anti-Congressism. The Congress Party during its long years of rule over the country aroused hopes and expectations among people which it could not fulfil. The low economic growth and its uneven spread left large sections of people dissatisfied. This in turn led to the erosion of the party's widespread influence and the emergence of dissident and antagonistic groups and leaders. The centralization of its leadership thwarted the ambitions of some Congressmen, who swelled the ranks of the Janata Dal. The Janata Dal thus came to consist of a variety of representatives of special interest groups and disgruntled Congressmen.

However, despite this miscellaneous character, the Janata Dal did have a hard core of its own. The core element consisted of rich and middle-income farmers who form the new social groups which have emerged in the wake of the economic development of the last three decades. They have replaced the old and historically entrenched zamindars and substituted their age-old and institutionalized inequality with their own brand of dominance over the rural poor. They have achieved this astonishing feat through a combination of caste linkages, and populist programmes and slogans, and by the use of caste tensions in their favour over elections, especially in state assembly elections. They have in this way secured the support of the social strata of rural society whose interests are otherwise opposed to theirs.

It was the hard core that made the Janata Dal a sizeable political formation but it continued to be a loose grouping of regional and caste parties with narrow social bases even when it came to power. Most of these parties are the political fronts of caste formations which depend on generating collective animosities to gather electoral support. The main objective of these parties is somehow to capture the state and reap the benefits of power, prestige and patronage for their constituents. Disregard of constitutional norms and preference for confrontational politics are explained by them and their ideologues in the idiom of Jayaprakash Narayan or Ram Manohar Lohia, as suits the occasion. It is not surprising that Bihar, where both these leaders wielded their largest influence, has become a cauldron of seething caste animosities. The emergence of powerful landowning dominant castes has effectively sabotaged land reforms in a rich state like Bihar where they continue to coerce the landless and the Dalits. With their sense of deprivation enhanced, poor communities have become easily available for extra-constitutional and agitational politics which are increasingly degenerating into violence.

The Janata Dal leadership has not been able to overcome the limits imposed by the special interests supporting it. They are too spellbound by their narrowly conceived 'mission' to have a vision of the national interest. The conception of a worldview in which to integrate the national interest is beyond the mental horizons of the fragmented, regional and caste elites from which its leadership draws electoral support and political inspiration. Their inherited backwardness never gave them an opportunity to gather the strength, insight and self-confidence needed for the assumption of a leading role in society. Their entire experience has been confined to a struggle to carve out a place for themselves in the political spectrum and gain sectional economic advantages.

Since the Janata Dal was not able to integrate the separate interests of its various constituent groups into an internally consistent economic programme, it remained politically unstable. Under these circumstances the party had to constantly adjust policies and manipulate groups to keep them in its fold. The result was political unpredictability and contradictory pulls and pressures in place of a steady pursuit of well-thought-out policies. This is what happened in 1977–9, in 1990, and yet again in 1996–7. In 1988 the chieftains of its various factions failed to produce a united leadership and cheerfully splintered the party. Laloo Prasad Yadav and, later, Naveen Patnaik left the party to set up their own separate regional formations and the party lost heavily in the 1998 general elections. All these manoeuvres have belied the hope of the Janata Dal becoming a national party. The way politics has taken shape under the Janata reminds one of the remark Graham Wallace made long ago: 'It is the growing and not the decaying forces of society which create the most disquieting problems.'

Our political system has now reached a stage where we need to rethink the concept and practice of democracy in the light of our experience and specific needs. Such an attempt was made during the Emergency by the Swaran Singh Committee but its deliberations got distorted in the authoritarian environment of that time. The regimes that followed had neither the time nor the inclination to make another attempt. Meanwhile democracy is running its course in a manner that has made governance of the country more and more difficult. The Nehruvian consensus based on parliamentary democracy, central planning (socialism), secularism and non-alignment no longer exists.

Parliamentary democracy based on the Westminster model has worked in Great Britain because of the existence of two parties. In India it worked for nearly four decades because of the dominance of an overarching national party. In its absence the model is producing hung parliaments, frequent elections and unstable governments. It is not that our constitution-makers were unaware of these dangers. In a memorandum which he had submitted to the States and Minorities Sub-committee of the Constituent Assembly, Ambedkar had with unerring instinct foreseen such possibilities. He wrote:

The British Cabinet system has undoubtedly given the British people a very stable system of government. Question is: will it produce a stable Government in India? The chances are very slender. In view of the clashes of caste and creeds there is bound to be a plethora of parties and groups in the Legislature in India. If this happens it is possible, nay certain, that under the system of Parliamentary Executive like the one that prevails in England, under which the Executive is bound to resign upon an adverse vote in the Legislature, India may suffer from instability of the Executive. For it is the easiest thing for groups to align and realign themselves at frequent intervals and for petty purposes and bring about the downfall of Government. The present solidarity of what are called the major parties cannot be expected to continue. . . . Constant overthrow of Government is nothing short of anarchy.[6]

The Constituent Assembly had a lively debate on the parliamentary versus presidential system of democracy. Summarizing the main points of the debate Ambedkar in his address, while introducing the Constitution Bill, explained the reason for the assembly's preference for the parliamentary system. While the presidential system emphasized the stability of the executive and the legislature, the parliamentary system stressed responsibility. Evidently the assembly preferred responsibility or accountability to stability. It seems now that our democratic system has reached a stage where it lacks both accountability and stability.

Centralized planning worked reasonably well for the first two decades of independence. Its substantial achievements are the creation of a network of institutions of development, the establishment of basic industries, and a significant increase in trained manpower and technological capabilities. But all these achievements notwithstanding, centralized planning failed to solve the basic problem of poverty. Again, the pursuit of secularism gave India communal peace for several years after the Partition, but no longer. Hindu revivalism and Muslim and Sikh fundamentalism have exposed the weaknesses and limitations of

[6] *The Framing of India's Constitution*, Selected Documents, vol. II (New Delhi: The Indian Institute of Public Administration, 1967), pp. 103-4.

the policy of secularism as practised in India. The policy of non-alignment, which served India's interest well during the era of the cold war,
ceased to be relevant after the collapse of the Soviet Union and the end
of the super-power confrontation. All these developments have gravely
weakened the consensual basis of Indian democracy. A new consensus
is yet to be arrived at.

It was hoped that coalition governments would develop a culture
of mutual accommodation between parties; alliance partners in such
governments were expected to learn the art of give and take and develop common policies and programmes to run the government and
even evolve an alternative national consensus. But this has not happened. Coalition governments beginning with V.P. Singh's National
Front in 1989 suffered from in-built infirmities. They were either
minority governments dependent on outside support or, as in the case
of the Vajpayee government, were dependent on alliances with minor
state sataraps who had their own personal and parochial agenda to
pursue. Under these circumstances, no coherent framework of national policies could emerge. In fact the circumstances in which the
Vajpayee government fell exposed the perverse dialectic of Indian
coalitions.

His government fell when the prime minister had succeeded in
containing the extremist section of his party's supporters; when he had
taken bold initiatives in search of peace with Pakistan; when negotiations in the wake of Pokhran II were at a final and decisive stage; when
the budget had led to recovery in economic confidence and the economy
was buoying up, and when the government was preparing for a second
generation of economic reforms. In sum, the government was brought
down at a time when it had got its act together and was gathering
widening support for its economic, security and foreign policies. And
the reason for its collapse by one vote was no weightier than its inability
to satisfy the extravagantly selfish demands of the self-styled Puratchi
Thalaivi (revolutionary leader), Jayalalitha.

How has this situation come about? Paradoxical as it may seem, it is the result of the success of democracy itself. A lopsided democracy no doubt; a democracy where the principle of representation has gained precedence over its other aspects. Electoral politics has emphasized primordial bonds to the neglect of civic ties. Successive elections have only intensified the self-awareness of voters within the narrow limits of caste and community. With the passage of time, the search for identity and representation has inexorably shifted from caste to sub-caste, from sub-caste to sub-sub-caste, and so on. The result has been political fragmentation and the emergence of a large number of small parties. Many of them are small pressure groups and others are simply an individual politician's outfit to promote his own career. These are hardly the conditions which make stable coalitions possible. The larger political formations that have to depend on such small parties are plagued with dissidence, defection and party-hopping. In these circumstances, coalition governments lack political coherence and become unstable and shortlived. Since its institutional framework continues to be weak, democracy in India will continue to be inchoate, bringing with it turbulent unpredictability.

Most political parties seem to have accepted these prospects of Indian democracy as inevitable. India has entered the phase of coalition governments—this is a conundrum which is repeated day in and day out without any thought being given to the question of how to prevent such governments from being dysfunctional. When ideologically disparate parties combine to fight elections, they certainly enhance the chances of their electoral success but for that very reason they cannot form stable governments or follow coherent policies.

Sometimes the fatalism about coalition governments is presented in terms of historical inevitability. According to one such interpretation:

intra-social conflicts are not only inevitable but it is through these that the rule of law would rule the roost. In the short run it may look disruptive but given the historical experience of India there do not seem to be any short-cuts. Before individuals become the autonomous political units the stage to be undergone would have to be the federation of communities. India has achieved the political federation—a union of states—which is a vertical contraption. To complete the process a horizontal federation would as well have to be achieved. The dalit, backward caste and minority rights movements that are now rocking the country would eventually be the catalysts. That would complete the process of legitimacy of the Indian state.[7]

Such theoretical underpinnings for accepting things as they are, are very soothing to our politicians because they are thereby absolved of their duty to find solutions to the problems they create.

It has become part of political correctness to adopt anti-elitist postures. But history teaches us that successful attempts at basic structural changes have everywhere been accompanied by the rise to power of an elite group or groups who made such efforts possible. In the process of reorganizing society the elites have necessarily to work with materials provided to them by history and within the social situation they inherit. But their success depends on their ability to transform their inherited factors into a system directed towards their new goals. The anti-elitist rhetoric rationalizes the existence of political groups which are too parochial, too divided and too circumscribed by old habits of thought and behaviour to lead India to modern times.

Democracy is more than elections and the cobbling together of majorities to share power. Power is what power does, which means that power has to be used within a certain framework of principles, norms and conventions which together constitute what may be called democratic culture. What has happened in India in recent years is the gradual erosion of this culture, which in any case was not firmly rooted in the country. The degeneration of standards is visible in the attitudes and behaviour of all political parties. They do not hesitate to set up known criminals to fight elections so long as they are sure to win. In a sample survey of people who contested the 1996 elections for the Lok Sabha, the Election Commission found that out of the 13,952 candidates

---

[7] See Partha S. Ghosh in *Legitimacy of Conflict in South Asia,* edited by S.K. Mitra and D. Rothermund (Delhi: Manohar, 1997).

1,500 were facing criminal charges of rape, dacoity and murder—more than half of them hailed from UP and Bihar.

Upon assumption of office, it has become customary for chief ministers and their ministerial colleagues to order wholesale transfers of officers on considerations of caste. In states like UP, where governments have changed too frequently, officers have been transferred several times in a single year. In such a situation officers can hardly concentrate on the jobs they are supposed to do. As a consequence, the morale of the civil service has sunk low, corruption has become rampant, crime has increased and the administration is losing even the limited autonomy it had in the decisionmaking process.

When charges of embezzlement of hundreds of millions of rupees in what is known as the 'fodder scam' were brought against him, Laloo Prasad Yadav, a former chief minister of Bihar and a product of the JP movement, claimed that he was innocent because the 'people's court' had given that verdict by giving him a huge electoral victory. To demonstrate his continued popularity with the electorate he organized a mass rally in Patna in March 1997. Addressing the rally, which he called 'garib' rally (rally of the poor), he spoke on social justice and demanded, '*hummay adalati nyaya nahin, samajie nyaya chahiye*' (We do not want justice as administered by the courts; we want social justice), an echo of the slogans of the JP movement. With populism gone wild it is not surprising that the principle of intercaste equity is invoked in black humour to justify corruption; since the upper castes have been corrupt in the past, it is now the turn of the lower castes.

Party loyalties have become tradeable commodities; disrupting the work of the state assemblies and even parliament is accepted as a legitimate form of protest; the use of state agencies like the income tax department or the investigating agencies to harass political opponents is part of political competition. The stand of the parties on crucial issues depends on where they sit in the house. Sitting on the treasury benches, they favour economic reforms which they oppose when occupying the opposition seats. They are ready to apply Article 356 of the constitution to dismiss a state government which they vehemently condemn when not in power.

In a properly functioning democracy parties are expected to adhere to certain basic principles of behaviour. Since the right to disagree is a cardinal principle of democracy, it is important to have agreed forms of dissent and the rectification of grievances which can be enforced by democratically established authority. Thus, the tension between the expression of dissent and the acceptance of authority can be resolved within a democratic framework only if agreed limits are built into the very concept of freedom. But democracy in India has not come to terms with the concept of authority. It gives the government the right to rule through the mechanism of periodic elections, but it denies to it the capacity to rule. The decisions and rules made by the government are often challenged in the name of democracy itself. Thus democracy is not looked upon as an arrangement to restrain the exercise of arbitrary power, but rather as a technique to prevent the exercise of even legitimate power—by every disgruntled group. In Gandhiji's time, an alien state was seen as an evil to be resisted. He called the British government in India 'satanic'. In free India too, the image of the state as an oppressor has persisted, though not entirely without justification. Repeated defiance of the rule of law and continuous attacks on the apparatus of the state have been dignified as appropriate democratic instruments for the redress of real or imagined grievances. The odd thing about this situation is that it is not only the dissenters who think that defiance is the proper way to relate to the state. Rulers themselves lack faith in the rule of law and often bow to the violators as if they were the representatives of a superior morality.

These problems have resulted from the rapid spread of electoral democracy unaccompanied by a commensurate development of constitutional liberalism. While elections decide who will rule, political culture determines how that rule is exercised. A mature democracy's political culture is based on liberal values, general acceptance of the rule of law and respect for the constitution. A liberal political culture internalizes a sense of discipline and restraint in the government in its use of power, and at the same time makes citizens in general and opposition parties in particular accept the legitimacy of the political authority of the elected representatives of the people.

In the absence of a liberal political culture, free and fair elections can produce illiterate, unenlightened and oppressive regimes—as has happened in many countries. For there is nothing to prevent demagogues from being elected by appealing to caste and religious animosities. It was the fear of such results that made John Stuart Mill argue in *Considerations on Representative Government* against granting the vote to illiterates and to recipients of parish relief, even though he believed that 'No arrangement of the suffrage . . . can be permanently satisfactory in which any person or class is peremptorily excluded . . .' To safeguard liberal values Mill proposed giving multiple votes to 'qualified' people, e.g. the educated. In modern times, when universal and equal suffrage is accepted as a basic human right, Mill's suggestion would be rejected outright as elitist. But the problem that worried Mill still remains with us.

During the last fifty years some political reforms have been introduced in India as their need arose. The Constitution has been amended seventy-eight times. Legislation has been enacted to prevent defections and floor crossings. A Lok Pal Bill has been drafted. Codes of conduct have been laid down; value-based and issue-based politics have been talked about, but there has been no improvement either in the quality of public life or in the governance of the country. It is time to make a comprehensive review of the past experience and prepare a programme of reforms that will suit India's specific needs. Such an exercise should include a review of the constitution, reform of the functioning of the legislative bodies, electoral reform, greater autonomy of the civil service, strict and more impartial enforcement of the rule of law and democratization of political parties. Unless these reforms are undertaken, India cannot be said to have established a viable democracy which is also an effective system of governance. Only then will it have fulfilled Jawaharlal's Nehru's dream. When asked by the British journalist Norman Cousins about his legacy to India, Nehru replied, 'Hopefully, it is 400,000,000 people [now a billion] capable of ruling themselves.'

The Indian political class will also have to ponder over questions raised long ago by Alexis de Tocqueville: 'Shall we attain—as some prophets, perhaps as vain as their predecessors, assure us—a social transformation more complete and more profound than our fathers foresaw and desired, or than we ourselves were able to foresee? Or are we about to enter an intermittent anarchy—that chronic and incurable malady well known to ancient peoples?'

Which way the wheel of history will turn and in which way India will find its solutions to its problems will depend, in the main, on whether and how soon the newly arrived in politics will overcome their myopia, and their reformer opponents the diffidence that inhibits them.

Index

INDIRA GANDHI,
THE 'EMERGENCY'
and INDIAN DEMOCRACY

The 1970s were a tumultuous decade in the Indian subcontinent. Indira Gandhi dominated politics like a Colossus. Bangladesh came into existence and Sikkim merged with India. India and Pakistan fought a war, followed by the Simla Agreement. Bhutto, Mujib and Jayaprakash Narayan reached heights of success and depths of defeat in this period.

P.N. Dhar was closely associated with Prime Minister Indira Gandhi for most of these momentous years. In this book he provides an insider's account of the major political events, decisions and personalities that made up the 1970s.

This is the first book to carry a detailed account of confidential negotiations between Indira Gandhi and Jayaprakash Narayan during the 'Emergency'. It also deals with the economic and political developments that fed into Indira Gandhi's declaration of an 'Emergency'. It provides a close picture of Mrs Gandhi's trauma in relation to the Bangladesh refugee problem and the Bangladesh war, and later in relation to her son Sanjay Gandhi. In its account of the confidential negotiations between Indira Gandhi and Zulfikar Ali Bhutto over the Simla Agreement, it offers unrecorded information which is likely to provoke strong reactions in both India and Pakistan.

P.N. Dhar's delineation of Sikkim's relations with India since Nehru's time, culminating in its merger with India, is the most lucid account of that controversial political event. His analysis of Indian